FREE CULTURE AND THE CITY

Hackers, Commoners, and Neighbors in Madrid, 1997–2017

Alberto Corsín Jiménez and Adolfo Estalella

W0010218

CORNELL UNIVERSITY PRESS   ITHACA AND LONDON

First published 2023 by Cornell University Press

Library of Congress Cataloging-in-Publication Data

Names: Jiménez, Alberto Corsín, author. | Estalella, Adolfo, author.
Title: Free culture and the city : hackers, commoners, and neighbors in Madrid, 1997–2017 / Alberto Corsín Jiménez and Adolfo Estalella.
Description: Ithaca [New York] : Cornell University Press, 2023. | Series: Expertise : cultures and technologies of knowledge | Includes bibliographical references and index.
Identifiers: LCCN 2022012868 (print) | LCCN 2022012869 (ebook) | ISBN 9781501767173 (hardcover) | ISBN 9781501767180 (paperback) | ISBN 9781501767197 (pdf) | ISBN 9781501767203 (epub)
Subjects: LCSH: Social movements—Spain—Madrid—History—21st century. | Protest movements—Spain—Madrid—History—21st century. | Political participation—Spain—Madrid—History—21st century. | City and town life—Spain—Madrid—History—21st century. | Hacktivism—Spain—Madrid—History. | Madrid (Spain)—Social conditions—21st century.
Classification: LCC HN583.5 .J56 2023 (print) | LCC HN583.5 (ebook) | DDC 303.48/40946410905—dc23/eng/20220822
LC record available at https://lccn.loc.gov/2022012868
LC ebook record available at https://lccn.loc.gov/2022012869

Contents

Preface

The fieldwork on which this book is based began in 2010. Our project started when Alberto relocated from the University of Manchester to the Spanish National Research Council in 2009 and was awarded funds to carry out ethnographic research at Medialab Prado, a digital arts center hosted by the Department of Culture at Madrid's municipality. Shortly after, Adolfo joined the project as coresearcher. The project was meant to be a study of the culture of a citizen hacklab, an investigation inspired by the anthropology of organizations and social studies of science. Two months into our fieldwork, however, we became distracted. The Tobacco Factory (La Tabacalera), an abandoned industrial factory at the heart of the city, was occupied by squatters. The occupation was hailed as an epochal moment in the history of squatting in Madrid. What took us by surprise, however, was that everyone at the Medialab seemed to be involved in the occupation. In Madrid, as in Rome, you do as they do, so we followed suit.

At La Tabacalera our attention was drawn for the first time to the specificity of *cultura libre*, free culture, as an urban sensibility. Although at the Medialab we had come to take for granted the center's endorsement of free culture principles as part of its technical and design philosophy, we were surprised to find the same principles invoked by squatters when speaking of a "copyleft social and self-managed space." So it was that we found out about the history of the free culture movement in Madrid and the long history of intimate associations between hackers, squatters, neighborhood activists, and museum curators. The situated nature of cultura libre as urban consciousness and habitus, weaving and imbricating itself across spaces, collectives, and dispositions in the city, slowly began getting under our skins, too.

It took us almost a decade to sense our way through and weave a story out of the many stories and trajectories entangling our paths. The result is, in some respects, an exercise in writing *ethnography as a matter of sense*, to invoke one of the book's central concepts: an exercise in wayfinding and storytelling—through journeys and *détournements*, histories and assemblies, archives and footwork, biographies and infrastructures—the huffs and the puffs, the frictions and the frissons, of learning together.

Long before we had a project, however, we had a time-traveler. At the turn of the century, Adolfo worked as a trainee journalist in the newsroom of Spain's leading daily newspaper, *El País*. There he became one of the country's first reporters on all matters digital. He took an interest in the development of various cultura libre initiatives, including the organization of the first Dorkbot workshops in Spain and the mobilizations against the introduction of the digital canon (both described in chapter 2). These and other accomplishments merited his appointment as one of a handful of editors of the free software and technology news website Barrapunto. Although in time Adolfo would leave the field of journalism for the excitement of anthropology, his time travels to those early pioneering days have proved an invaluable source of insight and connections for writing this book.

Our fieldwork proper began at Medialab Prado, where, between February 2010 and February 2011, Adolfo regularly attended meetings, participated in design workshops, and joined members of staff in trips to present the work of the media lab at other cultural organizations or events. For his part, Alberto similarly attended design workshops and laboratories, and between 2015 and 2018 he was a permanent member of the lab's task force on social innovation. At the squatted social center of La Tabacalera, Adolfo joined various teams from the earliest days of the occupation in March 2010, and he remained involved for over a year, attending assemblies, helping clean, build, and repair the space, organizing events, and so forth.

Our work with the 15M movement and popular assemblies began with the occupation of the square at Puerta del Sol on May 15, 2011, and lasted well into 2012. In the early days of the movement, both of us regularly attended meetings at assemblies in the neighborhoods of Lavapiés and Prosperidad and the Puerta del Sol General Assembly. Once the main encampment at Puerta del Sol was dismantled and the movement took root for good in the barrios, Adolfo joined the facilitating task force in charge of organizing the weekly gatherings of the Lavapiés assembly and contributed to the workings of the assembly in that capacity for just under two years. Either jointly or individually, we attended hundreds of assemblies, preparatory meetings, working groups, demonstrations, and direct actions.

As we made preparations to start writing this book, we turned to some of our friends and interlocutors for in-depth interviews. Over the course of four years we carried out over sixty interviews with hackers, curators, guerrilla architects, cultural mediators, journalists, squatters, neighborhood activists, artists, civil servants, historians, and participants at assemblies, to name but a few. Unless otherwise stated, all translations from Spanish sources, including academic texts, interviews, archival materials, and ethnographic exchanges, are our own. Except when spoken by an interviewee, we will not be providing sources for colloquial phrases or terms in common use in conversational contexts.

In January 2012 we teamed up with two guerrilla architectural collectives, Basurama and Zuloark, in a funded research project on the material architectures of the assembly movement. We met weekly for six months, visited vacant lots and occupations, participated in auto-construction workshops, built a dome, organized seminars, and wrote papers together. What began as a formal collaboration developed over time into a friendship and a shared problematization about the mutual designs of complicities and complexities for our runaway world. This is an insight we have come to treasure: how complicities alloy complexities and how complexities ally with complicities, in the city, in anthropology, and beyond.

This book is the culmination of many such alliances, comradeships, and amalgamations. We have respected our friends' and interlocutors' decision to have their real names used in the text, unless otherwise stated. This is in keeping with the free culture philosophy that intellectual work is always choral and embodied, and we have tried to capture some of these expressions of relational and dynamic thinking in the text itself.

We would like to thank Juan Carrete and Marcos García for making our fieldwork at Medialab Prado possible. Our gratitude toward Marcos, as the pages of the book testify, extends in endless directions. To this day, the Medialab remains a second home for us, thanks in no small measure to the boundless hospitality of Mónica Cachafeiro, Sonia Díez Thale, Patricia Domínguez Larrondo, Laura Fernández, Raúl González, Javier Laporta, Gabriel Lucas, José Miguel Medrano, and Daniel Pietrosemoli. Jara Rocha embodied like no other the joy of prototyping as a means for delirious conspirations.

It is a hopeless task to keep a tally of all the people who over the years have enriched, thickened, and textured our understanding of cultura libre as an urban sensibility. Carla Boserman, Nerea Calvillo, Jordi Claramonte, Gloria Durán, Montfrague Fernández, Amador Fernández Savater, Ana Franco, Juan Freire, César García, Igor Gónzalez, Bernardo Gutiérrez, Patricia Horrillo, Rocío Lara, Tíscar Lara, Carmen Lozano Bright, Jaume Nualart, Mar Núñez, Juan Martín de Prada, Ignacio Priego, David Rodríguez, Lorena Ruiz, Olivier Schulbaum, José Luis de Vicente, and Carlos Vidania have all, at one point or another, over beer, conversations, interviews, or discussions, helped us entangle, disentangle, and re-enchant our story further.

The history of libertarian municipalism in Madrid, like the history of most social movements, risks fading into yet another history about the accomplishments of big men. We treasure the time we have spent with some of the protagonists, who have reminded us that the vicissitudes of history work in other ways. We are grateful to Carlos Alberdi, Rubén Caravaca, Jesús Carrillo, Javier de la Cueva, Jesús González Barahona, Pedro Jiménez, Azucena Klett, Margarita Padilla, José

Pérez de Lama, Manuela Villa, and Miguel Vidal for taking the time to retrace with us the romances, agonisms, and misencounters holding the commons, the public, and the libre sometimes together and sometimes apart over these past twenty years.

The hope and joy we experienced during the exciting years following the 15M movement (from 2011 onward) remain with us. We shared time and learned from our comrades in the assemblies in which we participated. The neighborhood assembly in Lavapiés is of special relevance for this book, and we are grateful to our many friends and colleagues there: Ander Contel, Esther Reyero, Pablo Gutiérrez del Álamo, Martha Viniegra, Daiana Bertucci, Aurora Gómez Delgado, Anita Botwin, Ernesto García López, Estela Montejo, Paco Fernández García, Laura Hidalgo, Ion Urkola, Héctor Vizoso, Enrique Flores, Lucía Gutiérrez García, Amanda Figueras, Ángeles Olivia Díaz, Mariano González Mariscal, Estela Montejo, Mai Gredilla, Juan Coino Rodriguez, Gonzalo Maestro, Pepe Callejo, Guillem Marpons, Doris Palacín, Carlos Ferreiro, Elena Jiménez, Pilar Ventin Castro, Luis Ventin Castro, Óscar Eslava, Pablo André, Rakel Pereira, Andrés Muñoz, José Miguel Fernández-Layos, Mario Munera, Miguel Ángel Chumo Mata, Maribel Calero, Asunción, and Amaya Sanz.

Around 2012 our project took a big turn. We realized then that it was moot for us to study the making of free culture prototypes if we did not rise to the challenge of turning our research project into an anthropological prototype for free culture itself. We owe our encounter with guerrilla architectural collectives Basurama and Zuloark this gracious awakening. "If ours is a practice invested in the auto-construction of architecture," they subtly insinuated to us, "what would the auto-construction of anthropology look like?" This gentle prodding has since changed the whole edifice of our methodological and epistemic craft. For this and countless other hours of inspiration, solidarity, and sheer happiness, we are indebted to Juan López-Aranguren Blázquez, Mónica Gutiérrez, Rubén Lorenzo Montero, Alberto Nanclares, and Manuel Polanco Pérez-Llantada (Basurama); Aurora Adalid, David Berkvens, Manuel Pascual, and Luis de Prada (Zuloark); Diego Peris (Todo por la Praxis); Enrique Espinosa; Pablo García Bachiller; Esaú Acosta, Mauro Gil-Fournier, and Miguel Jaenicke (Vivero de Iniciativas Ciudadanas); Jacobo García Fouz and Jorge Martín (El Campo de Cebada); María Álvarez, Juan Martín Blas, and Fabio Silli (La Mesa); Raquel Congosto and Isabel Arenas (La Galería de Magdalena); Domenico di Siena (Think Commons); and Pablo Rey Mazón and Alfonso Sánchez Uzábal (Montera 34).

We are particularly grateful to all the artists, photographers, and friends who generously gave us permission to use their work: Julio Albarrán, Daniel Bobadilla, Luis Daza, Enrique Flores, Alberto del Río, El Campo de Cebada, Zoohaus, and Zuloark.

Sections of this book have appeared in print before. Portions of chapter 5 appeared in 2014 in "The Interior Design of [Free] Knowledge," *Journal of Cultural Economy* 7: 4, 493–515, https://www.tandfonline.com/doi/full/10.1080/17530350.2013.859632, Taylor and Francis Ltd. Some parts of chapter 6 appeared in 2014 in "Assembling Neighbors: The City as Hardware, Method, and 'a Very Messy Kind of Archive,'" *Common Knowledge* 20: 1, 150–71, Duke University Press. Some passages of chapter 7 have been reproduced from the 2016 chapter "Matters of Sense: Preoccupation in Madrid's Popular Assemblies," included in *Urban Cosmopolitics: Agencements, Assemblies, Atmospheres*, eds. Anders Blok and Ignacio Farías, London and New York: Routledge, pp. 147–63. And chapter 8 was first published as "Auto-Construction Redux: The City as Method," *Cultural Anthropology* 32: 3, 450–78. All materials are republished by permission of the publishers.

The book developed through numerous research grants and awards. We are grateful to the Spanish National Research Council (Proyecto Intramural de Incorporación 2009101002) and the Spanish Ministry of Science (CSO2010-17735, CSO2014-51970-R and FPDI-2013-17115) for helping fund the research for this book.

Over the years we have been lucky to have numerous colleagues read, comment, and discuss with us different parts of the manuscript. Georgina Born, Hernani Dias, Michael Guggenheim, Chris Kelty, James Leach, Javier Lezaún, George Marcus, Alain Pottage, Lucy Suchman, Fred Turner, and Alex Wilkie were part of the "Cultures of Prototyping" conference that we convened at Medialab Prado in 2010 and where we first presented some of our very preliminary thoughts regarding the design of free culture prototypes. The organization of a second conference in 2012, "The City as an Open Interface," allowed us to present some very preliminary findings regarding the culture of assembly as an infrastructural culture. We are thankful to Maribel Casas, Sebastián Cobarrubias, Mike Crang, Ignacio Farías, Stephen Graham, James Holston, Hannah Knox, Miguel Ángel Martínez, and Ramón Ribera-Fumaz for their careful listening and provocative engagements.

Tomás Sánchez Criado has seen this project grow from its earliest days, and his own work on experimental collaborations has been an inexhaustible source of inspiration. Daniel Curto-Millet, Candela Morado, and Teresa Tiburcio kindly read a very rough draft of part 1 and helped trim down its wild arborescence. Ignacio Farías and Anders Blok commented on some of the materials that found their way into chapter 7, while Morten Nielsen, Tomás Sánchez Criado, and Marilyn Strathern dazzled an earlier version of chapter 8 with their insightful generosity. Marisol de la Cadena read a first draft of the introduction and offered much-needed encouragement. John Postill's own work on media activism has been a constant reference for over a decade now. Miguel Ángel Martínez's intellectual and activist engagement with the history of squatting in Madrid has been a beacon throughout this project. Miguel Ángel also read part 1, which has been greatly enriched by his suggestions. Chris Kelty and Gabriella Coleman went out of their way in reading earlier versions of the whole manuscript. This book would not be what it is without their lucid engagement, perspicacity, and support. Dominic Boyer graciously welcomed our project into the intellectually vibrant home he has curated for Cornell's Expertise: Cultures and Technologies of Knowledge series. Jim Lance's editorial hospitality, guidance, and accompaniment at the press have been likewise a gift. We are immensely grateful to Nicole Balant, Cheryl Hirsch, and Mary Kathleen Murphy for fabulous copyediting and production work, and to J. Naomi Linzer for her enlightening work indexing the manuscript.

Our final thanks go to Antonio Lafuente. We can only hope our pages retain a fraction of the warmth, joy, erudition, and commitment he has brought to the free culture movement in Spain.

Alberto dedicates the book to Alejo, Jara, and Laura. Whatever glimmers of delirious hopes and autonomous aspirations shine through its pages, they express the warmheartedness of a movement that brewed in the streets and was embraced at home.

Adolfo dedicates the book to his parents, Rafael and Sacramento, for all their efforts and sacrifices liberated in him the drive to learn.

Abbreviations

15M movement	May 15 movement
ACP	Agencia en Construcción Permanente (Agency under Permanent Construction)
AECID	Agencia Española de Cooperación Internacional (Spanish Development Agency)
ARP	Áreas de Rehabilitación Preferente (Preferential Rehabilitation Areas)
CHS	Center for Historical Studies
CSIC	Consejo Superior de Investigaciones Científicas (Spanish National Research Council)
ECN/Isole Nella Rete	European Counter Network/Islands in the Net
ETA	Basque terrorist group
ETSAM	Escuela Técnica Superior de Arquitectura de Madrid (Madrid's School of Architecture)
EZLN	Ejército Zapatista de Liberación Nacional (Zapatista National Liberation Army)
FRAVM	Federación Regional de Asociaciones de Vecinos de Madrid (Madrid's Regional Federation of Neighborhood Associations)
GNU	GNU's Not Unix
IC	Inteligencias Colectivas
IMF	International Monetary Fund
MACBA	Museo de Arte Contemporáneo de Barcelona (Barcelona's Contemporary Art Museum)
MLP	Medialab Prado
NGO	Nongovernmental Organization
OTICAM	Oficina Temporal Inteligencias Colectivas Arganzuela-Matadero
PP	Partido Popular (Popular Party)
RoS	Rompamos el Silencio (Let's Break the Silence)
SGAE	Sociedad General de Autores y Editores (Spanish General Society of Authors and Publishers)
SMS	Short Message Service

TAZ   Temporary Autonomous Zone
UNIA   Universidad Internacional de Andalucía (Andalucia's
                        International University)

FREE CULTURE
AND THE CITY

FREE CULTURE AND THE CITY

**It must be said today that the critical task still . . . requires work
on our limits, that is, a patient labor giving form to our impatience
for liberty.**

—Michel Foucault, *What Is Enlightenment?*

Omnia sunt communia. On June 13, 2015, Guillermo Zapata took his oath of office
as a new member of Madrid's city council with a formula never heard before. The
secretary taking minutes was caught by surprise and, feeling perplexed, asked Zapata to repeat his oath again. *Omnia sunt communia*—All things in common.[1]

Zapata had been elected to office a few weeks earlier following the surprise
victory of Ahora Madrid, a grassroots alliance of community activists that, in
the 2015 municipal elections, broke up the two-party system that had dominated
electoral politics since Spain became a democracy in 1977. Hailed by some as a
sea change in Spanish politics, the rise of so-called municipalist confluences
opened up a new political landscape where neighborhood dynamics of urban
and social justice took center stage.[2]

A documentary filmmaker and screenwriter, Zapata had developed an interest in the cultural significance of free software, and copyleft licenses in particular, around the turn of the century, when he realized the impact that these new
legal and technical frameworks were likely to have on his profession. He joined
the ranks of a then loosely articulated *cultura libre* movement, a movement for
free culture that had come to be in the late 1990s in response to widespread corporate efforts to extend patent protection and copyright enforcement of cultural works in the digital age. By the year 2000, the cause of free culture had
been widely adopted by squatted social centers in Spain, where autonomous activists imagined provocative extrapolations of cultura libre to the urban landscape at large. In this context, Zapata joined Patio Maravillas, one of the city's
better-known squatted social centers, where the slogan omnia sunt communia

was often invoked during occupations. The battle slogan of the Reformist priest Thomas Müntzer, one of the leaders of the German Peasants' War in the sixteenth century, this phrase had become an established motto of commons movements across Europe.

Fast forward to 2011: on May 15 the Indignados movement takes to the streets.[3] For many people, the protests signal the collapse of the constitutional pact underpinning the transition to democracy in Spain following the death of the dictator Francisco Franco in 1975. Commentators speak of the May 15 (15M) movement as sparking the downfall of a thirty-five-year-old "culture of transition" paradigm.[4] "The fight against the culture of copyright," wrote Zapata for a volume analyzing this point of inflection, "was the main trigger for the articulation of a novel public space which led to the May 15 movement."[5] The movement for free culture, he intimated, was at the heart of the constitutional crisis that hit Spanish society in 2011.

Cultura libre, urban commons, and the crisis of democratic culture: What made it possible for a young scriptwriter-turned-activist to conjure these diverse imaginaries of struggle and hope into a unified narrative of collective action and political liberation? When and how did a hacker philosophy inspire the occupation of plazas and spearheaded a municipalist revolution? What scenarios and practices of "patient labor," as Foucault called them, had come together to mold the city into a form capable of expressing the "impatience for liberty"?[6]

Free Culture and the City traces the rise of free culture in Spain over the past twenty years. We explore how a set of technologies, legal arguments, and pedagogical tools that were devised at the end of the twentieth century to define and defend the reach of digital liberties in the age of the internet were unexpectedly reworked over the course of the following two decades into activist designs and problematizations against austerity urbanism. The book is also an ethnography of Madrid, a city caught between near-Norths and near-Souths, between fatuous regimes of modernization and the legacies of postdictatorial peripheralizations, yet also driven by joyful uprisings in pursuit of enlarged experiences of cityness.[7] The story about the ways in which free culture carved out a space for itself as a political project between the digital and the urban, between bricks and bytes, is therefore also a story about the stuff of politics and the stuff of cities today—what they are made of, how they are remade, and what living in them feels like. What does "the return of the political" look like in the wake of ecological and austerity crises? This question is often asked by social and cultural critics, and we hope to offer a partial answer in these pages.[8]

Broadly speaking, free culture activism in Spain stands at the crossroads of three liberation agendas: the liberation philosophy of free software hackers, the libertarian aspirations of autonomous activists, and the struggles over the right to the city of neighborhood activists. Drawing inspiration from all three agendas, we develop a conceptual proposition that aims to encompass the pressures, undercurrents, and reorientations of what we call *free/libre urbanism*. Free or libre urbanism inchoates an image of the city that is premised on aspirations that are vastly different from those encapsulated by the liberal city and public urbanism. But it is also different from the revindications for an urbanism of the commons, although in parts it overlaps with them. The questions that drive free/libre urbanism revolve not so much around modes of governance, scale, or organization as around trajectories of experiment, apprenticeship, and sensing-together: What horizons, practices, and commitments galvanize the promises of freedom and autonomy in urban life today? What glimpses or forms—what senses, systems, and assays—outline or anticipate the free city?

Unlike the right to the city or the urban commons, the notion of the free city has remained largely untheorized in urban studies. In *Free Culture and the City*, we develop an argument about the free city by lifting the concept of free culture out of its traditional location in the history of free software and digital media and placing it in a richer canvas of urban struggles for autonomy, municipalism, and liberation. By navigating two decades of ethnographic and historical work with free culture collectives in Madrid, the pages that follow show how, in its journey from the digital to the urban, the practice of liberating culture not only called for the participation and entanglement of legal licenses, coding practices, or digital infrastructures but also required the mobilization of, and alliances between, public museums, neighborhood associations, squatted social centers, hackers, intellectual property lawyers, street artists, guerrilla architectural collectives, and 15M assemblies, to name but a few of the protagonists that populate the pages that follow. By staging a conversation between urban studies, social studies of science and technology, critical media and design studies, and anthropological theory, we describe how the freedom in cultura libre became entangled with other conceptions of liberty and social welfare, neighborhood fraternity and autonomous culture, and digital democracy and technical expression to shape an urban sensibility and an urban sensorium that would animate the limits of the city as a space of liberation.

The rest of this introduction is in three parts. In the first part, we introduce our conceptual treatment of the free city. In the second part, we offer an overview of the rise and significance of the free culture movement. Readers who are conversant in urban theory may not be familiar with the history of free software; similarly, scholars familiar with the history of hacktivism and digital rights may not be fluent in the details of urban activism. Our book tells the story of how these two movements found one another in Madrid at the turn of the century and describes their subsequent synergies, symbioses, and singularities. In the final part we describe some aspects of recent Spanish cultural history that help place in context what kind of culture the movement for free culture was trying to liberate itself from.

The Free City: Public, Commons, Libre

We were among the first to arrive at the orchard. It was a gorgeous summer afternoon. The dry weather lent the garden a slightly untended appearance, although the colorful graffiti on the adjacent wall was a majestic soul-shifter, and under its shadow one's mood was swiftly captured by the garden's delightful and joyful ambiance. The urban community garden of Adelfas lies along a stretch of land by the city's southern railway lines, which have long cut across the fabric of Madrid's southern neighborhoods with incisive and segregating class lines. The wall separates the railway lines from the orchard, which stands as a delicate acupunctural intervention in an otherwise neglected interstitial space (see figure 1).

We had been invited to Adelfas to join a meeting that summoned grassroots and community initiatives from across the city. By the time we attended this meeting in July 2013, we had already been conducting fieldwork alongside free culture activists for over three years. What had started as an ethnography of a public media lab—where free software hackers, data scientists, visual artists,

FIGURE 1. Adelfas Urban Community Orchard. Photo by Alberto del Río.

architects, lawyers, and journalists came together to tinker with electronics, law, and cooperative social forms—had, to our surprise, mutated over the years into a citywide collaborative project on autonomous citizenship. The liberation technologies, methods, and sensibilities of cultura libre activists, we had found, were traveling out to the city, seemingly permeating and modulating autonomous projects everywhere.

The meeting at Adelfas was convened by the leadership of Madrid's Regional Federation of Neighborhood Associations (Federación Regional de Asociaciones de Vecinos de Madrid, or FRAVM). It was attended by more than twenty people representing some fifteen community initiatives, including Madrid's Network of Urban Community Gardens, food cooperatives, environmental groups, squatted social centers (more about them in chapters 1–3), public cultural centers (chapters 3–5), guerrilla architectural collectives (chapters 5 and 8), neighborhood assemblies (chapters 6 and 7), and citizen-managed public spaces (chapter 8). The leadership of FRAVM was eager to come into contact with what they described as a "new cohort of social movements," an array of autonomous projects and grassroots initiatives that had taken to the city in the wake of the 15M demonstrations. They felt these movements deployed repertoires of *saberes técnicos* (technical know-hows) that were drawing, mapping, and resourcing novel landscapes of political autonomy for the city. These included architectural auto-construction techniques, digital cartographies, open-source energy and infrastructure projects, or forms of documentary video and graphic storytelling. The proliferation of such vibrant autonomous designs sparked a debate among activist groups about the urgency to collaborate in drafting a statute to help empower these manifold initiatives vis-à-vis the city's municipal administrations. To this effect, the groups and collectives attending the meeting, as well as many others that had not attended in person, joined ongoing efforts for building a Network of Citizen Spaces (Red de Espacios Ciudadanos), which, over the following three years, worked arduously to produce the Common Statute for the Defense of Self-Management Citizen Spaces and the Development of Urban Commons in Madrid.[9]

The meeting at Adelfas had various moments of tension, but it also had a certain mood of festivity and discovery about it. We sat for almost three hours in a circle discussing the practicalities of the confederate network that we wished to bring into existence, acutely conscious that at stake was the very nature of the political body whose contours we were painstakingly drawing out there and then.

With the notable exception of the work of Murray Bookchin and Manuel Castells, the concept of the free city has largely stayed under the radar of urban scholarship, even though the struggles for the free city have done anything but subside since the 1960s.[10] Our research and collaborations inspired us to recuperate the conceptual valence of the free city, one that takes the practices of liberation of free culture activists as its point of departure. The free city, as we think of it here, is not a jurisdictional or political entity, nor is it model of community or association. It is not bounded to specific political geographies, economic formations, or organizational systems. It inchoates a form of urbanism whose signature trademarks are neither simply liberal consensus or public values nor grassroots resistance and commons alternatives. Rather, we think of the free city as a system and sensibility involving liberation—an *urbanization of liberation*. By paying attention to free culture activists' concerns about complex descriptions, affective aesthetics, archival consciousness, and sovereign infrastructures, we reorient our gaze toward sites, methods, and bearings that tense, hardwire, and undulate the city into experiments and experiences of joyful autonomy.

Of course, these tactical maneuverings and orientations are very often energized by and connected to well-known struggles against the financialization, privatization, and commoditization of urban space, and in this sense they are deeply imbricated with scholarly debates about the right to the city and the urban commons. Therefore, although we will explore some aspects of these struggles in the chapters that follow, let us briefly engage with them here to situate the specificity of our argument regarding free/libre urbanism vis-à-vis the liberal city and the urban commons.

Starting in the mid-nineteenth century, rapid industrialization changed the contours of the city and the nature of urban life. The spatial and temporal matrix of capitalism hacked up the social and material fabric of the city, tearing up the richness of urbanity and the experiences of dense encounter and urban friction and shuffling and relocating people into dispersed productive peripheries and residential habitats. Historians of urban life have described how the deployment of infrastructures of transport, sanitation, and public lightning around this time, as well as the use of censuses, statistics, and maps, shaped novel modes of governmentality in Western cities, where the "freedom" of their inhabitants was engineered at a distance through the regulation of their habitats and modes of comportment, association, and expectation. This was the age of the liberal city and public urbanism.[11]

From a different angle, the story of how the urban condition became hollowed out of its experience of "inhabitation" and transformed instead into a landscape of "habitats" was famously told by Henri Lefebvre in his influential "Right to the City."[12] Cities were once works of art, Lefebvre argued, "'beautiful' *oeuvres* of urban life," not only where "products" were exchanged, but also where "knowledge" and "techniques," "streets and squares, edifices and monuments" were used in "*la Fête* (a celebration which consumes unproductively, without other advantage but pleasure and prestige)."[13] People's expulsion from the intensity of urbanity produced a spectral experience of the city, where "urban consciousness will vanish."[14] Our only hope for a return of the experience of urbanity, Lefebvre insisted, was to organize politically and thus reclaim "a transformed and renewed *right to urban life.*"[15]

Notwithstanding its radical poetics, it has never been very clear what substantive politics the right to the city, or the right to urban life, was meant to make way for. As David Harvey recently put it, "the right to the city is an empty signifier," a placeholder for disparate aspirations and revindications.[16] Some may see it as a human right, others may believe it is a right for distributive justice, and yet others will think of it as a marker of civil liberties.[17] As the anthropologist James Holston has observed, the conceptual framework of the right to the city describes a historical experience of urbanity, urbanization, and countermobilization that does not necessarily resonate with the histories emerging from the Global South.[18] In places such as Brazil, the residents of urban peripheries often invoke their own efforts at building the neighborhoods and houses they live in as claims on their very status as urban citizens: "Residents argued that those who make the city have a claim to it—what I call a contributor right."[19] The right to the city, in other words, is auto-constructed through specific material projects in infrastructure, housing, or community-building.

For Holston, such vectors of auto-construction posit the right to the city as a specific right to urban citizenship, whose prerogatives and duties are distinct from those of national citizenship, and are defined and circumscribed by membership in the political community of the city.[20] What the recent wave of metropolitan rebellions shows us, Holston contends, is that from Tahrir Square to Gezi Park, from the Spanish 15M movement to the rise of sanctuary cities in the United States, the terms and conditions of membership in the political community of the city are changing. A sense of the political is emerging that is "intimate yet common; material yet in between," where the expression and settling of contributing rights permits the "commoning" of politics.[21]

In invoking the notion of commoning, Holston draws on the recent interest expressed by scholars of urban and social movements in the political theories of the commons. The original theory of the commons, we show in part 1, was developed to account for modes of management of common-pool resources that were neither private nor public goods, such as fisheries, forests, or irrigation systems. In this context, the commons designated systems of property and self-regulation that stood in opposition to nationalized or privatized resources. The study of the urban commons, on the other hand, has largely focused on material spaces and sites that stand in defiance of or resistance to the hegemonic logics of capitalist urban development, such as urban community gardens or social housing complexes.[22] In these and other cases, scholars have noted how practices of commoning have effects that can hardly be circumscribed to questions of property or governance. Rather, the urban commons have been deeply entangled in the production of critical forms of "material space, knowledge, and meaning."[23] Not unlike the interstitial vulnerability of the urban community garden at Adelfas, these are territories of liminality, "threshold spaces," as the urbanist Stavros Stavrides has called them, "which escape the normalizing urban ordering of the city of enclaves."[24] As we describe in detail in chapters 3 and 4, in this light the commons have reinvigorated the languages of description of the city—its spatial registers, experiential forms, and experimental designs.

What Politics Is Made Of, How It Is Remade, and What It Feels Like

As the sun set, first into placidly pink colors and then into lazy crepuscular shades, we took a couple of breaks to stretch our legs and relax. On these occasions, our hosts at Adelfas would bring out some beer and show us around the orchard: the toolboxes and spare parts used in the construction of beds and benches, the seeds and compost used in urban horticulture, the handbooks and instruction sets they had prepared for novice gardeners.

Our open-air garden assembly was in many respects a classic instance of direct-action democracy: the ends of our political project prefigured by the means through which we were embodying it. As we discussed aims and goals, task forces and resources, timelines and challenges, we "assembled" a political project for ourselves through the assembly of our representational bodies and voices. Moreover, to a large extent the tenor and tone of our discussions, their cadence and rhythm, were in important ways modulated by the serene ambiance of the orchard, the beer and the sunshine, an atmosphere of peacefulness that mellowed the urgency.

Attending to the role that these ambient elements play in the composition of a political moment is characteristic of the perspective that scholars of social studies of science and technology (STS) have brought to bear on what has come to be known as "assemblage urbanism."[25] Unlike the assemblies of classic representational politics, these other assemblages are attentive to the overlaying dynamics that bring affects and materials, sympathies and corrosions, intimacies and frictions together in shifting choreographies of objects, people, and environments. These polyvalent and often diffracting dynamics are not always easy to describe in the representational vocabulary of classic urban theory. Rather, as the STS scholars Ignacio Farías and Anders Blok have pointed out, attending to an assemblage sensibility has often "required the development of a non-scalar language to grasp new urban topologies involving multiple relations, flows and atmospheres that tie together actors, institutions, sites and processes."[26]

The assemblage of a political moment at Adelfas offers us a point of entry into the complex swirl of formations, undercurrents, and agonisms animating the urbanization of liberation. We offer three choreographic principles—matters of sense, bricolages of apprenticeships, and climates of methods—that together articulate our inquiry into the stuff of contemporary urban liberation. We may think of these principles as orchestrating a specific formulation of urban ecocriticism and degrowth imaginaries in the Spanish context.[27] Yet ours is a proposal that dwells in the *longue durée*—the messiness, the huffs and the puffs—of ethnographic conceptualization. We have therefore devised these notions as strategies for introducing different kinds of platforms, tensors, and gatherings. While each redescribes and partially weaves into the other two, we separate them here for heuristic and explanatory purposes. Let us briefly introduce each strategy in turn.

What Politics Is Made Of: Matters of Sense

At times, our circular assembly at Adelfas felt as if it were reflecting the etiquette of parliamentary democracy. The emphasis on oratory, rhetorical performance, rational argumentation, and representational diplomacy ticked all the right boxes of parliamentary politics. However, most of the people in attendance had long been involved in autonomous movements and were well acquainted with the rituals and expectations of participatory deliberative assembly aimed at open and horizontal exchanges in pursuit of consensus. In truth, however, it was not always easy to distinguish which registers one had to use and when, for the art of patient and attentive listening was often followed up by the agonist dramaturgy of rhetorical confrontation.

These distinctions between the assembly and the assemblage of politics, between parliamentary and autonomous diplomacies, echo the opposition that Bruno Latour once drew between Realpolitik and Dingpolitik.[28] The former defines the real weight of politics by owning up to and adjudicating over "matters of fact," while the latter airs and breathes life into a political moment through the ongoing problematization and mediation of the "matters of concern" that compose and hold a collective together.[29] Drawing partial inspiration from the feminist practice of some of the autonomous activists whose stories we present in chapter 1, the scholar of feminist science studies María Puig de la Bellacasa recently added an ethos of care into relations of assemblage, directing our attention toward the "matters of care" moving, attaching, supporting, or obliging us to make particular ethicopolitical commitments and situations.[30] A caring disposition, de la Bellacasa has taught us, is not simply a mode of compassionate action toward others; it is also a troubling engagement with the diversity of materials and agencies that hold and sustain lives-in-place.

What brought us together at Adelfas that evening was certainly a *concern* for other stories, feelings, and experiments in urban assembling. It was also an urgency and desire to *care* for the interstices, vulnerabilities, and marginalia of the city's ecologies. However, the meeting itself also required on our part a considerable effort at attuning, tending to, and enriching a shared sensorium and sensibility of connectedness and participation. The tour around the orchard effectively primed such a mood. As we discuss at length in chapter 7, such modes of assembling rehearsed a collective mattering of empathy, sympathy, and anticipation that at once solicited and redistributed the material sensibilities of the city.[31] We were theatricalizing a common sense (*con-sensus*) of sorts. Therefore, this was an assembly and assemblage that not only performed a mattering of concerns or care but also functioned as a vehicle for and anchorage of *matters of sense*. To be sure, this sensing for and sounding out of the consilience and affinities of forms of life was not simply the search for a homogeneous synchronicity of sentiments, for a wholeness of community. Rather the movement felt more like an effort at getting our bearings, an orientation of sorts—an experiment in drifting, salvaging, and reckoning-with together.

How It Is Remade: Bricolages of Apprenticeships

The name given to the confederate network of activist projects founded at Adelfas was Hacenderas, an old Spanish term designating those collective tasks that traditionally required for their completion the participation of every neighbor in a municipality. One of the first task forces appointed by Hacenderas was charged with developing an online database of the different tools, resources, materials, and infrastructures kept by the activist projects in the network, from garden hoses and wheelbarrows to shovels, sanders, and computer servers. The idea was for the database to function as an *intercambiadero*, a digital exchange space where community projects could lend and borrow from one another as needed.

The idea for the *intercambiadero* had been floating around activist circles for a while. The platform was one of numerous free software digital infrastructures and archives built by activists during this time. Guerrilla architectural collectives and members of urban community garden cooperatives in particular had long been discussing ways to design a circular economy of skills, resources, and apprenticeships. These were collectives largely dedicated to furnishing marginal spaces and grassroots projects with sustainable and affordable urban infrastructures, from garden beds and benches to playgrounds or geodesic domes. When sitting down to talk about the way to furnish a particular urban site, architects and gardeners would often speak of *diseños para habitar controversias*, designs for inhabiting controversies, for they were well aware that they were not simply building makeshift infrastructures for marginal spaces but actually assaying material systems for convivial livelihoods—tools for conviviality, as the theologian and social critic Ivan Illich famously put it.[32] Taking a cue from the work of James Holston referred to earlier, in chapter 8 we will see how, for architects and community gardeners, these projects in auto-construction served not just as initiatives in self-building and self-maintenance nor simply as exemplars of social innovation, resilience, or self-organization, but rather as methods for grasping the uncertainties, requirements, and obligations of shared apprenticeships in the city. The circulation of auto-construction as method, platform, and exemplar—as a charter for the entwinned crafts of storytelling and storymaking in the city—points to an arts of living founded on what Eduardo Viveiros de Castro recently dubbed the arts of "bricolage."[33] In the age of Gaia, Viveiros de Castro notes, we should do well to challenge the modeling infatuations of engineers with the compositional artistry of bricoleurs, for bricoleurs make do with whatever is at hand and available, patching and repurposing apprenticeships rather than engineering solutions. The bricolage of apprenticeships becomes an "essential element of . . . the effort to 'unpredict the world' . . . and to invent after the fact."[34] The speculative horizons of the city of dreams are intuited and groped for through the rubble and the desires of urban bricolage.

What It Feels Like: Climates of Methods

Some eight months after the 15M demonstrations took the city by surprise, the grassroots philosopher Amador Fernández-Savater wrote a blog post where he described the reasons why he felt that, despite the decline in people's involvement in popular assemblies and rallies, the spirit of the movement remained alive and kicking. "The 15M is not just the name of an organizational structure," he noted, but also "a state of mind . . . that traverses society like a wind. We used to know how to organize social movements, but do we know *how to organize a climate?*"[35]

Fernández-Savater's appeal to the climatic designs of the 15M movement has a distant echo of Murray Bookchin's concern with the "ecologies of freedom," the scales of participatory sensibility and political mutualism that are required to make one *feel* part of an urban environment.[36] We recognize that some aspects of Bookchin's anthropology are problematic today, yet his interest and that of Fernández-Savater in the complex designs of sympathetic ecosystems give us food for thought.[37]

We wish to explore how such climates of liberation gain traction and are operationalized in and through concrete methods, in terms not dissimilar to how the philosopher of science Isabelle Stengers has spoken of the "ecologies of practices" circumscribing milieus of action and response:

> The ecology of practices is defined first and foremost by the fact that the way those practices are introduced and justified, the way they define their requirements and obligations, the way they are described, the way they attract interest, the way they are accountable to others, are interdependent and belong to the same temporality. . . . But the . . . ecology of practices also requires the viability of a register of intervention . . . that affirms the possible, that actively resists the plausible and the probable targeted by approaches that claim to be neutral.[38]

Inspired by the work of Fernández-Savater, Bookchin, and Stengers, we propose the notion of *climates of methods* to signal and draw together the dynamism, tentativeness, and fragility of the political worlds that activists struggle to bring into existence. The term refers to the practical logistics of breathing, imagining, and inspiring together—"to conspire," as the Italian autonomists famously put it in the 1970s, "is to respire together."[39] The concept of climates of methods captures the breeze of impending situations in a new "climate of history," to echo Dipesh Chakrabarty's poignant formulation.[40]

We are interested in particular in the multiplicity, heterogeneity, and promiscuity of the material systematics through which activists inchoate and gamble on the risks and affordances of specific transformational projects and trajectories. In this we describe a history of struggles for the free city that not only seeks to bring to light the moral subjectivities, political positionalities, or discursive formations through which activists claim urban social justice but also accounts for the methods, tactics, and assays—the "rapidly generated hypotheses for how to act," in the words of the urbanists AbdouMaliq Simone and Edgar Pieterse—through which they inhabit their predicaments and problems.[41] What atmospheres of distress, excitement, or joy sustain the imagination of fugitive and insurrectionary designs as enduring and convivial habitats?

Climates of methods are therefore systems of hope whose forms of agency and possibility are not exclusively embodied in the actions of individuals, institutions, or collective organizations, nor are they simply facilitated by the use of technologies, networks, or infrastructures. Moreover, they are also not exhausted by the circumscriptions of rights, entitlements, use values, or identities. Instead, methods operate as assemblages of materials, techniques, revindications, and aspirations that at once carry *and* ground the affordances and reach of the claims at stake. These methods travel as concrete devices with which activists test the limits of their demands and experiment with the material durability and political durée of every right and every freedom, while providing the infrastructures, perceptual systems, and moodscapes for sounding out potential extensions or extrapolations. In the words of the scholar of autonomy Stevphen Shukaitis and the anthropologist David Graeber, they are "methods for liberating life as lived imagination."[42]

The Culture of Free Culture

This book describes our encounter with free culture as a technical and design philosophy in 2010 and our gradual rediscovery, over the course of the following decade, of its imbrication in the city as a climate of methods for autonomous citizenship. The book charts an unexpected ethnographic journey from the squatted laboratories where free software hackers experimented with open infrastructures and legal licenses to the plazas where a new generation of municipalist activists reimagined the free city.

But what is free culture? Where does the movement come from, and what is distinctive about the Spanish case? Let us offer a brief genealogy to set the scene for the rest of the book.

There was a time by the mid-1990s when one could still speak of the internet as a "world that all may enter without privilege or prejudice accorded by race, economic power, military force, or station of birth," as John Perry Barlow famously put it in his Declaration of the Independence of Cyberspace; a world where the "legal concepts of property, expression, identity, movement, and context do not apply."[43] At the heart of Barlow's cyber polity was an architecture of networked democracy made possible by the intuitions and experiences of free software hackers because, as the anthropologist Chris Kelty put it, for a number of years "the Internet look[ed] the way it [did] because of Free Software. Free Software and the Internet are related like figure and ground or like system and environment."[44]

Unlike proprietary software, free and open-source software is software that is free to run. It is also free to access the source code and study how the software works, to redistribute one's own copies of the software, and to change, readapt, and improve the program, and also to release such improvements to the public. As the software engineer and free software activist Richard Stallman famously put it, this makes software a matter of liberty, not price, for free software is "free as in 'free speech,' not as in 'free beer.'"[45]

As we show in chapter 2, in the late 1990s struggles over the management of intellectual property rights, and over peer-to-peer sharing of music files in particular, were pivotal to the rise of what the media studies scholar Hector Postigo called the "digital rights movement."[46] At stake was the nature of cultural works in the digital age: how to define their materiality, what to bind their authorship and ownership to, and how to trace and circumscribe rights and entitlements to their economic royalties and legacies. Over time, digital rights activism evolved from an initial concern regarding conflicts between author and consumer rights in digital content to, in later iterations, larger questions about net neutrality, free speech, and the defense of fundamental liberties—a "free culture movement" largely concerned with liberating "access to the 'cultural commons.'"[47]

The term *free culture* was proposed by Lawrence Lessig, one of the cofounders of the Creative Commons licenses, to describe the potential for liberal democracy inscribed in the technological architecture of the internet.[48] While it is helpful for illuminating how political liberties are framed in the digital age, Lessig's vision of free culture takes a rather partial view of social process by focusing almost exclusively on the roles of technology and law as driving forces of social change. Moreover, it is a vision that uses a largely US-centric cultural matrix for understanding what counts as liberal and libertarian attitudes to digital freedom. As the anthropologist Gabriella Coleman observed, however, there are in fact different geographical and historical traditions of liberalism at play in hacker politics, from anarcho-capitalists to libertarian socialists, with "southern European hackers," for example, following "a more leftist, anarchist tradition than their northern European counterparts."[49]

Despite the importance of the free culture movement in shaping both the technical architecture and the cultural persuasions of digital democracy, there is actually very little comparative scholarship on its development as a situated social and historical movement in different parts of the globe. Thus, while scholars have written insightfully about the "poetics of hacking"[50] and the "cultural logics of networking,"[51] about the values of wit, humor, or craftiness embraced by hackers, or the systems of decentralized and nonhierarchical organization and decision making endorsed by alter-globalization activists, we still know very little about what happens to free culture when it leaves the world of intellectual property lawyers, free software geeks, and networked politics. As Chris Kelty has asked, "What is happening to Free Software as it spreads beyond the world of hackers and software? How is it being modulated? What kinds of limits are breached when software is no longer the central component?"[52]

In his recent book, *The Rise of Nerd Politics*, the anthropologist John Postill has offered an initial response to these questions by engaging in a wider comparative look at the forces and trends that have shaped digital activism into a larger political force across the globe.[53] His comparative survey leads him to identify a class of actors whose skills are not limited to computing or hacking but include media activism, social protest, and formal politics, and among whose members one can also find "artists, journalists, economists, lawyers, politicians and many other specialists, even anthropologists."[54] Postill, whose fieldwork coincided with parts of our own, dedicates a substantial piece of his study to the case of free culture activists in Barcelona, and in light of his findings he alerts his readers to "the importance of paying attention to Spain as an extraordinary laboratory of democracy, in which nerd activism and scholarship have intermingled and co-evolved with the 15M movement."[55] His observations echo Hector Postigo's own concluding remarks about the global transformation of the digital rights movement into a broader political force, "with activists in Europe taking the lead in articulating the flows of a global technolegal regime that seeks to circumscribe the public domain . . . such as Isaac Hackimov [*sic*] and the Hackademy in Spain."[56]

Our own present work provides a historical and ethnographic argument for understanding how digital activism in Spain became this "laboratory of democracy" that Postill talks about. We offer an account of some of the key legal battles and moments of political organization that free software hackers and digital activists in Spain have been involved in over the past twenty years. However, our account departs from the literature on network and digital politics in that we also strive to provide a thick description of how these various debates and struggles circulated and were shaped by specific brick-and-mortar contexts, at squatted social centers and public museums, in plazas, academic spaces, or abandoned industrial factories. In so doing we pick up on the questions posed by Kelty about what happens to free culture when it spreads beyond the world of hackers and networked activism. The relation between free culture and public culture—as incarnated, for example, in public museums or public universities—is one that we pay particular attention to, as we describe how they worked at times as analogues, antagonists, or even enablers of one another and in so doing textured, thickened, and complexified the imbrication of welfarist promises with autonomist hopes.

Freedom from Culture: Inchoations of the Intransitive

When we began fieldwork in 2010, the financial crisis was pushing the Spanish economy into the darkest corners of the European periphery. By 2011, the meltdown of the property market had dragged the urban middle and working classes into an abyss of precariousness and desperation, with unemployment hitting

21.4 percent of the working population, or 5 million people, and 42.3 percent of workers under the age of twenty-five.[57] In June 2012, the Spanish government requested external financial assistance from the European Financial Stability Fund for an estimated 100 billion euros (€) over an eighteen-month period. The assistance was granted subject to extremely harsh conditions, including reforms of the pension system (freezing pensions and raising the age of retirement) and the labor market (drastically reducing the cost of dismissals), as well as massive retrenchments in health care and education.

Our ethnography took place in this context of austerity and precarity. Many of our friends and ethnographic counterparts have moved in and out of precarious employment for as long as we have known them. Many others were pushed to set up alternative cooperative or associative networks just to make ends meet; and yet others were pushed out from their homes by escalating rents and mortgage rates and forced into squatting.[58] We will relate their stories later, but for now, suffice it to say that our fieldwork certainly gives credence to the geographer Jamie Peck's observation that "austerity is becoming a new urban condition."[59] However, notwithstanding the very real drama of economic hardship and insecurity of these years, our book aims to strike a different tone. In the aftermaths of austerity, one can also witness, as the sociologist Fran Tonkiss has observed, "a mode of urban practice that works within the cracks between formal planning, speculative investment and local possibilities."[60] We offer here one such interstitial ethnography, an account of the cultures of inventiveness and methods of futurity that snaked their way through the ruins of austerity; an account of how free culture collectives responded to the neoliberalization of the city by way of the urbanization of liberation—the tentative inchoation of a free/libre urbanism.

While the political economy of austerity no doubt helped nurture such a culture of resistance and rebelliousness, it was also partially entangled in a longer series of tectonic shifts in the cultural matrix of Spanish historical consciousness, shifts that made the occasional appearance in people's arguments, expositions, and self-perceptions during the course of our ethnographic work. We refer to the legacies and memories of the country's dictatorial past, which, as several commentators have pointed out, were still actively shaping—when not overdetermining—the structure of its liberal public sphere. These are issues that have inflected Spanish cultural history and theory since, which is why we briefly engage with them here too.

Following the death of the dictator Franco in 1975, the country transitioned to a parliamentary democratic system over the next five years. Popularly known as la Transición (the Transition), this period saw the molding of an ideology of political consensus and democratic culture—the so-called Culture of the

Transition—which was in effect simply a prolongation of the narrative of modernization and development set in motion during the Francoist dictatorship.[61] As the cultural historian Germán Labrador put it, "Starting in 1977, the discursive production of historical discontinuity [vis-à-vis the dictatorship] became the State's key politico-cultural task, which helped found, in turn, the cultural logic of Spanish democracy as a project born *ex nihilo*."[62]

The ghosts of the Francoist social system have haunted Spain's cultural and political history ever since. Notwithstanding the far-reaching influence of the Culture of the Transition as "the legitimating framework of a project of neoliberal transformation which mainly uses [a] modernizing, pro-European discourse," there were, of course, sites and expressions of resistance and opposition to such a project.[63] The histories of these countercultural ecologies and lifestyles, however, is only now being unearthed and written. The recent work of Germán Labrador is very important in this regard, for it has given voice to an underground vanguard of musicians, writers, and artists who gave themselves to experimenting with drugs, sex, and a poetics of life that violently placed them at odds with the liberal consensus of Spanish postdictatorial society, thus shaping their own "transitional lives as works of art."[64] These transitional subjects, Labrador suggests, may be thought of as inhabiting a space of critical self-detachment from the consensual myth of Spanish democratization. Activist historian Gonzalo Wilhelmi has similarly drawn attention to the oppositional and insurrectional operations of numerous autonomous, neighborhood, and workers' movements that throughout the late 1970s struggled against the pact of silence and amnesty that finally led to the Culture of the Transition and the establishment of a liberal democracy and parliamentary monarchy.[65] Yet all such "grassroots actors," as the historian Andrea Davis has explained, "were coerced into dropping the memory and legacy of the dictatorship from the popular agenda."[66] These actors struggled to "break the consensus," as Wilhelmi puts it, and their embrace of direct democracy aimed at the establishment of a socialist republic. Theirs were grassroots struggles that, amid the death rattles of dictatorship, "came together as a commons to the defense of the public."[67]

The situated legacies of this commons-public complex are central to the story we tell in this book. In particular, we follow Labrador in defining such commons-public assemblages as expressive of an undercurrent of "intransitive culture" brewing in Spain since the last years of the dictatorship.[68] Silenced and ostracized by the metanarratives of neoliberal Europeanization, such intransitive cultures gestured toward modes of life nervously posed between the near-Norths of modernization and the near-Souths of peripheralization. The history of such an intransitive stance toward democratization is important for our own account of free culture activism because it helps situate what exactly activists were seeking to liberate themselves from at the turn of the century. As the cultural theorist Luis Moreno-Caballud suggested, in the context of the mobilizations leading up to the 15M protests, the practices of free culture activists—including the use of free licenses and editorial systems for collective authorship, cultural remixing, collaborative work, and autonomous digital infrastructures—played a key part in the process of "cultural democratization" that challenged the interlacing of "cultural authority" and "neoliberal logic" silently sustaining the myth of Spanish political modernity for the past forty years.[69] Put somewhat differently, the liberation of culture that free culture activists aspired to and wrestled with was a liberation from the Culture of the Transition. In this context, cultura libre rekindled the faded aspirations of intransitive democratization. Therefore, this was a practice of liberation with very specific cultural and historical roots, a situated exercise in both negative and positive freedom: *liberation from* the legacy and memory of post-Francoist culture, including the structures of feeling harnessed by, and for the production of, modernizing, elitist, and Enlightened subjectivities; as well as *liberation to* experiment with new forms of direct democracy, infrastructural solidarity, and autonomous expression. Thus, the "cry of the streets" during the 15M demonstrations, as the historian Kostis Kornetis put it, "rendered the *Transición* a synecdoche for Spanish society agonizing between past and present, remembrance and oblivion, exemplary processes and unfinished ones, reconciliation and ongoing traumas."[70] Or, as we shall pick up later, in the Conclusion, for over twenty years, the histories and stories of the urbanization of liberation, from the pleas for free culture to the glimmers of the free city, drifted and drafted currents, contours, and moodscapes for an *intransitive urbanism*: a coming together as a commons to the defense of the public through the tools of the libre.

Part 1
THE CULTURES
OF THE FREE CITY

When Margarita Padilla first walked into the Laboratory on July 1997, a joyful image crossed her mind: "A rhizome." Margarita had long read Gilles Deleuze and Félix Guattari but, as she put it to us, she had "never quite grasped what a rhizome might look like outside its botanical forms. What might it mean to experience a rhizome?" As she walked into the Laboratory, however, she felt "overtaken by a profound ambience of multiplicity and joy (*gozo*)," and noted to herself, "This is what a rhizome must be. I need to stay here and live this."[1]

The memory of the Laboratory holds a special place in the history of autonomous and countercultural collectives in Madrid. A self-managed squatted social center (*centro social okupado autogestionado*), the space opened on April 19, 1997, following a tumultuous period of violent evictions in other centers in the previous years. The Laboratory was founded by an alliance of the evicted in defiant response to what some people believed were gratuitous acts of state repression. Over the course of the following six years, and notwithstanding its closure and subsequent reincarnation at three different sites, the Laboratory faithfully stood up to its name and enabled a multifaceted examination of the conditions and challenges underpinning the practice of autonomy in between the rise of network politics, the dawn of informational capitalism, and the daunting logics of urban dispossession. Spanning the turn of the century, between 1997 and 2003, the lifespan of the Laboratory thus contributed to reformulating an illustrious legacy of autonomous activism and occupation into an expansive ecology of urban experimentation and liberation.

On July 1997 Margarita had arrived in Madrid from Barcelona to attend the Second Intercontinental Meeting for Humanity and against Neoliberalism, a follow-up to the Zapatistas' call in Chiapas a year earlier to form an intercontinental network of resistance. The Laboratory hosted the Madrid node of the meeting, which was the first international encounter to be attended by members of the EZLN (Ejército Zapatista de Liberación Nacional, the Zapatista National Liberation Army).[2] Margarita was forty years old at the time. In her youth in the late 1970s she had militated in workers' autonomous groups in Barcelona, when Spain was battling to forge a new horizon for democracy after a forty-year dictatorship. Yet she had a bitter memory of those years, of promises and expectations forgone. As she recalled in one of our interviews, her political militancy went "dormant" for the best part of the "long, dark political tunnel" of the 1980s, only to resuscitate in the wake of the appearance of new squatter movements in the 1990s.

Remaining faithful to the impression that the Laboratory first made on her, Margarita was one of a small core of people who became full-time squatters at the center. A computer engineer by training, she had been involved in a number of counterinformational networks throughout the 1990s. For a while she worked at Nodo50, the first "antagonist telematics" in Spain, which was set up in 1993 as a networked coalition of local nongovernmental organizations (NGOs) to coordinate their contribution to the worldwide protests against the International Monetary Fund (IMF) and World Bank on occasion of the fiftieth anniversary of the Bretton Woods agreements (which took place in Madrid in fall 1994). Shortly after settling in the Laboratory, Margarita decided to put her skills as a software engineer to good use. She helped set up the center's hacklab, and over the course of her stay she also played a leading role in the creation of sinDominio, a free software server that quickly became the preeminent countercultural digital platform in the country and hosted email lists and webpages for squatted social centers, autonomous collectives, hacklabs, and disobedience groups over the following decade.

At once a gentle but also subtly self-critical observer, over the years Margarita developed a certain discomfort with the digital utopianism of some hacker communities. "There is a compositional game to how our bodies come together, how we touch one another," she wrote in one of a number of texts that she penned around this time, "that carries a political premium . . . a type of trust and complicity that in my experience one does not find in telematics. . . . There are practices that challenge you to put your own experiences at risk, that call for experimenting with the risks of experience."[3] Thus, she set out to discover, play, and experience with new languages, venues, and tools of expression; she peeked into the joys of exploring the city as a climate of methods. To name but a few of the projects she became involved with, in the early 2000s she joined the broadcasting team of one of the first women-only internet-based free radio stations. Around that time, she also helped bring into existence a "hacking in the neighborhood" project (hackers de barrio), whose objective was to inhabit and "incarnate the conflict of proximity that holds the digital and the organic at once together and apart."[4] In 2004, shortly after the Madrid train bombing, which killed 192 people, Margarita joined a horizontal space of dialogue, reflection, and accompaniment that included victims of the attack and their kin.

The story of Margarita, her militancy in anarchist and autonomous movements, her involvement with squatted social centers, and her unflinching embrace of free culture as a complex technical and social form—such a story informs the history of free culture activism that we wish to essay here. The story of Margarita, along with others we shall be hearing about, is a story of the weaving and unweaving of digital and material liberations in the fabric of the city, a story about the designs and vitalities of autonomous experience. These stories inform the history of free culture that we outline in part 1, where free culture reveals itself not just as a philosophy of technical expression or a networked movement but also as an urban culture. In this story of Spain and Madrid, free culture turns out to be entangled in a wider narrative about autonomous and libertarian movements, about the struggles for the right to the city in squatted social centers but also in arts centers and cultural organizations. True, it is a story about networks and technology, but it is also a story about plazas and assemblies, about barrios and rave parties, about guerrilla street artists, intellectual property lawyers, and curators. It is a story, then, about the urban ecologies of free culture.

Ours is not an attempt to provide a full historiography of this period, which is an effort well beyond the scope of this book, but rather to give a feel for the debates, issues, and challenges that shaped free culture into a singular urban movement. As such, chapter 1 traces the history of autonomous movements in Madrid and their entanglement with the struggles for housing rights and neighborhood politics of squatted social centers, as well as the ties that university students established with Italian autonomia collectives in their fight against precarity in the 1990s. Chapter 2 provides an overview of the birth of so-called self-defensive telematics in squatted social centers and the debates concerning the nature of autonomy as a space of vitality between network rights and affective needs. Chapter 3 then tells the story of how autonomous projects and public art institutions mutually allured one another, and in so doing generated a tension between a certain intellectual avant-garde and a burgeoning experience of the city as commons. All in all, part 1 seeks to describe how digital autonomous projects in Madrid found their way out into the city and in doing so chartered novel territories of encounters, diffractions, and antagonisms between the public, the commons, and the libre.

FREE NEIGHBORHOODS

On March 12, 1977, the police stormed into the broadcasting studio of Radio Alice in Bologna, the first free radio station in Italy. A day earlier a student had been killed in the city during massive student demonstrations across the country. Radio Alice had immediately broadcast news of the death, sparking the mobilization of one hundred thousand people. Students set up barricades and declared "free zones" around the city. One of the founders of the radio, Franco "Bifo" Berardi, had been arrested a year earlier on charges of "inciting rebellion." That evening, the police broke into the studio and "made eight arrests for incitement of delinquency and subversive association, but they were unable to find Bifo. The next day, March 13, Bologna was under siege."[1]

In 1976, a year ahead of the violent police attack on Radio Alice, Bifo and the radio collective wrote *Alice Is the Devil*, a short book about the radio station's experimental ecology of telecommunications.[2] The book was at once a denunciation of the circumstances that had led to Bifo's arrest, an account of the internal political tensions experienced by the radio's collective, and a theorization of workers' autonomy through a Dadaist exploration of technology and language:

> The experience of Radio Alice has been caught between two poles: on the one hand, an expression of the politics and desires of a core group of people . . . and on the other hand, the expression of the movement's tendency towards experiences of liberation. . . . This is the reason why it's time to resume a Dadaist orientation: to critique and overcome the

separation between art and life . . . to recompose transversally the movement's subject. . . . Writing texts in the plazas, painting red all life forms, transform the colors of the city and the language of relations. . . . The central question for the revolutionary process amounts to nothing else than the liberation of the worker's life vis-à-vis salaried employment, the collective transformation of free time and the spaces of life, and of language.[3]

When *Alice Is the Devil* was published in French a year later, in 1977, Félix Guattari wrote the preface to the book. "The viewpoint of autonomy towards the mass media of communication," he explained, "was that a hundred flowers should blossom, a hundred radio stations should broadcast."[4] As Bifo later noted, Guattari was drawn to the Italian free radio movement in Italy as "a precursor of libertarian cyber culture."[5] The ecology of Alice—the airwaves, the streets, the bodies—embodied for Guattari the molecular revolution that would become his theoretical signature only a few years later: "A whole engagement of theory—life—praxis—group—sex—solitude—machine—affection—caressing."[6]

Alice Is the Devil was translated and published in Spain in 1981. An autonomist movement had blossomed there in the late 1970s amid the ashes of the Francoist forty-year dictatorship (1939–1975). As Lester Golden put it in 1978,

> forty years of living in a political strait jacket have left Spanish society with too many groups with unredressed grievances that will not stand for being "temporarily" ignored while the "consolidation of Spanish democracy" is engineered by the PCE and PSOE "pactistas" [Communist and Socialist Parties' deal makers]. The PCE and PSOE have distanced themselves from the growing feminist and gay liberation movements, attempted to prevent or slow down neighborhood organizations' occupations of unused apartments, closure of polluting industrial plants, and land occupations by unemployed landless laborers in Andalusia.[7]

The end of the dictatorship crystallized a period of associative effervescence that sowed its seeds in the late 1960s. By 1977, a survey conducted by the National Department for Youth and Sociocultural Development noted that 51 percent of the country's youth were unequivocally in favor of workers' self-management cooperatives, compared with just 8 percent voting for a capitalist mode of organization. When asked about property regimes, 27 percent of youths said that private property should only apply to "personal goods (housing, cars) and not to production goods (businesses, land), while 20 percent were against private property altogether."[8]

The vibrancy of the associative, neighborhood, and libertarian movements in Madrid was famously described by Manuel Castells in his magisterial *The City and the Grassroots*.[9] In this ambitious cross-cultural theory of urban social change, Castells identified the citizen social movement that took to the streets in the 1970s as "the most powerful and innovative neighborhood movement" of any European capital.[10] In the early 1970s, the movement spearheaded the struggle for housing rights by establishing a vibrant coalition of "*gentes con inquietudes*" (concerned people) that included *vecinos-trabajadores* (neighbor-workers), communist militants, grassroots Catholic activists, lawyers, and architects.[11] While for many years the movement struggled for basic neighborhood rights (the legalization of slums, water and sewage infrastructure, public schools and transport), toward the end of the 1970s it had developed a broader urban consciousness of its struggle as a "school of democracy."[12]

Thus, between 1976 and 1978 the movement organized the occupation of some five hundred vacant houses, while "trade-union anarchists also occupied buildings that they considered their legitimate properties confiscated by the fascist Franco's regime," giving birth to "an active network of Ateneos Libertarios [Libertarian Athenaeums] [that] emerged in the transition to democracy."[13] The Madrid Citizen Movement, about which we say more in the conclusion, epitomized for Castells the capacity of social movements not just to vindicate specific rights or resources but also to "produce qualitative changes in the urban system, local culture, and political institutions in contradiction to the dominant social interests institutionalized as such at the societal level."[14]

By the early 1980s, however, the movement had lost much of its impetus. For one thing, the elite negotiations that established the terms for reforming and transitioning the dictatorship into a democracy were designed to mute and delegitimize "the grassroots narrative of the popular conquest and defence of democracy."[15] Over time, la Transición, the process of institutional democratization, co-opted much of the movement's energy, with some of its leaders and members taking jobs in municipal governments or rising the echelons of political parties.[16] Marxist, anarchist, or libertarian groups survived here and there, pullulating across the city with little or no relationship to one another. Their horizons of political action and hope were also diverse, spanning environmental, feminist, and antimilitarist aspirations. Slowly, some of these groups began sounding out spaces of mutual complicity and collective action. For example, in 1983 a group of free radio stations signed the Villaverde Manifesto, thus claiming a sense of autonomy and common purpose vis-à-vis the proliferation of unlicensed pirate radio stations. Free radio, they proclaimed, differed from pirate radio in the adherence to principles of self-management, nonprofitability, and decentralization in telecommunications.[17] In 1985, the editorial collective behind the punk fanzine *Penetracción* joined a band of university and high school students in squatting in a vacant building in the neighborhood of Lavapiés in Madrid. They were moved by "the struggle for the right to housing in the city, which they feel is especially pressing for the youth."[18] Theirs was a movement defined by "a certain punk aesthetic, marked by a preoccupation with the future of work for the youth, the values of music as an open form of expression, and a general antisystemic ethos."[19] The squat was evicted only ten days later, but that was long enough to have a play put on by a local theater group, organize a carpentry workshop, equip the space with a modest library, and provide rehearsal spaces for local bands.[20] However, rather than to their libertarian forefathers, these groups looked up to the aesthetic and cultural influences of budding German and Italian autonomist collectives for inspiration.[21]

Despite their diverse provenances and sensibilities, the experience of squatting offered many of these groups a shared environment for organization, encounter, and experiment.[22] They tried out modalities of engagement and worked toward designing spaces of complicity that were often explicitly antagonistic to partisan politics and cadre formations, that foregrounded the embodied experience of participants and groped tentatively toward horizons of direct democracy and action. The sociologist Cristina Flesher Fominaya (née Eguiarte), who studied autonomous movements in Madrid at the turn of the century, described these various cultural practices as amounting to a "logic of autonomy," and the history of autonomous groups in the European context has indeed found these to be widely shared cultural values and aspirations.[23]

A key referent in the Spanish scene in this context was the squatted social center of Minuesa, which operated in Madrid from 1988 to 1994. A former print shop, the premises were occupied by its workers in 1988 following the firm's declaration of insolvency. This led to a strike where workers were joined by a variety of neighborhood and student collectives in protesting against real estate speculation and demanding the right to housing. One of the leading historians of the autonomist movement in Madrid, Gonzalo Wilhelmi Casanova, described Minuesa as a "watershed" in the history of autonomism in the city.[24] Whereas throughout the 1980s squats served as reclusive spaces for countercultural communities, in particular radical left-wing and antimilitarist groups, Minuesa found a somewhat different place for itself in the urban landscape. The squat offered a platform where an eclectic cohort of grassroots initiatives recognized their respective needs and capacities and offered each other mutual assistance. Local neighborhood associations, trade unions, groups like Mothers against Drugs, and collectives of precarious workers found in Minuesa a venue for collaboration.[25] The claims of these and other groups layered onto the original printers' and students' demands for social housing and, in the process, articulated a textured and intricate network of complicities and complexities that shaped the urban landscape anew. It is this experience that led historians to describe Minuesa as "the first squatted social center in the city."[26]

Precarity

In 1949, the Spanish poet and critic Luis Rosales published *La Casa Encendida* (*The House in Flames*), perhaps his most ambitious and complex collection of poetry. Rosales returned to the text repeatedly over the following two decades and published a much revised and expanded edition in 1967. A close friend of Federico García Lorca, Rosales was haunted all his life by the assassination of that poet, who in the hours previous to his detainment had, in fact, sought refuge in the Rosales family home. The Rosales's household was profoundly conservative and some of Luis's brothers were well-known members of the Falangist Party, an influential National-Catholic movement that espoused a fascist ideology during the Spanish dictatorship. The Falange Party was the only political party permitted by the dictatorship, and it was designed as a totalitarian, integrated system, where workers and employers stood side-by-side in a so-called *sindicato vertical*, a "vertical" trade union. As we noted in the introduction, the cultural memory of such a hierarchical, fascist, Catholic society deeply pervades Spain's ideological spectrum to this day, where it has modulated, and still modulates, the experiences and orientations of countercultural action.

In *The House in Flames*, a work that is deeply intimate and lyrical, Rosales found comfort and hope for the torments of memory and nostalgia in the safe haven afforded by the home as a space of family and friendship. The metaphor of the house in flames is one that the critical sociologist Jesús Ibáñez returned to in his 1994 book, *Por una sociología de la vida cotidiana* (For a sociology of everyday life).[27] The house in flames, for Ibáñez, is no longer a space of conservative and bourgeois morality and sentiment but a space of centrifugal expulsion and dispersion.[28] The warmth of electrified consumerism has replaced the warmth of the hearth. We can no longer feel at home in our houses, notes Ibáñez, for "our very own bodies are in exile at home."[29] What were once spaces of repose have been redesigned anew into "combinatory games" of "ambience," "brightness," and spectacle.[30]

A staunch critic of modern, consumerist life, Ibáñez was professor in the Department of Sociology and Political Science at Madrid's Complutense University. He is widely regarded today as one of the founders of a distinctive school of Spanish critical sociology, one of a few, moreover, who drew a dedicated body of student followers in the 1980s.[31] Ibáñez, like most postwar intellectuals, had been brought up within the academic circles of the Falangist Party, although over the course of his life he migrated to radical left-wing political positions. Better known among his colleagues for his work on the epistemology of the social sciences, and in particular his introduction of the focus group as a methodological-cum-ideological innovation in the Spanish context, Ibáñez's students were drawn to him for his erudition and commitment in all matters of political theory and action.[32] Ibáñez's reputation as a fiercely independent intellectual had few equals in the Spanish intellectual landscape of the 1980s.[33] In the late 1970s, Ibáñez had been involved, as he himself would later put it, in some "guerrilla politics" in Madrid aimed at opening up spaces of autonomous and creative political action outside the increasingly constraining framework of the Communist and Socialist Parties, which monopolized the language of democratic institutionalization in the postdictatorship years.[34] In this context, he drafted an umbrella manifesto under which a disparate variety of radical left-wing parties, including the Communist movement, the Communist Revolutionary League, the Workers' Party, and the Workers' Revolutionary Organization, attempted to produce a unified political program for the general elections in 1977, although in the end this proved a futile effort.

Under the inspiration of Ibáñez in the 1980s, not a few of his sociology students took to the streets and joined the ranks of autonomous collectives across the city. "Many of us found our way into Minuesa," noted Miguel Martínez, now a professor of urban sociology at Uppsala University, "through Ibáñez. He introduced us to a branch of libertarian and autonomous Marxism that stirred quite a few of his students to get involved in squat and autonomist collectives."[35] It was a group of Ibáñez's students in the Department of Sociology and Political Science that set up the counterinformational bulletin *Molotov* in 1986, which would in time become the preeminent radical news agency in the city.[36] Some of Ibáñez's students also helped organize Lucha Autónoma (Autonomous Struggle), the coordinating network for autonomous collectives in Madrid.[37]

The presence of students, in particular sociology students, had far-reaching implications for the self-representation of autonomy as an urban, theoretical, and transformative project. Students were caught up in a double bind: energized by their intellectual and academic studies, they roamed the city for models of working-class consciousness that were, however, hardly representative of their own experiences. The statutes of Lucha Autónoma declared the "subject position" of the collective "as that of the working class, modeling them after those of the CNT [Confederación Nacional de Trabajadores, the National Workers' Confederation, which was the preeminent anarchist trade union in Spain]." However, "70–80% of the founding members were university students, or had recently completed their university education," and of course had little or no experience of working-class activism themselves.[38] With no experience of factory-floor politics, students searched in books and in the streets for an emerging style of autonomous consciousness.[39] They debated and discussed heatedly the nature of autonomy as a body of theory and praxis, its genealogical connections to the Italian *autonomia operaia* (workers' autonomy) or German Autonomen traditions, and the pull and push forces that energized the movement between the fabric of the city and wider dynamics of global protest.[40] "We would hunt the city for books recommended to us by Ibáñez," wrote Miguel Martínez, "and would often find them in the sales of squatted social centers. It seemed an obvious connection to us at the time: from the university to the squats via autonomy as a theoretical and practical project."[41] The space of the university thus animated and outlined the space of autonomy as an urban orientation.

In 1991, two members of Lucha Autónoma traveled to Italy and came across the use of the label *social centers* in reference to squats for the first time.[42] Among the materials they brought back from the trip was a copy of *Alice Is the Devil*. Although the book had been translated and published in Spanish in 1981, its rediscovery by the young militants of Lucha Autónoma had profound consequences:

> We suddenly found ourselves with a repertoire of concepts—"to conspire is to respire together," "the practice of happiness is subversive"—that were, true, a little abstract, almost Dadaist, yet introduced an element of rupture with the classic, militant approach to activism that we found profoundly refreshing. We had been schooled into an imaginary of radical autonomy where direct action and confrontation were central to its practice. When we found these texts in 1991, where autonomy was described as an intimate entanglement with the territory, as a generative form of sociability—where neighborhoods and *vecinos* [neighbors] are identified as the new subjects of relation—well, what a fascinating and liberating read that was![43]

Inspired by the promises of their recently found Dadaist toolkit, in 1993 some members of Lucha Autónoma organized the first of many visits to Italian squatted social centers.[44] The visits allowed them to witness in person the plurality and heterogeneity of sensibilities and tools that were being mobilized, without too much concern, apparently, for the purity of their autonomous provenance.[45] The visit "provided us with a first-hand account of a large variety of experiences, some with an incredibly potent expression of autonomy—which one may not recognize in otherwise more classic structures—such as Leoncavallo [a squatted social center] or cyberactivism. . . . They [Italian social centers] were in fact the first ones to report on the Zapatista insurgency because of their connection to the Internet. We were awestruck."[46]

The Italian trip introduced the Madrid-based collectives to the question of "transversality," in the terms described by Guattari and quickly picked up by Bifo and his colleagues at Radio Alice.[47] What, then, would it have meant for these ideas to be uprooted from their Italian bearings and transported into the Madrid context? What might transversality have meant there?[48]

In fact, this question burdened autonomous groups for the best part of the 1990s. In 1986, Spain had entered the European Community and, under the terms of the Single European Act, the Spanish state embarked on the full liberalization of the national economy. "The surge in FDI [foreign direct investment] since Spain joined the European Economic Community in 1986," an international policy analyst observed in retrospect over a decade later, "has been such that it seemed at times as if the country was up for sale."[49] Indeed, over the following decade this led to the introduction of measures for the "deregulation and flexibilisation of capital and labor market, control of nominal wage increases, and an accelerated privatization of public enterprises."[50] The labor market in particular was hit like no other country in the European economy. In 1988, the then ruling Socialist Party presented a proposal for labor reform aiming to introduce flexible contracts, which were popularly labeled as *contratos basura* (garbage contracts). The project was met with a general strike in which "more than 95 percent of the active population stopped working" under the "call to fight 'precarious contracts.'"[51] By 1994, however, the government succeeded in introducing these and other measures to deregulate the labor market, and the effects were catastrophic, with unemployment reaching a record high of 24.17 percent and youth unemployment peaking at 42.33 percent for the 20–24 age group.[52] It is in this context that student activists first declared their resistance to corporate and transnational globalization—a few years ahead of the alter-globalization protests in Seattle in 1999—by reclaiming the legacy of political autonomy and liberation from the spatial and temporal dictates of capital.[53] It is also in this context that the conceptual framework of "precarity" was first invoked by these young autonomists to make sense of their conditions of disenfranchisement and ruination.[54] The rise of autonomism in the 1990s was a direct response to these transformations. As the lawyer and labor movements scholar José Luis Carretero (himself an active participant in the autonomist movement) put it, "the 'autonomist scene' ... was an attempt at organizing an emerging precarious workforce. ... Precarity; new forms of existence; a relation (a little ambivalent on occasions) with the labor struggle; the development of its own cultural sphere, at once plural, transgressive, and creative; a commitment towards its imbrication in the neighborhood fabric; a dense sociability—these and many more things is what the urban autonomous movement accomplished in Madrid in the 1990s."[55]

The experiences of precarity and fragmentation and the urge to respond by organizing networks of autonomous resistance echo the well-known description that social theorist Alberto Melucci made of the rise of "new social movements" in Italy in the wake of postindustrialization in the late 1970s, and in particular his characterization of a then-emerging form of collective action carried out by a generation of young "nomads of the present": "These Italian developments exemplify a more general change in the dominant form of collective action. In the 1980s collective action came to be based on . . . the form of networks composed of a multiplicity of groups that are dispersed, fragmented and submerged in everyday life, and which act as cultural laboratories. . . . The submerged networks of social movements are laboratories of experience."[56]

The alliances that squatters, students, immigrants, and unionized workers established in the face of increasing unemployment and precarity around the "laboratories of experience" of Minuesa and the Laboratory responded to such a logic of submerged networking and cultural experimentation. As Michael Hardt put it back in 1996, the "experiments of laboratory Italy are now experiments on the political conditions of an increasing large part of the world . . . due partly [to] new forms of production that involve more immaterial and cybernetic forms of labor, flexible and precarious networks of employment."[57] The Madrid autonomous scene was no different. In fact, it is arguable that the numerous visits and exchanges between Italian and Spanish squatted social centers throughout the 1990s laid the grounds for a heightened consciousness about the radical potential of autonomy as a source of transversal radical praxis.

It is significant that the 1980s also saw the rise of a social movement in Spain that was unique in the global landscape of resistance and had a profound influence on the local culture of autonomy: the movement against obligatory military service, locally known as *insumisión* (insurrection). Back in the 1980s, it was mandatory for all young males over the age of eighteen to serve twelve months in the army (in 1991 the period of service was reduced to nine months and in 2001 it was finally abolished). Students were allowed to postpone conscription until graduation, when a few opted for insurrection, running away and hiding from the state in squatted social centers and autonomous circles. By the time the military service was abolished, some fifty thousand youths had declared themselves *insumisos* (disobedients) of which one thousand ended up imprisoned.[58]

It was not uncommon for these young rebels to be highly educated, and some went on to develop well-known careers as artistic provocateurs. In this context, although originally a carrier of antimilitaristic and antifascist sentiments, the phrase *vivir insumiso* (insurrectional life) soon became a metonym for antisystemic aspirations and desires and, to the dislike of many activists, a synonym for the joy of autonomous living more broadly.[59] The polysemy of insurrectional living signaled an ethos of experimentation that stretched from electronic music to drug consumption, from squatting to raving—"If there ain't no dancing," activists would say, echoing Emma Goldman's famous aphorism, "it ain't my revolution."[60] The delirium of vivir insumiso aspired for an overflow of desires, affects and *gozo* (joy), as Margarita put it in the opening vignette of part 1, into a total experience of liberation for which the city was the canvas.

Over time, however, the project of joyful liberation produced some disaffections. Some regarded it as the expression of a self-affected, masculine vanguard, represented for the most part by insumisos men, who bragged about their own capacity to "refuse work" (a classic autonomous concept to which we shall turn in a moment). As the activist historian Gonzalo Wilhelmi explained, "There was a profound split between those who despised work—to the extent that they would speak of labor precarity in positive terms, as an 'opportunity' for liberating oneself from the chains of employment—and those who got implicated in the self-organization of precarious workers."[61] The split had also an important gender dimension and triggered an acute problematization of the identity of feminism within autonomous spaces, between "those young women, probably university students, claiming that there was nothing better than to live without working, and those women who had come from the other side of the world and would give anything for a shit job."[62]

Barrios Libres

One of the key concepts of the 1960s workers' autonomous movement in Italy was the "refusal of work": the aspiration to subtract oneself from capitalist relations of production and imagine alternative forms of sociality sustained on non-waged labor—affective labor, immaterial and material labor, desiring labor, or the labor of care that reproduces society. Among autonomists, such a project was often conceived as an "exodus" or "defection," as Paolo Virno put it, from the institutions of the capitalist state and the relations of waged labor—a defection not to "a spatial 'frontier' but [as] an abundance of knowledge, communication, and acting-in-concert implied by the publicness of general intellect. The act of collective imagination that we call 'defection' gives an independent, affirmative, high-profile expression to this abundance."[63]

In *Fragments of an Anarchist Anthropology*, David Graeber recalls the history of the Italian autonomous movement to underscore the importance that "the broad refusal of factory work among young people, the flourishing of squats and occupied 'social centers' in so many Italian cities . . . [had] as a kind of laboratory for future social movements," including the theory of exodus that autonomists developed.[64] For Graeber, the spatial imagination underpinning the theory of exodus is part of "a history which has largely yet to be written" on the minor yet expansive compositions of revolutionary practice, which includes, among its exceptional "glimmerings,"[65] the concept of the "temporary autonomous zone" developed by Peter Lamborn Wilson (aka Hakim Bey).[66]

The essay on the temporary autonomous zone (TAZ) has acquired somewhat of a cult status in anarchist circles since it was first published in New York in 1990. With its insurrectional aesthetics and poetic vision—"The TAZ is an encampment of guerrilla ontologists"—and not least with its embrace of the anarcho-libertarian stream of hacker philosophy, Bey's topological vision for autonomy has inspired the prefigurative and practical imagination of radical movements at the turn of the century.[67] However, there are to this day few empirical studies of actually existing TAZ, if for no reason other than, as Bey himself put it, "as soon as the TAZ is named (represented, mediated), it must vanish, it *will* vanish, leaving behind it an empty husk, only to spring up again somewhere else, once again invisible."[68] Instead of TAZs, therefore, political scientists have turned their attention to the study of so-called free spaces as zones of refuge and aspiration that—within the bounds permitted by the liberal framework of political science itself—somewhat approximate the laboratories of autonomy.

In their classic study of free spaces, the political theorists Sara Evans and Harry Boyte studied, for example, the safe havens afforded by black churches under slavery; the role played by prayer groups, mothers' clubs, or benevolent associations for widows and orphans in the women's movement; and the importance of union halls and secret societies for the workers' movement.[69] Whereas Evans and Boyte originally deployed the term *free space* to refer for the most part to social dynamics taking place in a material setting, the political theorist Francesca Polletta has more recently drawn attention to the "social structural dimensions of several cultural dynamics" that in her view characterize different types of free spaces.[70] She speaks, for example, of "transmovement" structures whereby activists find a suitable form for federating and networking—across geographies, organizations, or agendas—their capacities and resources; "indigenous" structures that are not initially founded on an oppositional agenda but on the basis of a community of interests and complicities; and "prefigurative" structures, through which activists' organizational projects themselves model the world they are trying to build.[71] In other words, it is the cultures of organization, trust and intimacy, and distributive justice and economy, rather than their material setting, that shape a free space.

One of the central arguments we wish to develop in this book is that in the case of the free culture movement in Madrid, the "microcosm of that 'anarchist

dream' of a free culture," as Hakim Bey described the spatial aspirations of autonomy, was shaped and modulated by an assemblage of techniques, infrastructures,
affects, and methods as much as it was by dimensions of structure, organization,
and culture.[72] Activists spent as much time discussing and debating political
philosophy or organizational strategies as they spent designing, furnishing, or
repurposing buildings, tools, archives, licenses, servers, and protocols. It is significant that the uses, redeployments, and configurations of these various resources and equipment had consequences that traveled across the city, either
enabling or disabling, aligning or disrupting, particular kinds of relationships
and environments. Therefore, rather than thinking of it in terms of free spaces or
TAZs, we wish to think of free culture here as an ecology or climate of methods—
an ecology that was activated with and as an urban orientation and problematic.

Indeed, central to such an ecology was the experience of the *barrio*, the neighborhood, as both a habitat and a habitus of encounter, exchange, and experiment. The question of the neighborhood is one that we shall return to often
throughout the book. One of the arguments we pursue is that neighborhoods—
and the neighborhood of Lavapiés in particular—became trading zones where
activists explored, negotiated, and navigated the boundaries and interstices between network culture, autonomist politics, and insurrectional aesthetics. Neighborhoods became spaces of assay and trial for articulating a new type of
freedom—the freedom of "free culture"—as a specific form of urban liberation
born from the exchanges and frictions between civil, infrastructural, and digital rights.

The political struggles over housing rights and public infrastructure that took
place in Lavapiés at the turn of the century exemplify this notion of the neighborhood as both a space of hope and a problem-space of insurgent inquiry, experiment, and liberation. A brief historical recapitulation can serve to further
situate our argument.

In the wake of the country's membership in the European Union in 1986, the
early 1990s witnessed Spanish cities joining the branding spectacle of "global
cities," with Barcelona, Seville, and Madrid hosting the Olympics, the Universal Exhibition, and the European Capital of Culture, respectively, all in 1992. In
1997, the so-called Bilbao effect of Frank Gehry's Guggenheim museum transformed the politics of urbanism into trend-setting agendas in iconic architecture.[73] These projects in urban megalomania gave the green light to the "prodigious
decade of Spanish urbanism," which, starting in 1997, saw over 5 million new
houses built in the period up to 2006, an average of 13.3 for every 1,000 inhabitants and twice the European average for the same period.[74] Between 1997 and
2002, Madrid alone received an estimated 1 percent of the world's total foreign

direct investment,[75] which, not surprisingly, provoked a spiral of escalating prices and led to an accumulated increase in the price of housing of 345 percent between 1987 and 2002.[76] As the urban sociologist Miguel Ángel Martínez López put it, a "global class of well-off employees and investors, the rise of urban tourism, the city-backed processes of gentrification in the inner areas and the big infrastructural projects aiming to attract the Olympics, all engendered one of the most speculative real estate markets in the world."[77]

More to the point, starting in 1997, a succession of right-wing governments set in motion a series of dramatic urban reforms that inaugurated an age of gentrification and dispossession, triggering in turn the history of neighborhood resistance and activism that we wish to retell here. On April 17, 1997, Madrid's regional government signed a new General Urban Development Plan for the city and its hinterland. Two days later, on April 19, the Laboratory was occupied in a carefully staged public stunt. Although the occupation was not designed as a response to the government's plan, the proximity of dates was no coincidence either. The central motif of the new plan was "to exploit the city's spatial resources to the limit of their capacity."[78] The plan changed the status of land uses in the city and its hinterland, making most land available for urbanization, with "less than 10% in the hands of the public sector."[79] Moreover, it further introduced a "flexible" program of land-use changes that empowered politicians to carry out "fragmentary, punctual, and conjunctural" interventions, often "outside or against the plan."[80] As the urban geographers Julio Vinuesa and José María De la Riva put it, the plan's design set the stage for "real estate interests and neoliberal and deregulatory projects facilitating the 'pro-development' (*desarrollista*) vision of local politicians, who thence viewed the 'urban agenda' (*urbanismo*) as an easy way to leverage the city's economic and financial resources."[81]

The 1990s further saw the approval of a long-standing claim on the part of neighborhood associations and activists regarding the renovation of the architectural and residential patrimony of the city's historic quarter. This entailed the declaration of certain districts as Preferential Rehabilitation Areas (Áreas de Rehabilitación Preferente [ARP]). For years, the municipal government had neglected the conditions at the heart of the city center, where many of the historic buildings and much of the infrastructure was in a ruinous state. In the case of the neighborhood of Lavapiés, for over twenty years activists had protested the deliberate designs of such "policy by neglect," where landlords were allowed to take no responsibility for the ruinous condition of their premises, over time pushing tenants to relocate elsewhere.[82] Widely perceived as a strategy of complicity between the municipal government and real estate speculators, the designation of Lavapiés as an ARP on July 16, 1997, was therefore welcomed by neighborhood activists as a long-overdue victory—although it also brought in its wake some unanticipated and unwelcome consequences.

It is in this social climate of neighborhood effervescence and activist pride that the Laboratory was occupied on April 1997 in a carefully staged stunt of territorial "transversality."[83] One of the central aims of the Laboratory was to rethink its own interface with the surrounding Lavapiés neighborhood as a complex ecology of encounter and inclusion, solidarity and exchange, cooperation and support. As expressed in the idiom of the time, participants strived for an "opening toward the social" (*abrirse a lo social*).[84] The key references in this orientation were the second-wave of Italian autonomist projects of the late 1970s, the so-called "diffuse" and "social autonomy" projects, of which Radio Alice had become an emblematic precursor: a view of radical consciousness that aimed to incorporate the experiences of subaltern groups beyond those of the working class, including feminists and gay activists, ecologists, even Dadaist artists, out in the streets, in the plazas, and on the air waves.[85] In this context squatted social centers offered a privileged site for radical investigation: at once at the heart of a neighborhood's social dynamics but also outside the norms and strictures of the city's political and economic conventions, they offered an ideal laboratory for social and political experimentation. The neighborhood and the neighbors thus became figures of complicity but also of strangeness, horizons of hope and tension all at once.

The figure of the neighbor that autonomists encountered in the late 1990s was essentially an antipolitical machine. Since the 1970s, local neighborhood associations (*asociaciones de vecinos*) had been in the hands of the cadres of the Communist Party. In the minds of these young autonomists, the ebullient life of the neighborhood was asphyxiated by the anachronistic politics of the old left. As they saw it, neighborhoods were territories that were calling out for transversality. Reflecting on the singular and situated trajectory of the Laboratory over its six-year history, activists Carlos Vidania Domínguez and Margarita Padilla penned a provocative problematization of "the neighborhood" as, precisely, the line of both fugue and resistance for the diffuse autonomy of squatted social centers:

> Who is a "neighbor" today? Are Chinese residents our neighbors? How about Moroccans? Or the people who are evicted from their homes, drug traffickers, squatters, precarious workers? Yet local neighborhood associations stick to that generic fiction: "neighbors." We feel this is a legacy of old associational politics, the cultural politics of a party system working the factory floor. . . . There are multiple compositional logics to how territories are weaved together, and the logic of the neighbor is

just one of them. Yet these other logics have difficulties in finding spaces of expression of their own. The Laboratory 3 [that is, in its third incarnation following two evictions] aimed for just that: to open up a space of encounter and coincidence. . . . A social center is nothing if it is not a sense-making machine . . . a machine for weaving the complicities with which to sound out a shared experience.[86]

In a similar vein, members of La Eskalera Karakola (The Snail [Spiral] Staircase), a feminist squatted social center that opened a few months ahead of the Laboratory, likewise theorized their own emplacement in the neighborhood as an operation in the "reorganization of the territory":

> Squatted social centers emerge as specific forms of political intervention at the heart of the urban condition—forms for the "reorganization of the territory." . . . The [Spiral] Staircase must be understood as part of such a complex context—for the center is in some senses "squatting" within the neighborhood itself, and therefore we must situate our own practices as constantly traversing, and being traversed by, the power relationships that modulate our surrounds. . . . We are witnesses to the very real marginalization and expulsion of some of the most so-called "conflictive groups" in the neighborhood (namely, the elderly, migrants, squatters, low-income families) through processes of renovation and gentrification that aim for a younger, bohemian, multicultural, and "alternative" public. . . . We must therefore find ways to set in motion collective assemblages that are open to contamination, to their fluctuation, and to the creation of unheard-of forms of intervention and making of the urban world we want and desire.[87]

Against this background, the occupation of the *casa de mujeres* (women's house) La Eskalera Karakola enabled "squatter-sister interactions," as the historian Roberta Gold put it for the New York context, which were aimed at transforming the conditions of the neighborhood as a territory of transversal feminist praxis and imagination.[88] In particular, some members of La Karakola developed pioneering tactics for understanding the choreographies of precarity and *cuidados* (care) crisscrossing the fragmentary impulses of the neoliberal city. These two concepts, as shown in subsequent chapters, were central for articulating a sensibility of liberation among free culture activists in later years. Enlisting housemaids and nurses, immigrants and precariously employed young women, activists from La Karakola developed original action-research projects whose exploratory and situationist methods had a long-lasting influence as operations for *inventar barrios* (inventing neighborhoods).[89] The centrality of the neighborhood as a topology of autonomous improvisations was not lost to the anthropologist Montserrat Cañedo Rodríguez, who carried out ethnographic fieldwork at the Laboratory between 2002 and 2003. "The neighborhood," she wrote, "is a fundamental anchor for understanding the history of the Laboratory. . . . It is the everyday context of neighborhood life that generates the cultural atmosphere wherein the Laboratory bubbles up its own projects of expansion and contraction."[90]

An example of one such topological design was the Red de Lavapiés, the Lavapiés Network. First formed in the fall of 1997, the network brought together a loose coalition of activists, neighborhood and immigrant associations, educational projects, squatted social centers, and art-activist collectives that were activated by the Laboratory shortly after its opening, and which embodied the center's agenda for a diffusely autonomous "opening toward the social."[91]

One of the network's earliest and perhaps most successful interventions picked up on the designation of the neighborhood as a ARP, which had been welcomed in the first instance and yet was bringing about some unanticipated and undesirable effects. Under the plan laid out by the municipality, the designation of a district as a ARP came with important financial incentives, albeit incentives skewed toward the interests of rentiers. The owners of buildings were entitled to 100 percent subsidies on the renovation of their estates, whereas the owners of individual properties were only allowed up to 60 percent of the expenses incurred in renovating their homes. Therefore, "with over thirty percent of all homes [in the Lavapiés neighborhood] being rental properties, and one out of every three being vacant," it did not take long for activists to realize that such a system was all but designed to set in motion a logic of real estate depredation whereby landowners leached on public subsidies only to evict their tenants once they had improved the look of their assets.[92]

In these circumstances, on November 13–15, 1999, the Lavapiés Network organized a public and participatory art festival under the name Rehabi(li)tar Madrid (Re-habitat /Rehabilitate Madrid), which partook of the spirit of street and public art interventions that were gaining currency at the time such as Reclaim the Streets in the United Kingdom. At the time the neighborhood had become home to a number of direct-action artists who were experimenting with notions of autonomy and public space, and who warmed to the festival as a unique opportunity for rethinking the mise-en-scènes of art and politics.[93]

One of the art-activist collectives that took part in the festival was La Fiambrera Obrera (The Workers' Lunchbox). Set up by a group of young insumisos in Valencia in the early 1990s, who then dispersed and took up residence across the country, the collective had a history of critical art practices in and around public space and housing issues.[94] In the context of the Rehabi(li)tar Madrid festival, La Fiambrera organized a witty but also very effective "anti-ruins" campaign aimed at signaling the ruinous state of certain buildings in the Lavapiés neighborhood. These were buildings whose maintenance had been deliberately neglected by landowners in the hope that the properties would be officially declared structurally damaged and unsuitable for occupancy. Under the law, such declarations enabled owners to evict tenants without compensation as well as claim substantial municipal subsidies toward the buildings' renovation. However, if the attention of the municipality was drawn to their ruinous state before the buildings underwent a technical inspection, then it was the municipality's legal responsibility to undertake the renovation and subsequently charge and bill the owners for negligence.[95] The Contest of Ruins (Concurso de Ruinas) that La Fiambrera organized successfully mapped many such ruinous properties around the neighborhood. The contest was organized as a festive stroll around the quarter that enabled a jury of neighbors and participants to both jointly gain awareness of the gradual deterioration of the area as well playfully award different prizes to the most ruinous properties. To this end, as they toured the neighborhood, the march of juries plastered the facades and columns of the ruinous estates they found on their way with flamboyant posters and signs, calling attention to the specific materials and structures that were falling apart. They further produced a map and census of the identified properties, which were made available online by hosting them on the Laboratory's own free software server (described further in chapter 2), as well as archiving the documents (flyers, posters, photographs) of the whole event.[96] It is significant that, as a public record of negligence, which was attended by residents and the media and publicly documented on the internet, the spectacle succeeded in drawing the municipality's attention.[97]

Complicities and Complexities for Liberation

In his comparative history of urban squatting, the geographer Alexander Vasudevan described two major historical vectors of squatting in US and European cities. Surveying histories of squatting in New York, London, Vancouver, Amsterdam, and Copenhagen, as well as various Italian and German cities, Vasudevan observed that squatting projects that often originated in long-standing struggles over housing rights developed over time into wider intersectional movements capable of mobilizing complex agendas on issues of race, gender, environmentalism, or sexuality, which aimed to reinvent the city as a space of autonomy and experimentation.[98] Despite apparently diverse trajectories, the double agency of squatting—aspiring for decent housing, on the one hand, but also struggling to bring into existence creative autonomous spaces—would often find in the "neighborhood" a placeholder of shared complicities and complexities. Thus, while some squatters would speak for example of building "a self-determined neighborhood infrastructure that prevents livable homes from remaining empty and falling into disrepair," others would proclaim their visions for realizing "in our house . . . a collective form of life and work that preserves and extends existing neighborhood structures."[99] Thus, the neighborhood did double duty as both domicile of community and organon of experiment. As Vasudevan summarizes for the case of the Italian Autonomia movement of the 1970s, "The turn to squatting and other occupation-based tactics within the wider Autonomia movement testified to a desire to build bases of worker autonomy in the city. But it also formed part of a new urban geography that treated the whole city as a stage for radical happenings, spontaneous encounters, creative interventions and other insurgent practices which, in their eyes, pointed to a new urban movement for the creation of 'free spaces.'"[100]

Scholars of urban squatting have commented on the cycles and waves of protest that have inflected such transformational dynamics in Europe and North America since the 1970s.[101] Although, of course, social movements are always situated in and responsive to local circumstances, they have also been shaped by similar experiences of resistance to wider global processes, including capitalist dynamics of urban restructuring, displacement, and gentrification; the flexibilization and deregulation of labor markets, with the concomitant precarization of youth employment; predatory dynamics of urban financialization; the criminalization of public protest; and recent policy reforms for austerity urbanism in the provision of public goods and services.[102]

These larger global processes were also at work in the Madrid context.[103] When the Laboratory opened in 1997, it did so in part as a response to the global dynamics of neoliberal expulsion and precarity that Spain's membership in the European Union had set in motion a decade earlier. By 1994, unemployment rates among the youth had reached an all-time high of 42.33 percent, locking large sections of the population into "garbage contracts." The rise of urban autonomous collectives was partly a response to these circumstances. These young autonomists, who often had a strong academic background and were deeply immersed in the traditions of Italian and German autonomy but were also haunted by the memory of the grassroots and libertarian movements that struggled for the right to the city during the country's forty-year dictatorship, took to the streets to explore alternative figurations of radical liberty and imagination. In their pursuits, they discovered the Dadaist toolkits of Italian social and diffuse autonomy, and under their influence, they visited and learned from the second generation of squatted social centers in Milan and Rome, where autonomy seemed to be constantly reinventing itself. They learned about transversality and sought to imagine ways of "opening towards the social" by diving deep into the associative logics and textures of neighborhood life. The neighborhood became a central ecology of their problematizations, at once an operation against dispossession and gentrification and also an aesthetics of joviality and insurrection, a space of struggle and contestation as well as a "sense-making machine."[104]

It is our hope that the brief history of the autonomous movement in Madrid that we have sketched in this chapter will help readers frame for the rest of part 1 the wider context wherein free culture activism was born at the turn of the century. Chapter 2 describes the role that the autonomous movement played in hosting some of the first experiments in infrastructural sovereignty by hackers and free culture activists. In this milieu, the language, praxis, and alliances of autonomia offered free culture activists a provisional template for making sense of their own tinkering with the assemblages of liberation. Yet the underground passages from autonomy to free culture still resonated and conveyed some of the stories we have told here about the struggles for building decent habitats for the city or the situated imaginations of the barrio as a space of conviviality, refuge, resistance, and experiment. These are stories, in sum, about the neighborhood as an intimation of the free city.

THE COPYLEFT AND THE (COPY) RIGHT TO THE CITY

On September 29–30, 1994, the World Bank and the IMF organized a summit in Madrid on occasion of the fiftieth anniversary of the Bretton Woods agreements. Sometime earlier, toward the end of 1993, several NGOs and anticapitalist groups came together to organize a countersummit under the slogan Foro 50 Años Bastan (50 Years Are Enough). It soon became obvious to them that their campaign would benefit greatly from the use of a telematics infrastructure. To this end, a coalition of academics, solidarity groups, and the autonomous counterinformational agency UPA agreed to set up a bulletin board system (BBS) under the name Nodo50.[1]

The experience of setting up Nodo50 encouraged many of these activists to establish annual counterinformation gatherings across the country. At these meetings, participants debated the future of the internet and "autonomous telematics," organized workshops on free radio and cryptography, and exchanged ideas about funding, the ongoing problems of precarious and voluntary work, or the communicative aesthetics and sensibility of counterinformation.[2] In format and content, these meetings prefigured the "hackmeetings," which, starting in 2000, would become the preeminent point of encounter for hackers and free culture activists in Spain. The language of autonomy pervaded these vibrant encounters about telematics and political change. This was also the time when the philosophy and technologies of free software began to circulate widely in squatted social centers and some people began speaking of "digital self-defense" (*autodefensa digital*), a wink to the Italian poet and writer Nanni Balestrini, who in his novel *The Unseen*—an emblem of the Italian *autonomia* movement—had written of organizing "the self-defense of the conquered territories."[3]

It was in this context that participants at the annual national counterinformation gathering in 1998 agreed to look into the possibility of setting up a server independently of Nodo50. The shift was motivated by what some thought was a misunderstanding by the NGO world of the coalition's philosophy and capabilities. Two years earlier, in 1996, Nodo50 had made a decision to become an internet service and access provider, driven by the understanding of some solidarity groups and NGOs that it was part of the organization's mission to guarantee universal access to the internet in the Global South. By 1998, however, the liberalization of the telecoms industry meant that most telecoms were already offering free access to the internet as part of their sales deals. Some activists noted that Nodo50's commitment toward a southern telematics would be better served if the coalition shifted its aim from "access" to "source code," in particular through the use and endorsement of free software and infrastructure. Margarita Padilla, whose story opened part 1, was one of the most vocal opponents of Nodo50's politics at the time. Margarita had long been involved in the project, at one point becoming one of a handful of Nodo50 employees. In an essay titled, "Why Nodo50 no longer interests me" she explained:

> It seems that all that Nodo50 cares about today is providing the technical means for the circulation of certain progressive, left-wing ideas and content on the Internet. Such a view misses the point that technical infrastructures are themselves "content"; that every choice and decision we make as to how to build such infrastructures is a political decision. These are political decisions both in the way they summon specific power relations and in the terms through which they enable the construction of the real, the things that are and are not possible. . . . My critique of Nodo50 should be read in this context as a commentary about the possibilities of critique today: about the ways in which our projects are built and un-built, the prisons that constrain every expression of hope, in sum, about what it means to do autonomy (*hacer autonomía*) in a society mediated by technology.[4]

Margarita was giving voice to a feeling that had gradually taken root among the wider autonomist and squatting circles about the importance of self-defensive telematics. This had led some collectives to modestly invest in their own telematics infrastructures—their own hacklabs, as they would come to be called. The Laboratory led the way in setting up the first *área telemática* (telematics zone) of any squatted social center in Spain, within days of the first occupation of the building in spring 1997. Margarita herself played a leading role in this effort, along with the hacker Miguel Vidal, some of whose crucial contributions to the shaping of free culture we will discuss shortly.[5] It is in this context that the idea of setting up a server independently of Nodo50 gradually gained currency. "We felt," Miguel Vidal explained in a retrospective interview in 2005, "that there was scope for opening more than a virtual space for politics. Our aim was to build a truly hybrid community, fusing the best from the hacker culture and the best from the world of self-managed political spaces."[6] In this spirit, between 1998 and 1999, a group led by the Laboratory's hackers and members of the Barcelona squatted social scene approached the Italian counterinformation network ECN/Isole Nella Rete (European Counter Network/Islands in the Net) for advice and guidance in setting up a hosting service and infrastructure. The reputation of the Italian hacktivist scene was well known. As Alessandra Renzi noted in her extraordinary history of the network of pirate television channels Telestreet, "Italy was the first country in southern Europe to organize hackmeetings and set up spaces for hackers," often in squatted social centers too, whose commitment and concern for "the socialization of political life through activities of social reproduction" warranted that technology was "never a virtual affair but a material social entangling of bodies and machines."[7]

The Spanish and the Italian hackers had first met during the Second Intercontinental Meeting for Humanity and against Neoliberalism, which had been hosted by the Laboratory in Madrid in July 1997 under the auspices of the EZLN, the Zapatistas National Liberation Army. During the time it took to acquire the machine, the ECN hosted an email list that the Spanish hackers used to establish the constitutional assembly for an independent server. They called the assembly, sinDominio (NoDomain). They registered the domain with the Anarchy Organization and purchased a Pentium II 450MHz 256Mb RAM computer that was jokingly referred to as "Fanelli," in homage to the Italian anarchist Giuseppe Fanelli, the emissary that Mikhail Bakunin sent to Spain in 1868 to set up the local branch of the International Working Men's Association (the First International).[8] The joke could hardly be overlooked: the strong Italian autonomist connection, cultivated over years of visits and exchanges between squatted social centers in both countries, had overseen the rite of passage of the Spanish autonomous movement into the international free culture community. The world that Fanelli stood for gestured toward the complex modulations and transformations between the worlds of autonomy and the incipient worlds of digital liberation.[9]

The story of how the Zapatistas' insurrection of 1994 sparked new forms of network politics has been told many times before, and there are echoes of that story in the account of sinDominio's birth. The Laboratory hosted one of the nodes of the second Zapatista encounter after some of its members attended the first

Intercontinental Encounter for Humanity and against Neoliberalism, which the EZLN hosted in Chiapas in 1996, where the liberation army called for the founding of an "intercontinental network of alternative communications" that would in time inspire the likes of Indymedia or the European Counter Network—or indeed of sinDominio itself.[10] In his history of digital activism, the media anthropologist Todd Wolfson has charted the influence that the EZLN played in the articulation of network struggles across the globe, as well as the way in which social movements scholars have since described the role played by communication technologies, transnational and multiscalar alliances, decentralized modes of organization, and a philosophy of direct democracy in shaping networked cultures of resistance.[11] However, Wolfson decries the normative interpretations that scholars have largely made of what were once tactical and adaptive responses on the part of the EZLN to the specific nature of their struggle. For example, the Zapatistas' invocation of direct democracy harked back to the culture of patience and listening of Mayan communities, while their use of tactical media and networked communications was a way to circumvent the Mexican state's media industry. Therefore, when social movements such as Indymedia adopted direct democracy and new media as procedural toolkits, they often did so by uplifting and redeploying a philosophy of action that was foreign to their own context of resistance.[12]

In her work among hacker activist collectives, Gabriella Coleman has similarly expressed concern for the way in which scholars have sometimes pigeonholed digital activism under the "myth of sweeping hacker libertarianism," failing to note how these protest movements are, always and everywhere, inflected by their participation in a specific and situated community of practices and social spaces—"mailing lists and image boards, code repositories, free software projects, hacker and maker spaces, internet chat relays, and developer and hackers conferences." She draws on Francesca Polletta's work, which we encountered in chapter 1, to describe these sites as "free spaces," and further notes how in the European context many of these hacker movements, as opposed to their North American counterparts, are associated with projects for social transformation that enlist artists, anticapitalist groups, or autonomous collectives and have communal aspirations that stand at perpendicular angles to the ethos of libertarianism.[13]

Our history of the free culture movement in Spain dwells on the climates of methods that modulated a movement originally organized around self-defensive telematics and independent media, which developed into a larger urban sensibility. In this chapter we show how the exigencies for free culture were first shaped by the politics of assembly and autonomy of squatted social centers. However, over time the conceptual vocabulary and technical tools of free culture offered hackers, intellectual property lawyers, musicians, squatters, and cultural managers a much more adaptable resource for working on the limits of their shared political intuitions and vocations. Questions about the nature and assemblages of free labor, public knowledge, and common infrastructures led to the use of free culture as both a descriptor of and incipient methodology for emerging forms of urban collective action. The idea of free culture as a culture of methods is one that we develop further in part 2, where we explore how certain conceptions around the forms and energies of public institutions and public space shaped free culture into an impulse and an outlook for a free/libre urbanism.

Care for the Net

From its earliest formulation as a *sin dominio* (without domain, free of domination), the project for an independent and autonomous server was conceived not as an infrastructure or technological platform, but as a political community. As Miguel Vidal put it,

> We aimed, and I think it is fair to say we accomplished, to go beyond the usual separation between geeks and users. Our aspiration was to move sinDominio beyond the classic conception of a service provider towards its articulation as a learning space, a space that would work its way outwards from the experience of squatted social centers through and into novel interface spaces—where people with a political background in telematics, in particular the hacker and free software communities, could share experiences with those with a more traditional social movements background.[14]

The central vector in the articulation of this novel learning interface was the assembly. SinDominio first saw the light as an assembly and only later as an infrastructure. The assembly was itself conceived as an experiment of sorts, for it was organized through an email list. What kind of political space could such an assemblage or assembly of the technical, the social, and the affective produce? This was the experience and the experiment that sinDominio set out to assay.

The first project hosted by sinDominio—by the assembly and the server—was the Agencia en Construcción Permanente (ACP), the Agency under Permanent Construction, a self-regulating bulletin board whose software enabled anyone to publish news or content directly, without the intermediation of news agencies or editors, as well as allowing people to comment, enrich, or debate every entry. Along with sinDominio, the idea for the ACP was presented at the annual counterinformation gathering in April 1999, and it was launched in summer 1999, predating by a couple of months the foundation of the now famous Independent Media Center (Indymedia) during the alter-globalization protests in Seattle in November 1999.[15]

Within months of having launched, however, the ACP became a huge problem for sinDominio. Unmonitored and unedited, the site had become a pothole of venomous accusations, incendiary exchanges, and internet trolling. As a result, a decision was reached to close the ACP early in 2000. The decision was wildly contested and eventually tore the assembly apart as a technical and political project.[16] For a start, it was unclear who had made the decision and under what kind of political prerogative. Many voices complained that it responded to the partisan and conspiratorial politics of the Laboratory's hackers, their invested interests in shaping the narratives of counterinformation in the Spanish context. As it turned out, the Madrid activists had indeed taken the somewhat unilateral decision to shut down the news portal. However, in their view this was simply an acceptance of the realization that they had not paused to consider what the nature of a digital assembly entailed. Theirs was a call to problematize anew the assemblage, and the assembly, of politics and infrastructure in the digital age.

To these activists, the experience of the ACP had shown rather dramatically that there was both a technical and an affective dimension to what "giving voice" meant for a digitally mediated political community. In one sense, this was a technical issue because it became painfully evident that the software did a poor job of organizing how the different "voices" addressed each other. There was simply, as Miguel Vidal put it, too much information, resulting in a "problem of noise."[17] However, the experience of the ACP had also shown that the nature of the assembly as a political body was poorly understood. What was at stake was not simply the representativeness of voices or the cacophony of information. For some, there was a deeper issue at stake about the assembly as a political space able to effect change, to move and align bodies and emotions into a common project. This was beautifully captured in an interview with Margarita Padilla, who had been involved in both the ACP and sinDominio since the start. We quote at length:

> An assembly is not the place, should not be place, where people get together to make decisions, not in the first instance at any rate. An assembly is all about creating an autonomous space and time where values are arrived at collectively. The assembly is a space of enablement. "Enablement" is a specific form of "power." We are not talking about the "power" to make decisions. Rather, it is the "power" to decide what kinds of decisions need to be made, the power to decide the language in which

they are enunciated, the power to deconstruct those decisions . . .
power, then, as a form of enablement.[18] I am afraid the assembly of
sinDominio had no such power. . . . However, that is also the foundational legacy of sinDominio: it created an experience of emptiness, of
impossibility, the realization that you have no "power" whatsoever to
organize an experience. But that, in retrospect, is a wonderful lesson,
because it undermines the assumption that one can aim for something, that you can orient a body towards an objective. Rather, it is the
"something" that orients you. . . . So yes, shutting down the ACP responded to your average "we do it because we want to, period" decision. How could we reach such a decision, and whom or what prompted
the decision to be made? I have no doubts: In my case it was the experience of the squatted social center. It was that experience that composed
our energies as a collective body, and that enabled us to resist—I would
even say to love—the criticisms we knew would come our way. . . . In
sum, and notwithstanding that sinDominio was a virtual project, one
of the lessons I learned from participating in the project is that there is
a compositional game to how our bodies come together, how we touch
one another, that carries a political premium. In other words: being together (*estar juntos*), seeing your face, to recognize you, to know that
when you say something it's you who is saying it, to have experienced
the Laboratory. . . . That builds a type of trust and complicity that in my
experience one does not find in telematics. . . . It is that experience that
was summoned when we shut down the ACP.[19]

The experience of sinDominio affected different people differently. Margarita
chose to reorient her capacity to inhabit the network by developing a free internet radio project together with a friend. She took upon herself the challenge of
exploring the possibilities for affection and care afforded by the use of free
technologies.

In the aftermath of the ACP's closure, Miguel Vidal joined a team of hackers
intent on developing a new software architecture for the platform, one that would
allow for the technical remediation of the problems of filtering and noise.[20] The
ACP opened again in 2002 as the Madrid node of the global Indymedia network.
The software of the now branded Indymedia-Madrid portal was unlike anything
else on the network. Algorithmically curated and moderated, the project was se-
verely criticized from all quarters, accused of censorship and manipulation,
although, ironically, and as Miguel Vidal had predicted, the design of the ACP
prefigured the ecosystem of "likes" and "dislikes" of future social media platforms.[21] For Vidal, this signaled a misconception of what "free" stood for in the

digital age: "There's no such thing as censorship in the Internet, because if you don't get it published here you will publish it there. . . . Hacker and free software communities have known this for a long time. No technical system will purify politics. If you talk politics it will get messy. All the system does is organize the visibility of the mess."[22]

At the turn of the century, then, the experience of sinDominio's assembly and the ACP triggered a healthy dose of skepticism toward the allures of free technologies as tools for political liberation among free culture activists in Madrid. In different ways, Margarita and Miguel both recognized the need to develop complex navigational systems—in between method and technology, complicities and complexities, affects and apparatuses—for nurturing the capacities for political engagement. The experience prompted activists to think carefully about the complex articulation between the politics of assembly and the politics of assemblages, their frictions and interactions, and the different ways in which bodies, technologies, and affects leveraged or disturbed one another.

The Labor of Free

The debates and tensions that traversed the rise and fall of the Agency under Permanent Construction—debates about the economies of attention and care that striate the technologies of liberation, about the spaces of autonomy and friendship that are sometimes asphyxiated by the noises of overabundant information, about the cyborg nature of labor lurking behind all such manifestations—these were concerns that loomed large over the free culture community at the turn of the century. One episode in particular helps place in context the situated nature of these concerns when confronted with larger global dynamics of immaterial and networked labor. This is the case of the Spanish forking of Wikipedia.

On February 26, 2002, the then nascent community of Spanish Wikipedia editors decided to move the content they had written for the online encyclopedia to a server hosted at the University of Seville. The reason was that there had been a row with Wikipedia founders Jimmy Wales and Larry Sangers over the latter's intentions to incorporate advertising to fund the work of the encyclopedia. For some time, the Spaniards had expressed uneasiness about the use of a dot com domain for Wikipedia (as opposed to dot org), as well as discontent with the fact that all international Wikipedia sites (all but the American Wikipedia) were running obsolete software. In conversation with Jimmy Wales, they suggested that the project set up a foundation for every international site, but Wales refused on grounds that this would entail too much administrative fuss. "We were all working for free," one of the editors leading the revolt recalled to *Wired* magazine, "in a dot com with no access to the servers, no mirrors, no software updates, no downloadable database, and no way to set up the wiki itself. Finally, came the possibility of incorporating advertising, so we left. It couldn't be any other way."[23] The Spaniards thus forked the Wikipedia project and launched their own Enciclopedia Libre Universal, which in time prompted Wales and Sangers to rethink their commercial aspirations for the future of the world's favorite encyclopedia.

For the communications scholar Robert Gehl, the Spanish forking represents the first "free labor strike" of the internet age, a momentous occasion where a group of "free laborers . . . recognized their status as such and withheld their labor to have a greater say in the shape of the nascent Wikipedia."[24] The notion of a "free labor strike" is developed by Gehl, who builds on Tiziana Terranova's seminal essay on free labor in the digital economy.[25] For Terranova, free labor is labor that is "simultaneously voluntarily given and unwaged, enjoyed and exploited," including, for example, "building Web sites, modifying software packages, reading and participating in mailing lists."[26] Terranova is at pains to emphasize that free labor is but the latest phase in a "longer history of experimentation" in the capitalist extraction of value from social and cultural processes as it is "totally immanent to late capitalism."[27] What free labor has helped made visible today is the unmooring of labor from its traditional location in the realm of production and its spilling over into the domains of consumption.[28] Said somewhat differently, free labor is what culture looks like when our engaging in infrastructures of play, desire, and knowledge-making loops back into the circulation of capital.

In theorizing the ambiguous nature of free labor as a social relationship, Terranova draws on the legacy of the Italian autonomists, for whom, as we saw in the case of Radio Alice, it was paramount to take the struggles of the factory out to the streets and the airwaves and thereby overcome the separation between life and work, between labor and waged labor.[29] However, the capacity for carving out such spaces of autonomy within networked capitalism, where free labor is now an immanent part of its infrastructure, remains doubtful at best. As Franco "Bifo" Berardi recently put it, in a somber tone, today the "worker does not exist any more as a person. He is just the interchangeable producer of microfragments of recombinant semiosis which enters into the continuous flux of the network."[30] There seems to be little hope for autonomy in this melancholic economy, except perhaps, in Berardi's intimation, where the "dissemination of self-organized knowledge . . . create[s] a social framework containing infinite autonomous and self-reliant worlds."[31]

It is this historical juncture that Gehl wishes to illuminate in his study of the Spanish forking of Wikipedia. The promises that the infinite flights of self-organized knowledge have opened up for autonomous experience, or indeed the horizons of hope that have been attributed to the general intellect of a net-worked multitude—these are poetic visions of political change, notes Gehl, that are somewhat difficult to apprehend from a pragmatic perspective.[32] On the other hand, in Gehl's view, the free labor strike of the Spanish Wikipedia editors speaks of a very concrete design for remedial action. The Spanish editors cleverly and laboriously engineered their own autonomy by making sure that the legal, technical, and infrastructural requirements of the encyclopedia safeguarded their own labor, and the labor of all future contributors, as free laborers. The status of the site as a foundation, its use of free software, its technical and archival decentralization—these various requirements enabled the editors to "engineer" their labor into a "class for itself"—a class of free laborers.[33]

The attorney, academic, and hacker Javier de la Cueva was one of the four editors who led the Spanish forking of Wikipedia. De la Cueva is one of the leading experts on internet law and technology in Spain today, who is well known for his advocacy of free intellectual property licenses. He first pointed us to Gehl's text, although he himself entertained a somewhat different interpretation:

> I am not sure I share Gehl's view that this was a "free labor" strike. Strictly speaking we had no contractual relationship to Wikipedia—it is therefore unclear on what grounds we could have gone on "strike." We just wanted the cultural capital we had collectively put into the project to remain just that: a free/libre, public, and universal good. We didn't have the word for it at the time, but I guess one would say today that we were worried for the preservation of a *procomún digital* (digital commons).[34]

De la Cueva's resort to the language of the commons is worth noting. We wish to signal here to the specific inflection through which de la Cueva chooses to reconceptualize free labor as a *procomún*—a free/libre, public, and universal good. As it turns out, subtending such a conceptualization is the fact that the migration of backup files and archives to the new Enciclopedia Libre Universal was supported and hosted by servers at the University of Seville. This was made possible because one of the four rebellious editors was a professor of information technology at the university and thus facilitated access to the university's infrastructures. Although both Robert Gehl and Nathaniel Tkacz mention the donation of server space by the university in their respective accounts of the forking, neither pauses to reflect on the fact that it was a *public* institution that enabled the migration.[35] The point was underscored to us by de la Cueva, who noted that the university was instrumental in setting up the alternative site.

Free culture, the commons, and public knowledge: where are their boundaries and where are their gray zones? What are their entanglements, their labors, their mutual irradiations? Central to the rise of free culture in the Spanish context was the role played by a number of public institutions—universities, cultural centers, and museums in particular—which both funded and cleared the space for articulating novel and subversive institutional relations. The sometimes explicit, sometimes self-effacing, and at any rate always fragile relations between public organizations and activists helped shape the "culture of 'free culture'" into an ecology of practices, methods, and infrastructures that extended well beyond the realm of the digital. These relations rekindled the history of intransitive culture that we described in the introduction: a coming together as a commons to the defense of the public through the tools of the libre. Indeed, as we have seen, the Spanish forking of Wikipedia was made possible by a dense entanglement of relationships between hackers, academics, lawyers, free culture activists, and public institutions, which made it plausible for the Spanish editors to imagine a network of care for their content—a digital commons, as de la Cueva put it—beyond the language of network rights, licenses, and telematics.

Autonomous Dynamos

De la Cueva's encounter with free culture activism was very much happenstance. In the late 1990s he taught himself Linux after repeatedly losing his digital archives to the notorious Windows "blue screen of death" system error. "I remember reading the details of the Windows license and feeling infuriated: not only did Windows assume no responsibility for damages occasioned to loss of files but users were in fact called-out for 'piracy' if they attempted to tinker and solve whatever software troubles they had."[36] He bought some magazines, read around here and there, attended the meetings of various Linux user groups, and in the year 2000 decided to install the Debian operating system on his computer. As some of these Linux user groups grew in size, de la Cueva, who was one of the few lawyers around who understood the technology, was asked to help with the legal paperwork to change the status of the groups into not-for-profit associations. By 2003 his skill with free software was such that he joined a national Linux news server as one of its system administrators.

At the turn of the century, free software developers and intellectual property lawyers were part of a transnational conversation about the uncertain legal status of digital rights. In the United States, the passing of the Digital Millennium Copyright Act in 1998 spawned, first, a movement for consumer rights over what was deemed an excessive copyright legislation and, later, a broader cultural movement for a digital commons economy—the digital rights or free culture movement.[37] In Spain, a comprehensive reform of the Law of Intellectual Property in 1995 enabled author societies to collect levies (popularly known as *canons*) as a result of private copying carried out through digital media and CDs. Although little happened on this front for a number of years, in 2002 a judge sentenced a manufacturer to pay the Spanish General Society of Authors and Publishers (SGAE), the country's largest authors' guild and copyright management entity, €0.22 for every CD sold since 1997.[38]

While in this context software engineers and hackers had a clear understanding of the purchase of free software licenses for distributing digital content, an acrimonious debate ensued over the production and distribution of cultural works such as music, video, educational, or scholarly resources. Free culture communities agitatedly discussed the "modulations," as Chris Kelty has called them, of free software into more specific cultural "experiments," discussing the legal licenses, technical requirements, and conceptual vocabulary needed to speak about and distribute free textbooks, music, or typography.[39]

In Spain, these debates centered originally on the music industry and the increasing role that copyright management entities played in overseeing the design of fiscal, penal, and compensatory legislation on all matters related to emerging digital technologies. A key episode in this context was the filing of a complaint by Javier de la Cueva on August 30, 2003, at the Spanish Competition Court against the passing of new intellectual property legislation that enabled copyright management entities to receive fiscal compensation for the sale of digital media (CDs and DVDs). Known as the "digital canon" affair, the lawsuit became the centerpiece of the free culture movement's struggle for digital rights and liberties for well over a decade.[40]

The year 2006 marked a particularly momentous point of inflection in these struggles. Only a year earlier, under the slogan of Rompamos el Silencio (RoS, Let's Break the Silence), a broad confluence of autonomous collectives, neighborhood associations, squatted social centers, and social movements agreed to instate an annual Week of Social Struggle and civil disobedience across the city. As the bioinformatic and science software developer, musician, and copyleft activist David García Aristegui has documented, the movement reached its zenith in 2006, when a newborn Eje de Cultura Libre (Axis of Free Culture) within RoS organized the occupation of the headquarters of SGAE in one of the city's most exclusive districts.[41] The occupation signaled the free culture movement's coming of age as a forceful urban presence.

Back in 2003, in proper free culture spirit, de la Cueva had made the template of the lawsuit available on the internet, which included a guide explaining how others could file their own claims.[42] As he put it to us, "This was a revelation to me, and central to how I have operated since: to use the internet, not as a political vitrine or media for spectacle and reclamation, but as a procedural tool—a tool where 'freedom' is inscribed in the procedure itself—thus, a *procedimiento libre* (free/libre procedure)."[43] In truth, the canon affair proved anything but a reality check for de la Cueva, for only fourteen people followed suit and filed their own complaints. In his words: "I realized then the distance separating the law and the streets as spaces of political action, and the difficulty entailed in designing tools of political transformation that can act as a bridge between them."[44] It would indeed take a dense entanglement of urban alliances and complicities for such designs and methods to trigger wider political change.

One such pivotal moment, during which de la Cueva himself played a crucial role, was the so-called case of Ladinamo, in which a group of activists took up a legal fight with the mighty SGAE and won. The story of Ladinamo takes us back once again to the struggles for autonomy of university students in the early 1990s. Manuela Villa was one of these students. Adolfo had first met Manuela in the year 2001 at the editorial offices of Spain's leading daily paper, *El País*, where they were both trainees in the newsroom of the paper's then incipient "cyber supplement."

Manuela had studied sociology at Madrid's Complutense University, and in her second year, along with some fellow students, she founded the collective Autónomos y Autónomas, "which was directly inspired by our readings on the Italian *autonomia operaia* tradition, as well as our relationships to the local squatted social scene."[45] She moved to London for a fresh start only a few years later, where she registered anew for a sociology degree and moved into a squatted social center. "I moved quite a bit in those years. I don't think I knew what 'free culture' meant at the time, but I was drawn to different libertarian traditions: I spent some time with the Traveler movement in France, and moved for a while to Ibiza for work, too."[46] Manuela returned to Spain at the turn of the century, where she enrolled in a postgraduate degree in journalism and worked as a trainee at *El País*. During that time, she resumed contact with her friends from the university and the autonomous scene. In 2002 she joined a group of friends in exploring "how to make a sustainable livelihood from our militant activism"—how to turn the urban atmospheres of autonomy into a project for collective living.[47] Thus, Ladinamo was born: a cultural association dedicated to investigating and promoting cultura libre. It served as "a dynamo: a generator that uses the energy that is put into it to transform the energies around it."[48]

Originally a publishing project for a cultural magazine, Ladinamo quickly drew in a wider array of energies, at first by transforming itself into an editorial collective and in due course developing a dance company, a theatrical project, a choir, and finally a cultural center that housed all of these efforts. The project provoked some resentment in the squatted social scene, in particular among members of the Laboratory, who only a few months back had been close allies but now judged the project "politically bland and highbrow."[49] The project was very modest but required a modicum of economic resources: "We paid very little rent to a religious order and ran a bar that sold drinks for a marginal profit. We made social security contributions for everyone that worked there, of course. However, notwithstanding the ludicrous economics of the project, all this was anathema to the squat scene."[50]

Ladinamo opened up a space for autonomous creativity outside the established circles of autonomous practice, such as squatted social centers or university autonomous collectives. Ángel Luis Lara, one of the friends with whom Manuela launched the project, was one of two lead singers of the hip-hop and acid jazz band Hechos Contra el Decoro (Facts against Decorum), whose fourth album, which came out in 2000, included an epigraph by the sociology professor Jesús Ibáñez: "A bird dreaming is worth more than a hundred sleeping." The band attained a certain amount of fame in Spain in 1998 when it recorded the soundtrack for the award-winning film *Barrio* (Neighborhood). Some of the band's members (including its lead singers) had been actively involved in the autonomous and squatted social scene throughout the 1990s, and their lyrics captured the anger and frustration, but also the resilience, of life in the city's peripheries. The connections that Ángel Luis Lara had to the music world enabled Ladinamo to imagine the construction of a material space, aesthetic languages, and relational economies that could work with, but not feel constrained by, the dictates of the autonomist tradition—including paying rent, salaries, or social security payments, and therefore entering into relationships with the state and the economics of exchange value, gestures largely repudiated by anarchist collectives. For example, a conscious choice was made by Ladinamo to employ the graphic team behind Hechos Contra el Decoro's records to design the artwork for the magazine. The resources of Ladinamo were scant but the group thought it important to invest in crafting an iconic aesthetic for the magazine. "Looking retrospectively," Manuela Villa told us, "I think there was a shared feeling that we needed to expand the cultural frontiers of the neighborhood. Sometimes Lavapiés feels like a ghetto—it's a steep walk up and out into the center of Madrid—and it felt imperative to open up new spaces of respiration. The music world was one way out—we opened up the space to community organized *bachata* and *reggaeton* dance lessons, for instance. The hacker world opened up another way out."[51]

In the early days of November 2004, Adolfo walked into Ladinamo with plans to write a journalistic piece on the first Dorkbot meeting taking place in the city—an informal encounter between scientists, engineers, and amateur technologists gathering to explore the then-emerging possibilities of electronic art.[52] To his surprise, he recognized two friendly faces among the meeting's conveners. As he roamed around he recognized, first, Manuela Villa, once a fellow trainee at

El País, calmly preparing drinks behind the bar. Minutes later he bumped into Javier Candeira, who was running up and down and giving directions and explanations to every new arrival, and who turned out to be the meeting's promoter.

Adolfo and Javier had first collaborated in Barrapunto, the Spanish version of the free software and technology news website Slashdot. Javier had cofounded the portal in 1999, and over the years he gained a reputation as a formidably skilled and knowledgeable advocate for free intellectual property licenses.[53] The website quickly became a key referent for the free culture community in Spain and a treasure trove of information for lawyers, hackers, and indeed journalists. Adolfo himself had contributed often to the site and in 2001 was invited to become one of a handful of the site's editors. Some members of the Barrapunto community—including Adolfo, Javier, and Miguel Vidal—were also involved in the Creative Commons email list that was set up in February 2004 to organize the translation of the free culture licenses into Spanish.

The chance coming together of Manuela, Javier, and Adolfo at Ladinamo was therefore expressive of a political momentum whereby a young generation of technologists and autonomists, journalists and artists, musicians and lawyers recognized in certain urban ecologies a natural habitat for relation, discovery, and apprenticeship. Indeed, by 2007 *El País* ran a brief reportage on Ladinamo that offered a neat synthesis of the project's eclecticism: "They describe themselves as a 'delirious group of *mileuristas* (precarious workers), hackers, and the unemployed, who have just managed to pull their way in huffs and puffs.' The fact is they are a band of some one hundred people in their thirties, mostly journalists, sociologists, and historians."[54] The first issue of Ladinamo's magazine nicely captured this eclectic admixture of traditions and trajectories, between the academy and the street, between musical fusion, *autonomia*, and free software, including for example an intellectual biography of Antonio Negri, a piece on the resistance and performative movement, Reclaim the Streets, and a permanent section on Conocimiento Libre (Free Knowledge) with questions and answers on the GNU/Linux operating system.

One particular episode in the story of Ladinamo illustrates the special place that music, technology, and intellectual property played in the shaping of free culture as an urban social movement. Sometime in 2004 a representative from the leading copyright management entity in Spain, SGAE, visited Ladinamo's cultural center. "One day a suited-up guy dropped by asking questions about the type of activities we organized," Manuela recapitulated for us. "I explained to him that we were a free culture association, committed to airing and liberating free cultural works. He was rather nice and seemed to understand the project, so when he left I thought to myself, 'that went surprisingly well. . . .' A few months later, however, a package arrived in the post with a letter stating that we were being sued by SGAE for €829.70 for infringement of copyright law."[55] The package had a DVD inside. Manuela and her associates at Ladinamo played the DVD to discover that it included a recording of a show that the art group La Más Bella had performed at the cultural center. Someone from SGAE had sneaked into the show with a video camcorder with the hope of proving that the center aired and played copyrighted materials. "The poor souls failed to notice that no music played at that particular show [it was an art performance with no live music]. Yet they thought that because the video recording showed we had a sound system, that was enough proof of us playing music whose rights were managed by SGAE."[56]

The judicial actions placed Ladinamo in a delicate situation, for they had no economic resources to cover the costs of litigation. At that time, however, Javier Candeira (who had been organizing the Dorkbot meetings) was an active participant in a variety of free culture forums, including the Creative Commons email list, which had been created to function as a working group to translate the licenses into the Spanish legal framework, and a national copyleft email list. It is in the context of these various groups that Candeira knew Javier de la Cueva and that he introduced the latter to Manuela Villa.

When Javier de la Cueva was approached by the staff at Ladinamo to become their attorney in the court case against SGAE, his eyes glimmered with excitement. He had been waiting for such a case to land in his hands for quite some time. "I told the guys from Ladinamo that we had a double objective. Of course, our short-term objective was to clear them from having to pay the SGAE. But derived from this, and in the long term more important, we had to make sure that the court explicitly mentioned the word 'copyleft' in its ruling."[57] Anticipating that one such case would sooner or later come his way, in 2004 de la Cueva had teamed up with the copyleft musician Ani López (aka Defunkid) in writing a letter to the subdirector general of intellectual property at the Ministry of Culture. In the letter, the musician noted that as a copyleft artist he did not wish to affiliate with a copyright management entity and was therefore requesting the ministry to pay him directly his share of the digital canon. The ministry swiftly responded that there was no scope for such a request as these were collective rights managed by the corresponding entities. "However, our job was already done, for our intention all along had simply been to slip the term *copyleft* into the ministry's archival registry."[58]

Therefore, when de la Cueva developed his procedural portfolio for Ladinamo, the first thing he did was to ask the judge to include Ani López's request for copyleft rights from the Ministry of Culture, whereupon he used it to build a case for copyleft exemption *using the procedural regime itself*. "The first thing that the law understands," de la Cueva said to us, "is the law itself. The files lodged within the Ministry of Culture paved the way for a procedural explication of what 'copyleft' stands for. It was all very well for us to point to Lawrence Lessig's writings, or to the GNU General Public License long in use in free software projects, yet these were references that meant little to the judges. On the other hand, the file lodged within the Ministry of Culture appealed to a natural argument that the correspondence itself gave credence to."[59] In other words, copyleft had first to become a bureaucratic procedure in order to enable its legibility as legal discourse.

The court eventually ruled in favor of Ladinamo, "the first ruling ever to cite 'copyleft,'" as the broadsheets put it, and de la Cueva used the sentence to expand the suite of *procedimientos libres* (procedural libre tools) he had been painstakingly developing in an online digital archive.[60] As he put it to us, "scarcely two years after Ladinamo's ruling, judges from all over Spain had naturalized the term *copyleft* as a conceptual operator, therefore gradually establishing it as minor jurisprudence."[61]

The case of Ladinamo illustrates the complex assembly and assemblage of political and material practices that free culture activists mobilized at the turn of the century. From lawyers to musicians, from journalists to academics and technologists, Ladinamo transformed free culture activism into a broader urban ecology, whose endorsement and support was no longer simply a matter of digital rights and freedoms but had truly become an economy and habitat for "a delirious group of *mileuristas* (precarious workers)."[62] This was a delirious community of activists who resisted their fateful destiny as free laborers in the digital age and ventured instead to imagine and care for a different networked environment—an environment at once digitally mediated and urban in character. It was an imagination of free culture, then, no longer as just a question about copyleft matters but also about the (copy) right to the city.

Climates of Methods

In January 2017, we traveled from Madrid to Seville to interview José Pérez de Lama (aka osfa), professor of architecture at the University of Seville and founder and first director of its Fab Lab. In his early fifties, tall, skinny, forever humorous and smiling, Pérez de Lama comported his bohemian and quietly erudite persona with affability, graciousness, and an endlessly embracing hospitality. Although we had exchanged correspondence over Twitter and other media for quite some time, this was the first time we met in person.

Pérez de Lama is well known in architectural and activist circles in the Spanish-speaking context for cofounding in 2001 the agitprop collective, hackitectura (a portmanteau of the words *hacking* and *architecture*), whose work paved the way for an imaginative application of the philosophy of free software to both architectural design and urban studies. When we arrived at the School of Architecture (Escuela Técnica Superior de Arquitectura) it was unusually cold and rainy so we took refuge in a nearby café, where Pérez de Lama warmed us with his wide-ranging curiosity, learnedness, and recollections.

Born in Seville in 1962, the son of a onetime mayor of the city, Pérez de Lama studied architecture in his hometown, although he was soon "travelling the world around."[63] By the time he completed his degree in 1987, he had developed an interest in bioclimatic architecture, which, as he put it to us, "is how, back in the day, architecture modulated its own intermediary position between technology and the environment."[64] As an undergraduate student he contributed to the Master Plan for Seville's Universal Exhibition by designing the bioclimate for the exhibition's open-air spaces. He quickly realized, however, that he was poorly equipped for the task at hand, so he applied for a scholarship to further his research on bioclimatic architecture under the supervision of Baruch Givoni, a leading expert in urban climatology, first in Israel and later at UCLA. In Los Angeles he came into contact with various artistic and technical collectives, whose flirtations with psychedelia, entrepreneurialism, and techno-utopianism were then fermenting into the so-called Californian ideology. In a later visit toward the end of the 1990s, Pérez de Lama befriended media artist Natalie Bookchin, who introduced him to various members of the Critical Art Ensemble. (Pérez de Lama would later write his PhD thesis on his encounters with the networked urbanism of Los Angeles, blending his interests in the bioclimates of inhabitation with the then-emerging dynamics of social movements' cyber- and counterinformational tactics.)[65] On returning to Spain in the early 1990s, he teamed up with Antonio Sáseta, a professor of architecture known for his interest in anarchist theater and scenography, and together they took their university classes outdoors, getting their students to design a number of open-air architectural choreographies and theatrical climatic interventions.

Some of these early experiments in climatic architecture—outdoors, scenographic, agitprop, ephemeral—took place in the context of ongoing struggles against the gentrification of the La Alameda neighborhood in Seville. As described in chapter 1, in the wake of the urban spectacles of the 1992 Barcelona Olympics and Seville's Universal Exhibition, Spanish cities had entered a "prodigious decade of urbanism" defined by urban restructuring, displacement, and gentrification.[66] The Big Mess of La Alameda (El Gran Pollo de la Alameda), as the neighborhood struggle came to be known, lasted over a decade, and mobilized residents, social movements and civil society support groups (drug users, immigrants) alongside architects, cultural producers, hackers and insurrectionary artists such as La Fiambrera (mentioned in chapter 1).[67]

The Big Mess first gained traction in 1998 in opposition to the construction of an underground parking in the neighborhood. The project for the parking was part of the Urban Plan, a larger European Union–funded program for "urban revitalization" that the municipality had signed into implementation in 1994.[68] By 1998, however, "the Urban," as it had come to be popularly called, had failed to reach every one of its social goals (reducing unemployment, urban marginality, youth delinquency) yet had stimulated direct private investments by over 50 percent, thus provoking a dismal escalation in house prices.[69] Therefore, when the plan for the underground parking was unveiled, the Big Mess quickly garnered intersectional support for a wholesale rejection of the Urban's designs for the neighborhood.

Pérez de Lama and Antonio Sáseta would often invite their students to prototype, test, and rehearse their interventions and installations for the Big Mess at the Instituto del Teatro (Centro Andaluz del Teatro), where they were allowed to use the center's rooms and equipment. In one of these rehearsals, Pérez de Lama met architecture students Pablo DeSoto and Sergio Moreno (who was also a free software geek and amateur network manager), whose tinkering with streaming technologies and prankster aesthetics caught his attention and with whom he would shortly team up to form hackitectura.

One of hackitectura's earliest tactical prototypes was a so-called "media tank," whose design already displayed their interest in blending electronic art, architectural atmospheres, and situated activism. In their book, *Wikiplaza*, Pérez de Lama and Sergio Moreno describe with amusement and candor the origins of the media tank in the promiscuous entanglement of autonomous struggles, public universities, and hackers' crafty imaginations:

> One evening in—was it 2001?—found us on Alameda de Hércules avenue in Seville (pre-gentrification, when it was still a dark city), with a contraption consisting of wheels, a seat, a projector, audio equipment and a computer, which we dubbed the "media tank". We projected materials that people brought along, images and video, onto a huge improvised screen that the platform Alameda Viva [the anti-gentrification neighborhood movement] had strung up between the trees that the City Council wanted to cut down. . . . Our equipment had been borrowed from the university's audiovisual service. . . . The idea we were toying with was to build a self-propelled vehicle that could move through (anti) globalization demonstrations while transmitting video in real time, projecting images and making noise. . . . By that time we had begun experimenting with live internet broadcasting (video streaming), and we had already tested the first GPRS telephones that made it possible to

do it from anywhere, often with low kbyte bandwidth that we would laugh at—or rather cry at—today. That same summer, our team touched down at Tarifa Border Camp, along with legendary Barcelona art collective Las Agencias [described in chapter 3] and their "Media Bus." . . . Even so, nobody could manage to make the streaming work until the "hippies" from Seville turned up with the Volkswagen Polo packed with gear—again borrowed from the university, which obviously had no idea of its exact whereabouts. Using the latest generation of GPRS phone[,] . . . they soon set up a cross stream between Tarifa and Germany, which was simultaneously projected at Tarifa's boulevard with Africa visible in the background. The phone acted as a modem; we used Real Producer—we were still having to use proprietary software then—to send the signal, and broadcast through an account that had been set up for us on the piratetv.net server. Streaming—using almost DIY [do-it-yourself] means to send real time video to the global network, as only TV had done in the past—was a slightly addictive pastime.[70]

The term *hacktivism* was coined in 1995 by journalist Jason Sack (nom de plume Jason Logan) in a piece reviewing the work of New York–based multimedia artist, Shu Lea Chang.[71] Logan echoes the artist's own characterization of her first feature-length 35mm film, *Fresh Kill*, "as a work of eco-cybernoia," where, he explains, an "environment in which the inability to access the media of change causes the uprising of low-fi activism and hacker mentality, or 'hacktivism' if you will."[72] Notwithstanding this early formulation of the hacktivist complexion as modulated by ecological consciousness, technical craftiness, and artistic drive, scholarly attention to hacktivism has largely focused on the application of technical media skills to subvert the global flows of informational capitalism. In 1994, the Critical Art Ensemble famously alerted us that "streets are dead capital!" and called instead for "electronic civil disobedience," a modality of political engagement that, they admitted, was "still science fiction" because "no alliance exists between hackers and specific political organizations."[73] The times were a-changing, however, and by the turn of the century the media scholar Tim Jordan could faithfully describe hacktivism as "activism! running free in the electronic veins that enliven our 21st-century, global socio-economies."[74]

Perhaps not surprisingly, such a view has tended to confine hacktivist politics as the latest vanguard in a distinguished tradition of rebellious communication and radical media activism, with hacktivists theorized as liberation technologists working hard within and against the networked realms of digital capitalism.[75] However, as Stefania Milan observed in her comparative study of "radical techies," the "emancipatory communication practices" of these movements "become more visible when they step out of cyberspace," such as in the "media centers at major protest events."[76] Said somewhat differently, there is always a brick-and-mortar context to where and how hacktivist projects gain traction, and, as Milan herself notes, "in Europe, in particular, they emerged in the milieu of the squatted social centers and street activism, with strong links to the more radical and the autonomous/antagonist scene."[77]

The example of hackitectura is a case in point. At once influenced by the California ideology and environmental architecture, net-art and anarchist scenography, but also weaving joyful complicities and intricate solidarities with neighborhood movements, squatted social centers, and insurrectionary artists, the work of hackitectura epitomizes the singular transformation of free software hacktivism into a broader neighborhood concern, where the neighborhood is no longer a territorial demarcation but an ecological and atmospheric space too—a theater for hopeful climates.[78]

The story of hackitectura joins our brief history of sinDominio, the ACP, the Spanish forking of Wikipedia, and Ladinamo in showing the central role played by questions of design, procedure, and methods in the liberation practices of free culture activists. No issue was broached by activists that did not entail them thinking joyfully and caringly through the affective, material, and political dynamics orienting their intuitions, desires, and hesitations toward different configurations of freedom. In this vein, the formations of freedom that they tentatively set forth often demanded that they were simultaneous inscribed *and* liberated as procedural tools, for example, in the infrastructures of software and the archives of law, but also in the designs of systems and dramaturgies of attentiveness through which they anticipated future horizons of action, or the ecologies of intimacy and responsibility through which they assayed neighborhoods and infrastructures of care. The Enciclopedia Libre Universal was one such system, as were the modulations of sinDominio's assembly and the ACP.

The cases of Ladinamo and hackitectura also anticipate an ethnographic argument we develop in part 2, about how these systems of attentiveness grew over time into larger theaters of action, modulating the media and equipment through which we tell stories about the city, the systems that we use to inscribe, store, and archive these stories, as well the registers that we use to communicate and make them available to others. They are stories, in other words, about the experience of the city as a climate of methods.

THE CITY IN FLAMES

On the morning of March 11, 2004, Adolfo was on his way to London to visit a friend from his hometown in Extremadura. The bus that was taking him to the airport drove past the train station of El Pozo in the south of Madrid. There was an unusual amount of traffic that morning. As the bus approached the station, a dense and chilling sound of sirens suddenly filled the air. Breaking news of a terrorist attack had been on the airwaves starting in the earliest waking hours. Ten bombs had exploded on four trains in the Madrid commuting rail network, including a train stationed at El Pozo. As the bus drove past the station, amid the sounds of sirens, car horns, telephone calls, and radio news, the passengers turned their heads to witness for a few and flashing seconds a city in flames. One hundred ninety-two people were killed that morning and over 1,800 were injured, making this the deadliest jihadist terrorist attack in European history.

The bombings took place just three days ahead of the country's general elections, on March 14. In the wake of the attack, amid the confusion, the mourning, and the devastation, the Spanish government rushed to declare the Basque terrorist group, ETA, as the prime suspect for the attacks. The right-wing Popular Party, which then led the government, had invested its electoral campaign with a nationalist rhetoric organized around fighting Basque separatist terrorism, and the bombings were immediately mobilized to serve this cause. The mainstream media and national newspapers united in confirming the government's story. However, insights from international news agencies and on-site reporters gradually trickled in with versions that at best were ambiguous, if not wholly contradictory. As time went by, rumors of a media blackout were on the rise and a widespread sense of frustration and misinformation took root, eventually leading to the use of various counterinformational and digital networks and tools (SMS, email lists, blogs) in staging "the first case of a political 'flash mob' or smart mob protest in Spain."[1] Over the weekend, thousands of people marched in protest against the government's partisan and manipulative use of information, building up a wave of indignation that, contrary to polling expectations, finally pushed the ruling Popular Party from office on March 14.

While the use of new information technologies has rightly been highlighted as signaling a turn-of-the-century techno-political awakening among social movements and countercultural activists, the sentiment in response to the Madrid bombings also nurtured a deep feeling of shared affection and emotion that called for an experience of "togetherness": an experience of *estar juntos* (being together) and *sentir común* (feeling in common).[2] Such an experience modulated previous engagements with autonomy into a pathos of sublime commonality, one that was at once inflected by and weaved into specific geographies, media, and organizations of engagement and obligation—into specific *matters of sense*. The existential indignation felt about the inhumanity of the attacks merged with the indignation felt about its political and informational mishandle, which merged in turn with preexisting trajectories of autonomous liberation. Out from the ashes of a city in flames rose a phoenix culture of urban commons and solidarity.

The House in Flames

When Alberto Nanclares woke up late on the morning of March 11, 2004, his cell phone registered over a dozen missed calls. Alberto had been working well into the night preparing the grand opening of Basurama's first exhibition in the cultural center, La Casa Encendida. The art-architecture collective, which had been founded three years earlier by a frenzied and self-determined group of architecture students, had made a joyful appearance on the city's cultural scene with their use of trash and recycled materials for designing ingenious metabolic installations. Then in their early twenties, the collective had been organizing a yearly *festival de basura*, a trash festival, at Madrid's School of Architecture since 2001, whereby the school's central patio was turned into a dumping ground for a week, after which students, artists, and passersby were invited to compete in a furious one-day session of creative reappropriations with a prize for the most original recycled design.

The invitation by La Casa Encendida to host the 2004 edition of their trash festival signaled the recognition by the cultural establishment of Basurama's promising work. Named after Luis Rosales's famous poetry collection, "The

House in Flames," the center had opened its doors in 2002 to national acclaim. Founded by Caja Madrid, the oldest of the Spanish savings banks and at the time a nonprofit owned by Madrid's regional government, the center was designed to fulfill part of the bank's four-pronged social responsibility agenda, its so-called *obra social*, which spanned the areas of education, environment, solidarity, and culture. As such, La Casa Encendida occupied an unusual place in the local landscape of cultural institutions: handsomely funded by a financial organization, its remit was, however, defined by the social agenda of a public institution.

On waking, the first call that Alberto Nanclares responded to that fateful morning was Carlos Alberdi's. Alberdi was in charge of cultural programs at La Casa Encendida and had overseen the preparations of Basurama's exhibition. It was Alberdi who told Nanclares about the train bombings and about the decision to postpone the opening of the exhibition. Alberdi had joined La Casa Encendida's team of program directors after a long career working for Spain's Network of Cultural Centers in Latin America. Starting in the 1980s, Spain had embarked on the modernization and internationalization of its cultural legacy, a modernizing impulse that participated in setting in motion what recent commentators dubbed a "Culture of the Transition."[3] The forty-year dictatorship that came to an end in 1975 had left an indelible and embarrassing inferiority complex among the country's intellectual and political elites. The country's membership in the European Union in 1986 was seized on by the literati as an opportunity to align once and for all with a tradition of European progress and modernity, which in this context was unashamedly articulated around the golden age of Spanish empire and colonial rule—a narrative, incidentally, first propounded by the intelligentsia of the dictatorship. In the minds of its proponents, the history of Spanish colonial rule in the sixteenth and seventeenth centuries offered an ideological framework—centered on the dubious splendors of cultural hybridity and *mestizaje*—to reawaken and consolidate commercial and diplomatic relationships with Latin America.[4] In this light, the Spanish Development Agency (Agencia Española de Cooperación Internacional [AECID]) was founded in 1988, a reworking of the organizational structure of its predecessor, the Institute for Iberoamerican Cooperation. For over a decade the institute had set up local cultural centers alongside most diplomatic delegations, despite lacking a clear agenda of their mission or purpose. In an effort to turn this unstructured lattice of cultural agencies into a sustained and coherent program of cultural diplomacy, the Network of Cultural Centers Abroad was established in 1998.[5]

Carlos Alberdi arrived in Buenos Aires in 1988 to work in the local cultural center, becoming its director only a few years later. In the mid-1990s he went on to join a team of high-level civil servants tasked with lending organizational coherence to the Network of Cultural Centers Abroad, of which he would become its first director. As he explained it to us, the Latin American experience was formative for a new generation of *gestores culturales* (cultural managers) in Spain:

> The Network of Cultural Centers Abroad (and in Latin America in particular) developed an approach to cultural work that was rather special. Unlike other international cultural agencies (say, the Goethe Institut or Alliance Française), we worked with and for the cities where we were emplaced (*trabajamos para la ciudad*). Inevitably, part of the work we carried out responded to a classic style of cultural management, say, organizing exhibitions, seminars, readings, or book launches, and in particular enabling a transatlantic conversation between the Spanish and Latin American literary worlds. But of course this could only keep the centers busy for so long, and it was only a matter of time before the centers drew in an eclectic cohort of local artists, architects, and provocateurs of all types. Importantly, for a long time the centers enjoyed considerable political autonomy. This has shifted over the years, but in the late 1990s and early 2000s the Network of Cultural Centers operated in some respects at the margins of, if not actually in direct opposition to, the cultural politics of diplomatic missions.[6]

When the project for La Casa Encendida was set in motion in 2002, the cultural philosophy that guided the initiative was deeply influenced by the Latin American experience of the Network of Cultural Centers Abroad, which Alberdi had helped to shape as one of its chief designers. It was equally significant that La Casa Encendida's founding director, José Guirao, had an undisputable reputation as one of the country's leading cultural managers, having recently completed a six-year term as director of the Reina Sofia Museum, Spain's leading contemporary arts museum. During this time, he served also as chief adviser to the Ministry of Foreign Affairs's international cultural politics division, where he witnessed firsthand the dynamic urban transformations of which the network of Latin American cultural centers was part and parcel: at once emissaries of a new modernist and neocolonial program of cultural hybridity, but also attentive venues facilitating local grassroots projects in cultural experimentation.

Madrid's New Cartographies, the first large-scale exhibition marking the inauguration of La Casa Encendida in October 2003, crystallized this conflicted and conflicting vision of urban cultural change. The exhibition showcased work by a variety of emerging and established artists and activist collectives whose work touched issues of immigration and gentrification in the city—a collective meditation on the sociology of art as/in a neighborhood complex.[7] The exhibition included work on border migrations by La Fiambrera, whose work as part of the Lavapiés Network we described in chapter 1, and in this sense it addressed a much-contested topic for La Casa Encendida regarding its own role as a gentrifying agent in the neighborhood of Lavapiés. It is significant that this was a topic La Casa Encendida was intent not to shy away from. In fact, in writing and in speech, José Guirao, the center's founding director, had made it public that he found the cultural politics of the Laboratory inspiring.[8] This was no rhetorical ploy. The third incarnation of the Laboratory sat right next door to La Casa Encendida. "The day we opened," Alberdi told us, "activists from the Laboratory 3 dropped by our opening party. We soon realized we appealed to a public that would visit the Laboratory on the way out from one of our exhibitions, and vice versa."[9] Indeed, less than a month after the center had been inaugurated, El País, the country's leading daily paper, published an article that drew a direct parallel between La Casa Encendida and the Laboratory, noting that "never had the neighborhood of Lavapiés witnessed such a rich abundance of cultural programs, let alone in the same block." Moreover, it added, "some people and collectives from the Laboratory have already collaborated in some of La Casa Encendida's projects, but it is yet to be seen if the collaboration extends in time, or indeed whether it goes both ways."[10]

The exchanges between the Laboratory and La Casa Encendida signaled to a then nascent conversation about the conditions of possibility for a *nueva institucionalidad* (new institutionalism) among museum curators and cultural managers in the Spanish context. At stake here was the spatial and material politics of art centers and cultural institutions, not only as patrons of art but as themselves complicit partners in processes of radical transformation. The movement was in part a response to the proposals for a new "relational aesthetics" and "participatory" or "community art" projects, which were gaining traction in the international art scene, where the agency and labor of artists were scrutinized in terms of the everyday challenges and aspirations traversing them.[11] The peculiarity of the Spanish case was that it was not only the artists that were held accountable for their sociological or political engagements, but also the institutions themselves.

The landmark for this new institutional framework was the project known as Las Agencias (the Agencies), which was commissioned by Barcelona's Museum of Contemporary Art (MACBA) in 2001.[12] Led by La Fiambrera, whose art-activist work with the Lavapiés Network had drawn the attention of the Spanish art world, the project interrogated the conditions of "agency," as one of its leading proponents explained, enabling a contemporary art museum to imbricate itself in the "molecular organization" and "self-learning processes" of society.[13] Las Agencias, for example, was actively involved in the anticorporate globalization campaign against the World Bank that took place in Barcelona in 2001. The anthropologist Jeffrey Juris, who was doing fieldwork on network activism in the city at the time and whose interlocutors included members of Las Agencias, was drawn to the collective's "tactical media projects" and use of "digital technologies to create and distribute posters, flyers, stickers, videos, and Web-based content . . . [combining] guerrilla communication, culture jamming, civil disobedience, and corporate sabotage."[14] Widely praised in the international arts scene, Las Agencias "situated MACBA as a collaborator of social movements by defining the art institution as a working space for social activists," culminating, in the view of some commentators, in a "singularly unique accomplishment, unlikely ever to be repeated, involving the collaboration between activists, artists, and museums."[15]

While the work of Las Agencias captured the "emerging networking logic" of activist practices that so intrigued Juris, it is important to keep in mind the situated urban history of disaffection and insurrection that brought artists and museum curators, autonomous squatters and hackers, together in exploring novel terrains for liberation.[16] Free culture, we have been suggesting, offered one such terrain, for it offered both a political vocabulary and an aesthetic imagination as well as a technical medium for grappling with fundamental shifts in the nature of the urban condition. Part and parcel of this movement, the agenda for a new institutionalism responded to the widely felt perception among activists, artists, and curators that they were sharing energy and momentum, a feeling that the time was right for exploring crossovers and synergies—commonalities and commons—between the cultural avant-garde, global and networked alliances of protest and solidarity, and tactical and territorial operations of neighborhood survival.[17]

It is against this context that the figure of "the house in flames" emerges as an apposite metaphor for a city that is at once in decadence but also up in arms, caught up in a spiraling process of ruination and dispossession, but also shining with sparks of joyful insurrection. It extends from Luis Rosales's original poetic vision of the house in flames as a familial refuge for the tribulations of the soul (a vision of a conservative hearth in the midst of an authoritarian regime) to Jesús Ibáñez's visceral repudiation of the flaming tele-accelerations of capitalism (a vision, in turn, of charismatic and defiant confrontations to the turmoil of alienation); and against these visions, the story of free culture activism in the early years of the twenty-first century speaks instead of the precarious yet exploratory partnerships that artists, curators, hackers, and autonomous activists formed as they sounded out the depths, contradictions, and hopes for *estar juntos*, for togetherness, in a city in flames.

The Commons and the Avant-Garde

When the Laboratory hosted the third annual national hackmeeting in Madrid on October 4–6, 2002, a number of activists felt that the time was ripe for exploring in greater depth the fragile relations between precarity, networked labor, and autonomy that were increasingly gaining hold over their lives. Toward the end of November they called for a meeting to discuss the organization of a two- or three-day workshop on "capitalism, copyright, and the new economy . . . when the immaterial (affects, communication, care, language, the de-codification of symbols) becomes the key factor in the valorization of capital."[18] While the response showed that there was plentiful enthusiasm and momentum, it was also felt that such an event ought to engage a wider public. Someone suggested asking the Laboratory's next-door neighbor, La Casa Encendida, to collaborate in the organization of the workshop. Few decisions were made that evening except setting up an email list under the name Copyleft to serve as the organizing and networking tool for the group.

The idea for the workshop had been promoted by a militant research collective that operated under the name of La Universidad Nómada (the Nomad University). Made up by a group of (mostly male) young philosophers and critical thinkers who were mostly in their mid- to late twenties, the group had first come together in June 2000 as an "open and processual political laboratory" with the aim of producing collective theorizations on the changing regimes of capital, labor, and knowledge.[19] By the time "the Nomads" (as they often described themselves) suggested to La Casa Encendida the joint organization of the Copyleft workshop, the group had already convened a workshop against patents in 2000 (where Richard Stallman gave the keynote) as well as a workshop in 2001 on migration, capital, and labor, with Tariq Ali, Walter Mignolo, Giovanni Arrighi, and Yann Moulier Boutang as keynote speakers.[20]

Despite their youth, the Nomads had quickly gained a reputation for themselves as intellectual provocateurs. This was due in part to their membership in a generational alliance of student activists who, in the late 1990s, very ably established an international network of activist exchanges and mutual support in Spain, Italy, and France. Riding on the back of "the Erasmus exchange program" and cheap airline tickets,[21] activists visited one another at squatted social centers, learning about local histories of struggle and protest as well as wading into situated genealogies of critical theory. In the wake of the alter-globalization protests in Seattle, activists further came together to coordinate larger networks of activism and resistance, mounting up to such iconic demonstrations of disobedience as those of Prague in 2000 or Genoa in 2001.[22]

Notwithstanding the Nomads' ability to mobilize the local intelligentsia, their ability to garner the support of public institutions such as La Casa Encendida also was related to the class and family status of some of its members. Some autonomous activists were the children of well-established university professors and public intellectuals—as was the case, for example, with Jesús Ibáñez, whose younger son was a "key member of the squat and *insumiso* movements," as Ibáñez himself put it in a short memoir.[23] These class and kinship relations enabled the Nomads to gain the favor of patrons who would have otherwise been out of reach of their youthful and insurrectional aspirations.

On occasions, the social and intellectual background of the Nomads generated moments of tension and confrontation. In her dissertation on Madrid's autonomous collectives, Cristina Flesher Fominaya (née Eguiarte) reported, for example, how the Nomads mobilized their academic and networking credentials to fashion an identity for themselves as an intellectual vanguard. Writing of the role that the Nomads played in the constitution of a Disobedience Lab in 2002, she notes:

> One fundamental contradiction was attempt[ing] to simultaneously uphold the notion of an intellectual vanguard that could direct and set an agenda for a "mass" movement, and a commitment to a heterogeneous, open, horizontal assembly. Linked to this idea of intellectual vanguard was a critique of spontaneity and "brainless activism," the adoption of an abstract theoretical discourse, and the use of discourse to score political points rather than to communicate with other members of the assembly. The commitment to theory-based action (institutional left) was in tension with an alternative vision of action-based theory (autonomous). The institutional left practice of credentialism was also in evidence: members of the Nomad University set up implicit membership requirements which included theoretical sophistication, demonstrated membership in a valid political group, and bona fides.[24]

The echoes of an intellectual avant-garde resonated many years later, on occasion of the twentieth anniversary of the Laboratory's first occupation, on May 11, 2017. The event was a joyful and memorable celebration of the legacy of the Laboratory in the city, attended by many of the activists who made the occupation possible. To our surprise, at the meeting, one of the Laboratory's founding squatters made a candid opening statement where he emphasized that "it would be wrong to remember the Laboratory by its writings and theoretical production. The Laboratory was much more than that, and in some respects, it is doubtful whether it was even that." Another attendee added that she "never understood much of what the Nomads said we were supposed to be doing," that she never recognized her own experience of the vibrant mutuality of the Laboratory in those terms. In a gracious mea culpa, one of the founding members of the Nomads took the opportunity to recognize the group's intellectual self-indulgence, while partially justifying it as an expression of the burgeoning global autonomous consciousness taking shape at the time: "The Laboratory hosted the Second International Zapatista meeting. We hosted the first hacklab at any squatted social center. We were a central node in the European protest-network against new migration policies. We did all these things for which we had no vocabulary, no language. We were trying to stay afloat."[25]

The organization of the Copyleft email list and the workshop that ensued were no exception to the tensions between intellectual avant-gardists and pragmatists. When the idea for the workshop first circulated, its remit was described as centered on "the centrality of immaterial capital and the general intellect in the collective making of knowledge," and it named Bifo Berardi and Wu Ming as possible keynote speakers for the event.[26] However, only a few hours later Miguel Vidal wrote with a slightly different proposal. Instead of focusing on the insurrectional aesthetics of autonomy, he noted, "I'd rather take inspiration today from the Creative Commons project, and their development of a suite of specific tools for cultural creation."[27] Wrapping up the somewhat different sensibilities and outlooks expressed in the email exchange, another contributor offered a palette of alternative titles for the workshop: "infolibremeeting, the Soviet cognitariat, a critical meeting on intellectual property."[28]

The Copyleft workshop was a success on various counts. On the one hand, the event was widely covered by national newspapers, at a time when questions of piracy and intellectual property in the music industry—and the role of copyright management entities thereof—had long been monopolizing the terms of the debate. To this end, the event convened dedicated seminars to a large variety of topics, including patents on life, higher education, and trade unionism.[29] Bifo Berardi and Wu Ming were indeed invited, but so were Glenn Brown, managing director of Creative Commons, and Las Agencias, among others. (Brown's visit prompted the opening of the Spanish chapter of the free licenses project.) It is significant that the event also helped consolidate the alliance that activists had established with public cultural institutions. As a follow-up to the first Copyleft workshop, two public institutions, UNIA (Andalucia's International University) and Arteleku (an art center set up by the provincial government of Gipuzkoa in the Basque country) offered to sponsor a second round of itinerant workshops around the country. These institutions had recently joined Barcelona's Contemporary Art Museum (MACBA) in a research project that aimed to "trace the plurality of practices, models, [and] cultural counter-models that do not respond to the hegemonic structures, politics and practices . . . of the country's alleged modernization."[30] Partly inspired by MACBA's experiment with Las Agencias and the new institutionalism agenda that it had given birth to, the research project found in the work of the Nomads, La Fiambrera, and the hacking and art-activist initiatives of squatted social centers a fertile ground for the types of countercultural practices that it had set out to investigate and document. In this spirit, Arteleku and UNIA funded a second and third run of Copyleft workshops in Málaga and Barcelona in 2004 and a fourth run in Donosti in 2005.

Thus, the Copyleft email list that activists had set up in 2002 to help organize the original workshop at La Casa Encendida became, over the following years the preeminent digital forum where free culture activists in Spain met, discussed, and proposed new developments and projects. As time went by, on top of practical logistical matters regarding the organization of workshops, people wrote to the list with questions about all sorts of technical curiosities: for example, about the types of legal licenses to be used in graphic designs for sign language; about the legal status of the iconography used in urban public spaces; about the intellectual property underwriting a (presumably universal) mathematical language for tap dancing; or even about the intellectual rights in the religious icons used by confraternities during Easter week. Musicians, designers, visual and digital artists, schoolteachers, architects, editors, librarians, software engineers, journalists, academics: all turned to the list as a clearinghouse on matters regarding the technical and legal implications of copyleft licenses.

The list also opened up a space for discussing some of the tensions, contradictions, and uncertainties that made free culture activism something larger than just a digital affair. While some of these discussions were technical, many others pointed outward to the modulations of free licenses as an urban problematic, such as the overlap or coextension between the public domain, the social functions of property, public space, and urban infrastructures and equipment. These debates prompted an intense discussion about the use of "copyleft" as a suitable label for such extradigital practices. It is in this context that activists tried out novel conceptual assemblages for their work and sensibility and that the terms *cultura libre* and *procomún* (commons) first circulated as alternative coinages.

For example, when Javier de la Cueva was preparing his lawsuit against the digital canon imposed by copyright management entities, he consulted widely with various free culture communities. He immersed himself in the preparation of an appeal to the Constitutional Court in the expectation that his original demand would be dismissed. He circulated sections of the text to email lists and engaged in detailed explanations and discussions of the legal arguments he was elaborating. A couple of exchanges are particularly illuminating for understanding the wider cultural context shaping the arguments about digital liberties that free culture activists were trying to articulate at the time.

On June 11, 2004, de la Cueva announced to the Copyleft list that he was drafting an appeal on the unconstitutional nature of the digital canon. In exploring the issue, he had come to the realization that there could be scope for arguing for the unconstitutional nature of copyright management entities more broadly. He explained: "I believe the structure of copyright management entities may be described in terms analogous to the vertical trade unions of the Franco dictatorship [an allusion to the hierarchical unions of the Falangist movement]. There is no constitutional doctrine establishing how these entities are to operate. All that is said is that they are to be non-profit and associational, leaving therefore unmarked the question of possible conflict of interests between associates."[31]

The message prompted a lively discussion in the list over the work that copyright management entities were carrying out and the types of interests, conflicts, and agendas they pursued and represented. It is well known, as de la Cueva pointed out in later correspondence, that "the voices of all authors are not equally represented in such corporations, and that, in a manner analogous to how 'vertical trade unions' operated, the pressure of the voices of those 'above' (employers, famous authors) carry more weight than the voices of those in weaker positions— this is what made vertical trade unions unconstitutional to start with."[32]

De la Cueva was drawing here on the Falangist imagery of Catholic, hierarchical unionism that had been a model for corporate organization during the dictatorship. There was a general consensus that the image of "vertical integration" was a felicitous one in the case of copyright law because it showed how it encroaches on the "horizontality" of peer-to-peer transactions and constrains its "commons."[33] The vertical "cuts" into the horizontal, so to speak. In this light, de la Cueva further advanced that he was developing a legal argument that built on the doctrine of the "social function of property," and in particular its application in urban law, to prove the unconstitutional nature of existing copyright legislation. It was surprising, however, that in this line of reasoning the city became a template for the commons.

> I am making use of the legal argument about the social function of property, which is established and recognized by Article 33 of the Spanish Constitution, whereby:
> 1. The Constitution recognizes the right to private property and inheritance.
> 2. The content of the aforementioned rights will be delimited by their social function, in accordance with the law.

In this sense, I am trying to develop a legal argument that illustrates the social function of property in terms analogous to how Urban Law limits the extension of private property. That is, when it comes to intellectual property law we need analogous "common spaces" (the equivalent in Urban Law would be green areas, urban equipment, natural parks . . .) because inasmuch as intellectual property law is just one kind of the property genus, then of course it only makes sense that it, too, is limited by the social function of property.[34]

The complexion of free culture as a social function—a social function for which the ecological joviality and multiplicity of the city provided its most suitable metaphor—thus gradually empowered activists to imagine conceptual and practical alternatives to the delimitative and punitive directives of copyright legislation. The Copyleft email list and the Creative Commons list for Spain (founded in 2004 to discuss the adaptation of the CC licenses to the Spanish legal context)[35] became vibrant forums for discussing these and related matters.

One fascinating development was the way in which the urban condition provided resources for problematizing and redescribing property relationships and copyright entitlements. For example, activists were quick to enlist the cooperation of public libraries in their fight against the implementation of a digital canon on the loan of library materials such as CDs or to garner the alliance of municipalities to redesign the iconography of urban equipment.[36] There was an acute consciousness that the ecosystem of digital rights was calling out for a thicker and richer description of requirements and obligations than those strictly delimited to the technical and juridical apparatuses of the net. There was also increasing awareness that the sensibility and orientation of their practices could only be represented poorly through the legal and hacking idiom of "copyleft" and that there was a singular and specific trajectory to the "culture of 'free culture'" in Spain that merited an alternative formulation.

For example, in a long exchange that took place between June and July 2004, the members of the guerrilla street art collective Suéltate/Pankahackers made an appearance on the Copyleft list expounding the somewhat extravagant accusation that the discussions in the list were elitist mumbo-jumbo.[37] For Suéltate, these were times that called for a more radical and performative "hacking" of public space, as their own Situationist and irreverent shout-outs in public plazas and streets demonstrated. While the intervention of Suéltate was widely acknowledged to be "surrealist" and "performative craziness," and some even called for the collective to be expelled from the list, it nonetheless raised the question of what it would mean for free culture to travel outdoors and outside the strict realms of the digital, the technical, and the legal.[38] In two crucial contributions during this exchange, Miguel Vidal cleared a space for distinguishing between liberation, freedom, and the commons in different, and admittedly not-always-easy-to-separate, technical, legal, and political contexts. In fact, it was during this exchange that Vidal first suggested the use of the Spanish term *procomún* to describe how the imaginary of free software licenses, and the political philosophy of copyleft more broadly, might be given generic political valence in the Spanish context. These are important contributions that deserve to be quoted at length. Apropos the distinction between freedom and liberation, Vidal offered the following terminological and conceptual precision:

> In a strict sense (that is, as defined by the GNU Project), and if we abide by the use that the free software community has been making of the term for the past twenty years, copyleft is NOT a legal term, but a political one. It refers to the use of copyright legislation for promoting the liberty of users and *making sure that everything that is free will remain so*. . . . We are dealing therefore with a concept, an idea, that is open to different types of implementation (that may use different types of licenses). . . . For instance, we could imagine non-juridical implementations of copyleft, such as a political decision aimed at protecting the commons. . . . What we are seeing today, however, is an extension of the idea of free software to other domains, and the correlative extension of "copyleft" as a descriptor for the non-commercial copying of things. Copyleft works very well as a meme, easily understood by anyone ("to turn copyright inside out"). Thus, we face a situation today such that what must work as a requirement in the case of free software (the four liberties) [i.e. (i) to run the code, (ii) access its source code, (iii) redistribute it, and (iv) redistribute the changes] may no longer apply when we are talking about other forms of cultural expression. And yet for practical reasons we still refer to these modulations as "copyleft" . . . because they somehow respond to our overall aspirations, namely, to expand the *procomún* and make sure that nothing that enters it will ever leave it (will be "re-appropriated" by third parties). . . . I think it is fair to say that is the state of affairs to-date. Now my personal opinion: the way I see it, it makes sense to speak of "copyleft" so far as we use the term as a generic, as a political referent of the movement, and as long as we do not forget the term's original meaning. Because if we were to forget it, we would be losing a crucial dimension of its purchase—*que lo libre siga siéndolo*, that free things remain so—and we wouldn't be getting anything that isn't already contained in the terms *procomún* or *libre*.[39]

Vidal's clarification, however, only seemed to generate more disagreement and confusion: What gets liberated when we speak of hacking a plaza or *autogestión* (self-management) in a squatted social center? What technical, legal, and sociological dynamics bring freedom, autonomy, and liberation together or apart at different conjunctures and in different arrangements? In this context, Vidal tried once more to essay a notion of *procomún* that operated as a singular Spanish version of liberation, between-and-betwixt—at once more and less than—the commons, freedom, and copyleft:

> "*procomún*" is a genuinely Castilian term and of very old origin. . . . There are documented appearances in the XVth, XVIth, XIXth and XXth centuries. . . . In every case its use is similar to the way we use it today ("that which is common and useful at the same time"). The Dictionary of the Royal Academy of Language has an entry for it in every one of its editions, including the last one where its usage as "public utility" is accepted (from "pro," benefit or advantage, and "común," common). In other words, the term has long been used in a very similar way to how we use it today to denote "that which is of public use." Therefore, *procomún* would serve as a good translation of "commons" (although there are even more precise translations such as "ejido") and it has the advantage over other translations—such as common property, common goods, or public goods—that it is both short and that it can be used as a generic . . . *procomún* does not refer to forests, land, nor irrigation systems. Nor does it refer to culture. It is sufficiently generic to encompass all of the above; it is intuitive, one doesn't need the dictionary to understand its meaning; and it has the term "común" (common) embedded within (which gestures to "communal," "community," even "communism"). It's not as if we want to impose one term above others, nor to show off our philological expertise. . . . We just want to see how the term serves as a political tool enabling the circulation of a concept that can do just what we aspire for. What matters is the concept rather than the word that embodies it (copyleft, commons, procomún, ejido . . .).[40]

By 2004, when these lines were written, discourses on the commons were anything but a local phenomenon. Elinor Ostrom's influential treatise on the governance of the commons, which was published in 1990, had already become a canonical text in institutional economics and political theory.[41] Ostrom's important text surveyed empirical cases of successful self-organizing and self-governing alternatives to market and state management of natural resources. On the basis of such cases, she developed a model of common-pool resource management based on practices of situated strategizing, commitments, and compromises that could not be characterized in terms of either central regulation or privatization. Ostrom's argument quickly found its way into neighboring disciplines. In 1998, the legal scholar Yochai Benkler published an influential article on the regulation of wireless transmissions as a public commons.[42] Shortly after, Lawrence Lessig, an intellectual leader of the free culture movement in the United States through his early writings on the regulatory power of code, built on Benkler's work to speak more broadly of the commons as an intermediary "balance" between the "ills of communism" and the drive to "privatize everything."[43] In 2001, Naomi Klein described the antiglobalization movement as a movement for "reclaiming the commons."[44] By the turn of the century, therefore, the notion of the commons as a political alternative to both capitalist relations and state paternalism was well established. More broadly, the commons had become a figure that also invoked the promise of a certain sociological autonomy, beyond the spectacles of possessive individualism and the associative logics of identitarian communitarianism. The concept now functioned as both a repository of wealth and a reservoir of virtue.

Benkler's writings on networked commons circulated amply among hackers in Spain. In 2003, the journal of the association of information technologists published a special issue dedicated to the commons, which included translations of works by Benkler and the writer and commons activist David Bollier.[45] However, the invocation of *procomún* in the Spanish context signaled a slightly more tensile infrastructure. The commons that people referred to and articulated through their practices were neither a form of property nor a community-managed resource. They were neither a tool for autonomous digital organization nor an affective reservoir for collective action. As the above exchanges make clear, by 2004 autonomous activists had intuited, and were struggling to find adequate idioms for, a new language of political aspiration and material hope, at once inspired by the technical and legal affordances of free software, the libertarian practices of *autogestión*, and the political theory of the commons. This language, however, pointed to a rather unstable horizon of action, which appeared and disappeared in complex, provisional, and tentative alliances across the worlds of squatted social centers, public art institutions, and technical hackers. In the interstices between these worlds there emerged, here and there, glimpses of a "free culture," a culture of autonomy and experimentation that often found in the city, across its insurrectional landscapes and assemblies of joy, a privileged site of enunciation. The idiom of cultura libre was therefore used in this context as a spotlight that helped silhouette such an urban landscape; a tentative idiom for grasping the urbanization of liberation: the inchoation of an impetus for intransitivity, where people came together as a commons to the defense of the public through the tools of the libre.

When, in 2008, Miguel Vidal and Javier Candeira (the founder of the Dork-bot meetings in Madrid) engaged in a historical reflection on the nature of co-pyleft activism in Spain (after a long silence in the Copyleft list, and apropos a new subscriber's inquiry into the ambiguous meaning of the term "copyleft"), they remarked with a dose of irony and capitulation:

> [JAVIER CANDEIRA, JC]: The very name of this email list (Copyleft) is misleading. I've lost count of the number of times I've had to explain that "copyleft" has two different meanings: a strict, technical mean-ing, and then a somewhat laxer meaning.[46]
>
> [MIGUEL VIDAL]: Right, I couldn't agree more. And I take part of the blame for it (including setting up the email list over five years ago). Hence my penitence of clarifying the matter every time that someone brings it up. I don't think there is much we can do, though, Javier . . . except explain its polysemy "ad aeternum," the way you would do with the meaning of other words that have mutated over time. Ex-cept this time, rather exceptionally, we have witnessed the mutation firsthand. Our only hope—and correct me if I am wrong, Javier—is that this seems a specific development of the Spanish-speaking world, for the Anglo-Saxon world does not seem to have picked up the meme the way we have.[47]
>
> [JC]: You are right: there is no such usage in the Anglo world. In fact, they look at us strangely when they hear about it.[48]

In Flames

The hours following the Madrid bombings on May 11, 2004, were a time of chaos, confusion, and mourning. Within just a few hours of the blasts, the government rushed to call for a public demonstration the following day, whose slogan—"With the victims, with the Constitution, against terrorism"—provoked widespread in-dignation and condemnation as it was believed to insinuate that the attacks had been carried out by the Basque nationalist and terrorist group ETA. The slogan deliberately conflated and manipulated a collective pathos of grief with the ruling Popular Party's antinationalist and pro-constitutionalist electoral rhetoric. Shortly after noon, the Ministry of the Interior further confirmed at a press con-ference the conviction that the attacks had been carried out by ETA. As time went by, however, "leaks from the security forces on the day of the bombings soon began to suggest doubts about ETA's responsibility and the possibility of the involvement of al Qaeda."[49] There was a growing feeling of confusion and resentment as people circulated snippets of news trickling in from foreign correspondents and radical news agencies that cast doubts on the government's version, on blog posts, email, and a variety of activist forums. By the late hours of the afternoon, the Editorial Collective of Madrid's Indymedia network issued a statement denouncing the government's media strategy and its insidious appropriation of the voice of civil society: "Was it ETA? Was it Al Qaeda? The answers offered by some come oh so fast!"[50]

When Alberto Nanclares woke up on the morning of March 11, 2004, ready for the opening of Basurama's exhibition at La Casa Encendida, his cell phone registered over a dozen missed calls. "I returned one call after another and people just expressed a desire to be together (*la peña quería estar junta*)." The bombings triggered a shared feeling of mutuality but also a feeling that the government's manipulative tactics at such a devastating moment should not go unremarked. As the old *Alice is the Devil* adage had it, "to conspire is to respire together":[51]

> Within the Madrid-based social networks, the government's call for a public demonstration, together with what was felt as a need to engage in a collective reflection over what had happened, prompted a number of meetings. The first such meeting took place on May 11 at Ladinamo's venue, where over fifty activists from various Lavapiés-based squatted social centers came together, as well as members from two telematics operations (Indymedia Madrid and Nodo50), some antimilitarist and disobedience groups, and the Nomad University.[52]

Some activists felt it was important to show up at the demonstration as an expression of solidarity with the victims, while others thought there were other means for doing so that did not require endorsing the government's actions. By the morning of March 13, however, when the Ministry of the Interior affirmed yet again that the main suspect remained ETA, activists had had enough. As Cristina Flesher Fominaya reported it: "Activists called each other, trying to come up with some way to express their anger and to demand that the government come clean about the evidence they had regarding the responsibility for the attacks. Five activists met in a café in Madrid and decided to send out a call for a protest in front of the PP [Popular Party] headquarters at 6 p.m."[53] The SMS message that activists put out quickly went viral and prompted a protest in front of the Popular Party's headquarters—"the first case of a political 'flash mob' or smart mob protest in Spain."[54]

As it turned out, we were both in the United Kingdom when the SMS was sent out. Adolfo was in London visiting a friend and Alberto was at work at the University of Manchester. We both received the SMS under conditions that signal the significance of its situated nature. Adolfo got the message immediately, through connections and friends in the free culture movement, but he found it unintelligible as he was unaware of the context of indignation that was brewing in the streets. Alberto only received the message many months later, when he turned his Spanish cell phone on during a brief visit to Madrid.

The SMS summoned people to attend a flash mob that was exceptional in more ways than one. On the one hand, it contravened the so-called *jornada de reflexión*, the day previous to an election when political demonstrations are deemed illegal. However, it was also exceptional in that, as expressed by some Spanish political scientists, "We may well be facing the first popular manifestation mediated by new informational technologies that (in a manner complementary to the work of mainstream media and, admittedly, in a singularly unique context) had immediate effects upon a consolidated democracy."[55]

It is significant that the success of the flash mob further showed how far the autonomous movement in Madrid had come in weaving a successful network of complicities and complexities around counterinformational and self-defensive telematics. A study of the communication networks used during the circulation of the call showed the central role played by counterinformational agencies in the propagation of the message: that it was Nodo50 that first put up the call on the internet, which was then picked up and redistributed by five news outlets from the Indymedia Network.[56] Although the response to the flash mob certainly reached out beyond activist circles, it was the latter's culture of network politics— cultivated over years of work in antagonist telematics, in complex alliances with the art world and public institutions, and in expansive associations with neighborhood communities—that enabled and shaped its original momentum. Some activists even described the protest as the zenith of the autonomous movement. For Jacobo Rivero, one of the founding residents of the Laboratory, "The coming together of people on March 13, regardless of their political affiliations, whether they voted for this or that party . . . such coming together was a sheer expression of absolute autonomy."[57] In the same fashion, a choral memoir and analysis published a year after the bombings, among whose authors were members of the Laboratory and the Nomad University, neatly synthesized a view of free culture as at once a social vector of mutuality and empathy, an economy of information, and a pulsation of freedom and liberation:

> [In response to the media blackouts over the attacks,] thousands of people resorted to communication technologies as vehicles for creating common spaces for discussion, thought, and *sentir libremente* (feeling freely) . . . a meeting of multiple spaces and singular subjects, in forums and weblogs—as well as many other physical and virtual places—led to a gradual empowerment over the moral blackmailing that we were

being subjected to. . . . Only the multiplication of viewpoints, of discussions, of molecular encounters weaved around spaces of affect and care radically different from the ones available to us from mainstream media—only then was it possible to articulate timid and fragile testimonies at first, then critical reflections and statements, and finally manifestations, exigencies for truth. . . . [Because] access to the true plane of creation, of thinking and doing, is always to be found at the bottom (*abajo*). Deep down. We keep forgetting about such a plane, its collective process, which always gets lost in the society of spectacle. . . . This book, on the other hand, offers a key to access the source code (*una llave de accesso al código fuente*) of the production of an alternative imaginary.[58]

The year the city rose in flames and tears, then, signaled also the coming of age of the free culture movement as an urban movement, its deep entanglement in the sentimental, technical, and political fabrics of the city. The exhilaration felt in seeking out for one another, in the calls for *estar juntos*, *sentir común*, and *sentir libremente* (being together, feeling in common, and feeling freely), was an exhilaration unleashed from the shackles of political normativity as well as from the informational economies and dictums of mainstream media. It was a dramatic exhilaration that had found in the experience of free culture a novel articulation of liberty and sociality. This was free culture thrice unleashed: free as in freedom, free as in free access, and also free as in liberation.

Part 2
CLIMATES OF METHODS

The Ice Palace was designed in 1922 by the Spanish architects Gabriel Abreu and Fernando García Mercadal for the Belgian hotel entrepreneur George Marquet. The palace stood at the heart of courtly politics in Madrid, directly opposite the Palace Hotel that Marquet had opened ten years earlier and only a few blocks away from parliament, the stock exchange, and the Prado Museum. The building was originally intended to house an ice-skating rink and an automobile museum but in 1928 the Spanish government bought the property and commissioned an alternative use for it as the new home for the Center for Historical Studies (CHS).

The CHS had been founded in 1910 with a view to bringing scholarship in the humanities in Spain in line with its European counterparts. It was directed for many years by Ramón Menéndez Pidal, whose influence in shaping a distinctive tradition of Spanish philological research would be far-reaching, inaugurating a historical and ethnological comparative approach to the study of Spanish language and literature. In the aftermath of the Spanish Civil War, however, many of Menéndez Pidal's students were forced into exile, and under the aegis of the national-Catholic agenda of Franco's dictatorship, the CHS was integrated into the newly founded Spanish National Research Council (CSIC).

When Alberto first walked into the CHS in September 2006, the building vaguely retained the aura of its magnificent past. Worn-out and faded, the facade stood slightly at odds with the splendor of the surrounding scenery at the heart of administrative and bourgeoise seat of power in Madrid. On their way to the Prado or Reina Sofia museums, tourists often walked past the CHS with indifference, their gaze occasionally diverted toward the elegant showcases of its ground floor bookshop. Inside, the building also belied its grandeur, displaying an atmosphere of abandonment and resignation—the lights dimmed, the wooden floors squeaking with every step, the air thick with the smell of old books. Alberto had arrived in Madrid earlier that summer on a research sabbatical from the University of Manchester to do an ethnography of humanities scholars. After clearing access with the leadership of CSIC, he settled on doing fieldwork in the CHS among Hebrew and biblical philologists on the one hand and historians of science on the other. In this context, some six months into his fieldwork, he met the historian of science Antonio Lafuente.

In his mid-fifties, with short white hair, sparkling brown eyes, and a strongly built body, Lafuente was warm and joyful but also measured and thoughtful. The door to his office in the CHS was always wide open. He welcomed any interruption, engaging generously and warmly with visitors. He spoke lucidly, in studied and calm sentences, with an air of tranquility that veiled his vivacious curiosity and erudition.

Born in the southern Andalusian city of Granada in 1953, Lafuente moved to Barcelona in the early 1970s to pursue an undergraduate degree in physics. In the city he quickly became active in a number of communist and left-wing circles where discussions about the "failed modernity" of Spain were a recurrent topic—questions, for example, about the presence or absence of local versions of the Industrial Revolution or the Enlightenment. The failure of the Spanish modern period was often associated with the decadence of its imperial period and its fatuous reincarnation in the national-Catholic agenda of the Franco regime. Discussions about the contemporary state of Spanish science were part of this gloomy and pessimistic diagnostic, whereby historians of science joined the ranks of historians of government, historians of the church, and historians of labor in articulating a history of their respective disciplines as exemplars of a grander narrative about the doomed history of Spanish exceptionalism.[1] While still a young postgraduate student, Lafuente decided to enter this wider debate by writing a master's dissertation on the introduction of Einstein's relativity theory in Spain. Very quickly, however, he became skeptical of such a historiographical sensibility. "Even before submitting my dissertation," he noted to Alberto in 2007, "I was already aware that I wasn't really writing a history of science but a history of Spain; that mine was a portrait about the idiosyncrasy of Spanish science, rather than an account of the specific assemblage of encounters, machines, or laboratories through which the theory of relativity circulated at the time."[2]

It also became obvious to Lafuente that as a historian of twentieth century physics, he was very much left to his own devices in the Spanish academy. There were few interlocutors for his work, few if any academic departments or spaces of debate where he could present his research. Therefore, for his doctoral work he decided to shift research interests to the history of science in the eighteenth century. His first book, *The Geometrization of Earth* (1984), was a study of the scientific expeditions that first measured the shape and size—the geodesy—of the Earth.[3] The study of the Spanish-French expedition that traveled to Quito in 1736 to measure the longitude of the meridian gradient on the Equator soon alerted Lafuente to related questions about the tensions between colonial science and metropolitan science and, crucially, to the all-important part played by *criollos* (creoles) in the production of scientific knowledge.

The problem of creole science shaped Lafuente's historiographical sensibility thereafter. Rejecting narratives of metropolitan diffusionism and progress but also narratives of postcolonial resistance and identity, Lafuente sought to clear up a space for reckoning with that which took place in between the "two shores of science": the fictitious shore of geographical distance between the metropole and the colony and the equally fictitious shore of epistemic distance between experts and laypeople.[4] By the turn of the century, Lafuente was trying out different ways to conceptualize the gray zone of reconnaissance and invention lying between the two shores. For a while he settled on a notion of discovery as a "popular" project, by drawing, for example, on the work of Georges-Louis Leclerc, count de Buffon, whose *Histoire naturelle, générale et particulière* (1749–1804) was one of the most widely read books of the Enlightenment.[5] For Lafuente, Buffon's idea of science (or natural history, as it was called then) was not a project in the description or revelation of nature but rather a project in the rediscovery of our capacity for experience and sensibility—a popular or shared project if there ever was one. A few years later, Lafuente opted for a new conceptual regime, that of *common sense*, to describe shared orientations and expressions of curious awakening, feeling, and experience in the production of knowledge.[6]

In the early 2000s, a group of young software engineers were employed by the CHS to upgrade the center's information technology infrastructure. The group would often gather for a coffee break by the coffee machines in the building's basement, where they held enthusiastic and loud exchanges on free software, copyleft licenses, and peer-to-peer networks. Lafuente was drawn to these casual discussions and would in time become party to them. It was through these young engineers that he first heard about free and open-source software and that he met the hacker Miguel Vidal (mentioned in part 1), who would, in turn, introduce Lafuente to the old Castilian term *procomún* (commons).

The idea of procomún that hackers were busy exploring and articulating was an eye-opener for Lafuente. It resonated with his own vision of science as a "common sense" and, crucially, offered a concrete placeholder for his interest in the archival and material trading zones of scientific exploration. The commons was not a culture, a political ideology, or a sensibility. The commons that hackers spoke of was an infrastructure of feeling and *tâtonnement*, a sociotechnical assemblage of legal licenses, software packages, and shared apprenticeships designed to function as an experimental collective system.[7] It was a technology of enunciation and visibility as much as an archive of descriptions, which resonated in intriguing ways with Lafuente's own historiographical work on eighteenth-century expressions of popular and creole science. These were projects of inquiry that moved between the cracks and crevices of authorship, property, and possession, neither strictly public nor private and neither individual nor communitarian, although of course they clashed with these regimes of power and authority in different ways at different times.

Lafuente found the idea of procomún inspiring and went to work immediately. He retrieved his previous studies and analyses on creole and imperial science, revisiting them with fresh eyes on the lookout for glimpses of procomún. Soon enough he found himself revisiting the question of the archive. The world's natural history museums, Lafuente observed, are full of objects whose patrimonial value lies in their mundanity, anonymity, and replaceability: the bones, rocks, fossils, plants, fibers, textiles, butterflies, ceramics, and shells that one finds in every museum in the world, which made every museum at once different and the same. Such artefacts arrived at the museums through scientific expeditions of empire, the legacies of imperial ambition, dispossession, and accumulation. Often collected by indigenous peoples, if not stolen from them, they found their way into the botanical gardens, curiosity cabinets, and anatomical collections of the metropolis, where they were classified into taxonomies, series, tables, or ages and transformed into objects of state knowledge and, in time, heritage and public goods. For a brief moment, however, they were also objects caught at the crossroads of empire, Enlightenment, and indigenous or creole experience—objects that drew around them an emerging and uncertain trading zone, whose energies and qualities "belonged at once to everyone and to no one."[8] At that uncertain point, the objects irradiated an energy and were intensified by a furious "trafficking between [their] symbolic and ontological qualities."[9] Just there, at that overwhelming moment of experience and experiment, the commons were made visible, informed by the cosmopolitan dreams of Enlightenment science, only to be violently erased thereafter by the forces of the state. The history of "the management of the commons," Lafuente concluded, "was a technological mission whose costs only the state was able to assume, and whose controversies only the state was in a position to dissolve."[10] The promises of the Enlightenment made the commons visible in the eighteenth century only to have them erased in the same gesture by the promises of the state.

The study of the commons as an object of the history of science, where complex networks of instruments, expeditions, missionaries, illustrators, or indigenous people were brought together to grant ontological and archival stability
to new discoveries, offered Lafuente a source of inspiration for charting the emergence of contemporary commons. He already knew about the legal licenses and
technical solutions of free software and also began to explore novel articulations
of property rights in new genetic materials and the disputing of claims over planetary commons such as water management or air pollution. Developing his
newfound interest in the configuration of the contemporary commons, in 2004
Lafuente convened for La Casa Encendida a public series of roundtables on "hybrid
objects," objects whose affordances "exceed the regimes of the techno-scientific"
and that in this capacity, "claim for themselves new political and juridical
natures."[11] The event enlisted public intellectuals, novelists, psychiatrists, biolo-
gists, lawyers, and hackers in what was arguably the first public event in Spain to
ever showcase a discussion about the commons not as property regimes or environmental or digital resources but as techno-scientific problems.

Talk about the political challenges of digital technologies and free culture was
in the air in those days, too. Thus, while in some respects the encounter between
Antonio Lafuente and Miguel Vidal at CHS had been a serendipitous one, in
other ways it was expressive of the latitudinal imaginations that the parlances
of procomún and cultura libre were setting in motion. The city, once again, became a template for such cross-pollinations.

For one thing, struggles for the right to the city had anything but subsided at
the turn of the century. In 1999, for instance, the monumental building that
housed La Tabacalera (the Tobacco Factory) in Lavapiés closed its doors for the
last time. An architectural icon of popular culture, the building housed tobacco
production in the city for over 170 years. The building was an emblem of the labor
and women's movements, with some of the most famous feminist labor leaders
of the 1930s rising from the ranks of the cigarreras (women cigar workers). These
women worked and lived in the neighborhood, which was in many respects
transformed by the rhythms of labor and hope of the factory floor. Therefore,
no sooner was the building closed than autonomous and neighborhood activists from the Laboratory where already demanding that the municipality have
it repurposed as a local community center. When the Laboratory itself was finally evicted in 2003, the aspirations of activists turned once again toward La
Tabacalera, which by then was in a dreadful state of abandonment and neglect.

By 2004 the movement reclaiming La Tabacalera had scaled up. The Ministry of Culture had announced the transformation of the building into a flagship
visual arts museum, a strategy that reawakened the fears of gentrification that
squatters and neighborhood activists had long been struggling against. Building

on the Laboratory's grassroots networks (and the Lavapiés Network in particular), activists set in motion a campaign calling for a public debate on the future of the factory.[12] Over a period of four months, public intellectuals, academics, neighborhood activists, architects, and curators came together to discuss global and territorial dynamics of cultural production and urban democracy.

The organizers of the campaign included members of the Laboratory and the Nomads, among them Miguel Vidal and the grassroots philosopher Amador Fernández Savater, who had themselves organized the Copyleft symposium at La Casa Encendida two years earlier. They were both well aware of Antonio Lafuente's science studies approach to the commons and had, in fact, promoted the "hybrid objects" workshops that Lafuente convened at La Casa Encendida only a year earlier in activist circles.[13] It was in this context that they invited Lafuente to deliver a talk in a public plaza in Lavapiés to a packed audience of neighbors, activists, and passersby on April 9, 2005.

Under the title "The Museum as a House of Commons," Lafuente's talk articulated a set of ideas that would become foundational for the free culture movement in the years to come. Lafuente built on his historical work on the Enlightenment's natural history collections to outline an idea of the commons not as a resource or property form but rather as a problem-space, one fundamentally animated by questions of archive and documentation, writing and inscription, and caretaking. "The commons," he would articulate there and repeat dozens of times elsewhere, "are first made visible when they come under threat. It often takes a regime of technological exploitation for the commons to come under threat; but it also takes a complex assemblage of technical and aesthetic languages to make such threats visible and envisage alternative solutions."[14] The talk further made an audacious proposal for relocating the problem of the commons away from the patrimonial sites and modernist enclaves of resource management and cultural curation and straight into the experimental confines of the laboratory: "I asked myself: Where is there space for everything? Where can I fit a galaxy or a desire? And the answer I kept coming back to was: a laboratory. Laboratories are places where objects have no frontiers, where they are at once situated and yet undefinable. Our challenge, then, was figuring out how to get the commons out of the museum and into a laboratory."[15]

The story of Antonio Lafuente's inquiry into the history of science as a history of the commons, and in particular his encounter with hackers' and squatters' projects in urban autonomy, offers a point of entry into the specific practices and scenarios through which the free culture movement in Madrid began its journey out into the city at large. In public plazas and abandoned industrial factories; in public museums and elite academic centers; in scholarly texts, activist pamphlets, and hybrid objects, the language of procomún began modeling a novel ecology of claims, commitments, and responsibilities. This new ecology was modulated by a sensibility for the archives and infrastructures, the material designs and legal instruments, the sensors and methodologies inchoating the city as a complex assemblage of objects, standards, resources, and interests— as a climate of methods. Moreover, the story about Lafuente's research activism is also a story about the crossing-over of autonomy into the public sphere through the unsuspected alliance between scholars and hackers, curators, and squatters. This story and others in the following chapters offer us a glimpse into the dynamics of complicity and complexity that, for a while, brought ideas about public culture, free culture, and the commons to test each other's limits, and in the process intuit and imagine shared vicinities of liberation.

Part 2 dwells on these stories of technical designs and urban encounters. In chapter 4 we examine the centrality awarded by activists to practices of description and documentation. Activists engage in profuse descriptions of their projects, sometimes in literary form and sometimes in other registers such as photography, sketches, technical drawings, filmmaking, and so on. These complex descriptions, which they refer to as *prototypes*, aim to provide both technical and legal guidelines for others to replicate the designs, and also pedagogical directions so that users can understand the contexts to which the designs originally responded as well as orient them toward potential re-functionings. It is significant that the prototypes also incarnate a cultural history of intransitive designs: situated assemblages of the commons, the public, and the libre. Chapter 5 shifts our focus on prototypes, viewing them not just as sociotechnical devices but as archival assemblages more amply, which mobilize ecological sensibilities, material exigencies, and contextual obligations. In this way, we draw attention to how activists seek to liberate culture *in three dimensions*, not just by freeing it from the shackles of discursive normativity or the technical and legal constraints of intellectual property rights, but also by understanding the role that atmospherics, physics, and kinesthetics—ambience, infrastructure, and interior design—play in bundling practices of knowing into specific climates of action and experience.

MORE THAN MANY AND LESS THAN ONE

It's a chilly afternoon late in November 2010, and I (Alberto) am walking briskly to Medialab Prado (MLP) for a meeting. It's getting cold and I look forward to getting refuge. As I approach the space, my body registers a familiar thrill. MLP is hidden away in a basement under a small and snug square in Madrid's old historic quarter. It is a most unusual location. Presiding over the square is the Belgian Sawmill, the ruins of a beautiful early twentieth-century industrial structure that have been under renovation for a number of years now. The Sawmill stands at the heart of the city's so-called Art Walk, in front of the Royal Botanical Gardens and the Prado Museum and within walking distance of the Reina Sofía Museum. Once its refurbishment is completed, the Sawmill will be MLP's new home, joining a glamorous and spectacular landscape of art venues.[1] Everything shines on this urban plane. Where I am heading, though, is an underworld of sorts. As I walk down a long metallic ramp into the square's basement, the sounds of the city fade away. The city lights dim, too. With a little effort I swing open a heavy, portentous black door. For a second I stand at the doorway and my body registers, again, that familiar thrill, a little excitement and a little trepidation, as I recognize a crowd of friends and strangers—engineers and artists, autonomous activists and university professors—who are busy chatting, tinkering with electronics, or quietly working away at their laptops. There are no urban sounds here anymore, but the atmosphere vibrates with its own soundscape of anticipation.

We have been asked by Marcos García, head of cultural programs at MLP, to help its staff evaluate the interim progress of a series of workshops launched earlier in the year. Under the title "Thinking and Doing Medialab," the workshops have brought together a cohort of well-known artists, hackers, and intellectuals to meet four times over the course of the year to take stock of a decade of MLP activities, but also, and perhaps more important, to advance new lines of research and action in light of MLP's forthcoming relocation to the Belgian Sawmill.[2]

> The meeting has been convened at relatively short notice. I could sense a hint of concern in Marcos' voice when he called me on the phone. As I walk into MLP I am greeted by Juan Carrete, MLP's director, who is having an animated conversation about the nature of the civil service with a fellow member of staff. "Ah, a civil servant," jokes Juan as he sees me approaching; "you are surely one not to complain these days, are you?" His sardonic tone alerts me to the nature of the conversation. Two years into the financial and economic crisis, it has become commonplace for casual chitchats to include discussions on the politics of austerity, crisis, and precarity. In this context, Juan is calling attention to the stability of my civil service job. I note to Juan that universities and scientific institutions have seen huge cuts to their budgets too, so we are hardly exempt from the consequences of the crisis. Yet Juan's mind has drifted elsewhere already, for his rejoinder is not addressed to me but enunciated with a certain absent-mindedness: "Time and productivity in the public sector: they are unmanageable. For over a year, our hands have been tied, without monies, without resources. And then, at no notice, we are pressed to spend a budget we didn't even know we had. No wonder civil servants mock the notion of productivity—a whimsical political idiom if there ever was one."
>
> Alberto's Fieldwork Diary, November 30, 2010

Marcos García was in his early thirties when we first met in 2005. A tall figure with a gentle demeanor and a reputation as an attentive listener and generous conversationalist, Marcos was then responsible, along with his partner Laura Fernández, for the educational program at MLP.[3] The job suited him, for Marcos is a tireless pedagogue. He had graduated in 2002 from Madrid's School of Fine Arts, to which he had been drawn not so much by an artistic vocation as for his interest in art theory. The school's well-known project-based pedagogy, whereby students are encouraged to try their hands at new tools and resources, suited his penchant for experimentation: "I look back at my projects from art school and they are not good; they are pretty awful, I'd say. But we were given absolute room for experimentation and that was something I relished, and for which am grateful."[4] Toward the end of their studies, Marcos and Laura spent a year in Kassel, Germany, working at documenta 11, the celebrated quinquennial art exhibition, where they were employed as exhibition guides. The experience, Marcos has often told us, was fundamental in shaping his view of the exhibition of art as a larger and richer process of accompaniment and mediation. At documenta they were given the opportunity to witness artists assemble and install their works, gaining firsthand insight into their workings and artistic intentions. Marcos and Laura used these insights in their own explanations to visitors, subtly reorienting their jobs as guides to experiment with a function of mediation. Shortly after their return from Kassel, Marcos and Laura both applied for jobs as exhibition guides at MLP and included in their application files a project for rethinking the role of guides in terms of a more ambitious educational program.[5]

MLP opened in 2002 as the premier digital arts center in the city.[6] Operated by the Department of Culture at Madrid's municipality, for a number of years the center showcased exhibitions at the vanguard of the digital arts. These exhibitions, so-called banquets, showcased leading work by national and international artists, often with an interest in the organicist and biological metaphors of digital and networking visualizations (which were common tropes at the time). By 2004, however, Marcos and Laura had expressed an interest in the participatory dimensions of digital commons projects and in cultura libre as a political program for the liberation of the arts. This was the time when the advent of new institutionalism swayed the Spanish art world, thrusting public museums and cultural centers into a praxis of critical and organizational self-reflection. Most famously, Barcelona's Museum of Contemporary Art (MACBA) upended its entire exhibition logic by holding a temporary experiment in insurrectionary logistics, whereby a number of social movements and autonomous collectives were allowed to take over the museum as their center of operations for a few months. In the context of these various transformations, Marcos and Laura had been particularly impressed by the results of an introductory workshop on the open-source hardware platform Arduino, which was held at MLP in November 2005.[7] Over the years Marcos has often singled out this particular Arduino workshop as a turning point in his philosophical approach to digital culture. The workshop, he has told us innumerable times, awakened him to the realization that there were ways to translate the collaborative dimensions of free culture into the physical realm:

> It wasn't so much the fact that Arduino is a free culture project as the fact that it focused on tinkering with technology as an educational process. You have to remember that back in the day Arduino was described as a microcontroller platform enabling "physical computing." The physical dimension is crucial. We came together to build a technological prototype and in so doing laid out the material procedures—online documentation, how-to guides, and associated archival infrastructure—for others

to build it too. It brought people together to do a particular kind of critical work by tinkering and rearranging their own social and techno-material relations as sources of freedom.

The results of the Arduino workshop prompted Marcos and Laura to overhaul the entire artistic project of MLP, abandoning its mission as an exhibition and curatorial space and turning it into a *critical making* workshop instead—a workshop dedicated to the production of so-called prototypes. We shall be hearing more about the culture of prototyping at MLP shortly, but suffice to say for the moment that under the inspiration of the philosophy of free software, the practice of prototyping became not just a practice of technical design but an organizational ethos at large: an attempt at working through the "source code" of public participation within the center itself.

The series of Thinking and Doing workshops was part of this ongoing critical effort at reckoning with the center's participatory culture. To the surprise of everyone, one topic dominated the year-long series of discussions in 2010: the nature of the state as a purveyor of public goods, and in particular the relationship between digital culture and public culture. Marcos had called us to an urgent meeting that afternoon because he was concerned about the direction that the fourth and concluding debate might take. At the previous meeting (the third one in the series), there had been a controversial discussion recalling the recent firing of a temporary worker due to austerity cuts in the municipality. Both the firing and the ensuing discussion provoked much distress among MLP's staff. Some people felt this was not a matter that ought to be discussed publicly, whereas for others it was the very fact that a public discussion could be had that distinguished MLP's organizational culture. During the seminar some activists invoked the infamous episode to question MLP's long-standing fidelity to the philosophy of the commons, and in particular toward a culture of *cuidados* (care) that they felt had been neglected. In response they pressed for opening up the notion of "the public" undergirding the nature of MLP as a state institution. As one person put it: "We speak of MLP as an 'open-source organization' or a 'commons project.' We invoke loosely 'free culture' as a sanctimonious ideal. Yet the truth is we have ultimately no ownership over the projects that are developed here, there are strict boundaries and limits to what we can and cannot do. Nobody would ever think of sweeping the floors here. There is no *autogestión* (self-management) here."

The tone and subject of the conversations that we had with MLP's staff that cold November afternoon has stayed with us all these years. The sacking of the employee had been just the tip of an iceberg, the latest in a long series of structural reforms designed to contract out the cultural agencies of the municipality to commercial enterprises. There was a communion of experience but also a communion of vexations, that MLP's staff shared that afternoon over the ambiguous nature of their work as both a free culture project and a state service: between their vocation as free culture provocateurs and their obligations as civil servants. "We owe ourselves to the public administration," a member of the staff noted, "that is what the Statute of Public Workers says, that we 'owe fidelity' to the state administration." "There is an expectation of 'office' for civil servants," someone else added, "a veneer of 'officialdom' that overdetermines our budget and hierarchical relations. We are not a squatted social center. There is no escaping the political responsibilities of our office." "And yet," someone else retorted, "not a few people think that MLP is a private firm, a technological start-up or public-private partnership, and some of us are indeed not on permanent or functionary contracts but on precarious employment contracts. One does wonder sometimes whose aspirations are we laboring for here."[8]

The meeting marked a point of inflection in our fieldwork, a shared and somber appreciation that the very foundations of public culture were cracking under our feet. But it also flagged a discovery of sorts: the sudden realization that public culture and free culture often worked as analogues for one another; that there was a veneer of complicities and complementarities, of mutual dependencies and symbiotic exchanges, to which they both contributed.

Feral Methods

"Documentar, documentar, documentar," Jara Rocha mumbles to herself as she takes a seat in front of a computer; "Document, document, document," she says again, her quiet murmur inchoating both a mandate and a ritual, as her lips circle around the one word that MLP's staff utter most times a day. Jara is twenty-six and always has a breezy smile and inquiring eyes, which are only slightly disguised by an elegant demeanor. She has been working as a *mediadora* (mediator) at MLP for just over a year, first as a postgraduate intern and more recently seconding the leaves of absence of permanent members of staff. She was raised in the countryside, in a small village "with less than one thousand inhabitants, in a school with fewer than eight children per classroom: a feral environment for a feral girl," she notes with a distant glimmer of pride in her eyes.[9] She first moved to Madrid to pursue an undergraduate degree in law and journalism but quickly realized she had no interest in either and registered anew for a humanities degree. On completing her degree she worked for a while in film festivals—"I truly thought I'd find my place in the world of film production"—but again quickly grew tired of the work and decided to further her studies by completing a master's degree in cultural and critical theory. Halfway through her studies, however, she already knew there was only one place where she could work. "There wasn't really any other place in the city where one could experiment with net-art, so I braced myself one morning and cold-called at the front door asking for a job." She stares at her laptop: "And so it is that I landed an internship at MLP, and so it is that I am overwhelmed with all this documentary stuff today: videos that need to be classified, tagged, and archived; files that are pending meta-descriptions; wikis awaiting to be trimmed and organized."[10]

The drive to document is at the heart of MLP's philosophical approach to prototyping. While MLP has no real expectation that teams working on a project will develop demos of their proposals by the end of a prototyping workshop, the center does, however, make stringent demands on teams to exhaustively document their design processes. Such an approach is part of MLP's effort to overhaul the philosophy of free software and change it into a radical liberation pedagogy. Three features define MLP's conception of the prototype: (i) a mandatory use of free intellectual property licenses for every design; (ii) an archival consciousness, such that the technical specifications and processual flows for every design must be documented and made available on open-source platforms; and (iii) a radical pedagogical aspiration, whereby an attempt must be made to explicate every design (through the use of text, drawings, photos, technical specifications, and so forth) to facilitate its use and replication by third parties.

It is the first week of June 2010 and everyone is busy preparing for Interactivos?, the oldest and most established of MLP's prototyping workshops, which is scheduled to start in under a week. Jara is readying the infrastructure for documenting the workshop, making sure that each team has a wiki to work on; other people are setting up posters and information leaflets for every project, while yet others are tidying up and rearranging the room, wheeling tables and chairs around to accommodate cables, multiple socket outlets, and laptop bags. "If you don't trip over a cable, it ain't hectic enough!" Jara declares with a smile.

Interactivos? is MLP's flagship program, whose methodology, which has been fine-tuned over the years, has been used as a benchmark for all other programs, and has traveled to and been replicated in media labs all over the world, in London, Lima, Mexico, and Ljubljana. There was a particularly festive mood in the air in 2010, for only a few days earlier Marcos had been notified that Ars Electronica, the world's most prestigious media arts festival, had awarded an honorary mention for interactive art to the collaborative methodology developed at MLP's Interactivos?

The organization of Interactivos? follows the same pattern every year. Once set on a theme, MLP issues an international call for projects. The theme for 2010 was "Neighborhood Science" and was inspired by a blog post written by the historian of science Antonio Lafuente (whose biographical sketch opened part 2) in

2006.[11] Other themes have included explorations of "Technologies and Magic" (2007), "Garage Science" (2009), and, more recently, "Inhabiting Recycled Territories" (2018). In 2010, out of some forty submissions, ten projects were shortlisted, including projects from Canada (two), the United States (two), Mexico (two), Colombia (two), the United Kingdom (one), and Venezuela (one). (For the first time, there were no projects from Spain.) There was a considerable variety of projects and not all were narrowly focused on electronics or media art. There were, for instance, proposals for establishing a Society of Urban Naturalists, for developing a telephony system to record biographical stories of secondhand objects, and for developing open-source solar circuits. Once a list of projects has been selected, MLP issues a second call for collaborators, where people with different skills, backgrounds, or experience express interest in helping develop one project or another. Close to one hundred people registered to collaborate in the workshop in 2010. Most collaborators are based in Madrid, but sometimes people fly in or travel at their own expense from outside the city. For every workshop, MLP further invites a cohort of mentors, tutors, and speakers: artists, designers, engineers, or academics who are internationally recognized for their work in fields relevant to the workshop.[12]

The aim of Interactivos? is to interrogate and explore the interactive nature of digital media (hence the question mark) using free software and hardware as social and material leverages for relationality. At Interactivos?, references to *abrir los proyectos* (opening up projects) are constant, and almost obsessive. While proposals are initially submitted by individual researchers, one of the most important criteria for selecting projects is the willingness, as expressed in the original proposal, to forgo authorship and radicalize the collaborative and documentary dimensions. This is the one topic that most concerns mentors and tutors: the gravitational tendencies that, in their view, pull projects apart between their "artistic" and "collaborative" vocations, with the former being driven by a principal researcher's agenda and his or her refusal to let go of their authorial sense of ownership over the project. Since there is no obligation for collaborators to stay with a project throughout the duration of a workshop, it is not unusual for "artistic" projects to be left with no collaborators by the workshop's end. In the eyes of the MLP staff, a project's success will be measured by its capacity to enlist collaborators; to produce documentation; to showcase a variety of sensibilities, skills, and registers (photography, text, code, audio); and to demonstrate conviviality among its participants. It will be deemed a failure if these qualities are not present, no matter how accomplished or virtuous its technical output.

Prototyping workshops at MLP rehearse a type of experimental pedagogy that scholars have recently come to describe as "critical making."[13] Critical making builds on the tradition of constructionist approaches in critical design and social studies of science, but unlike these approaches, it focuses on the pedagogical importance of developing "shared construction itself as an activity and a site for enhancing and extending conceptual understandings of critical sociotechnical issues," rather than the making of functional or "evocative objects."[14] In a critical making project the material construction of an object becomes a means for conceptual exploration. The object made is not an outcome or reflection of prior design assumptions and expectations, nor is it valued for its capacity to work critically as a piece of design. Rather, critical making double backs on the design process to interrogate the forms of knowledge that its own material construction has elicited.

In 2010, Adolfo registered for Interactivos? as a collaborator on re:tag, a project whose original proposal had been submitted by Sandra Dávila, a Mexican designer who lives and studies in New York. During the project's public presentation, Sandra showed some photos of her apartment in New York, recounting how she had picked up and recycled most of the furniture from the street. Rooted in her personal experience, the project addressed those moments of vacillation when one bumps onto an abandoned object and wonders about its history and provenance. As she put it, her aim was "to get those objects to tell their own stories, to make them familiar, so that if one comes across them on the street, you will no longer hesitate to take them."[15]

Sandra's original proposal presented a relatively straightforward technological challenge. The aim was to set up a local installation of Asterisk, an open-source telephony and switchboard system, for people to record and listen to the biographical stories of secondhand objects: You find an object on the street with a label and a phone number on it; you dial the number and listen to its story; and now that you know the object's biography, you find it easier to take it home and give it a second life.

Seven people joined the project, including a telecommunications engineer, a systems administrator, a graphic designer, two photographers, and two anthropologists (Adolfo and an MIT student doing fieldwork for her MA thesis). While the installation of Asterisk presented some difficulties, the group soon realized that the real challenge was pairing an object's identifier with a unique registry in the telephony system. One could hardly expect people to run their own local installations of Asterisk and update the database with a new entry every time they wanted to give an object away. Would it be reasonable, the group started to wonder, to organize local collection points and have them operate their own installations? No sooner had the group started deliberating on these matters than some of MLP's mediators pointed them in the direction of Basurama, an art and architectural collective who had been working with garbage and recycled materials for well over a decade and made the necessary arrangements for the group to pay them a visit to their studio in the outskirts of the city. (We first described Basurama in chapter 3 and will return to them in chapter 8.)

Housed in a lightly repurposed garage, Basurama's studio is a fanciful combination of a flea market and *Charlie and the Chocolate Factory*. Hundreds of discarded objects are cluttered on the floor and walls and hanging from the ceiling. Surrounded by tires and cardboard, pallets and crates, theater billboards and an abandoned industrial oven, the re:tag group walked around the studio in wonder, their marveling eyes silently conceding that they had come to the right place.

Over the course of the visit, the members of Basurama explained to the re:tag group how the legal status of trash changes and mutates as it moves across the city: "Once our garbage bags are out on the street, they become the property of the municipality. The latter grants charity organizations, churches, and social inclusion agencies the right to pick up and recycle certain types of abandoned property, such as furniture or clothes, while benevolently permitting cardboard and waste collectors to sort out through other stuff and take their picks."[16] There is a social geography to how trash circulates around the city, Basurama explained. They recounted their experience organizing "trash safaris," during which they roam around a neighborhood on the lookout for planks, plastics, and other types of materials that might prove useful in future design and auto-construction workshops. These safaris go out to the city at night and offer participants an opportunity to engage with the otherwise invisible materiality of the city's residual wastelands. In homage to the Situationists' urban *deambulations*, the term *dérive* is applied to these drifting walkabouts around a neighborhood, which in Situationist fashion are also therefore somewhat aimed at recuperating the psychogeography of neighborly life that lies outside the circuits of capital.

The art and architecture collective further recounted their own experience with using geolocation devices to develop a digital cartography and networked community for promoting the reuse and exchange of secondhand objects. As it turned out, some members of Basurama had developed their own software for such a purpose many years earlier at a workshop in MLP.[17] Paraphrasing Mary Douglas's famous motto, "Dirt is matter out of place," they explained that sometimes all it takes is to move garbage from one place to another—by bundling together objects that are the same color or perform similar functions—to change people's perception of trash.[18] All in all, in conversation with Basurama, the re:tag group confirmed their intuition about the importance of understanding the metabolic agencies of the city in order to design a software that could somehow graft itself onto the systems of urban trash circulation rather than simply focus on the idiosyncrasy of individual objects.

Thus, shortly after returning to MLP, the re:tag team reached a decision to designate "local nodes" (charity shops, cultural centers, city hall delegations) where people could drop off the stuff they wished to give away. These nodes would each have to be assigned a virtual phone number whose Asterisk switchboard would be configured by the re:tag team. All that would be left for local nodes to do would be to allocate each object an individual code and then have this added as an extension to the virtual phone number. The group made two additional decisions. The first was to set up a web platform and digital archive to host the biographical stories. The second decision was reached by the group after testing various prototypes out on the streets. The group went out to the nearby neighborhood of Lavapiés and, in three different experimental setups, left different objects on the street for people to interact with. Observing at a distance, the team noted how people were variously drawn to the objects depending on their emplacement as well as the visibility of an informational label that had been attached to each item. In light of these experiences, they resolved to design hand-made labels for each object (see figure 2) for, as they explained in the documentation produced for the project, "The devil is in the details, and we really concluded that the material of the tag was really important when objects were left on the street." It is a feral environment out there, they realized, so you really need feral methods to stand out.

FIGURE 2.   Label tagging an abandoned toy duck. Photo by Sandra Davila, re:tag project.

I went for beer today with a group of Interactivos? participants. At least four or five of the people in the group asked for the price of beer before ordering, uncertain that they could afford it. Some of them ended up sharing drinks. It's not something that people talk about but it is obvious that a large number of collaborators are on a shoestring budget. The precarity is generalized.

Adolfo's Fieldwork Diary, June 15, 2010

Mónica and Nerea (MLP staff) both headed to a nearby supermarket today to help organize the catering for one of the workshops. They had discussed whether to shop online but decided in the end not to because they had to pay €7 for delivery. There is no money at MLP for hiring fancy catering services, or at any rate that is not what they want to spend their budget on. There is no money for cleaning services either: staff take weekly turns to take the bathroom towels home to have them washed.

Adolfo's Fieldwork Diary, May 27, 2010

We are heading to a nearby restaurant for dinner. We are a large group: over twenty of the participants in Interactivos? have joined us. It is a warm night and everyone is enjoying the stroll. I walk with Jara. We resume a conversation we've been having, on and off, for the past three months, about conditions of employment at MLP, about her precarity, about the general nature of precarity among people of her age. As an intern at MLP she was earning just under €600 per month, though she is no longer an intern proper: hers is now an "annex contract" that for a limited amount of time has extended her internship's conditions of employment. She is not alone. Quite a few of MLP's staff are self-employed, while others have been renewing temporary contracts for years. Things are unlikely to get better now that the municipality has subcontracted its employment services to a commercial firm.

Adolfo's Fieldwork Diary, June 17, 2010

The workshop is close to finishing. We are only a couple of days away from wrapping up, but there is already a sense of exhaustion up in the air. Some collaborators have left, others do not come in until late in the day.

A nearby squatted social center, La Tabacalera, which opened a few months back following almost a decade of demands from neighbors and activists, has extended an invitation to MLP to present the results of Interactivos? at the center. Quite a few of MLP's members of staff and users have been heavily involved in the occupation of La Tabacalera. There is only a fifteen-minute walk between the two centers and there's been a constant traffic of activists from La Tabacalera to MLP and back again. Some activists speak of the importance of having La Tabacalera develop methodologies modeled after some of MLP's own methodologies. There is even a "copyfight" guide that describes how to turn La Tabacalera into a *centro social autogestionado liberador de cultura*, a self-managed social center that is a liberator of culture.[19] Some of the passages of the guide—on how to work with Creative Commons licenses, or how to escape the mandates of copyright collection societies—have been drafted by people long involved in these debates at MLP.

I (Adolfo) got myself drawn into organizing a weekly open mic night at La Tabacalera that was modeled after one of MLP's open workshops. Two mediators and two artists put forth a proposal to organize such sessions, and I got dragged along as the ethnographer-in-residence. The session has taken on a life of its own now and over the past months there have been talks by a lesbian video-art collective; a community of hackers that teaches IT skills to unemployed people by recycling old and abandoned secondhand computers; a pirate radio station; and another group of hackers who a few years ago helped phreak a phone for Patio Maravillas (another squatted social center) and have plans to do the same for La Tabacalera. They too used Asterisk for their hack.

The re:tag group has agreed to make a brief presentation of the project at La Tabacalera. As it happens, the Patio Maravillas hackers were in the audience for the talk and quickly approached the group to exchange insights and advice on their respective Asterisk installations. The hackers told us about how they phreaked phones to enable illegal immigrants to call back home, a story that resonates with re:tag's own vision for a more porous and textured understanding of the legacies and affordances of the city's metabolic infrastructures.

Back at MLP, I tell Jara about the conversation between re:tag's engineers and La Tabacalera hackers: "Methodological neighborhood trafficking: Someone should document it!" she says with a breezy smile.

Adolfo's Fieldwork Diary, June 10, 2010

In some respects, Interactivos? workshops have a family resemblance to hackathons. Workshops unfold over an intensive two-week period, during which time project developers, tutors, and speakers (but not collaborators) are hosted in a nearby hostel. Teams work through the day, generally very long hours, lunching and dining together, and often join other teams for evening outings into the city until late at night. Participants share some demographic and sociological characteristics. Most are in their early thirties and have a working knowledge of English and a university education. They all have an interest in new media, though by no means engineering or computing backgrounds. There have been unusually high numbers of social scientists registering for these workshops, as well as schoolteachers or architects. Several attendees are studying for postgraduate degrees in cultural management, social science, or design. Many have precarious jobs or no jobs at all, which is one of the reasons why they can afford to dedicate two weeks of their time to the workshops.

The atmosphere at the workshops is jovial and festive; the experience is intense, almost juvenile. Participants often describe it by recollecting their childhood summer camps, a vertigo of *communitas* and exploration that is partly intimidating, partly thrilling, partly antagonistic, and ultimately exhausting. If there are echoes of a rite of passage this is indeed how Marcos has often described MLP's approach to prototyping: "People come here to prototype a community as much as they come to prototype a technology."[20] At MLP, prototyping conjures a liminal imagination that is as much sociological as it is technological (see figure 3).

The analogy between social and technological sublimation is indeed proper of hackathons. In her work on hackathons in India, Lilly Irani noted how hackathons

FIGURE 3. Viernes OpenLab, November 12, 2010. On Friday afternoons, Medialab Prado opens its doors to anyone interested in freely experimenting with interactive electronics. Photo by Medialab Prado is licensed under CC BY-SA 2.0: https://creativecommons.org/licenses/by-sa/2.0/.

"*sometimes* produce technologies, and they always, however, produce subjects."[21] Irani is rightly skeptical of the theatricalization of hopeful and designed futurities staged at hackathons for they reproduce the siren calls of Silicon Valley's innovation evangelists and the enthusiastic mood of its entrepreneurial and technological zeitgeist with too much devotion. Hackathons, she argues, participate in a "politics of speed and vision" that appeals to a very specific middle-class subject: fluent in English, with a college degree in engineering, a situation of privileged employment that allows them to take several days off work, and often a dislike of the messy and empirical disturbances of the outside world.[22]

While it is no doubt true that the cultural form of the hackathon has often been deployed as an auspice of liberal pragmatism, techno-digital utopianism, and reformist volunteerism, Irani's attentiveness to the situated politics of design offers us another route for examining the specificity of MLP's prototyping workshops. At MLP projects often develop an orientation that is specifically urban, located and weaved into the situated metabolism of neighborhood dynamics and struggles. Prototyping teams go out to the city as a research strategy, seeking the advice or support of local activist networks, organizing visits to squatted social centers, or establishing contact with local academics. These are strategies that are actively encouraged and facilitated by MLP's staff, contributing toward a methodological mise-en-scène that is profoundly mediated by the cultural politics of urban autonomy. They are strategies of *porosity*, to echo a term used by the critical media scholar Alessandra Renzi to describe the Neapolitan autonomous media activism scene: "a way of tending to the activist field" by "repurposing" connective technologies that create "resonance by giving priority to acts that extend beyond themselves to become contagious."[23]

While MLP's prototypes may certainly summon candid visions of designed futurities at times, at other times they incessantly perform and practice into existence archival sensibilities and methodological orientations toward urban justice. One of the legacies of MLP's culture of prototyping has therefore been the cultivation of a dense network of resources, attentions, and understandings between and across numerous activist groups in the city. Not quite a technology and not quite a cultural sensibility either, the prototype appears in this guise as a climate of methods and orientations. We might say that this is a use of the city as a method.

The Future Has an Old Name

There is another aspect that differentiates the Californian ideology of hackathons from MLP's prototyping workshops in fundamental ways, namely, the role awarded to the public sector as a vector of futurity. At MLP, the future did not arrive in a temporal register—it did not arrive "sooner," as the anthropologist Lucy Suchman would often overhear her colleagues at Xerox's Palo Alto Research Center (PARC) say—but rather it arrived in a deeply reflexive historical form: the form of welfarist public value.[24]

Our opening vignette proffered a first example: a discussion about the values of *lo público* (the public) as a tension of office and dedication, a placeholder for aspirations often pulling in opposite directions, between *autogestión* and the Spanish Statute of Public Workers, between bureaucracy and the commons. There was certainly no consensus on what the public stood for in these discussions nor what its terms of engagement with autonomous practices ought to be. These were always hotly contested issues. Yet a culture of "public culture" always took root as a natural background to the projects of autonomy and liberation that the various free culture communities working at MLP were trying to articulate, inaugurating an exciting but also fraught experience in negotiating and accommodating diverse expectations and desires regarding the practice of public culture as free culture.

This notion of "public culture as free culture" is worth disentangling. Before we do so, however, let us briefly emphasize how very marginal the notion of public service has been in recent accounts of media and hacker culture. In his recent history of hacklabs and hackerspaces, the hacker scholar and activist Maxigas makes no mention of public culture or public institutions as vectors of contemporary media culture.[25] In an argument that concords with the narrative we presented in part 1, Maxigas observes how hacklabs have historically been founded by tactical media collectives within autonomist or anarchist movements, while hackerspaces respond to a more recent wave of entrepreneurial libertarianism. Whatever kind of liberty or autonomy is at stake here, there is no sense in which these political figures overlap with or accommodate a subsidiary sense of public value.

By contrast, such expressions of public value have been at the heart of MLP's cultural practice for the past decade.[26] They have modulated the terms in which the center has both hosted and promoted free culture projects. In this sense, they have articulated, through the favoring of specific interfaces, methods, and forms of sociality, how free culture and public culture have become at times analogues and at times enablers for one another—a singular expression of the "culture of 'free culture'" taking shape at MLP and gradually traveling out to the city at large.

Let us spell out in some detail the characteristics shaping this conception of public culture. We do so by going back to the discussions that took place in the context of the Thinking and Doing debates, and in particular the concluding session, which was carefully formatted to wrap up the whole series.[27] This last session was convened by the free software developer and activist Margarita Padilla and the grassroots philosopher Amador Fernández-Savater, who were appointed by MLP to develop an analysis of the whole series as well as moderate the ensuing debate (see figure 4).[28]

It is significant that the final session took place just two months ahead of the birth of the 15M movement, when a climate of protest and frustration was already brewing on the streets. The debate during the last workshop was therefore inevitably framed by this climate. The references that participants made to the shifting values of public philosophy and social democracy should be read in this context. We can sense in these discussions how participants were calibrating the capacities of free culture activism to confront the structural violence of the government politics of austerity that was ongoing at the time.

The workshop took off with Padilla and Fernández-Savater propounding a view of MLP as an ecosystem characterized by an "in-betweenness" (*estar entre*), a specific potency of ambiguity and indefiniteness that allowed the center to bypass various binary opposites: in between the state and the market, art and science, thinking and doing, and networks and communities. Building on their own research and contributions to radical autonomous thinking, Padilla and Fernández-Savater outlined the conditions of what they termed a "hypothesis of dispersion."[29] "We are witnessing the dissolution," they noted, "of the public-

FIGURE 4. Public seminar convened during the "Thinking and Doing" Medialab Prado workshops. November 14, 2010. Photo by Medialab Prado is licensed under CC BY-SA 2.0: https://creativecommons.org/licenses/by-sa/2.0/.

state matrix (*lo público-estatal*), and, in the best of cases, subsequent emergence of generative parasitical arrangements."[30] MLP's culture of prototyping, they argued, offered one such example of tactical counterpolitics, responding to the assemblage of a "self-organized public" (*público auto-organizado*): an interface and interstice where state-related resources and practices are mobilized and drawn from to empower self-organized initiatives.

The description of MLP as a self-organized public prompted a protracted discussion on both the nature of the public and the nature of self-organization and on the specific qualities shaping MLP as a situated project in between. In this framework, Padilla and Fernández-Savater drew on the year-long discussions of the previous Thinking and Doing workshops, as well as their own intimate knowledge of MLP, to explain the concept of "in-betweenness" in relation to the center's own singular context and climate of methods.

For example, it was widely felt that MLP's unusual underground location contributed to its maverick ethos. In particular, its spatial invisibility afforded the center an elusiveness that most people found enchanting and productive. There was a sense in which people felt that its hidden location enabled MLP to escape the grip of the culture of spectacle as well as the overzealousness of bureaucratic vigilance and audit. The sense of public value that was invoked here conveyed a certain intimacy of scale and familiarity, a refuge from the state's classic locus as a biopolitical iron cage of impersonality. During the debate, Marcos himself conceded that "the provisional nature of MLP's space suits the ideas of prototyping and experimentation that we hold dear here."[31] A material equation of sorts was therefore established between the center's spatial threshold, the culture of experimentation, and the nature of public value.

Another quality widely perceived as central to MLP's cultural practice was the notion of "hospitality," which was deployed to function in two interrelated registers: as a sociological trading zone and as a technological interface. Over the years MLP developed a culture of *mediación* (mediation) whereby staffers took on the role of *acompañantes* (companions), whose job was to walk visitors around the space, introducing and explaining the projects on display. Mediation was deployed in this context as a pragmatic theory for renegotiating the forms of stranger-relationality characteristic of public institutions.

However, the idiom of hospitality was further mobilized to redescribe a specific technological dimension of MLP's culture of prototyping. The prototypes developed at MLP are often artefacts or technologies that are in progress or incomplete, with few bells and whistles to showcase them through a spectacular display, and whose valence or promises lie therefore not in their designs but in their documentary or pedagogical legacies. As such, these are projects that are not immediately graspable or comprehensible by casual visitors. They demand ad hoc, often evolving, explanations. Given such a context, the practice of mediación was also devised to provide accompanying explanations for MLP's prototypes: it became an integral part of the culture of prototyping such that prototypes were not considered to exist in full outside such forms of companionship and storytelling. Thus, prototypes became technologies of hospitality in their own right.

Finally, participants during the Thinking and Doing workshops also coincided in highlighting the existence of a unique "culture of listening" (*cultura de la escucha*) at MLP. Partly this was again associated with the culture of prototyping—with the fact that one had to listen to the stories that *mediadores* told of prototypes if one wished to understand their designs—for embedded in the design of every prototype there was a story about its inconclusiveness and its promises, its forms of companionship and hospitality. However, in the thick of conversations and exchanges one would often hear people ascribe the culture of listening to a broader philosophy of feminist care (*cuidados*), whereby the practice of prototyping was said to echo the inexorable fragility of reciprocal communication. Prototyping was spoken of in this context as a movement of desires, needs, and commitments, a material technology enabling the coming together of people as both a community of caretakers and a community of problem-designers. Marcos coined a formula to explain this ethos of caretaking: "People come here to prototype a community as much as they come to prototype a technology."

The description of MLP as a self-organized public (*público auto-organizado*) therefore responded to the culture of prototyping that the center had cultivated over the years. Such a culture, it was argued, hinged on a specific climate of methods, where listening and caretaking, attentive description and storytelling, mediation and hospitality played key roles.

However, while there was widespread consensus regarding the role that prototyping played in this context, the description of MLP as a self-organized public provoked a heated controversy. There was confusion and bewilderment, and some people were even upset, regarding the terms through which Padilla and Fernández-Savater's theoretical framework provided an outlet for political transformation. Some questioned the framework's simplistic binary, the so-called hypothesis of dispersion, whereby the state and the market were framed in an agonistic confrontation in neoliberal times. "Where are the legal licenses in all this," they queried, "or the archives, or the networks? Where is the complexity that prototypes are indexes for?" For the historian of science Antonio Lafuente, the description of MLP as a self-organized public was profoundly troubling, for it effected a perverse elision of the commons as *bienes nacientes* (nascent goods), emerging political practices, at the same time as it reinforced the dualism of state-market or of public-private through the backdoor. For yet others, the description of MLP as something other than a public/state institution was also disturbing, insofar as it signaled a failure of the welfarist imagination of those doing the thinking: "If the state is not delivering the public goods we would hope for, then it is our task to make sure it does; we should defend the public rather than reinvent it." The culture of prototyping was imagined in this context, then, not so much as a placeholder for designed futurities, a technical horizon for transitional hopescapes but rather as an organon for pulsating the perdurance and desire of collective existence. The prototype stood as the symbol of a profoundly historical imagination, linked to philosophies and political theories of commonwealth and public goods. In a poignant statement, the artist and musicologist Miguel Álvarez Fernández synthesized this position thus: "There seems to be an urge for finding new concepts and terminologies to help us articulate the modes of relation and social transformation that organizations such as MLP are outlets for. However, what is wrong with our old words? I, for one, hear undertones of social democracy, the welfare state, or municipalism in everything that is being said here. The language of the future has an old ring to it."[32]

Complex Trajectories and Blurred Genres

In the first decade of the twenty-first century, the language and culture of prototyping in Madrid gestured toward horizons of autonomous hope, designs, and struggles that shifted and transitioned between insurrectionary, institutional, entrepreneurial, precarious, and avant-garde worlds. In direct continuity with the stories outlined in part 1, the feral methods of the prototype activated repertoires of action and response that relayed a longer history and tradition of urban autonomous struggles and socialist libertarian values. Prototypes mobilized people, technologies, imaginaries, and capacities across diverse urban territories and oppositional cartographies. The fragility of prototypes stood for the fragility of public services in times of austerity, for the fragility of precarious bodies and drowning relationships, for the provisional fragility of squatted aspirations, and for the leaky and bleak fragility of metabolic exchanges in the city. As a world and a word for the commons, for the public, and for the "liberation of culture," as La Tabacalera copyfight statement put it, prototypes relayed many worlds from the modesty of their never-quite-accomplished designs.

Such a vision of the prototype as a heterogenous assemblage of commons, affective alliances, and infrastructural solidarities echoes recent proposals for an expansive reading of the commons under contemporary regimes of sovereign austerity. The cultural theorist Lauren Berlant, for example, has taken issue with the conventional approach to the commons as a placeholder for hopeful belongings, a "manifestic function . . . always political and invested in counter-sovereignty, with performative aspirations to decolonize an actual and social space that has been inhabited by empire, capitalism, and land-right power."[33] Berlant is rightly skeptical of the role that the commons has hitherto come to play as a referential terminus of aspiration and flourishing as well as an index for novel arrangements of complicity and confidence. Theirs is instead a proposal for a commons that is neither a form of property nor a systematics of awareness; it is neither a refuge for decorous citizenship nor a site for the redemption of fugitive bodies or injured memories. The commons, rather, is "a transformational infrastructure" through which we move and stick together, a patterned orientation for holding on and creeping up through the tensions, the repulsions, the temptations or the thrills of every form of transitional yet indispensable companionship.[34]

Berlant's vision echoes anthropologist Anna Tsing's recent writings on the "latent commons" as the mobilization of a sensorium capable of noticing the "boundary confusions that mark the edges of alienation," where "muddling through with others is always in the middle of things."[35] Messed, muddled, and middled, the commons surface, if they do at all, in and through the *minima moralia* of turbulent symbioses, material alloys, and emotive synergies.

These visions of entangled commons are heirs to Donna Haraway's famous cyborg anthropology, where the cyborg stood as a codification of "potent and taboo fusions" between humans and animals, organisms and machines, the physical and the nonphysical—an index of the turbulent traffic and intimate and agonistic exchanges happening at the boundaries and interfaces between parts and wholes, nature and culture, male and female, and so on.[36] For Haraway, the cyborg was neither "one" nor "other," for "to be One is to be an illusion, and so to be involved in a dialectic of apocalypse with the other. Yet to be other is to be multiple, without clear boundary, frayed, insubstantial. One is too few, but two are too many."[37] As a "whole image but not an image of a whole," as Marilyn Strathern succinctly put it, the cyborg therefore summons a figure of complexity that can be "more than one and less than many"—a cipher for "complex trajectories" that sidesteps the perils of "blurred genres."[38]

As we bring this chapter to a close, we would like to take inspiration from the figurations of complexity of the cyborg to think about the complex trajectories of the prototype. Our ethnography of MLP gives us a basis to think about three dimensions of this complexity.

On the one hand, the culture of prototyping in Madrid has delineated a horizon of encounter for three traditions of institutional, infrastructural, and insurrectional solidarity: public culture, free software, and procomún. The prototype emerges as a historical form staging a thickly textured conversation between the structural transformations of the welfare state, the philosophy of free software, and the political theory of the commons. Chris Kelty has noted how free software geeks develop forms of interaction that are constitutive of a "recursive public" because their expressions of social and political solidarity are grounded in the designs and affordances of the infrastructures holding their interactions together in the first place.[39] In Madrid, the designs of prototypes are not only recursive (with the ultimate recursion devolved to the urban condition at large) but profoundly historical as well, modulated by their self-conscious filiation to traditions of welfarist social democracy and *autonomia*. Prototypes incarnate inchoations of the intransitive culture we outlined in the introduction: a coming together as a commons to the defense of the public through the tools of the libre.

Second, the prototype is also an ethos of design for the city. Its designs inscribe intuitions and desires for, as well as systematic inquiries into, the complicities and complexities of neighborly conviviality: an exploration of the material, technical, and aspirational "openings of the social" (*aperturas de lo social*) that are inscribed precariously in, and in the precarity of, everyday urban life. These explorations map onto shifting and contradictory cartographies of technological sovereignty, infrastructural affect, and material dispossession, which both spread across and take residence in public squares, squatted social centers, cultural organizations, and elite academic institutions. We may think of prototypes as transitional infrastructures for the perdurance of proximal attunement and companionship. Yet these are systems of perdurance that are always and everywhere carried through and sustained across specific spaces and locales, walks and deambulations, archives and interfaces, technologies and designs. Prototypes are systems of fragilities unashamedly oriented toward the attainment of urban justice, and thus they are indices for a free/libre urbanism.

Last, the culture of prototyping unfolds also as an experimental culture, as a systematics for assays, trial, and the joys of figuring out. This systematics involves documenting, classifying, tagging, phreaking, coding and licensing as much as it involves walking, squatting, recycling, mediating and getting lost. Undergirding everything is a radical material pedagogy of liberation. In this pedagogy, to "liberate culture," to investigate the conditions for "opening the social" and "opening up prototypes," as participants at MLP's workshops are incessantly invited to do, is to call for an exploration and exfoliation of the archival, technical, legal, and metabolic affordances inscribed within every practice and every design. True, these prototypes are often "failed" projects inasmuch as they do not lead to working demos. Yet this is not what they strive for. Theirs is a field of complexity intensified by their eluding and escaping of the exigencies of technical, authorial, and proprietary closure, through the use of free licenses, archival documentation, pedagogical workshops, and urban reappropriations tout court. The complexity of prototypes is not defined by the requirements of functional accomplishment or the urge for aesthetic effect as much as by the promises of a vibrant and cross-pollinating climate of methods. They are designs that deliberately shy away from "one" description by seeking to open the sources of the very capacities for description. Thus, they are more than many and less than one.

FREEDOM IN 3D

In September 2015, Marcos García, MLP's director, invited Alberto to join a task force charged with designing trajectories of apprenticeship to allow the municipal government to learn from the city's social movements. Against all odds, a coalition of grassroots activists and social movements had won the municipal elections in May 2015 and the task force was set in motion shortly after in an effort to cross-pollinate the rigid bureaucratic structures of the municipal administration with the experimental ethos and effervescence of free culture activists. The aim of the task, as Marcos put it then, was to design *dispositivos de escucha*, listening assemblages for pausing to better understand the needs of and desires for collective action.

The task force had an eclectic membership, and it enlisted civil servants, long-time autonomous and neighborhood activists, and academics in monthly meetings. Sometimes the meetings followed a conventional format whereby we sat down and talked and discussed for hours. But Marcos and his team also made an explicit effort for *instalarnos en la ciudad*, to find ways for installing or grafting ourselves onto the urban condition, and in this guise they arranged for going on neighborhood walking tours with community activists or holding our meetings at community spaces across the city.

Prompted by our conversations with activists as well as our own participation in community projects over the years, Alberto joined another member of the task force, the architect-activist Manuel Pascual, in exploring this supposed capacity for grafting onto the city's ongoing energies and lattices of mobilization. We decided to work on drafting a *caja de herramientas*, a toolbox of do-it-yourself skills, apprenticeships, and know-how that various grassroots and neighborhood initiatives had been assembling over the years. These often served as sophisticated research methods and systems of analysis in their own right, which, however, were little known outside very small circles. We therefore thought of the toolbox as a sort of inventory for resourceful improvisations, which included, for instance, accounts of how squatted social centers use social media; descriptions of the digital archives used by activists to file the minutes of their meetings or keep track of collaborative projects; and some of the tricks of the trade developed by long-term activists for upholding relations of care and affection amid the passions and agonism of assembly politics.[1] We discuss this platforming of methods into bricolages of apprenticeships in part 4.

Although a joint enterprise, the toolbox was, in fact, a natural extension of much of Manuel's previous architectural and activist work: pragmatic, action-oriented, community-driven, but also glowing with conceptual invention. It was also the sort of project that Manuel knows how to masterfully redeploy to enlist other people's attentions and energies. In his mid-thirties and an architect by training, Manuel is a formidable rhetorician, a natural-born storyteller with a talent for both analysis and punch lines. An easily identifiable figure, a tall young man with a surprisingly long Marxian beard, he is much loved among the city's grassroots movements, in part because he is a resourceful organizer and all-purpose, hands-on technician, but also because he is a political snake charmer and an unrelenting optimist. His stories always transform the city into another, previously unseen city.

We had first met Manuel a few years earlier, in the wake of the occupation of public squares that gave birth to the 15M movement. In the early days of the encampment, we had come across an online photographic essay on the architectural typologies and infrastructural requirements of the camps, whose insights into the material energies of the movement we found at once delightful and wondrous.[2] Yet it was not just the architectural reportage that caught our attention, but also the very archival infrastructure that its authors were using to host these materials.[3] We contacted them at once over Twitter and soon arranged to meet in person.

The photo essay on the encampment's infrastructure had been produced by the architectural collective Zuloark, of which Manuel was a founding member. The members of the collective, who were in their late twenties and early thirties, knew each other from their days at university. During the early 2000s, architecture students in Madrid would often share an apartment's rent and turn it into a studio where they would help one another in preparing their graduation projects.[4] They flourished on the energy of collective work but also shared a certain skepticism of—and in some cases outright hostility toward—the paradigm of the architectural star system and the urban financialization that it parasitizes. Indeed, when the economic crisis hit in 2008 and the real estate economy collapsed, many of these young graduates saw their prospects of employment disappear overnight. A survey carried out by the Architects' Trade Union in 2013 noted that almost 31 percent of architects in Spain were unemployed at the time, while 71 percent were making less than €1,000 per month.[5] In these circumstances, some of these young architects decided to turn their study groups into solidarity infrastructures for the joint navigation of precarity.

These solidarity infrastructures took various forms. Sometimes studios would pool resources and join their fragile forces in signing a project together; at other times they would group into larger associative networks for the purposes of sharing resources or apprenticeships. At yet other times, they embraced temporary modular or rhizomatic structures, drawing, patching, or loaning specific resources or capacities from one or another studio. This was a labile association of complicities that enabled a ductile navigation of complexity. The architectural establishment soon had a name for them, *colectivos de arquitectura* (architectural collectives); their signature dynamic was their capacity to work in various guises as "networks, connectors, and platforms" for precarious times.[6]

As we were soon to find out, the photo essay was hosted by one such solidarity infrastructure, a larger project on urban archival experimentation that Zuloark was part of. This larger project was coordinated by the multidisciplinary platform Zoohaus, which had been set up in the early 2000s to function as an umbrella operation for the many guerrilla architectural collectives and street artists that were popping up at the time. What distinguished Zoohaus from other such solidarity infrastructures was its explicit concern with recycled and repurposed technologies, grassroots auto-construction techniques, and the overall resourcefulness and sustainability of makeshift urbanism. In their own practice, the members of Zoohaus were particularly drawn to the use of open-source technologies for their own archival and design purposes, in part because they were free to use (and hence affordable on their precarious budgets), but also because they were an infrastructure they could tinker with and adjust to their ever-shifting networking and experimental projects. In this conjuncture, it did not take long for the Zoohaus family to start exploring the resonance that these technologies seemed to have with their interest in auto-construction urbanism, and they soon began to ponder what the contours and affordances of an open-source architecture might actually look like. Therefore, in 2007, Manuel and other members of the Zoohaus network set out on an adventurous exploration of the ways in which the philosophy and infrastructures of free culture were transforming the place of architecture in the city, including their larger role in rethinking and interrogating the material and ecological forms of the urban condition. This adventure

FIGURE 5. The Offfficina (aka the Dinosaur). Photograph by Inteligencias Colectivas—Zoohaus is licensed under CC BY-SA 4.0: https://creativecommons .org/licenses/by-sa/4.0/.

would, in time, lead them to design and build a "dinosaur" of sorts, as they would themselves call their creation, which is an infrastructure whose legacy would be at once enduring and condemned to extinction (see figure 5).

This chapter tells the story of the Zoohaus dinosaur, which is a story about the problems faced by a group of young architects trying to build a physical archive for open-source architectural techniques that would itself serve as an object of free culture. At the cusp of the financial and economic crisis in Spain, the question they put to themselves was simple enough: "What kind of architectural object is free knowledge?" Yet as they would soon find out, this was a question that shook the foundations of how politics grounds itself in the city and how freedom takes an urban and a material form.

Three Dimensions

Perhaps the most famous dinosaur in the history of science is the model of the Iguanodon monster inside whose mold Benjamin Waterhouse hosted a New Year's Eve dinner party at the Crystal Palace in 1853 (see figure 6). The historian of science James Secord has commented on the role that the three-dimensional (3D)

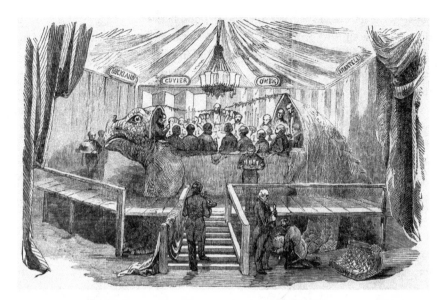

FIGURE 6.   Dinner in the Iguanodon Model, at the Crystal Palace, Sydenham. *Illustrated London News*, January 7, 1854, 22.

models of the Crystal Palace dinosaurs played in the context of Victorian attitudes toward science. In his words, the "Crystal Palace exhibits can . . . be understood as the apotheosis of a short-lived conjunction between commercial capitalism and rational education in the early 1850s," at a time, he reminds us, "when the very notion of the spectacle was under construction."[7]

The Crystal Palace dinosaurs were a remarkable public experiment in visual education. They offer a vantage point from which to reassess what the historians of science Soraya de Chadarevian and Nick Hopwood described as the "dimensions of modelling" in science.[8] Such objects open up scientific analysis and understanding to "the advantages of engagement in three dimensions."[9] They invite a kinesthetic, material, and wholesale bodily engagement with "knowledge" that places the dynamics of science in a novel educational and pedagogical terrain. It is significant that three-dimensional models also invite questions about their own internal construction, and thus about their relationship to representational techniques such as drawing, photographing, cataloging, indexing, or writing. The manifold tactics and practices through which these various techniques are assembled—sometimes painstakingly, sometimes with care, but often in a rush— brings to the fore as well the scenography and choreography that uphold every form of knowing as a model and every model as a form of knowing.

Not unlike the Crystal Palace's antediluvian monsters, the material corpus of Zoohaus' dinosaur signaled, too, a series of transformations in the relations between the nature of spectacle and the arts and between pedagogy and education, as well as shifting proprietary formations in an age of networked capitalism. Their interrogations about the liberation of urban culture—"What kind of architectural object is free knowledge?"—revolved precisely around the transformational effects of thinking about the practices of knowing in three dimensions: the scalar, material, diagrammatic, infrastructural, interventionist, and atmospheric properties of architecture. By placing these properties center stage, Zoohaus brought attention to the role that atmospherics, physics, and kinesthetics—as expressed in ambience, infrastructure, and interior design—play in bundling practices of knowing into specific forms of experience. They showed how a vision for the liberation of urban culture demanded an artful and skilled installation of a complex cohort of relations and associations—with public museums, neighborhood activists, or indeed the social networks of an architectural profession then undergoing a dramatic period of reinvention. The result is an inspiring monster for monstrous and uninspiring times.

Gathering Intelligences

The story of the Dinosaur began as a Zoohaus project back in 2007 when a group of people launched a project to document what they referred to as "architectural and constructive peculiarities" found in their travels around Spain.[10] They set up a website which then functioned as a repository of visual descriptions (photographs, videos, diagrammatic sketches) of do-it-yourself, retrofitted, community-driven architectural designs and adaptations.[11] They called the project Collective Intelligences (Inteligencias Colectivas; hereafter IC), for it is to the anonymous, collaborative, and do-it-yourself nature of the objects and devices that they found—and keep on documenting to this day—that their attention was drawn.[12]

Although IC was originally conceived as a visual repository, its first developments were made as an educational tool. In 2009, Zoohaus obtained funding from the Spanish Development Agency (AECID) to carry out a series of workshops on "grassroots construction techniques" at various design and architectural faculties in Latin America.[13] Throughout 2010, members of Zoohaus traveled the continent teaching students in Lima, Bogotá, Santiago or Buenos Aires, among other locations, how to identify and document local do-it-yourself constructive techniques. The workshops were convened to draw attention to the architectural intelligences behind mundane objects and technologies, making them visible but also, importantly, cataloging and diagrammatizing them and laying out the technical specificities and sociological dimensions of their designs.

In preparation for the workshops, Zoohaus developed a four-step methodology for documenting and describing such techniques. The steps were named, respectively: catalog, upgrade, prototyping, and human network. At the time of their Latin American tour, the pedagogical program designed by Zoohaus focused solely on cataloging and prototyping "intelligences." As they put it to us: "We felt there was an expectation from us to 'build' things. This is what we are after all: we're architects, we are in the business of construction. So it was important to have the students build a physical thing in the workshops. We taught them how to catalog an intelligence and then how to use that description to reassemble it into a new object."[14]

Step by step, the methodological itinerary was designed to work as follows: the first step is that of "cataloging" an intelligence. Attendees at a workshop are trained in exploring and perambulating the city's residual landscapes and wastelands, treasuring the inventive capacities of urban ecologies that more often than not are ridden by crisis and dereliction. Students are taught to develop and nurture an attentiveness toward unusual forms and materialities, a particular sensibility that seizes on the ways in which objects, technologies, and landscapes fold and camouflage into each other; an attentiveness, in other words, to the vibrations of matter, its inclinations and proclivities and its environmental affordances. With this in mind, participants are prompted to wander around their urban surroundings on the hunt for do-it-yourself, retrofitted, or community-driven architectural designs. If they find an intelligence they deem worthy of recording, they are told to document it down to its finest detail by taking photographs, making drawings, sometimes video-recording the workings of the device in question (see figure 7). These various files are all later uploaded to the IC website. The work of cataloging therefore involves documenting, indexing, and archiving whatever intelligences are found.

The second step involves "upgrading" such intelligences, although this has not always been part of the educational workshops. Upgrading an intelligence involves breaking it down into its constituent parts and documenting, step by step, its technical reassemblage. It is a complex, arduous task, which requires skills in technical drawing and 3D design and often requires expertise with Autocad architectural projections as well (see figure 8). The aim of an upgrade is to specify and explain the internal functioning of any device in order to make it replicable.

In this respect, the work of upgrading an intelligence echoes the technical descriptions entailed in patent specification. By drawing things together, the upgrade objectifies the intelligence as a representational—and potentially political—form.[15] The specification solidifies an artefact that up to that point was environmentally malleable and distributed. Unlike patent specifications, however, upgrades remain

FIGURE 7.   Catalogue of a Tetracyle. Photograph by Inteligencias Colectivas—
Zoohaus is licensed under CC BY-SA 4.0: https://creativecommons.org
/licenses/by-sa/4.0/.

open-ended processes. There are no standards or protocols guiding how an upgrade ought to be carried out, and indeed, to this day Zoohaus is still engaged
in an inventive exploration of the very methodologies to be employed in the
documentary production of an upgrade. As the architects put it to us, "We are
still learning what an upgrade may actually entail."[16] Some intelligences require
a multilayered combination of iconographic techniques to be rendered fully
legible, such as the use of photographs, architectural sketches, and even video
recordings, through which the internal functioning of their components are
properly explained. The nature of the media formats, files, and languages employed to describe an intelligence's internal pedagogics is also open to scrutiny
and debate; for example, regarding the use of Autocad, a proprietary and very
expensive software widely used by architects to produce 3D designs, which in
this form, however, restricts the circulation of designs to those with access to
the technology. For this reason, all upgrades port Creative Commons licenses
and are made freely available online at IC's website.

There are a number of reasons that explain the difficulties encountered in
defining the methodology of upgrading. For a start, most intelligences are singular constructions. They are unique adaptations to a local environment. Even
if materials, technologies, or design compositions can be replicated, it is unlikely that an upgrade can describe how and why an intelligence provided a

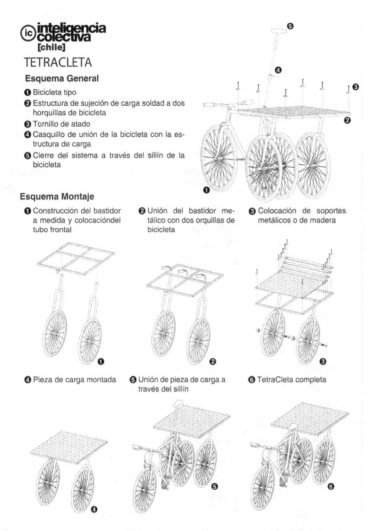

FIGURE 8. Upgrade of a Tetracycle. Technical drawings by Inteligencias Colectivas—Zoohaus are licensed under CC BY-SA 4.0: https://creativecommons.org/licenses/by-sa/4.0/.

constructive solution when, where, and in the manner that it did so. Moreover, sometimes the original development of an upgrade cannot be documented, perhaps because its makers are not around or because there are various problems to which the object is used as a solution and nobody quite knows what circumstances first prompted its manufacturing. Thus, although an artefact can, of course, be analytically deconstructed, it may not always be possible to reconstruct its contextual application.

The third step in the methodology entails the actual *prototyping*, or construction, of an intelligence. This is a hands-on activity in which students are required to make a physical object. Such objects, however, must offer a constructive solution for a context other than the intelligence's original context of invention. Students are here encouraged to, in the architects' idiom, "evolutionize" the intelligences, by which it is meant that they must look for ways to adapt the designs outside their original remit and location. In getting ready for evolutionizing such intelligences, they must learn to identify the carryover capacities of material interfaces—by looking at how materials vibrate with or mimic an environment—as well as learn to carry these vibratory qualities over to novel territories and contexts. Students must therefore develop a form of systems thinking that is at once analogical and digital, at once capable of imagining resonances, extensions, and analogies with technological appliances elsewhere but also capable of figuring out how to render them legible, how to digitize and graph them so as to enable them to travel. They must disembed the object from its original setting and stretch its design to adaptive solutions elsewhere. The challenge, as the architects put it, is to find "an enunciation that affords the prototype a contextually meaningful and productive application."[17]

Finally, the fourth step involves mapping the social relations of an intelligence. This is the "human network": the people who were involved in the original design of the intelligence or have become its custodians or transmitters. They are the people who know how to make such intelligences, how they work, where to source them from, and so forth. The task of describing a human network is implicit, of course, in the operation of prototyping insofar as a prototype is conceived as an intelligence that has been "evolutionized" out from its original context of invention. Knowledge of this context is therefore a requisite for the prototype's proper development. Ideally, such knowledge would take an ethnographic form. Descriptions of human networks, however, vary considerably. For some projects, the human network amounts to little more than a naming of the people who participated in the making of the original object and its prototypical extension. Other projects make use of video interviews; in yet other cases, an attempt is made to contextualize the territory, context or circumstances that prompted the creation of the intelligence. Most human networks, however, come to life as collections of digital media: video, audio, or image files.

Altogether, then, there are no standards as to how to catalog, upgrade, prototype, or map a human network. Different intelligences have, to this day, prompted different recollections. What perhaps best describes the state of the IC platform toward the end of 2010 was its redefinition from its original status as a project that aimed to document and map grassroots architectural intelligences to a collective exercise in networking and distributing social relations.

The IC project thus epitomized at this stage the kind of reorganization in the nature of experimental work that Latour has described as a transition from an enterprise in "data collection" to a "collective enterprise."[18]

Dramaturgies of Invention

In September 1594, the senate of the Republic of Venice granted Galileo a twenty-year "privilege" for a water pump. The historian of science Mario Biagioli has observed how the "entire description of the invention in the application and final text of the privilege boils down to two lines in which the pump is said to 'raise water and irrigate land, [and] with the work of a single horse it will keep twenty water spouts connected to it going at the same time.'"[19] The description that was demanded from Galileo as inventor was not intended to enable third parties to replicate his designs because, as Biagioli notes, this was a "function that was typically taken up by provisions about the training of workers and artisans to build and operate the invention in loco—a 'disclosure' through bodies rather than texts."[20] Not the dissemination of knowledge, then, but the maximization of local utility was what concerned sovereign rulers at the time.

The modern notion of patents emerged in the United States, France, and England at the end of the eighteenth century with the collapse of the Ancien Régime and the gradual conformation of liberal representative democracies. A process in which the system of privileges over inventions was granted by absolutist monarchs gave way to one whereby authors' rights were bestowed by political representatives. Whereas the granting of privileges had been subjected to exigencies and expectations of "reduction to practice" (that designs must prove to be practical and functional), by the early nineteenth century the rights inscribed in a patent were fulfilled to the extent that they provided a comprehensive description (textual and pictorial if needed) of its actual specifications.

The transition from the system of patent as privileges to that of patent as rights was, however, anything but smooth.[21] As the legal scholar Alain Pottage demonstrated, during the formative years of the US patent regime in the second half of the nineteenth century, patent lawyers would often argue their claims to an invention in the courtroom through "arguments [that] were materialized and articulated in demonstrations of working models, demonstrations which were designed to distinguish the 'mode of operation' of one machine from that of another."[22] Such 3D models provided a visual, material, and tactile representation of how a machine worked. The scale models assembled, staged, and theatricalized the drama of invention in the courtroom as a mechanical function. They offered a three-dimensional conceptual and performative rendition of how and what "invention" was supposed to be about. As such, scale models and textual descriptions pre-formatted the conditions of invention as a specific regime of material, iconographic, and instrumental processes. They "invented" invention through a process of modeling that, in this fashion, worked as "a kind of pre-conceptual condition for the formation and manipulation of legal concepts."[23] The object embodied the law *and* its invention.

By the end of the nineteenth century, then, the mechanics of patenting had come to sanction and exemplify a technical and expert regime of political representation: the terms by which "a politically sovereign 'public' set the conditions of possibility of the patent bargain—the contract between inventors and citizens."[24] Few other artefacts or discourses exemplified, the way the patent did, the technical imagination of liberal democracy.

We would like to think about the prototypes and archival intelligences of Zoohaus in the context of this wider narrative about the rise of technical and proprietary democracy. Not quite models and not just technical specifications either, Zoohaus's prototypes reposition the material sensibilities, tactical mechanics, and scalar flights of invention in a narrative about urban resilience, resourcefulness, and grounded improvisation. They are sketches or drafts of the urban-wide dramaturgy of invention. As such, they outline a technical and aesthetic regime for a body politic—the city—where knowledge can neither be granted nor claimed, neither transacted nor owned, but can only be liberated.

Self-Maintenance

On returning from Latin America in 2011, Zoohaus was invited to an artistic residence at El Ranchito, a curatorial project in Matadero, Madrid's largest contemporary arts center. The invitation expressed the art center's interest in exploring some of the wider implications of the IC project. The interest was part of the nascent and vibrant movement that was taking root in the city around questions of cultura libre at the time. "What would a 'free knowledge bank' look like," asked the commissioning invitation, "if it were to be designed as an architectural object? Could one build a meta-prototype that fed on all IC's projects to date and that would become, in turn, a space from where to promote the prototyping of further intelligences?"[25]

Zoohaus took the art center's challenge to heart and developed a proposal to extend and apply the IC program to Matadero's local neighborhood, Arganzuela. They proposed to construct an office space that would become an archival and intellectual platform for the development of a local IC program in the neighborhood. The office, the proposal suggested, would host a physical archive containing all the project's intelligences as well as a workshop space from where to launch a survey of Arganzuela's own local intelligences. The office proposal was named OTICAM to refer to IC's temporary office in Arganzuela, Matadero (Oficina Temporal Inteligencias Colectivas Arganzuela-Matadero).

The proposal that Zoohaus presented to Matadero spoke of IC as an object "without an owner, a tool in the service of everyone."[26] The text further described the office as a "physical and eventful materiality," by which it was meant that the office space would "host open events that will function both to recruit and enlist new intelligence-seekers" as well as "explain and publicize" the project's general program.[27] The office was thus conceived to work as an archive, workshop, and event space. It is significant that the project's identity was deliberately kept loose and ambiguous. Zoohaus insisted that this was the work of an open platform. "We want to give voice to the authors of the intelligences, and in so doing dilute the platform's own authorial identity. The platform should be thought of as an instrument rather than a model or project"; IC was at once an "infrastructure" and a "social network."[28] In its most succinct formulation, the office was imagined as a "prototype of and for collective intelligences."[29]

In the days prior to Matadero's approval of the project, Zoohaus sounded out a second idea with one of the center's curators: to develop an identity as Matadero's "maintenance architects." The idea was to apply a variety of intelligences to the art center's own infrastructure: to expose the repair work that goes into holding art together as an epistemic and material object. The proposal, however, was quickly dropped on approval of the project on July 2011 and Zoohaus turned their attention instead to the building of OTICAM.

The project was set in motion erratically and without much direction. Zoohaus started using the space provided by Matadero for all kinds of business, whether or not they were related to the IC project. Zoohaus had no office of its own so the workspace provided by Matadero was used at leisure by the architects for all kinds of work. "Visitors to Matadero," we were told in conversation, "dropped by our working space and were bedazzled at what we were doing there. We ourselves were not much better at explaining our own presence there." For a start, the architects struggled with the notion of an "archive": "We had this vague idea about spatializing onto a 3D object the affordances of a digital archive. We also wanted the archive to work as a sort of 'shelf for relics': a museum of intelligences, where people could touch and play with real artefacts. And of course we also wanted the archive to be a meeting place: a space itself enabling of new intelligences. Last, it was our hope that whatever we ended up constructing would stay in Matadero. We wanted to build something that would remain in the arts center past its exhibition date."[30] At meeting after meeting, the Zoohaus team deliberated how to build such an archive. Although their objectives were unstable and shifting, Matadero's own infrastructure soon became an obstacle itself: "We certainly hadn't much idea as to where we were going. But it didn't help that our own workspace in Matadero wasn't properly equipped for the task at hand. There were hardly any electricity sockets were to plug our laptops; sometimes, at a meeting, someone wanted to show the rest of the team a video, but we had neither a projector nor a screen where to watch them. We even had no archival space of our own, no storage proper. So it soon became obvious that we *really* had to build an archive."[31]

Zoohaus had hitherto imagined OTICAM as an intellectual platform: a free knowledge bank that acted as both a repository of local intelligences and an atelier for building up new communities of intelligence seekers. The project changed direction, however. At every meeting the architects ended up talking about the infrastructures that were lacking in Matadero: "One day, we suddenly realized that not one of the other artists in residence were working *for* Matadero. No one was working toward making Matadero a better place. No artistic project had taken Matadero as its own object of intervention. Why not, we thought then, build an office that will become an infrastructural enhancement for Matadero? *That* would be our prototype: a piece of infrastructure grafted onto Matadero's structural habitus, enabling its own activities."[32]

The idea of building up the archive as a form of infrastructure came as a revelation. The architects suddenly realized that what mattered in the construction of a "free knowledge bank" was the *construction*, and not the *freedom*: the design of infrastructural capacities, rather than simply the terms and conditions of access; a distinction reminiscent of the distinction drawn out by James Holston, which we cited in the introduction, that the right to the city be seen as a "contributor right" to urban citizenship rather than simply an entitlement to civil liberty.[33] Thus, Zoohaus's flippant proposal to become Matadero's "maintenance architects" returned in the reimagination of OTICAM as a platform enabling of the arts center's own curatorial projects. The office thus became a self-maintaining infrastructure.

Resources and Re-Sources

The new vision for the project opened up a whole new series of challenges: "Would it be possible, we asked ourselves, to build the office using the intelligences IC had collected the world over? Could we take an intelligence found in Palomino (Colombia) and retrofit it with one found somewhere else? That may sound rather banal to you, but it addressed a crucial challenge for us, namely, can architecture be open-sourced? Can an architectural intelligence be disembedded from its local context and material circumstances, and made to travel elsewhere?"[34] The question of retrofitting assumed a pivoting role in the imagination of the office as a structural assemblage. For Zoohaus, the open-source nature of the building required not only the use of Creative Commons licenses, but more importantly, the design of a constructive system capable of shifting scales. "We had to build an object capable of accommodating future needs. Thus, whose sources were open (open-source), but also whose own internal resourcefulness remained open. That was the point of the turn toward infrastructure: designing and building an object capable of transforming itself into a resource for others."[35] The inspiration here came from the auto-construction techniques that have become a trademark in the fringes of Latin American urbanization.[36] It is a topic to which we return in chapter 8, where we explore how in the practice of architects, free culture offered a palette with which to shift from a focus on *resources* (materials, infrastructures, objects) to *re-sources* (methods, techniques, pedagogies). For the time being, let us note how the office was imagined in this guise as a re-compositional object: made up with intelligences that can substitute for each other or even enhance and transform each other; structures that can anticipate future structures. It would be an object whose capabilities functioned also as instructions (for future and unexpected uses): a self-instructible object.

The construction of the office advanced at good pace over the following months. The building's design changed a number of times, such as when Matadero offered Zoohaus free wood with which to build the structure in exchange for their collaboration dismantling an existing exhibition piece. The wood allowed Zoohaus to develop a more ambitious plan for the building, but such transformations were in accord with their newfound program for a self-instructible construction. This newfound identity also prompted a change of name for the project. OTICAM was now renamed Offfficina, in homage to the image-bookmarking and web-based curatorial project, FFFFound!

The peculiarity of the installation that Zoohaus was building for Matadero was first brought to the attention of the art center's curators and management staff a few weeks prior to the exhibition's opening. All artists were then notified of the need to start moving their pieces from the workshop areas to their final residence in the exhibition hall. The news came as a shock to Zoohaus. The office built by the architects had been designed and dimensioned to their working area. It had never occurred to them that the structure would have to inhabit a space other than its own constructive space: "The thing is that we were building our own space. This distinction between a workshop space and an exhibition space was pointless to us. *Our workspace was our exhibit*."[37]

In the months to come, this vision of a self-built, autonomous space took a life of its own and contributed in important ways toward a further reconfiguration of the Offfficina's identity. A turning point was marked by Matadero's invitation to all El Ranchito artists to organize a series of workshops that would contribute toward publicizing their artwork. Without giving it too much thought, Zoohaus decided to organize the workshops at the Offfficina. They sent out invitations and scheduled the workshops appropriately. It was only later that they realized that not being under any obligation to ask Matadero's administrators to book a workshop space on their behalf or ask permission to use certain infrastructural equipment had suddenly turned the Offfficina into its own curatorial project. In their own words: "It was this sudden realization: 'Gosh, we have our own curatorial space here.' A place of our own, which is grafted onto Matadero's infrastructure, which parasites on Matadero, but that we manage. In fact, it becomes this tiny bit of Matadero that suddenly 'anyone' can manage, for anyone can join IC. So from one day to the next, you have this public space, run and administered by the state, and yet with a loophole in it, that allows anyone to manage it."[38]

From that moment on the Offfficina became a very different kind of object. Zoohaus opened up the platform to fellow artists and collectives, who started using it for a variety of purposes: book launches, academic seminars, parties, artisanal workshops, and so on. The Offfficina became an event infrastructure.

There were a number of restrictions, however, on what the Offfficina could be used for. The Offfficina was a free culture infrastructure, so all events hosted at the Offfficina were free as in gratis, but also free as in promoting free knowledge. Thus, if it was viable technically and organizationally, events ought to be streamed live over the internet and all related documentation and audiovisual materials likewise made available under Creative Commons licenses. Some members of Zoohaus spoke of "a natural evolution of the philosophy of openness that leads to the production of 'situations' or 'ambiences.'"[39] For instance, at a workshop organized for teaching how to build do-it-yourself rocking chairs participants were asked to source their designs from the needs of Matadero's back-office and maintenance personnel. Once built, the chairs were offered to the arts center's staff in appreciation for their ongoing support, and they have become today a recognizable item of the center's furniture-scape.

Throughout 2012, the platform also became a meeting point for Arquitecturas Colectivas, a network of young architectural collectives aimed at showcasing the work of emerging grassroots and guerrilla architects hitherto ostracized by the mainstream world of studio architecture. The Offfficina became a place for these architects and fellow interlocutors—artists, neighborhood activists, cultural agents—to hang out. Its infrastructure opened up a space where an emergent conversation about peer-to-peer urbanism, open-source architecture, and networked collaboration took root. Not unlike what the media theorist McKenzie

Wark has observed apropos de Situationists' visions for an urban world of pure possibility, the Offficina engineered the type of "atmosphere [that] gave [the Situationists] intimations of the future powers of an architecture it would be necessary to create as the ambiance for less mediocre games."[40] Over time, the Offffficina's open-source architecture became *the* place to talk about open-source architecture in Madrid. We may say that the Offffficina's infrastructure quite literally theatricalized—provided the dramaturgical and decorative context for—open-source architecture to take center stage. As a gigantic piece of interior decoration, the Offfficina supplied the atmospherics for making open source architecturally visible in the city.[41]

In April 2012, the curatorial project (El Ranchito) that hosted the Offfficina was scheduled to close. However, it soon became obvious to both Matadero's administrators and Zoohaus that the scale of the project would eventually pose a serious dilemma to the art center. The Offfficina's infrastructural intervention was unlike anything El Ranchito had commissioned. It was not so much the size of the installation, for the art center has housed considerably larger exhibits and pieces throughout its history. Rather, the Offfficina had literally opened up an infrastructural problematic within the center. It brought to attention some of the center's infrastructural and technological deficiencies, but perhaps most important, it did so by pointing to an alternative conception of infrastructure as a form of collaborative intelligence and ambience making.

For Zoohaus, the realization that the Offfficina entailed an infrastructural enhancement of Matadero meant that it was imperative to get the art center to keep the installation, but most important, to make sure it remained open and operative as an infrastructural center. At that point Zoohaus launched an imaginative campaign to "save the Dinosaur," as the Offfficina was affectionately renamed. The architects printed t-shirts with the Dinosaur's image, which were handed out for free among Matadero's staff, and embarked on a social media campaign to "mobilize empathy for the Dinosaur's cause," as they put it.[42]

There was more to the antediluvian monster than its affective qualities, however. At another time, members of Zoohaus noted that the construction of the Offfficina as a superposition and ensemble of different intelligences could be thought of as "the bringing to life of a kind of Frankenstein."[43] The formula echoes a remark by the makers of the Crystal Palace dinosaurs apropos the construction of such 3D objects as similarly "'Frankensteinic,'" which, as James Secord observes, expresses their concern for the way the models "posed an intricate combination of aesthetic, scientific, and practical problems."[44] For the scale of the Crystal Palace monsters was indeed of its time: a historical period that had a taste for "theatrical spectacle and extravagant stage sets," and that in this context placed a premium on knowledge conveyed through the senses: a philosophy of visual education where "the size, life-like character, and three-dimensionality of the restorations would appear as a revelation."[45] We bring this chapter to a close with some remarks on the idea of three dimensions.

Freedom in 3D

In 2016, the Museum Reina Sofia in Madrid, Spain's National Museum for Contemporary Art, hosted an exhibition on Constant Nieuwenhuys's New Babylon, an architectural vision for the city of the future that took the Dutch artist close to twenty years to complete (from 1956 to 1974). A founding member of the Situationist International, Constant imagined "not so much [a] utopia as an infrastructure for utopia," where humans, finally freed from the exigencies of labor through the advent of automation, would be able to enjoy a full life of nomadic play, leisure, and creative potential.[46]

On our way back from one of the interviews with community activists we were carrying out while researching the making of our toolbox of grassroots intelligences, Manuel and Alberto talked about Constant's project. Alberto quoted a reference to Constant's work that he had recently come across in a little book on the Situationist International by McKenzie Wark—"Constant is using multimedia to create an ambience, a space and time for desire"—and noted that the reference to ambience-making reminded him of Zoohaus's dinosaur.[47] Manuel grinned. He had not visited the exhibition but knew about Constant's work from his days at architecture school. "The thing about these utopian projects," he noted at one point, "is not the world they imagine for us, but the *aprendizajes* (systems of apprenticeships) that they leave behind for others to build on; not what we can learn from them, but what we can build with them. What we lack is manuals for a handmade, craft urbanism (*manuales para un urbanismo hecho a mano*)."[48]

Constant's infrastructure for utopia was, of course, part of a distinguished genealogy of urban avant-gardes, of which the Situationist International was indeed a fecund hotbed and inspiration in the late 1960s. Not a few of these projects found a program for political action in the image of enveloped infrastructures and floating ambiences. When in 1966 Jean Baudrillard joined Jean Aubert, Jean-Paul Jungmann, and Antoine Stinco, among others, to form the guerrilla urban ensemble Utopie, their vision for a new beginning for the world was clear: a world unhinged, free-floating, aspirational, elevated by the winds and dreams of inflatable and pneumatic architectures. Thus they drew, designed, and built worlds in plastic suspension.[49]

In some respects, these various worlds in suspension were creations of their time. They pointed to an outdoors of liberation that was contemporaneous with the aspirations of the civil rights movements but also with the asphyxiations evoked by the threats of nuclear escalation. It was a new world outside the world—where one could leave behind the pulls of mass media and the pushes of automation, the huffs of the military-industrial complex and the puffs of one-dimensional man. In the US context, as the media historian Fred Turner has persuasively documented, much of the energy dedicated to resolving these contradictions involved, too, the design of similar immersive and enveloping experiences of liberation.[50] Some of the examples that Turner dwells on include the famous Family of Man exhibition that traveled the world in the 1950s and the Human Be-In psychedelic gathering that took place in San Francisco in 1967. In their different ways, these events variously deployed and made use of multimedia setups, sensory environments, and cybernetic psychedelia to induce shared ecstasies of liberal fraternity. These "democratic surrounds," as Turner calls them, staged the conditions for a kinesthetic appreciation of democracy as a lived-in, interactive, and personal experience. They signaled a reconfiguration of democracy, in the words of science scholar Javier Lezaun, as a system of "arts of installation."[51] This was an experience of freedom in three dimensions.

Truth be told, in the case of Utopie, they were not just concerned with designing fugitive and experiential architectures for escaping the world. Their pneumatic constructions were not mere aspirational flights (of fancy). Their interest in the assemblage of atmospheres and exteriors was, importantly, informed by their concurrent interest in the deconstruction of interiors. A key notion of their programmatic vision was the concept of "disassemble" (démonter), which they employed to emphasize why understanding how objects are assembled is the necessary first step for disrupting and disassembling the logics of capitalism. Moreover, "to disassemble the manifestations of architecture, they argued, ran contra the Beaux-Arts understanding of architecture as an 'oeuvre,' 'creation,' or 'synthesis,' but also questioned the sufficiency of emerging ex-Beaux-Arts slogans, which sought to define architecture as a 'service to the people' or simply as 'a political act.' In the end, Utopie's 'rhetoric of disassembly' was an attempt to understand architecture as a particular type of product."[52]

The notion of disassembly is of course also at the heart of Zoohaus's archival experiments in free/libre urbanism. They, too, disassemble objects so as to have them reassembled as prototypes. Yet unlike their pneumatic and Situationist forefathers, it is a requirement of prototypes that they unfold as instructibles: that they are at once real and virtual operations of design, for it is their very composition as *resources* that furnishes their capacity as *re-sources*. They are descriptions of worlds-to-be that do double duty as worldings of the capacities for re-description. As described in chapter 4, prototypes outline possible worlds—more than many and less than one—because they are first and foremost designed, to paraphrase Manuel's words, as *bricolages of apprenticeships*. As such, they are not scaled representations in the way patent machines performed technical democracy in the nineteenth century, nor are they models-for in the way the Crystal Palace dinosaurs theatricalized a rational pedagogy for capitalist spectacle. Neither scales for the biopolitical organization of liberal citizenship nor models for an exhilarating refuge from the exigencies of labor, the stories that prototypes tell speak about how the city gathers itself together—how it lays out and reckons with its apprenticeships—in three dimensions.

Part 3
MATTERS OF SENSE

When Adolfo first met Ander Contel at the Lavapiés Assembly in summer 2011, things were going well for him. He was employed as a social educator in one of the city's peripheral neighborhoods, working in a big project funded by a bank. He had enjoyed a relatively comfortable life for the past few years, living with his girlfriend in a cozy apartment in Lavapiés. However, this was all about to change on May 15, 2011, when the intensity and vibrancy of our political commitments stormed our lives without warning.

Ander joined the Lavapiés Assembly as soon as it was first convened on May 28. Overnight his social life, which had once been taken up by concerts and cultural events, was filled with assembly meetings and gatherings. He stood out in every assembly, where he could regularly be seen with a sign saying *turno de palabra* (request the floor) while walking around writing down the names of those wishing to speak. The assembly where Adolfo and Ander first met was held at the Parque del Casino, the same place where years earlier Antonio Lafuente had given his talk on "The Museum as a House of Commons." By then, Ander was already a member of the assembly's facilitating task force, which Adolfo would shortly join. For almost two years they met weekly at the gatherings that the task force convened in preparation for the assembly a few days ahead of its celebration. Some twelve people made up the task force, at whose meetings they perambulated the neighborhood's plazas and open-air spaces, where they would sit to prepare the assembly's agenda, estimate time slots, and assign rotes and roles for the smooth running of the assembly, from moderator to timekeeper, minute taker, or *turnos de palabra*.

Many years before joining the Lavapiés's Assembly, Ander had had an intense experience of grassroots political activism. However, notwithstanding being well versed in assembly politics, he still expressed amazement at the dexterity of the methods with which the 15M assemblies brought people together to listen to one another. "How is it at all possible for something like this to happen?" he used to ask, with a look of amazement. During those years, Ander's relation to the neighborhood became profoundly mediated by the experience of assembly. As he put it to us, "You wake up early, you go to a really stressful but also really rewarding meeting, because making preparations for an assembly was a bit like preparing to go to war, such was its complexity. Next you go to the assembly proper, which may last four or five hours, and finally you go with other participants for beer and fun elsewhere. I remember some Saturdays when I would leave my house at 10 a.m. only to make it back at 2 a.m., and all this time I would have been talking politics—in a loose and ever-expanding sense—with other people."[1]

Born in a poor neighborhood in a rich, northern city—a conservative city, by his own account—Ander arrived in Lavapiés at the end of the 1990s. Having only just turned twenty-one, with no university education and no employment, he was introduced by his sister to the activist world of Lavapiés. One evening some friends dragged him to a concert in the Laboratory. Thereafter, he would visit frequently, drawn to the center's cultural agenda, until one day he finally decided to move in as one of the center's permanent squatters. Over three years, the center became his home and, eventually, his political project too: "I remember joining a study group one afternoon. And just like that, in my early twenties, with no education other than primary school, I began reading Toni Negri."[2] As a permanent squatter at the center, the Laboratory became an existential project for Ander as well as his "university," shaping and cultivating his political sensibility thereafter.

When Adolfo met Ander, he still lived in Lavapiés. He was ebullient and spoke of himself as being transformed by the 15M movement. His job as a social worker had long exposed him to handsomely funded and ambitious participatory social projects. Yet the assembly movement felt like a paradigm-shifter: "I had long embraced a professional vision, supported on text-book explanations and the designs of well-funded projects, where 'participation' was always pliable to some political framework or another. Yet along came the 15M movement to show us that we had been getting it all wrong. It came as a shock, even for those with a little experience in the struggles for and praxis of political possibility."[3] For Ander, the assemblies opened up a political sensibility that departed radically from his experience in militant activism: "It's the collapse of all boundary-policing, between expert and non-expert, professional and amateur, militant activist and people with no experience in activism. . . . It felt so liberating, not just for the underdogs, but for the alleged over-achievers also, the experts and the professionals."[4]

However, a menacing shadow lurked in the background of all that political effervescence. Amid a general climate of austerity, Ander's employer fell behind in paying his monthly wages. Along with other members of the assembly, Ander found himself having to move more than once, looking for cheaper rents and gradually sliding down into a state of precariousness. Failing to remunerate him altogether, Ander finally decided to quit his job. The economic crises was now in full swing, and finding a job proved a herculean task over the next few years. He moved yet again, this time to share an apartment with a fellow member of the assembly. Yet even this arrangement proved unsustainable, and well over a decade after having first moved into the Laboratory, Ander found himself squatting once again.

When Adolfo last met Ander in 2018, his prospects were looking somewhat better. He was sharing a flat with two other people (one of them a member of the assembly), had finally found (precarious) employment, and was trying to finish his university degree, which he had given up in the years prior to the economic crisis, when it hardly paid off to complete a university education. Always a shrewd political observer, Ander was somewhat skeptical about the municipalist confluences that had moved into power in 2015 while invoking the spirit of the 15M. He would rather reminisce about the times spent in the assemblies *cuando lo más importante era estar juntos*, when the thing that mattered the most was to be in the company of one another.

Part 3 takes as its central concern this notion of being and sensing together. We aim here to describe how the neighborhood assemblies that populated the city in the wake of the 15M movement breathed a spatial and political form of their own into the texture of the urban condition. In particular, we describe how the work of assembly articulated a particular right of inhabitation, an experience and knowledge of the city that accrued through movements of itinerancy and pre-occupation, nomadism and care, as well as modes of documentary and performative storytelling.

Chapter 6 examines in depth how assemblies took residence in the open air, in plazas and streets; how they negotiated the hospitality to strangers of public spaces; and how they had to furnish themselves with a paraphernalia of equipment (electrical hardware, boards and pens, chairs) and improvisational methodologies to become perdurable urban objects. This required assemblies to experiment with their own textual and archival forms, as well as their conditions as territorial boundary objects, where the material trafficking and political pressures of assembling often transgressed and redrew the geographical scales and dynamics of neighborhoods. In chapter 7 we turn to the art of politics at assemblies and examine how it was transformed from the voicing of reasoned arguments and practice of deliberation to the enablement of listening and the practice of mutual sensing and caretaking. Assemblies organized themselves into sensory organs that perambulated the city in marches and demonstrations but also through the everyday exploration of its local injuries and grievances. Assemblies worked as *political ambulatories*: perambulating the neighborhood's environments and sensing its frontiers at the same time as they delivered care to its outside patients or residents.

ASSEMBLING NEIGHBORS

The man sitting next to me mumbles unintelligibly. He always does. Over the weeks I (Alberto) have come to realize he is just repeating the words of the speaker to himself. It is an innocent gesture, but it is unsettling and distracting. Clara, who used to sit next to me at every assembly, now deliberately avoids him every Saturday.[1] "It's the last thing I need," she says; "it's exhausting enough having to make it through three hours of meeting without having to put up with all this hissing and mumbling." I was put off myself at the beginning. But then, some three Saturdays ago, he asked for the microphone. He stood up and started talking about the history of state schools in our neighborhood. It turns out he is a retired schoolteacher. His name is Jacinto. He was eloquent and engaging and lucid. He has made three or four interventions since, always concise yet enriched with the candor of hindsight and experience, and very often bringing a historical angle too, about the barrio's shifting demographics and the contradictory pushes of immigration, working-class impoverishment, and gentrification. I have tried to engage him a couple of times at the end of the assembly or during some of the assembly breaks, but it seems we are both a bit shy and I always feel lost for words. I despair at our mutual timorousness, which feels childish. Though perhaps it is not timidity that it is at stake. Our gathering in the open air makes for a strange social form. Whatever reasons bring people to the assembly, there is a sense in which they have to retreat the moment the assembly is disbanded. Over time we have come to witness each other with wonder and trepidation as we pulsate and sound out the limits and thresholds of a nascent social body. We sit, and we listen, and we witness, and sometimes we touch something, we find something, someone. In honesty, it is not always clear what remains at the end of the assembly.

Alberto's Fieldwork Diary, September 24, 2011

In the wake of the Spanish Occupy movement, which took to the streets on May 15, 2011, thousands of people gathered in the open air in plazas and public spaces all over Spain to deliberate and bring into action *Democracia real ya!* (Real democracy now!) at a municipal level. Over one hundred of such local popular assemblies blossomed in Madrid alone. Attended by professionals and the unemployed, the elderly and the young, people who introduced themselves as "feminists," or "hackers," immigrants or *vecinos* (neighbors) or simply passersby, the gatherings reproduced the conventional sociological dictums on urban cosmopolitanism.[2] Yet they did so in a format rarely seen before in public space. Assemblies dwelled in the open air and in doing so blurred the lines separating formal and informal sociability. They shaped themselves into a public body that was at once a permeable yet robust structure, a space of engagement and invitation as well as a device for programmatic decision making and action. As a specific type of get-together, the gatherings drew on the protocols and routines of conventional meetings (such as the use of agendas, minutes, or rosters of duties), yet their public orientation and openness charged these in fascinating ways. Assemblies challenged not a few of the spatial, temporal, and social qualities that hold together the qualities of urban space.

To begin with, the words *vecino* and *barrio* (neighbor and neighborhood) acquired a new political and social valence. The social form of the assembly inscribed the city with a revitalized practice of neighborly politics. Assemblies prefigured a social method and an infrastructure for dealing with, even reinventing, classical urban *topoi*, such as negotiations over relationships with strangers, the making of public spaces, and an understanding of the urban condition as a fuzzy territorial or deterritorialized form. Assembling mobilized a method and a set of devices that helped elicit the kinds of relationships and people (neighbors) through which the city, "as an artifact and generator of knowledge, comes to be understood."[3] In this sense, the fuzziness and messiness of the assembly—the difficulties that participants had at putting together, let alone understanding, the object of the assembly as an urban form—stimulates valuable insights into present-day discussions of the city as an object of political claims and rights. Moreover, the practice of assembling neighbors—of convoking a neighborhood assembly and of bringing and holding a disparity of relations together in the political and social figure of "the neighbor"—addresses wider issues about the possible forms that an urban commons may assume in the neoliberal metropolis. Should we approach the urban commons as a problem of urban scale? Or does it make more sense to see it as an experimental or improvisational form, an undulating assemblage of diverse elements, from archives to extension cables, therapeutic games, and affects? These are some of the questions that we address in this chapter.

Methods

Lavapiés is one of Madrid's old historic quarters. For instance, the neighborhood is home to La Corrala, one of the neighborhood associations studied by Manuel Castells in his groundbreaking study of grassroots urbanism, *The City and the Grassroots*.[4] Lavapiés retains today many of the cultural and sociological qualities that Castells identified in the late 1970s: it is "one of the oldest sectors of Madrid, a labyrinth of seventeenth-century streets populated by the elderly, craftsmen, small merchants, grocers, bars and cafés, petty bureaucrats, manual service workers, and, more recently, a handful of students and young professionals. It constituted a neighborhood with its own community life built around its physical charm and folk culture, as well as its poverty and dilapidation."[5]

Today Lavapiés remains the charming and rundown quarter that Castells described. The early 1990s witnessed the arrival of successive waves of immigrant communities, which have turned the neighborhood into one of Madrid's most vibrant multicultural wards.[6] Young people from Senegal, Morocco, and other African countries populate its streets; a dense network of grocery and electronic shops is in the hands of Pakistani people; and a great number of clothes and accessory stores are managed by Chinese businesspeople.

Like all May 15 neighborhood assemblies, the Popular Assembly of Lavapiés was first convoked on May 28, 2011 (see figure 9). For almost two years, the Lavapiés Popular Assembly met on a weekly basis on Saturdays. Between 2011 and 2012 the assembly's location migrated between various local plazas, sometimes in response to weather conditions (some plazas being more exposed to sun than others), sometimes in the hopes of attracting a wider audience. Although the turnout varied, meetings were rarely attended by fewer than thirty people, with an average number of around seventy people. The assembly was organized into a variety of working groups focused on topics such as housing, immigration, public water, finance, and culture and education. There were also two task forces—Communications and a facilitating group (*Dinamización*)—in charge of managing the assembly's logistical and organizational affairs. The assembly kept a

FIGURE 9.   Lavapiés Popular Assembly, June 16, 2012. Photo by Daniel Bobadilla is licensed under CC BY-NC-SA 2.0: https://creativecommons.org /licenses/by-nc-sa/2.0/.

public website where they published the minutes of all their meetings as well as forthcoming actions and events.[7]

Adolfo joined the Facilitating Task Force in September 2011 and remained a core member of the team for twenty months. The task force met one or two days ahead of every assembly to prepare the agenda and assign a rota of turns for each facilitator (moderator, minute taker, and so on). Its purpose was to organize and structure the temporality and rhythm of the assembly, anticipating controversies and discussions, designing participatory and mediation techniques, and overseeing its general functioning. However, as the following vignette shows, the task force's own internal dynamics often prefigured the tensions and ambiguities that traversed the composition of the assembly as a venue, infrastructure, and method for convivial politics in the city:

> It's almost 8 p.m. The Facilitating Task Force is meeting in the plaza just outside home. I (Adolfo) can see the group banding together from my apartment's balcony; twelve people altogether. I fly down the stairs to join them.
>
> First thing we do is talk about the agenda for tomorrow's assembly. We use the provisional agenda that was drafted at the meeting of the assem-

bly's working groups a few days back. We decide who's going to moderate at tomorrow's assembly: Lara will join Luis Miguel, who has ample experience by now.

We do a quick rehearsal by going through the motions. First, the members of the task force introduce themselves. They (that is, we) remind the assembly of the sign language at use (to indicate approval, disapproval, repetition, etc.); we run through the day's agenda (which we will be preparing this evening); and one by one we invite the various working groups to report to the assembly. The moderator is in charge of getting people ready and keeping their time. We decide to use our own very meeting tonight as a practice ground for tomorrow's moderation.

We have received a proposal by email to organize a meeting between the assembly and Noam Chomsky. The person who submitted the proposal has never attended an assembly. We discuss for over an hour whether it should be the Facilitating Task Force's prerogative to reach a decision on these matters: "Why not get that person to put the proposal directly to the assembly?"

As it turns out, he is unavailable to present the proposal in person at tomorrow's assembly. What is at stake, then, is whether we should read his email proposal to the assembly or discard it altogether.

Having touched on the topic of email, a related matter arises. We've been talking about the Chomsky proposal for a few days on the task force's internal email list. Some people expressed reservations about it, giving little credibility to the person that said he could clear access to Chomsky. Some of those exchanges have been leaked and copy-pasted onto another email distribution list. The messages were not compromising, but those affected queried about the privacy settings of our list and asked who had editorial permits for administrating the list.

The rest of the items in the agenda are straightforward, save for the last. The housing commission has submitted a manifesto on the "housing question" to be read at the assembly. It calls for price controls, among other measures for rent regulation. Some members of the task force expect it to cause an uproar and think it would be prudent to formally notify the police of our gathering. (Public meetings that expect to draw in over twenty people should in principle be notified to public authorities.) However, the very suggestion of calling the police causes a stir in the group: "I am a veteran activist and will never submit to police

oppression," Caroline notes. Miriam feels offended by such a statement: "I didn't know we needed activist credentials for this."

We call it a night at 11 p.m.

Adolfo's Fieldwork Diary, September 16, 2011

The role of the Facilitating Task Force was to anticipate controversies during the
celebration of assemblies and plan accordingly, drawing on mediating and methodological techniques. In this sense, the prefiguration of the assembly by the
task force had some prefigurations of its own. For a start, early on in Puerta del
Sol's encampment, the assembly format had already been construed by those attending as a specifically "urban" political object. A week into the original occupation of Sol, a neighborhood commission drafted a document known as the
"Methodology for Assemblies."[8] At the time the draft of the document was described as an extension of "the assembling method, the recuperation of public
space, and critical thought" to the larger hinterland of neighborhoods.[9] In the
weeks following, the draft was developed into a full document known as the
"Quick Guide for Facilitating Assemblies," which thereafter functioned as a manual for organizing assembly work everywhere.[10] The guide was compiled using
a variety of sources and expertise, including similar texts at use in the squatting
movement, field guides for community empowerment in developing contexts,
and insights from the autonomous governance of ecovillages.[11]

The role from its very inception, the method of the assembly was conceived
as an organon of social, political, and critical work in an urban context. The
"Quick Guide" included a sociology of roles, a praxis for conviviality, and a spatial and cultural layout. The document recommended that all assemblies be facilitated by "a moderator, a secretary in charge of taking minutes, someone
responsible for taking turns for questions, and a group facilitating the production of consensus."[12] There was also a role singled out for "interpreters," whose
function was to translate speeches or questions into sign language for the deaf.
The document further described a distinct kind of sign language to be used by
all for promoting conviviality within the assembly. Thus, approval of a proposal
or a comment was to be signaled by raising and waving one's hands, and indi-
cating that a speaker was talking in circles and not contributing to the discussion was signaled by a motion of circling hands.

The document also described the method for delineating assembly space,
which was meant to distinguish between "moderating space" and the assembly
proper. A "rectangular perimeter marks out the former with chalk or colored
tape on the floor, simulating a stage."[13] The moderating space was occupied by
whoever was speaking at any time. This person was flanked by the interpreters
and the rest of the facilitating team. Spokespersons for each of the assembly's

various commissions awaited their turn on one side of the moderating space. The other side was occupied by the team in charge of taking questions. The latter were to be located "as far away as possible from the team of secretaries, who are in charge of taking minutes, and who shall be close enough to the moderating space to request a repetition, a synthesis, or a copy of a document presented to the assembly."[14] The minutes of every assembly meeting were to be recorded by secretaries. Minutes should include the day's agenda and a record of the various reports received, proposals made, discussions had, and any consensus reached. The minutes were also to mention proposals or recommendations to be taken to Madrid's Popular Assembly (Asamblea Popular de Madrid), which was the name under which all the city's neighborhood assemblies met. The final version of the minutes was sent to the assembly's communications team, which would then post it on the assembly's website.[15] Much was made of the public and open availability of minutes over the internet.

Throughout, the methodological guide stressed the importance of keeping a "social climate of relaxation, listening, respect, and complicity."[16] A variety of supplementary texts suggested techniques and advice for doing so. For example, one leaflet noted how "when someone who is known to be sensible and positive finds herself constrained and incapable of reason, we embrace her and tell her: 'dear friend, we know what you are capable of. . . .'" In the same spirit, new members were to be greeted so they did not feel like strangers, poetry or other texts should be read aloud to enrich and enliven the affective character of the assembly meeting, and occasionally the gathering should end with a game.

The assembly format thus cultivated an aesthetics that was both therapeutic and ludic, through the unfolding of what we have called climates of methods. In the neighborhood of Coslada, for example, one of the attendees, who was a professional clown, regularly performed in the assembly space to break up and enliven the long hours of meetings. People were encouraged to attend dressed in fancy costumes as part of an attempt to draw in parents who might be roaming the plaza with their children. In Lavapiés and Dos de Mayo, children's assemblies (chiqui-asambleas) were organized for the young to discuss issues that were of concern to them while their parents attended their own assembly without having to worry about parenting. Children's assemblies themselves, however, also produced recommendations worthy of reporting to the general neighborhood assembly. Some assemblies organized parallel activities, such as barter markets and workshops, or they opened or closed with a meal at which the attendees shared the food they had brought. Because the assembly format structured both the assembly itself and the hospitality in public spaces, the two overlapped, blurred, and became difficult to distinguish (see figure 10).

FIGURE 10.   Urban spectacle at the Puerta del Sol encampment. Photo by
Julio Albarrán.

Central to the discursive production of hospitality in the assembly space was the
notion of consensus. It has been widely recognized that a defining characteristic of the 15M movement was the importance given by it to consensus as an expectation of the decision-making process. To the definition of consensus as
general agreement or concord in opinion, sometimes expressed unanimously by
a collective, the production of consensus in Madrid's popular assemblies added a
methodological and affective nuance. Consensus was defined in this context as
a nonquantitative operation: decisions were not voted on in the assembly space;
they were reached by a consensus that was meant to be the outcome of patient
listening, dialogue, and debate rather than of individual opinions held without
modification. The "Quick Guide" offered a technique or protocol for the "production of consensus":

> After the presentation of a motion or proposal, the moderator asks:
> "Any arguments strongly against the proposal?" Should there be any, a
> turn for questions and debate is opened: THREE arguments for and
> THREE arguments against the positions discussed. Having had an op-
> portunity for debate, the moderator turns to the assembly and puts the
> question back to it, inviting the assembly to pronounce itself for or
> against the proposal using sign language. If there is still no consensus,
> the moderator will allow 3–5 minutes of debate within the assembly,

such that smaller groups may be formed to discuss the matter internally. Following this, a new round of interventions is opened, where groups may put forward their new proposals for consensus. Failing this, two paths are opened: (i) if the proposal was originally made by a commission or working group, it shall be taken back to its constituency so that it can be properly reformulated; (ii) if the proposal was originally made by an individual, it is recommended that he or she take it to an appropriate commission or working group, where it will be discussed internally so that a first degree of consensus is reached at that level. In both cases, once properly reformulated, the proposals may be brought back to the assembly to be discussed anew.[17]

As this description suggests, reaching consensus took time, but the assembly movement rejoiced in its unhurried temporality, and indeed its slow pacing was often singled out as the movement's defining characteristic. The assembly was *not* a decision-making forum. Assemblies, as a number of participants told us, were "not operative or practical structures." Their ultimate aim was not to make decisions but to build *con-sensus*, modes of sensing together. The Quick Guide put the point somewhat differently: "the assembly's membership is its very *raison d'être*. They [the members] are [both] its principle and ultimate objective."[18] One of the most famous 15M slogans responded to this experience of political *longue durée*: "We proceed slowly because we aim highly (*vamos lento porque vamos lejos*)."

Although there was general agreement that the deliberate temporality of the assembly was among its greatest virtues, many attendees in practice dreaded the time it often took to build consensus. Some proposals that were expected to provoke controversy were postponed or deferred for a future assembly to which "experts" would be invited to help make better-informed decisions. Moreover, some methodological texts made a distinction between "urgent" or "unpostponable" consensus and more routine agreements. Whether a matter under dispute was unpostponable or not was decided on the spot by the assembly. If a protocol for urgent consensus was proposed, first "visual criteria" were to be employed to determine whether to proceed accordingly: the protocol was to be applied "so long as a visible 1/5 of the assembly does not oppose it." Two teams of five people each, one team for and one against the original proposal, had to agree on this visual count. If no agreement was forthcoming, a formal counting of votes was required.

The awkward prescriptions making up the protocol for urgent consensus typify the political complexity of the assembly as a neighborly urban form. After a month of occupying Puerta del Sol, and once the assembly movement had successfully spread across Madrid's neighborhoods, the pressure to dismantle the encampment mounted. The local authorities had already attempted to evict the protesters on a couple of occasions, and there were rumors and threats that more violent incursions might follow. There was also concern that, when its political purchase was most at stake, popular sympathy for the movement was declining. Some felt that the iconicity of a central encampment drew attention away from neighborhood assemblies, which were becoming increasingly successful. Faced with such demands, the assembly at the camp persistently failed to reach consensus on the convenience and timing of the camp's dismantling. The arguments for and against were many and complex, but it was the spatial qualities of the encampment as an urban public object—"a city in miniature," as it was often called—that many at the camp thought had been its greatest political innovation, so they resisted its disintegration (see figure 11). As a forum where strangers wove a web of neighborly ties from the discussion of their mutual affairs, the camp, the assembly format, and the process of consensus building had together reenvisioned *urban life as a climate of methods* and produced a means of making life in the city convivial. The insistence on conviviality helps explain the awkwardness of the protocol for urgent consensus. Even if a resort to clumsy representational techniques was a result, the endurance of the assembly format was understood to be the paramount concern of all its individual members.

FIGURE 11.   Puerta del Sol's "city in miniature." Photo by Julio Albarrán.

Hardware

Assembling is hard work; it is also hardware. In most assemblies an Infrastructures Commission took responsibility for keeping and maintaining the materials and equipment necessary for use in the assembly. Objects and devices such as audio systems, megaphones, long electrical cords, or simply writing paper and markers became infrastructural equipment that was crucial for an assembly to occur.

Making one's voice heard in an open space is an issue that all assemblies had to resolve. The use of a megaphone often proved unsatisfactory, for the sound is directed at an angle and therefore tends not to encompass the whole arc of participants surrounding the moderators' stage. It therefore became customary for assemblies to ask bars or cafés in the vicinity of a plaza to plug assembly audio systems into their electrical sockets. Doing so also made necessary the purchase of extensions to electrical cords (or sometimes the use of handmade extensions), capable in some cases of traversing a fifty-meter distance between the assembly space and an electrical socket.

The storing of these materials was, moreover, problematic. In Lavapiés, for example, the equipment was kept at La Tabacalera, the experimental squatted social center described in part 2. In Prosperidad, the equipment was stored at one of the local neighborhood associations (*asociaciones de vecinos*). These relations were not exempt from problems; negotiating was often a fraught process. La Tabacalera, for instance, was the latest reincarnation of one of Madrid's most famous squatter movements, the Laboratory described in part 1. Their radical political agenda had been cultivated over years of social mobilization, and there was a concern that, although it was praised by many, the assembly would simply import a cultural and political practice cultivated elsewhere.[19] Some local neighborhood associations, on the other hand, were known to have strong ties to the Communist Party. For these and other reasons, many assembly-goers repudiated the links to established organizations. "The assembly," one heard them say, "is an autonomous entity, representative of no one, and represented by no one." At a meeting in Prosperidad, someone observed that what ought to characterize the assembly format was that it was not "housed": "We do not, we should not have a place that we can go to, that can house us. We need to reassemble and reinvent ourselves at every meeting."[20] "The assembly is a *topos*," one of us overheard a participant say at a meeting in the Puerta del Sol Assembly, meaning, presumably, that it was a formula, belonging nowhere in particular, as much as it was a spatial form, and that its defining trait was its openness (to the city at large).[21]

In Lavapiés, the assembly met on a weekly basis, alternately at the Parque del Casino and the Plaza de Cabestreros. In Prosperidad, it met every two weeks at a plaza of the same name. The space of an assembly's meeting was a matter of dispute, at one time or another, in almost all cases. The Plaza de Prosperidad is an open-air space at the heart of the neighborhood, next to the local market and the subway station. The plaza is, as an attendee of the first assembly put it, "*the* point of passage (*lugar de paso*)" for the neighborhood. On a Saturday morning, it is where people bump into each other when going to the market or bakery, while waiting for a bus or an acquaintance at the metro exit, or on their way to have an *aperitivo* at a local bar. But the plaza is a dry, cemented space, with few if any trees, and therefore no shadows and hardly any breeze. During the first three weeks of assembly meetings in May and June 2011, it was intensely debated whether the plaza was the most suitable place to hold the gatherings. People were concerned that the lack of shade trees would make the plaza unbearably hot during the summer months. Some people suggested that the assembly ought to be relocated to the nearby Parque de Berlin, where esplanades of grass and tall trees would make meetings more tolerable and even pleasurable. But in the end it was decided that the assembly would stay in the plaza, for it was agreed that the plaza complied with the infrastructural, social, and political requirements that the visibility of the assembly as a piece of urban hardware demanded.

In Lavapiés, the weekly assembly meeting was signaled by a giant piece of yellow cloth with the words "Lavapiés Popular Assembly" written on it. The cloth hung near the entrance to the park where the meeting took place, although some people complained that it was not visible enough. There was a concern, it seemed, that passersby would not recognize the gathering as a "popular assembly." In Prosperidad, part of the debate around the assembly's location was focused on its "visibility"; it was thought that the plaza was more visible than the park. A participant put it eloquently at the time: "We cannot afford to become part of the urban equipment (*mobiliario urbano*). There are many reasons why we are here; but we are here to be seen also."[22] The naming of the assembly and its iconic quality thus testified to its own very particular status as a form of political hardware ("urban equipment") that should somehow both stand out from and blur back into the cityscape.

Even when a consensus was reached over the location of an assembly meeting, the space of the assembly format remained fragile and provisional. In Lavapiés, for example, at one of the assembly's first meetings, participants discovered that the plaza of the Parque del Casino was already occupied by a *batucada* (a large ensemble of percussionists). The assembly had to improvise a location for an alternative meeting place. On another occasion, a woman interrupted the Sol Assembly, desperately calling out that she had just been assaulted. A few people came to her aid and others left amid the confusion and fear. Furthermore, rain and bad weather generally were a persistent threat to all assemblies, and there was none that had not, at some point or another, discussed alternative locations for the winter months.

The assembly format was under constant pressure of these kinds—pressure on its political and material qualities, on its spatial and temporal registers. The assembly as an urban form was precariously but productively fuzzy, inchoate, porous, and in constant metamorphosis. The assembly format recruited a variety of local actors, who were not always consistent with one another. On the one hand, plazas and other public spaces were "wired": inscribed with devices and do-it-yourself circuitries that enabled a novel but manifestly temporary mode of urban encounter.[23] There were also political and autonomous collectives who made their presence felt in the assembly through different kinds of formats, channels, and capacities. On the other hand, local shops and bars, which were far less transient than these groups of people and sorts of hardware, made their presence felt as well. The assembly's porous and open nature was a source of frailty and instability but also of novelty, and some of the novel forms that emerged developed longer-term features and functions.

One feature that solidified over time was the meeting agenda. All meetings followed a roughly similar format. First, the team in charge of facilitating the meeting was introduced. As we saw in an earlier vignette, in Lavapiés the Facilitating Task Force met on the evening prior to an assembly meeting. Task force members went over the day's agenda and sometimes rehearsed and practiced techniques of facilitation. Such routines were important, for at least two reasons. First, the assembly proscribed permanent roles for individuals: volunteers had to rotate in their performance of various assembly roles. People who were new to a role, therefore, often required a little training before going live in front of an audience. Second, rehearsing the day's agenda helped the team anticipate controversial topics. The rehearsal offered a venue for sharing experiences of conflict management and resolution, which helped the assembly retain its identity as a neighborly forum.

On September 17, 2011, for example, the Lavapiés Assembly was discussing a "Housing Manifesto" that included criticism of "greedy landlords."[24] A woman stood up and interrupted the reading of the manifesto. She identified herself as a landlord and pointed out that since not all landlords are the same, it was unwise to generalize. A voice called out, demanding that she shut up and requesting a turn to make comments. The woman indeed shut up. But when the reader of the manifesto had finished going through the text, she approached, took him aside, and questioned him. Her doing so distracted the reader from questions and comments that members of the assembly were now addressing to him. The team of moderators felt at a loss, uncertain how to respond. One of the facilitators told the woman that her observations ought really to be addressed to the assembly at large and not simply to the reader. The issues debated in an assembly were or should become a matter of concern to all: the assembly's method of hospitality and inclusion warranted that issues of concern to one individual should be "assembled into" matters of concern for the neighborhood at large. People were assembled into neighbors around shared concerns, even if they held antagonistic or actually conflicting positions.

The Housing Manifesto itself provoked disparate reactions. Some people observed that the text was hardly different from one presented a week previously. The Housing Group (an established working group within the assembly) was encouraged to submit a new version once it had taken on board the objections raised by assembly members and had found ways to express the nuances desired. The Housing Group also had to take into account some quite specific concerns that members had raised. For instance, the manifesto made a demand for a 25 percent reduction in rents. This level of specificity troubled a number of participants, who suggested that no quantitative claims be made. The manifesto also called for a general strike in the autumn, which again was a sentiment unequally shared across the assembly. A group of about six people spontaneously decided to work together on the spot, redrafting the text for immediate reconsideration by the assembly. The group turned aside and dedicated itself intensely to the task, producing a text in time for the assembly to reach consensus on it later that same morning.

Archives

The speed with which the Housing Group produced a new version of its manifesto contrasts with the more typically *longue durée* of the assembly format, at least as described in assembly handbooks dealing with methodology ("we proceed slowly because we aim highly"). The relationship between the texts and the actual procedures is fuzzy. It appears to be less contradictory than perhaps supplementary, and anthropologist Tony Crook's term "textual person" may help to illuminate it. The term, he writes in a very different context, is meant "to characterize both the person-like relationships of texts, and the textual-like relationships of anthropological persons."[25] As an aesthetic artifact, a text is the composite outcome of disparate relational engagements. The text has a social efficacy that responds to and anticipates a world of relationships: "Recognition and currency for these objects—*the capacity to animate analytic and social relations in others*—is governed by exhibiting this aesthetic form. . . . The textual person is composed through combining distinct relations: although data/theory, spoken/unspoken, originality/analytic precedence, and literal/figurative are kept scrupulously separate, they are also combined according to kinship-like strictures."[26]

Texts are assembled and disassembled through the relationships that they themselves engender. The assembly format, as we have seen, was—in the methodological documents and guides, minutes, and reports that it produced—a textual corporate person. The assembly was as much produced by these documents as it had itself been productive of them and would be productive of more. The rush to produce a new version of the "Housing Manifesto" shows the extent to which a textual artifact can stand for the very life of a form. Although much was made in texts of the assembly's long-term agenda, which stressed the importance of its unhurried production of consensus, in practice there was an urgency about at least one facet of assembly practice: the constant reinscription of its living political presence through the production of documentary objects.

The documentary form that best exemplified the assembly's nature as a textual person was its minutes (*actas*). Minute taking was widely acknowledged to be the most important of these assemblies' activities. At a meeting in Sol, for example, a group of people brought forward a motion for convoking a national referendum. The group presented a document that explained its arguments and sought the assembly's endorsement. A number of people aired their concerns. Some were uncertain as to the document's origin: Who drafted it? Where do you meet? Where do you publish your minutes? The group remained silent, which prompted a robust exchange of accusations. A few voices suggested that the group belonged to an extreme right-wing party. A young man took the microphone. He held the document distributed by the group in one hand. He then pointed to its first page, which displayed a 15M logo. "You shouldn't come here," he said, "to wave around a document as if it had been produced by the movement. Nor should you come here and use this space to publicize a meeting that hasn't actually been approved by the assembly." A member of the group proposing the motion asked belligerently whether the young man worked "for the 15M's police force," while other participants pointed out that they had come merely as individuals to make a public announcement.[27]

This exchange vividly captures some of the tensions that functioned to negotiate the insides and outsides of the assembly format. These were brought into the open, in this particular case, by a documentary object: the motion for a national referendum. The textual artifact mobilized questions about the proposing group's authority, its representativeness, and its larger social engagement in and with the assembly format. A number of voices insisted on finding out more about the group, repeatedly asking about the minutes of the group's meetings: "Where do you publish your minutes? Where should we look to find out more about the nature of your meetings?" The group responded elusively. A group member said that they met weekly at a cafeteria and had a blog where they uploaded their minutes. The response was hardly satisfactory, and the assembly reacted with suspicion. Another group member added that they had worked with the assembly's Legal Commission and that the lack of minutes was characteristic of all of that commission's projects. A member of the Legal Commission then jumped up to observe that consensus over such a motion had never obtained within the group and that the lack of published minutes was no recommendation for the proposal to be elevated for consideration at the assembly level. The moderator finally ruled that "the methodological guide clearly states that all minutes must be sent to the Communications Commission, which shall then proceed to publish them on the internet."[28] In other words: in the absence of an archival record and adherence to a recognized methodology, there can be no politics.

In an important article, the urban scholar Vyjayanthi Rao suggested the concept of the "city as archive" as an aid to thinking through the complexity of the urban condition. The archive stands for the living memory of its urban experience.[29] It is through its archival deposits and infrastructure that a city faintly apprehends its own processes of understanding and becoming. The archive tenuously anchors the experience, and helps moor the memory, of the incessant vicissitudes and exchanges that otherwise would be lost in the city's intricacies: "Rather than highlight the archive's capacity to accurately represent a past, [I suggest] we use the notion of archive as a way of navigating the voids of the present, as a practice of intervening into and reading the urban fabrics created by these voids, not for reading the urban fabric as a quilt or a palimpsest of historical forms preserved within the archive.... The city-as-archive ... serves as a methodological intervention into the re-creation of everyday relations. . . . The city-as-archive works as a tool, re-fashioning our relation to the future."[30] While Rao finds in the archive a powerful conceptual analogy for the contemporary urban condition, participants in Madrid's assembly movement deployed instead the inscriptive and documentary practices of archiving as technologies of hospitality. The archive was both a methodology and *a climate of methods* for urban life. It was both a kind of documentation and a praxis that elicited new forms of relationship among strangers. The archive was an instrument that functioned both to stabilize the neighborhood commons and define the terms of recruitment into and membership in it.

The textual person, then, inscribed the assembly format in a circuit of documentary and archival practices that stretched out of the assembly space and in so doing publicized and questioned the terms of its internal democracy. "Who wrote this manifesto?" and "Where do you publish your minutes?" were questions that redescribed the spatial politics of the assembly format as archival politics. The relation that the assembly format claimed to establish with the neighborhood was therefore recontextualized across texts, inscriptions, and networks that challenged and blurred its spatial circumscription. The city and the neighborhood disappeared as spatial objects and reappeared as archival ones. In the process of assembling neighbors, the assembly format reinscribed the city in a novel archival and climatic landscape.

Territorialization and Deterritorialization

The territorial and spatial dimensions of the assembly format were the subject of numerous discussions in most assemblies. When the call for organizing neighborhood assemblies was first issued in May 2011, the people of Chamartín (a district of northern Madrid) showed up at two assemblies, in Prosperidad and Hispanoamerica, which had been separately convoked by groups of neighbors who did not know of each other's existence. Over the following days, each assembly discussed the advantages of merging with the other. The assembly of Prosperidad drew in more people and the local plaza seemed to offer a better infrastructural and social space: there were nearby bars that could offer access to electrical current, and the plaza itself was an open space that could be easily occupied. Thus, for a few days, Prosperidad became the point of assembly for the district of Chamartín. It seemed as if the territorialization of the neighborhood around the plaza had already made a sufficiently weighty political case for the assembly to meet there.

Soon enough, however, the case for the plaza began to lose weight. At Hispanoamerica, a group had already set up a website with their own neighborhood domain. A number of incipient working groups (on politics, education, economics, and so forth) had also set up their own email distribution lists and Google groups. The prospect of having to integrate or abandon these tools in favor of those initiated by the assembly of Prosperidad was unappealing. Hardly a week into the whole process, then, Hispanoamerica reclaimed its autonomy as a popular assembly. This episode was indicative of the territorialization and deterritorialization of the assembly format. Assemblies came into being as topological artifacts. There were a variety of factors that contributed to such topological immanence; to begin with, the politics of digital networking. As the present example illustrates, digital communications were crucial in the articulation of the assembly movement. Digital relations traversed and inflected street mobilizations. That the original encampment at Puerta del Sol was known as #acampadasol, a Twitter hashtag, is a testament to that importance.

Another important aspect of the topological territorialization and deterritorialization of assemblies was the heightened concern that one encountered there with scale and scale-shifting interventions. The case of the *chiqui-asamblea* is a poignant example because the term means "children's assembly" but *chiqui* also means "small." In Lavapiés, children's proposals were incorporated into the assembly's minutes: "Children ask for a play center; for the right not to wear uniforms in public schools; for getting people to throw cigarette butts in the rubbish; for public toilets, so we are not forced to pee in public; to be kind to one another; to have dog shit cleaned up; and for more flowers in the streets. They say they do not like churches because one cannot play in them. They like to play with neighbors. They further ask for a local swimming pool and a football field with grass."[31]

The assembly agreed to discuss some of these proposals in future assemblies and to make posters concerned with some of these issues and distribute them in the neighborhood. Children's issues are small issues, but they matter too. In both writing and speaking, there was continuous insistence that "little things matter," although this commitment led assemblies to ask vexing questions about the "sizes" of various political actions. The resources that assemblies could mobilize were scarce, so there were ongoing discussions about how best to deploy them. Discussion, for example, of the importance of making assemblies visible and iconic exposed some disparate assumptions not only about the aesthetics and location but also about the size of the political. Let us explain.

The suggestion made at the Lavapiés assembly to have a large yellow cloth identifying the location for passersby and the neighborhood at large, although it was welcomed, led to a discussion of who would take responsibility for finding a location for the banner. A few voices suggested the Information Commission, but it was quickly pointed out that the commission was understaffed and overworked. Someone suggested that neighbors with apartments facing the plaza be asked instead to hang the cloth from their balconies. A balcony location was iconic enough, but some people did not want to delegate out this or any political intervention. There was said to be a danger that the balconies would in time "naturalize" the assembly's political visibility: the banner would be absorbed into the neighborhood's landscape.

As a result, a new proposal was made for "small situated direct actions": assembly-goers would walk around the neighborhood advertising a meeting sometime prior to the date. Still another proposal came from a participant recalling how, in the early days of the movement, the assembly had had an "information point" in the plaza. The information point had been very successful at stabilizing the assembly's iconic and political visibility. Perhaps, it was remarked, it was no coincidence that attendance had started to decline once the information point was dismantled. The trouble with the information point, someone else noted, was that it had overworked those who staffed it: "We need to find a way to publicize the assembly that does not tax its members. That was the idea behind the banner: to liberate otherwise scant human resources from taxing activities."[32]

The question of the scale of political action was nowhere seen as clearly as in assemblies held in some of the villages surrounding the capital. In the assembly at Hoyo de Manzanares, considerable caution was exercised in the use of sign language to, for instance, alert a member that she had been speaking too long. In such small villages, we were told, relationships between participants were often inflected by kinship or friendship ties. "I have been approached by quite a few people at the village supermarket," a friend told us, "eager to express their support to me in person but who felt that, if spotted at the assembly," would be "liable" to bring "shame to their families."

Between the village structure and the urban plaza, the assembly format carved out for itself a fragile yet productive space of hospitality at the level of the barrio. Of course, it was this capacity to shift scales that, from the beginning, lent political agency to the assembly format: from an information point to a balcony or a poster or direct action, the assembly had the capacity to transform its political practices and political imagination. It recruited as many new objects, places, and actors as it deemed necessary, even if doing so blurred its own internal configuration as a political body and occasionally threatened it with dissolution.

Reassembling the Right to the City

It was Henri Lefebvre's original inspiration to think of our inhabiting the city not as the reclaiming of a right to political voice within the liberal juridical framework of a state-sanctioned or market-shaped urban geometry, but rather as an exploration of the very conditions that sometimes hold together the shifting horizon of our project for democratic-becoming yet more often let it recede into the distance.[33] As described in the introduction, Lefebvre's work on the right to the city has been revisited recently by authors who wish to reclaim the urban situation as a commons. For David Harvey, for example, the right to the city should be embodied in the "democratic management" of the forms of "surplus absorption" that cities generate: "Since the urban process is a major channel of surplus use, establishing democratic management over its urban deployment constitutes the right to the city."[34] In housing, water management, or transportation, the democratic management of these urban surpluses would help us delineate thresholds for the sustenance of commons: the appropriate scale or circumscription for the autonomous management of urban processes and resources.[35]

As the urban scholar Kafui Attoh has noted, however, there remains a certain vagueness to the right to the city, for it remains unclear whether the democratic management of surpluses entails the correct type of urban right, or whether democratic management should aim instead for, say, socioeconomic justice or the realization of a civil liberty.[36] Rights are always entangled with persons, spaces, technologies, and infrastructures, and for that reason they remain ambiguous, if productive, assemblages.

In chapter 1 we described how in the late 1990s, the autonomous movement in Madrid sought to articulate a vision for the city in terms of the liberation of its neighborhoods through the intersection of the struggles for the right to housing, antagonist telematics, and free culture. In the name of an "opening toward the social," neighborhoods were conceptualized as trading zones where activists explored, negotiated, and navigated the boundaries and interstices between network culture, autonomist politics, and insurrectional aesthetics.

Fifteen years later, neighborhoods remained central sites in activists' aspirations for a material ecology of urban liberation, yet they were now subtly reconfigured and partially displaced through the operations of assembly. Assembly offered an alternative site—conceptual and material—for exploring specific manifestations of public and collective action wherein expressions of the right to the city took place and grounded themselves.

For this to happen, assembly required, on the one hand, a strenuous investment in the material, textual, and archival production of "assembling" as an urban spatial form. The assembly defined itself as a particular kind of object—a piece of urban hardware that warrants its own temporal and spatial continuity by means of other objects, devices, and technologies that participants in the assembly mobilize. The assembly performs the urban as a climate of methods.

On the other hand, the process of assembling also produces a novel sense of urban neighborliness. Neighbors were "assembled into" social and political subjects through the process of assembling. As such, assembly distributes citizenship (for want of a better term) in terms of an archival, infrastructural, and methodical practice of conviviality. It performs a self-grounding democracy: an ongoing and deepening search, reinvention and reappropriation—*autogestion*, in Lefebvre's terms—of the radical and receding sources of political conviviality.[37] Assembly holds up its own claims at being a form that matters by "mattering" itself through archives, texts, and infrastructures for sensing together—for finding consensus.

AMBULATIONS

My house—it looks like the assembly's logistical headquarters. I (Adolfo) have made room for a number of boxes from Alejandra, including, for instance, one where she keeps her snorkeling suit, for which she has no room in her own place. I am keeping another box for Nuria, and only a few days back she took away a table that I had also been storing for her. I am keeping, of course, all kinds of paraphernalia from the Assembly: pens, copies of *Madrid15M* newspaper, brushes (which I need to hand over to Elena tonight, for a poster campaign). And as of yesterday I am also storing María's vacuum cleaner. It was meant to be given to her by Nuria at our latest assembly but they missed each other and I ended up with the vacuum in my living room. María should be around any minute now to pick it up. As if it weren't enough, Isabel is staying over at home this weekend.

Adolfo's Fieldwork Diary, June 8, 2012

Assembling has been likened to a novel form of public squatting and political liberation by activists, academics, and participants. Assembling performs a "right to appear," as Judith Butler has noted, whose very critical gesture resides in a gathering of bodies that is always precarious and vanishing: "Showing up, standing, breathing, moving, standing still, speech, and silence are all aspects of a sudden assembly, an unforeseen form of political performativity that puts livable life at the forefront of politics."[1] In the orchestrated arrangement of assembly, she argues, "a new space is created, a new 'between' of bodies, as it were, that lays claims to existing space through the action of a new alliance"—an aperture of the political that is embodied through the impetus of necessity and the infrastructures of precarity.[2] Assembly, Michael Hardt and Antonio Negri have suggested, is also the operation through which we can hope for the congregation and sustenance of commons today: "Assembly is becoming a *constitutive* right, that is, a mechanism for composing a social alternative, for taking power differently, through cooperation in social production. The call to assembly is . . . an exhortation to virtue."[3]

The operation of assembly functioned in Madrid as much as an operation for political liberation as a method for the composition of urban conviviality—as a climate of methods for the city. Although assemblies met publicly outside at local plazas or streets, the work of assembling stretched beyond their particular location. This "stretching" was spatial, but it was also temporal, social, and infrastructural. In the opening vignette, Adolfo's house was integrated into the assembly's logistical architecture: it became a storehouse and repository for stationery and multifarious equipment; it also became a social meeting point as well as a guesthouse. Assembling occurs in various places at different paces and tempos. It performs the work of a hospitable architecture, aimed at lubricating the wider conditions of urban relationality. It is significant that such conditions are also "rhythmed" out into the city in a variety of ways, including not only assembly meetings but also demonstrations, casual encounters, friendly visits, logistical preparations, and the incessant exchanges and interruptions of digital communications. The assembly is a rhythm as much as it is a collective, and in this capacity it distributes its presence as a sensory organon for navigating, anticipating, and caring for the city.

Listening

In May 2012, the Working Group for Migration and Coexistence of Lavapiés's Assembly held an open-air meeting to discuss a local incident that had become national news a few days earlier. Two policemen had been caught on camera chasing and beating an illegal immigrant who was peddling in the neighborhood. When confronted by a group of neighbors, one of the police officers panicked and fired a shot in the air. The images quickly went viral. The working group had called a public assembly to review the incident and, more amply, to discuss the structural violence against immigrants that was prevalent in the neighborhood. The following entry in Adolfo's fieldwork diary describes the meeting:

The Working Group for Migration and Coexistence is holding a meeting that is expected to draw large numbers because it will address the arrest last Sunday of a young immigrant, as well as the police beatings and shootings that surrounded the episode. The meeting starts at 8 p.m. in the Plaza de la Corrala. We are surrounded by metallic sheds on occasion of the Madrid Bollywood festival that the municipality is hosting later this weekend.

By the time I get there, just past 8 p.m., there are already over twenty people at the meeting, with more people gradually trickling-in as time passes. There are many young Senegalese in attendance. I count at least eighty people at peak time, with approximately thirty young black Senegalese. We meet for more than two hours, until 10:30 p.m. The assembly proceeds slowly because every time a Senegalese participant speaks it gets translated into Wolof. Natalia has the megaphone, and she is in charge of moderating the meeting. She asks for volunteers to keep the record of turns for speakers and for writing down the minutes. Salma, a young migrant woman who is engaged to Lucas [an assiduous assembly-goer], volunteers to keep the order of turns. Later, Raquel will write down the personal data of those willing to file a collective complaint against the police. . . .

I sit on the floor next to Natalia. She keeps the meeting's agenda in a small notebook. . . . There are three points on the agenda: to discuss the shooting and arrests on Sunday; to file a collective complaint against the police; and other business. Later we will talk about holding a rally but I am not sure if this was part of the agenda or came up during the discussion.

Natalia kicks off by explaining that the meeting is an assembly of the Migration Working Group. She asks a Senegalese participant to translate into Wolof and explain the language of gestures [indicating silence, respect, repetition, etc.] that we use at the assembly. . . .

The assembly is getting more crowded by the minute. On two occasions we have to open up the circle to accommodate new attendees. Groups of young Senegalese arrive, some of whom sit down while others stay standing. Some stay for the whole assembly, others leave.

In the background, by the square's stairs, a group of black men starts singing. It becomes a little difficult to listen to what's being said in the assembly. An Italian activist from the squatted social center of Cambalache approaches them. They bring down their voices, although it is clear that whatever she's said to them, it did not go down well.

Senegalese participants take turns speaking. They address the assembly in Wolof, which then gets translated into Spanish, or they speak directly in Spanish and then do the translation themselves. A young Senegalese says there is no need for translations, that he can speak in Spanish. But Natalia insists on the importance of translations because not everybody understands Spanish.

Several of the interventions by young Senegalese men show gratitude for the expressions of help and call for working collectively to solve the problem of police harassment. They acknowledge that street peddling is an illegal activity but note they have no other way to make a living. "Better this than other wrongdoings," one of them says.

Another person notes that the boy who got beaten and arrested did so for being black not for being a *mantero* (illegal peddler). He wasn't even peddling at the time. He was merely standing by the entrance to his house and "received a beating for being black." . . .

We are such a large crowd by this point that there are some rousing moments. But it is also tiring. The assembly comes to an end at around 10:30 p.m. with a round of applause. We have yet to decide what motto will be used at the demonstration, as well as drafting a statement to be read then. Some people want to get on with it now, while others prefer to leave it for tomorrow morning. We raise hands and on a quick count it is decided to leave it for tomorrow. Raquel asks some Senegalese participants for help in drafting the statement so that it is not the usual suspects who write the communiqué. As the assembly disbands, some of us head off for a drink at a nearby bar.

Adolfo's Fieldwork Diary, May 30, 2012

The assembly of the Working Group for Migration and Coexistence came to a close with a consensus to organize a rally against police brutality. Shortly after the assembly, the group drafted a public statement, for which they enlisted the help of some Senegalese participants at the assembly. Unlike other statements that came out from the assembly, this one had a marked stylistic plurality that captured the input from different groups. Perhaps for this reason the demonstration that took place some weeks later was crowded with immigrants. It was one of the few occasions in which immigrants had the opportunity to demonstrate, since it is otherwise prohibited for people without a residence permit to take part in political events.

Set up in the early days of the 15M movement in June 2011, the Working Group for Migration and Coexistence was busy on various fronts. The group's original membership was composed of Spaniards and Latin American immigrants, who had dedicated much of their efforts at putting together an archive of "evidence" for undocumented migrants, such as invoices, proof of enrollment in language courses, or census certificates, which lawyers could use to sustain the "rootedness" (*arraigo*) of migrants and argue against their deportation.[4] The group had also set up a system of *acompañamiento* (companionship) whose members assisted and stayed by the side of people who had been detained and taken into police custody or accompanied them to court hearings or visits to the hospital.[5] These interventions had been warmly welcomed by the neighborhood's local immigrant population, and soon enough membership in the group skyrocketed, with the group itself being largely run by undocumented, sub-Saharan migrants.[6]

Notwithstanding the group's scheduled reporting to the Lavapiés Assembly, it was unusual for its members to attend the assembly's weekly meetings for a variety of reasons, including the very real risks and fear of detention associated to the assembly's public visibility but also because of migrants' own complex negotiations of ethnicity and race vis-à-vis the rapidly and often confusingly intersectional politics of the assembly, where one could never be quite sure who or what would show up next.[7] Therefore, by any count, the assembly of the Migration and Coexistence Working Group that morning was a remarkable gathering. Rarely had an assembly been attended by so many immigrants, let alone required the need for translations. In the early days of the assembly movement it was not unusual for assemblies to employ sign language interpreters for people with deafness, and in the past the Lavapiés Assembly had to employ English translators on a couple of occasions. From the start, assemblies had been carefully designed to enable everyone and anyone to speak in public. For example, it was not unusual for passersby to join the assembly sporadically and intervene. On one occasion, in an impromptu act, a woman cut in line to complain about personal housing problems and the assembly made room to accommodate her disruption. Another time, the assembly listened to a group of four teachers who had come to explain the rallies against austerity they were organizing and whose petition was not on the agenda for the day. Whether making room for scheduled or improvised interventions, the design of the assembly strived always for the cultivation and furnishing of an attentive and accompanying atmosphere, where anyone could be listened to. With every installation in the open air, the

assembly reworked the conditions of the street, interrupting and reorchestrat-
ing its harsh pace and reorienting the urban soundscapes.

As it takes residence in public space, the assembly thus pulses with a particular mode of attention and exchange. The circle that is drawn as people take a
seat or stand around creates the conditions for a precise mode of interlocution
and speech: turns for addressing the assembly must be requested, a certain lin-
guistic style is observed (in relation to grammatical gender, for instance), and
the agenda dictates an order and temporality to follow. In this fashion, assemblies destabilize some of the cultural conventions that have guided etiquette between strangers in urban public spaces since the nineteenth century, such as the
right to be left alone or the right to silence in public, or implicit codes of comportment that conduce strangers to behave toward one another with civil inatten-
tion.[8] In its stead, the gathering of the assembly airs a different atmosphere, one
that renegotiates relations of civility in public space through the design of conditions for active listening.

For centuries, Euro-American notions of politics have been constructed
around the practice of speech. For Aristotle, language was the diacritical marker
distinguishing animals from humans, the "political animal," for "nature does
nothing in vain; and man alone among the animals has speech."[9] For the philosopher Jürgen Habermas, rational communicative action functioned as the
structural foundation of the bourgeois public sphere.[10] Deliberative democracy
is, to this day, organized around the natural political value of interlocution. And
yet despite the centrality granted to speech in our political imagination, its cor-
ollary, listening, has been largely relegated to the margins of theory. However,
as the political theorist Benjamin Barber has argued, a strong democracy is only
possible when listening is granted political relevance: "The adversary system . . .
puts a premium on speaking and a penalty on listening. . . . In fact, speech in
adversary system is a form of aggression. . . . It is the war of all against all carried on by other means."[11] There is no democratic premium to speech, in other
words, if no one is listening.

We know, of course, that over the last two centuries the development of liberal
democracies has run parallel to the construction of parliamentary (that is,
speech-enabling) architectures. We can describe the architectural history of par-
liaments in this sense as an effort to unfold the visual and acoustic conditions
of politics.[12] For instance, the architect Paulo Tavares described the chamber of
the British House of Commons as an example of "architectural speech-
machineries where air works as the medium that guarantees the voice of rhetoric and provides the adequate climate conditions for one to wait while listening
to the others."[13] He follows in the steps of the philosopher Peter Sloterdijk, who
has thought of democracy in terms of the laying out of the atmospheric infra-

structures for living in common.[14] In this perspective, parliamentary architectures serve as sensory chambers whose atmospheres are purposively designed to enable those who gather under one roof to better hear and see one another.[15] Therefore, the fact that listening has not received much attention in political analysis may well be attributed to it being a responsibility that our political systems have relegated to these silently docile architectures.

The architecture of the Lavapiés Assembly was anything but silent or docile. In its itinerancy and perambulation through the city, the assembly had to arrange and redeploy its own atmosphere every time it took residence in public space. As described in chapter 6, this was no easy task. It required wiring the assembly's body as a distributed presence with every new installation. Often this required mobilizing the complicity of neighboring activist organizations, who would lend materials and equipment such as amplifiers, microphones, or loudspeakers. On occasion it involved clashes with the police over this or that permit to use sound equipment or electrical appliances on the street. At other times, the echoes of the assembly would compete with the sounds of a nearby festival or celebration or the exhilarating screams and laughter of a children's playground. Neither a rally nor a demonstration, the assembly had to sneak its way into the interstices of regulatory and normalized public space, while in the process choreographing a distinctive soundscape of its own. Out on the streets, the assembly weathered its own sensory atmosphere, furnishing the urban condition with an architecture for political listening.

> We are having today's assembly at Plaza de Lavapiés, by the stairways to the National Center for Drama. I (Adolfo) arrive twenty minutes late. There's some people there already, included Emilio, who's been away for the past four weeks. . . .

> I speak to Emilio and see no agenda has been prepared. We were going to have a "thematic assembly" to speak about police repression but it looks like the people who volunteered to organize it haven't showed up either. . . .

> Emilio and I talk about how to improvise an agenda for today's meeting. Amparo joins us and notes that someone from Tetuán's Assembly has offered to drop by to give a talk on the new Employment Law and labour reform . . . We decide to draft an agenda on the spot, asking people for items to be included. . . .

> I get an SMS from Alicia saying that two police vans have stationed next to Austria's Assembly. We wonder whether we should report it out loud in the assembly, but in the end decide not to, for fear that people will leave.

Since there's no agenda proper, the whole assembly is dedicated to "other business." There are a couple of issues raised: about last week's police raids against the protests organized in opposition to immigration policy, and about the protests against foreclosures. There are a couple of announcements too: two fundraising parties to help support work in support of illegal immigrants and against housing evictions. . . . I take minutes and read them out loud. Emilio asks if there's consensus on the points raised. There is no dissent so we take that for a yes.

The person from Tetuán's Assembly is ready to talk about the labour reform. He talks for about twenty minutes. He is very clear and didactic. Quite a number of people stop by to hear what he has to say. By the time he finishes there are about fifty people seated and listening. . . .

We bring the assembly to an end with an anti-repression performance. A young man from an anti-repression group invites us to stand up. We're about thirty people now. A young woman holding a ball of wool calls her name out loud and throws the ball to another person while holding one end of the string. We're each meant to mimic her gesture. As the ball flies from one person to the next it weaves a web that connects us together. The performance draws the attention of numerous passersby who stop to watch. We're then handed a balloon each, which we have to inflate. When we're ready, we start walking and moving around the plaza. At that point, a couple of young men start to chase us bursting the balloons with needles. We are told to protect and care for the few people left with balloons. We run around trying to navigate the complex web and organize ourselves into some sort of caring structure. It has been lots of fun and we have pulled in quite a bit of an audience.

Adolfo's Fieldwork Diary, March 24, 2012

I (Adolfo) am on my way back home from work. Alba calls me. She's been trying to get hold of me all weekend. She tells me there is a poster campaign later at 10 p.m. I didn't know about it and agree to drop by. She also tells me that if I happen to bump onto Carmelo [a leading figure in La Tabacalera] I should remind him that the assembly has plans to meet at the center to paint placards for the 15M anniversary march.

I hang up the phone and minutes later receive a call from Marisol. I am temporarily acting as the assembly's treasurer. At our latest meeting we have decided to have various people, and not just one person, bank our money. Marisol is one of these people and wants to know at what time she can come by my house to take away the part she has agreed to take responsibility for. I tell her that am on my way to La Tabacalera; that I was meant to be there at 7 p.m. but am running late. Perhaps we can meet there? She can't make it that early, so we agree to talk later and make an alternative arrangement. I ask whether she'll be attending the poster campaign at 10 p.m. She will, so we agree to see each other then.

A little later Emilio calls me. He too has to come by to take his share of the money. He is not far from La Tabacalera right now so we decide to meet there. The reason I am heading for La Tabacalera is that we need to take back to Casablanca [another squatted social center in Lavapiés] some of the paraphernalia that we borrowed for organizing a market fair a few days back. I have been text-messaging back and forth with Nuria and Miriam all morning trying to find a time that suits us all. I thought I'd made clear that I could not make it before 7:30 p.m., but Miriam has already sent me a text saying "*Vecino!* [neighbor], did you call me? See ya in La Tabacalera at 7 p.m."

When I am done at La Tabacalera I call Emilio. He does not own a cell phone (I think he is among the very few in the assembly [who do not]) so it is not always easy to arrange a meeting with him. I get through, however, and tell him that am on my way home. I'll pick up his share of the money and we can meet in the plaza in five minutes time. Scarcely a second goes by after we hang up when Alba calls me. I tell her my whereabouts, so she, too, decides to *bajar a la plaza* (come down to the plaza).

Adolfo's Fieldwork Diary, May 7, 2012

On May 8, 2012, the Lavapiés Assembly organized a *pasacalles*, a street parade for handing out leaflets and flyers in protest of the forthcoming eviction of two immigrant neighbors, Hazim and Zahid. A group of assembly-goers had agreed to meet at 8 p.m. in Plaza de Lavapiés, the neighborhood's hub. Some people arrive with pots and pans and start banging them, a form of protest known as a *cacerolada* that became popular during the banking crisis in Argentina in 2001 (see figure 12). Andrea, who is heavily involved in Casablanca, brings pans and metallic plates from the squat for all to use. As soon as people get their hands on them they start banging them, with little concern for symphonic orchestration.

The parade formally kicks off with the reading of a manifesto that calls people to gather early next morning at Hazim and Zahid's flat in order to stop the eviction. But the noise made by the pans makes it impossible

FIGURE 12. Cacerolada in Lavapiés, May 8, 2012. Assemblies produced novel and creative documentary practices, such as the watercolors of well-known artist, Enrique Flores, a regular member of the Lavapiés Assembly. Watercolor by Enrique Flores.

to hear what the speaker, Javier, is saying. María walks around asking everyone to raise the intensity of their jamming and wait for her signaling a sudden halt. The concerted improvisation works beautifully, the metallic clangs assembling in crescendo until they erupt into a sonorous thunder, followed by an emptied-out silence. Javier then reads out aloud the manifesto. He intersperses it with the recitation of a romance he himself has composed. It is not the first time Javier has written a romance to be read aloud at assembly meetings or parades. He has also adapted Frank Sinatra's "My Way" to make it sound like a proper "indignant" song: it is time that the 99 percent have it "our way."

As the parade makes its way up north through Lavapiés's streets people stop to watch and some echo the *cacerolada* with applause. Others voice their support. Some of the streets are so narrow and steep that the noise bounces back from the asphalt and buildings, turning the march into a thunderous battalion. The parade circles the neighborhood, as if outlining the town's old medieval walls. It stops three times, and on each occasion Javier reads the manifesto and recites his compositions. The trail of the festive and blasting crowd maps out the neighborhood's sensorial and material contours. Back in the neighborhood's southern ward, there is some discussion as to where to head next. The various itineraries are all discussed in terms of atmospheric impact: which streets are more likely to welcome the march's festive mood at 10 p.m. In the end, someone suggests that it might be time to go to Hazim and Zahid's flat. A proposal had been made at the assembly some days previous to spend the night in their house in order to gather a crowd to confront the eviction squad the following morning. The march dissolves and some ten people make it to Hazim and Zahid's flat. I join them.

Once in the flat there is uncertainty as to how many people will eventually turn up. When the action was first discussed at the assembly, some twenty people committed to showing up—the larger the group, the bulkier the mass of bodies offering resistance to the police. But as the night goes by there is hardly any growth in numbers. An ambience of fear and risk takes over the spirit of those now squatting in Hazim and Zahid's flat's hallway. A debate opens up as to how best to make use of the flat's spatial layout: where and how to crowd together so as to impede the police's access; or how to distribute people's very different degrees of fear and risk across the mass of bodies. Those with experience in previous evictions place themselves in front; others, who are less experienced, or simply less inclined toward physical engagement, take a rear-guard position. The festive atmosphere of the parade has transformed into a local and unstable object of ambient care. The labor of assembling redistributes the geographies of care and risk that traverse the neighborhood.

Adolfo's Fieldwork Diary, May 8, 2012

Redistributions of the Sensible

How do activists relate to the future? How do their assemblies, rallies, or perambulations articulate a vision for social change or a philosophy of hope and imagination? These questions have been a source of incessant debate among scholars of social movements for decades. The theme of "prefiguration" has played a prominent role in these debates by noting how ideals of a future society are often pre-formatted and foreshadowed through specific modes of organization in the present: "the idea," as the social critic John Holloway has put it, "that the struggle for a different society must create that society through its forms of struggle."[16] The relation between the means and the ends of struggle, between tactical and strategic politics, between instrumental or experimental orientations to process—these have variously inflected understandings about the nature of time, knowledge, intentionality or imagination in activists' experiences of and attitudes toward social change. For the sociologist Marianne Maeckelbergh, for example, activists relate to the future through an orientation that is at once strategic but also experimental and open-ended, such that "practicing prefigurative politics means removing the temporal distinction between the struggle in the present towards a goal in the future; instead, the struggle and the goal, the real and the ideal, become one in the present" and prefiguration "posits a cyclical process of social change, in which means become ends, which in turn become the means to other ends, and so on."[17] For the anthropologist David Graeber, direct action may be similarly understood as "a form of action in which certain means and ends become, effectively, indistinguishable," a form, moreover, that also stands, no matter how tentatively or temporarily, for the immanent autonomy and creativity of collective imagination.[18]

In her important work with radical left activists in Denmark, anthropologist Stine Krøijer engaged anew with the literature on prefigurative politics by offering an original theory of collective action as temporally and materially redistributed agency. For Krøijer, while activist meetings and other direct actions are certainly expressive of an aspirational culture, they cannot be spoken of as foreshadowing the future in any obvious way. Take the case of meetings. For various reasons, including worries regarding police infiltration, security, and trust as well as a practical concern with facilitating consensus, the meetings that Krøijer participated in showcased no obvious direction of intentionality. Rather, most efforts went into warranting certain aesthetics and forms of exchange, including, for example, the gesturing etiquette for signaling agreement, for clarifying technical points, for making procedural comments or blocking decisions.[19] As Krøijer put it, at a meeting, "intentions are not the property of individuals or groups of individuals, but emerge in the particular relational space that the meeting offers."[20] Thus, there is no obvious sense in which meetings prefigure the radical democracy that they aim for, nor even the larger directional process of social change that they are allegedly part of. Rather, a "well-facilitated meeting is a 'figuration' rather than a prefiguration, which in my terminology means that meetings are the way in which the indeterminate (indefinite and uncertain) gain a determinate form."[21]

Meetings and other forms of direct action, such as building camps and designing street performances, operate therefore as complex and ambivalent distributors of sensibility. They choreograph and rearrange agency such that "intentions . . . are distributed and transposed between [human and nonhuman] bodies through different techniques that result in bodies and intentions becoming synchronized without belonging to single persons."[22] For Krøijer, these synchronizations, these concurrent alignments of bodies, are what define the future as a moment of action: "The future is not a future point in time, but a co-present bodily perspective."[23] The orchestration of this distributed and collective body, the style and form of its appearance, as the attention of activists oscillates between gatherings for "active times" and dispersals into "dead times," therefore shapes a theory of collective action as a theory of distributed rhythms.[24]

We are taken with Krøijer's elegant analysis of the styled rhythms of collective action and wish to extend it here to show how the work of assembly is grounded in the material distributions of the sensible afforded by specific urban assemblages and urban rhythms. Through the work of assembling, people in Lavapiés *look for each other* as they *look after one another*; they perform the neighborhood as a territory of attention and attentiveness. As it takes up residence in public space, the assembly weaves webs of care and deploys architectures of listening that modulate and define both its senses and sensibilities. Moreover, as its moves about, the assembly also feels and manipulates the limits of the neighborhood—its confines as a geography of experiment and discovery. There is a good example in the second vignette. Here the interactions between *vecinos* take shape in a fundamentally exploratory mode: they try out their own modalities of engagement, traction, and adhesion, by groping around for possibilities of encounter and dis/connection. They figure it out as they go. Relationships are expressed in a tentative, one could almost say "tempting" mode: a constant flux of calls, interruptions, intermissions, derivations, dislocations, superpositions, invitations, and mis-encounters, through which the work of assembling reticulates the neighborhood. The assembly aggregates and disaggregates through practices of *tâtonnement*, essaying and fumbling one's way through moments of anticipation, gathering, and disappearance. The work of assembling produces the spatial conditions of the neighborhood as a territory of tentativeness, accidents, and surprise. As Henri Lefebvre once put it, one wonders whether such arrangements may not "rhythm time as they do relations": whether the neighborhood that gradually emerges might not do so through surges and swellings of intuition and experimentation.[25]

The politics of the assembly is shaped by this experimental rhythm, this nervousness and candidness, this surging and enveloping of solicitousness and alertness. The assembly installs itself in public space, it grafts on and spreads across the skin of the neighborhood, through networks of awareness and responsiveness: through the difficult work of bringing and holding people together to debate or demonstrate; through the arduous task of keeping minutes, drafting statements, or reciting stanzas, and in doing so providing a public narrative of perdurance and persistence; through the imaginative redesign and redeployment of the layouts and atmospheres of public attention; through the explorations and systems of groping and communication that participants mobilize to reckon with the conjunctural, the serendipitous, or the unanticipated.

With this in mind, we wish to characterize the politics of assembly as a *politics of ambulation*. Ambulation echoes the invocation regularly made at assemblies about caring for the city, at the same time as it enacts an orientation toward uncertainty and unknowability, a concern for bringing unforeseen issues into life. Assemblies function as political ambulatories: assemblages that are ambulant or capable of moving, as well as capable of delivering care to outpatients or outside residents. Assemblies walk around the city—they ambulate across its landscapes— and in so doing furnish its environs with systems of sentience and concern. This is what Gilles Deleuze and Félix Guattari referred to when comparing the "royal sciences" to the "ambulant or itinerant sciences."[26] The ideal of the royal sciences, they argued, is that "of reproduction, deduction, or induction.... One is constantly reterritorializing around a point of view," whereas with the ambulant sciences "one is in search of the 'singularities' of a matter, or rather of a material, and ... the process of deterritorialization constitutes and extends the territory itself."[27] There is a bricolage of mediums, soundscapes, and embodiments—a bricolage of fumbling apprenticeships (as we further elaborate in part 4)—through which assembling gathers urban traction and finds its way. Assemblies, in sum, operate as shapeshifters for the city, as they ambulate and sound out the limits and affordances of shared insights and horizons.

Although most assemblies had specialized task forces, which often varied according to the specific needs of a local neighborhood, their work was never constrained by or delimited to particular thematic issues or topics. In Lavapiés, the structural violence and harassment suffered by immigrants was an issue of great concern for the assembly, along with the increasing number of evictions taking place in the neighborhood. These concerns were each taken care of by a dedicated working group. But the assembly was otherwise responsive and attentive to many other issues. In this sense, the assembly's openness to embracing and endorsing new causes displayed a political hospitality that went well beyond narrowly conceived matters of concern or public issues. The assembly dismantled the homology that is so commonly established between issues and publics when thinking of political participation.[28] At the assembly, participants came together not over a common problem but over a *common sense*: an attentive solicitousness to what was happening in the neighborhood—a state of being that took the form of an anticipatory preoccupation with city life.

Thus understood, the politics of ambulation gently displaces the locus of political action. Ambulation signals the moment when politics undergoes tension in anticipation of its "public" appearance. This is a politics that surfaces ahead of its recognition as a matter of concern, before issues are aired in public and streets are occupied—a politics whose "figuration of the future," as Krøijer would put it, takes place through a material redistribution of the sensible across the cityscape.[29] The ambulation of the assembly describes the efforts invested in anticipating issues that remain unknown and problems that are not even guessed, a hopeful expectation that thrusts the assembly into a readiness toward the not-yet. It outlines a politics of itinerancy and *pre-occupation*, a vectorial assemblage of nomadism and care. The assembly's pre-occupation is not a concern proper (a preoccupation) but rather a mode of engaging with the city in a state of solicitousness for what is yet to come (a pre-occupation, a prefiguration of other possible modes of inhabiting the city). Such is the assembly's common sense: a prognosis that emerges from its material navigation of everyday urban affairs. As such, ambulation assemblages a regime of perceptibility and a sensory organ for the city.

We have long understood the assertion of Bruno Latour, that before a thing is granted existence as a matter of fact it must be first brought into existence as a matter of concern; the ontology of the political is a tireless exercise in heterogenous composition.[30] We have also learned from the inspiring work of María Puig de la Bellacasa how the sustenance of any matter of concern is in effect subtended by attachments and affects holding it dearly as a matter of care.[31] The politics of ambulation, we wish to suggest, shows us another subtle displacement: before a concern comes (in)to matter or an issue is brought into light, we must be touched and moved first. Said somewhat differently, before a matter of concern is brought into existence, a *matter of sense* needs always to be assembled.

Matters of sense offer a different point of entry into the politics of consensus long posited as a central pillar of direct democracy. We have offered here a description of assembly whereby consensus stands not just for a common agreement on issues or for the common construction of problems. Rather, the assembly/assemblage of consensus stands for the material distribution of a common sense, the delineation of a shared regime of perceptibility, as the etymological origin of the word *con-sensus* indicates: a horizon and a landscape for feeling and intuiting together. In this guise, the occupation of plazas or street demonstrations do not serve only as expressions of direct action in public space. They are that, but they are also material redistributions of the city's sensibilities. Assemblies deploy themselves as sensory organons for the urban condition. They are political ambulatories—a mode of accompaniment, a mode of attention, and a mode of responsiveness toward the city.

Part 4
BRICOLAGES OF APPRENTICESHIPS

Aurora Adalid has been a friend and intellectual partner for almost a decade. In spring 2019, we sat down with Aurora on a couple of occasions to interview her about some of the most personal aspects of her career as an architect. By then, we had written texts together, jointly organized workshops and given seminar presentations, and worked together to design an ambitious open-source platform for urban pedagogies.[1] While there were aspects about her career that we wished to cast some light on, we also relished the opportunity to talk with her and reflect on the nesting and convergence of our shared interests and itineraries. Aurora had recently registered to study for a postgraduate degree in anthropology, partly inspired by our work together. We were eager to collaborate in thinking through this situated interlacing of architecture and anthropology in order to imagine possibilities and trajectories for the systems of reckoning-with that had brought a generation of guerrilla architectural collectives into close conversation with anthropologists, cultural mediators, and hackers.

Aurora was in her mid-thirties when we first met in 2012. Back then she was going through a difficult time personally, in part provoked by the cultural arrogance, machismo, and conservativism of the architectural profession in Spain. Aurora's love for architecture was at once tumultuous and ambivalent. When she was in her teens, she had imagined herself as a conservation biologist or ecologist. She remembers vividly the day when her preference switched to architecture: "My mother used to regret not being able to spend more time with my younger siblings. I was on the bus one day, reading Kleinbaum's adaptation of *Dead Poets Society*, ruminating about the whole 'take control of your life' thing, when it suddenly struck me that reconciling a family life with the commitments of biological fieldwork would in all likelihood not prove easy."[2] In this light, the prospects of an architectural practice seemed more manageable, not least because, in her imagination, architecture still offered a venue for environmental activism.

Aurora's commitment to architecture has since remained expansive and embracing. In her first year at architectural school, she registered for an undergraduate degree in contemporary humanities at the Universidad Nacional de Educación a Distancia (Spain's Open University), joined a theater class, and also founded a magazine, *Boutade*, "which I feel a little embarrassed about today—it was all-encompassing, we broached every topic, from poetry to graphic design, literature, architecture—yet [it] somehow offered me an expressionist outlet of sorts, a way of getting out all the energy that was boiling inside."[3] She would also often drop by local *copisterías* (small photocopying shops where university students leave and share their lecture notes for others to photocopy) and pick up copies of class notes from students in sociology or agronomy.

With her friends from Madrid's School of Architecture (ETSAM), Aurora would often meet for drinks and work in the house basement of one of them: an underground hangout of sorts (*zulo* in Spanish) that would in time come to designate the group itself. On their way to the zulo, they would travel across the city on the underground, each carrying their own computer workstation on their laps, flamboyantly nerdy and maverick all at once. At the zulo they first started experimenting with systems of collaborative work. Challenging traditional expectations of coursework at the ETSAM, they would often submit collectively authored assignments under the name of Zuloark. This offered them an opportunity to be more expansive, more daring, more audacious. "We would build much bigger scale models, or far more detailed ones, or we would submit beautifully colored maps. Or use the opportunity to turn a conceptual proposition inside out."[4] If asked to design a council housing project for a low-income population on the outskirts of the city, they would, for instance, redefine the problem of "housing" or "periphery" in terms of universal basic income, rent strikes, or immigration. Only then, once these premises had been justified theoretically, would they work up to outline an urban and architectural proposition. Some professors insisted on individually authored submissions, in which case members of the group would always add Zuloark to their surnames (Aurora Adalid-Zuloark), to underscore that all work was always and everywhere collectively coauthored. Working collaboratively, they produced files that could be easily distributed among the members of the collective, generally in the form of CDs. Perhaps not unsurprisingly, in time they found that copies of those CDs, or copies of the files of plans, sketches, or renders therein contained, found their way into the hands of other students (in junior years or different classrooms). Did this bother them? "Not at all. In fact, it felt rewarding to see people getting high grades for work that was—at least in part—your own! We were so tired of the culture of possessiveness and authorial integrity at the school. It was deplorable. Some students would use green biros [pens] for taking notes in class, making them no good for photocopying!"[5]

Over time, the practice of distributed authorship and collaboration became one of Zuloark's trademarks. In 2001, while still at university, the friends made a bold decision: they pooled resources and moved their zulo to a rented flat in Atocha Street, in the heart of Madrid's old historic quarter. It was an old and decadent, almost ruinous space. With large halls and ample rooms, it offered an ideal venue for students to set up their drawing tables and their workstations, their scale models and their installations. The space remained open for anyone to drop by and use. The atmosphere at Atocha was vibrant, collegial, and joyful. In the evenings, people came by after school for drinks, sometimes sleeping over. During the day, the space blossomed with activity, with people working together on class projects, painting, cooking or passionately discussing books or exhibitions. Attending the Medialab's electronic art and digital culture exhibitions, which premiered for the first time in 2002, became an obligatory experience. When an exhibition by videoartist Pipilotti Rist opened at the Reina Sofia Museum in 2001, her work became a constant topic of conversation at Atocha; Aurora confessed to us, "We organized some four or five trips to see it." The technical habitats of digital culture permeated the aesthetics and pragmatics of an incipient form of cultura libre architecture.

In 2004, the journal *Quaderns*, published by the Catalan Architectural Association, announced a competition for building four hundred thousand homes in three different Catalan municipalities (Salt, Amposta, and Barcelona). A group of people at the Atocha studio conspired to submit three projects, one for each site. It was an audacious proposal. The group lacked a formal structure: it was neither legally incorporated nor registered as an architectural studio. It was not even identifiable as a "group" as such: people moved in and out of the flat, sometimes attaching themselves to a project, sometimes disappearing without notice. But the energy was unstoppable. There was a friendly attunement of skills and crafts, a sympathetic consilience of visions and imaginaries. Submitted under the name of Zuloark, the proposals took the first prize in two out of the three competitions, to the surprise and delight of the Atocha community.

The competition brought instant national notoriety to Zuloark. They began getting small asks and commissions: curating exhibitions, providing graphic design capacities for larger and more prestigious studios, speaking at regional architectural associations, and so on. More important, it obliged the group to confront its own organizational form: what kind of entity was Zuloark? By then, several people had already graduated and obtained employment at established studios. For them, Zuloark was an after-work project, which enabled a certain amount of slack in how the group's resources and capacities were used. For example, it allowed the group to retain its networked informality and build on the synergies afforded by such a labile association of skills and talents. Such a form further allowed the group to preserve a distinctive cultural orientation to collective and distributed authorship, free intellectual property licenses, and the embrace of multiple and networked identities.

When the financial crisis hit Spain in 2008, with devastating economic and social consequences, the field of architecture took a massive blow. Architecture studios closed en masse. Zuloark's latticed structure proved surprisingly resilient, as they tactically realigned their capacities and resources in acupunctural and ad hoc collaborations with NGOs and development organizations, museums and art centers, schools and neighborhood associations, as well as affinal groups such as Basurama, Todo por la Praxis, Pez Estudio, Vivero de Iniciativas Ciudadanas (VIC), and PKMN. These were precarious and hardly sustainable arrangements, but through their grassroots abilities at shapeshifting and reinvention these *colectivos de arquitectura* (architecture collectives), as they were now called, suddenly became iconic references amid a landscape of architectural ruins.

It is significant that the sudden protagonism of the *colectivos* placed under the limelight practices that had long been pushed to the margins of the discipline. In 2009, the Zuloark members were appointed assistant curators of the Spanish Biennal of Architecture and Urbanism. In 2010, the members of Basurama were appointed curators of Madrid's White Night. Yet the spotlight came at a price, too, as Aurora explained to us: "I remember sitting next to this gentlemanly architect, well into his sixties, who upon hearing I was one of the assistant curators of the biennal turned to me with wondrous eyes and asked, 'Oh, well, so tell me, what have you *built*?'"[6]

The shadow of edification and construction has loomed large over the definition of architecture as a professional practice in Spain for most part of the twentieth century. "At the School of Architecture of Madrid," Aurora told us once, "people would say that 'if you're good, you're good, and if you aren't, you end up doing urbanism instead (*quien vale, vale, y quien no, a urbanismo*).'" The debate about what is and what is not architecture troubled Aurora for many years, especially since her own interest in the discipline was sparked by her sensibility toward environmental issues. Yet this was not simply a question about how to conceptualize architecture as an intellectual or logistical operation. At stake were much deeper issues regarding the modes of comportment and attention, the cultures of listening and engagement through which architects conducted themselves in the world:

> In the aftermath of the financial and economic crisis we were often asked to give talks at architectural schools around the country. All of a sudden, people seemed interested in our "model" or "solution" to the practice of architecture. And inexorably, someone would always raise their hand to protest that our practice didn't really count as architecture. More poignantly, at these and other forums, it quickly dawned on me that the mode of justification of one's arguments, the mode of delivering an idea, needed to be loud, accelerated, sharp, and authoritative. There was no time and no space to take stock of a question, to think about it, to problematize it. Let alone to doubt, to not know. And invariably it was always men, who rushed to occupy such positions, to raise their voices, to have an answer, always have an answer, to whatever was being asked.[7]

Slowly, Aurora decided to take a step back. The arrogance, the vociferousness, the spectacular virility of it all, was too much. She temporarily left the collective and took refuge at home. In this context of partial seclusion, Aurora returned to the perennial question of "What is architecture?" and pondered about the registers and formats through which architecture, as she put it to us, "has organized its modes of presentation to the world":

> Architects have a fondness for Charters and Manifestos, even Agendas, that function as sites of enunciation where problems are stated as circumscriptions, and as such, they can only become smaller and smaller, once you know how to zoom in on them. My experience was different. I zoom in on a problem only to discover that it gets bigger and bigger, that there are another twenty-five problems, another twenty-five voices that I must listen to and reckon with. So, I said to myself, "Perhaps what we need is a Declaration, a space for declaring, for people to state their worries and concerns, where the conjoining of all these voices hints where we might need to look next."[8]

Aurora thus conceived of a Universal Declaration of Urban Rights and immediately began working on it.[9] In her travels around the country she would roam a city's streets videotaping people's answers to three very concise questions: (1) What urban rights are worth protecting? (2) What urban rights are worth fighting for? (3) What urban rights ought to be eliminated? She opened a blog where she uploaded every interview. Very quickly she realized, however, that the technical infrastructure of the blog did a very poor job of coping with the scope and scale of the project, in particular the many possibilities afforded for organizing, tagging, and visualizing the interview materials. Aurora decided then to learn coding in order to build her own digital infrastructure. It was an exhilarating experience. She built mockups for the project's website and joined coding forums where she tested and discarded different frameworks and designs. Here she unexpectedly found a new language to talk about the city, a semantics and an ontology that cared little for "buildings" or "public space" because they enabled an expansion of the nuances, inflections, and associations through which people described and redescribed their urban concerns.

During our interviews, Aurora often drew a parallel between her apprenticeship as a web programmer and Zuloark's initial involvement, in the aftermath of the economic crisis, with art centers and cultural mediators, as well as her discovery of anthropology through our work together:

> This narrowmindedness about "What is architecture?" has long bothered me because it defines an inside and outside to the discipline, and I constantly find myself inhabiting a line of dispersion and centrifugality. It took me a long time to realize that the problem wasn't that I was "disperse," or that the regions I inhabited were regions of dispersion, but that people had largely taken for granted what the "center" ought to be. And this is a lesson, I think, that all of us at Zuloark have since learned: that we must do our best to redefine a problem of design in terms of the amplitude of its dispersion. We need to open the margins of design, to constantly interrogate their limits. Take anthropology. When one of my lecturers showed me his fieldwork diaries, this sprawling and never-ending register of vignettes, details and relations, my mind was blown away. It resembled so much how I myself had been taking notes about the city, about the ecologies of architecture. And yet I had always been told that such notes were "untranslatable," that they had no use, that they were dispersions. It turns out they are not. Turns out that some problems require other descriptions, different organizations of form. And that you have to think hard in each case about how you are going to organize collectively as a system of apprenticeships to reckon with those emerging forms (*cómo idear formas de poner en común y seguir siendo escuela entre nosotros*).[10]

Part 4 takes as its point of inspiration Aurora's concern for nascent systems of apprenticeships. In chapter 8 we follow closely in the steps of the guerrilla architectural collectives Basurama and Zuloark, which were described earlier in the book but whose work now takes center stage as we pay close attention to their practices of auto-construction, which function as methods for both building and navigating social and material relations in contexts of precarity and periphery and as recursive models for designing habitats and inhabiting modes of grappling-with. In close dialogue with our architect friends, we put forward the notion of *bricolages of apprenticeships*, a meditation on the recursive materiality of learning and its implications for both the city and social theory: What infrastructural, operational, or archival resources hold our fields together as sites of praxis, mutuality, and returning hermeneutics? What arts of bricolage and installation are involved in thinking the city together?

We draw the book to a close by revisiting some of the questions we posed in the introduction. We return to some of the elements of the history of Spain's transition to democracy in the 1970s, and by reworking them through the book's long ethnographic passage, we articulate a humble caution against recent transitional approaches to sustainable futures. Drawing a parallel between the skepticism of the 1970s neighborhoods movement toward the transitional arrangements of post-Francoist democratization and that of the free culture movement toward the so-called Culture of the Transition, we open up a space for imagining the contours of a modest theory of intransitive urbanism, one driven less toward transitional aims than toward intransitive becomings.

AUTO-CONSTRUCTION REDUX

"A monumental tool," someone suggested. "Hundreds of pages long," someone else noted. "The Processgram," a third person finally concluded, while providing a description that functioned as both nomenclature and mythical signature. It must have been 2011 or 2012 when I (Alberto) first heard these words, and the images they evoked have stayed with me over the years. I was mesmerized. It had never occurred to me that guerrilla architectural collectives might have developed a project management tool with the ability to register every action, every bifurcation, every photograph and drawing and sketch, every failure and insight garnered during a community project. At once a self-made archive and a social design interface, an organizational program and an urban directory, here was a tool that architects were using for auto-constructing the city (for building social and material relations) at the same time as they auto-constructed their methods.

The project in question was Autobarrios (literally, Auto-neighborhoods), a social community initiative led by the guerrilla architectural collective Basurama in San Cristóbal de los Ángeles, one of Madrid's poorest and most disenfranchised neighborhoods.[1] First initiated by Juan López Aranguren and Sarah Fernández Deutsch, the former a member of Basurama who had himself grown up in the community, the project signaled a departure from the collective's history of participatory and critical art interventions. On the cusp of the financial crisis, Aranguren took on the project when the very existence of Basurama was under threat. The art and architectural collective, which only a year back had curated Madrid's White Night (the preeminent summer arts festival in the city), was undergoing a profound personal, economic, and professional crisis. Basurama had measured up to the challenge of curating the event with a sardonic yet constructive proposition for engaging the ludic pulsations of capital—and of the capital. "Place Your Bets!," as they called the festival, took residence in the city's main arteries and public spaces by employing trash and discarded materials (the signature of Basurama's artwork) in the transformation of the cityscape into a gigantic open-air playground and amusement park. The installations thus built were designed to be dismantled and recycled for future use in the auto-construction of urban equipment in peripheral and marginal communities in Madrid's hinterland (see figures 13 and 14). However, the responsibility for curat-

FIGURE 13.   Giant swing, "The White Night," September 2010. Photo by Zuloark is licensed under CC BY-SA 4.0: https://creativecommons.org/licenses /by-sa/4.0/.

FIGURE 14.   Giant swing recycled at El Gallinero, December 2010. Photo by Zuloark is licensed under CC BY-SA 4.0: https://creativecommons.org/licenses /by-sa/4.0/.

ing White Night—a symbol, if there ever was one, of the "process of branding-based urban regeneration . . . [that is] complicit in the neoliberal attitude to the city" that characterized the architecture of spectacle and capital of recent Spanish urbanization—had split the collective.[2] Taking place in September 2010, just as the first wave of the financial crisis had sunk in and the miracle bubble of the Spanish real estate economy burst, Basurama's playful romance with the economics of desire drew little sympathy and took far too many punches, not least from radical and countercultural collectives, who viewed Basurama's involvement as a disappointing sellout to the seductions of capital. The city placed its bets and knocked Basurama out. In the event's aftermath, some members left the collective while others took a break and those remaining faced a glum horizon of precarity and depression. In this context, Aranguren set out to San Cristóbal with a project that was part therapy, part desperation, part calling. Autobarrios was conceived as a free-fall immersion into the conditions that shape autonomy as a practical design and political challenge in contexts of marginalization—where the use of the *auto* label gestured to the vague promises of both community and material self-emancipation.

As it happens, we never got to see the Processgram, although we encountered different versions of it over the following five years. Yet even though we never saw the object, we became party to the method. The method Basurama developed for Autobarrios became an important practice for their work elsewhere, in abandoned sites and vacant lots, working in collaboration with schools and neighborhood associations, in partnership with cultural institutions, other architectural collectives, or indeed academics such as ourselves. The method seemed to travel widely. Over time, however, we came to question this perception of the method as a traveling object. There seemed to be too much method everywhere. What if it was not the method itself that traveled as much as a particular cultural sensorium and material aesthetic? What if it was an emerging *climate of methods* that one encountered everywhere—and method was an infrastructure of feeling for the city?[3]

The story of Autobarrios is the story of how the struggles for autonomy in the city, which, as described in part 1, had been modulated since the 1990s by intermediations and contestations over the nature of infrastructural sovereignty, the thresholds of the neighborhood as a social territory, and the role and extent of the state's involvement in grassroots initiatives, gradually shifted toward the bricolage of collective action as a problem of method and apprenticeships. In particular, a concern for the autonomy of methods themselves became articulated in the language of "auto-construction."[4] Partly inspired by a tradition of grassroots urbanism and partly a reelaboration of the legacy of autonomy and *autogestión* in a material idiom, the language and method of auto-construction became a placeholder for the way in which grassroots projects thought and felt and grabbed hold of the city as a horizon of hope and responsibility, of intimacy and action. At a time of crisis and desperation, auto-construction provided a faithful and intuitive idiom for movements of aspiration and autonomy, for shifting (terra)formations of impatience and capability, for eclectic and wilding investigations into and out from the material depths of precarity. These manifold projects spoke about a city that accrued and proliferated through various languages, media, and interfaces of description; through archives, archaeologies, and technologies that deposited but also helped visualize and trace its memories and hopes; and through systems of apprenticeships, guesswork, and assay that exfoliated its various nervous systems. Auto-construction surfaced and circulated as a habitus and a habitat—an infrastructure and a sensory organ—for an experience of living-with and living-along in Madrid.

Auto-Dazzle

The story of Don Antonio is one we must have heard told dozens of times over the past years. Don Antonio is set in his ways. Now in his seventies and retired, he wakes up early in the morning and enjoys opening the doors of his balcony, which he leaves open for the remainder of the day. The soundscapes and breezes of the city visit his home, bringing along the gaiety and liveliness of a downtown location in Madrid's historic quarter. There are the sounds of motorbikes roaring past, of children shouting, of the maneuvering of bulky trucks offloading their cargo just opposite Don Antonio's building, at the popular market of la Cebada. Occasionally the rhythms and intonations of a musical performance or a theatrical play make their way into Don Antonio's living room. However, if the volume is too high, Don Antonio picks up his cell phone and calls Manuel, who will gently ask the actors or the sound mixers to quiet down their performance.

This is a story we have heard Manuel tell time and time again. Manuel was first mentioned in chapter 5, as one of the founders of the open-source archival platform Inteligencias Colectivas. Manuel is a member of the guerrilla architectural collective Zuloark, which was first involved, alongside local neighborhood associations, artists, activists, shopkeepers, and schools, in the transformation of a derelict and vacant open-air site in the heart of the La Latina neighborhood into a self-managed community project. We talk more about the story of this community space, locally known as El Campo de Cebada, later in the chapter.

The story of Don Antonio's relationship with the city is one that Manuel has recounted in front of multiple and variegated audiences. We have witnessed him dramatize the story before hundreds of people in an architectural salon at Madrid's Guild of Architects. We have also seen him deliver wonderfully colorful versions of the anecdote at various meetings with municipal delegates and policymakers. We have seen him rehearse an impassioned and charismatic version at a meeting of activists at a squatted social center and produce slightly different versions for talks at cultural centers and museums. He has also retold the story on camera for a video documentary, and of course he has staged endless similar performances for friends and colleagues. The story also exists in print, in texts that Zuloark has written for architectural journals and magazines and design portfolios the collective has submitted when competing for industry prizes and awards.

For Manuel, the story of Don Antonio exemplifies how grassroots community projects must continuously adjust and reproblematize the designs of method. In the case of El Campo de Cebada, this is shown in the collective's design of an ecology that attends to the interests and concerns of neighboring residents, including Don Antonio's particular sensibility toward the acoustics of the vicinity.[5] Members of El Campo will often say that theirs is an approach that *habita la controversia*, that does not shy away from dwelling in controversy, and that calls, correspondingly, for designs that inhabit every problem. In this light, Don Antonio's story rehearses many of the narratives and tropes that have become common in the classic literature on urban auto-construction: about the inventiveness, resilience, and resourcefulness of urban relations and their ability to operate under the radar of standardized market or state practices by sounding out horizons of mutual feeling and complicity, circuits of give and take that consolidate—sometimes erratically, sometimes fleetingly, yet also sometimes sustainably—spaces of convergence and productivity.

Yet there is another, complementary transcript to Don Antonio's story, which has circulated widely, in a variety of media forms, registers, and venues, as a story about methods; it is about the auto-construction of these methods but also about the method of auto-construction more broadly. Moreover, this story is only one of many other stories and anecdotes told about emerging experiments in auto-construction elsewhere in the city (such as the Autobarrios project with which we opened this chapter). Therefore, in print and in auditoriums, in public oratory and private conversation, these stories seem to function as both vehicles and anchors for an infrastructure of feeling for the city. The circulation of auto-construction as story, as metaphor, and as method surfaces as a distinctive and consequential economy and repertoire of urban skills, senses, and sensibilities. Borrowing a term from the urbanist AbdouMaliq Simone, we may say that auto-construction is slowly and gradually taking shape as a "perceptual system" for the city, a sensory organ that functions at once as an economy of attention and an economy of resources and that finds tentative anchorage in the city as a method for other methods. In short, it is a platform of stories that become methods and methods that become stories, quietly mixing and remixing them as bricolages of apprenticeships.[6]

Therefore, as we use it here the concept of auto-construction undergoes an important conceptual migration: from its original use in designating self-help housing in the Global South (auto-construction as object) to more recent usages signaling the inventiveness and resourcefulness of self-organized initiatives (auto-construction as process) and then to our proposal for thinking of auto-construction as a platform of inquiry, exploration, and grappling-with. In justifying such a transition, we set up a conversation with the comparative literature on urban auto-construction. We are aware that this is a risky strategy. The literature on auto-construction in the Global South is often a far cry from the community projects in political autonomy and democratic experimentation that we reported on in this book. There is a vast expanse between the cultural geographies and political economies of the peripheries of the urban South and Madrid's own vectors of peripheralization. Yet we believe the comparison is one worth pursuing because of what it can teach us about the status of social scientific methods today, and in particular about the consequences of their co-inhabiting—along with grassroots, autonomous, and indigenous methods—complex worlds of partial and interdependent descriptions. The literature on auto-construction has proven exquisitely attentive to the insightful and resourceful ways through which people furnish environments of desire and anticipation, action and existence, for themselves. In this sense, it has equipped us with a certain sensibility for unpacking how people's urban navigations function simultaneously as methods for questioning and experimenting, opening up new vistas on how the city auto-constructs its own worlds-in-analysis.

This interest in the mutual and recursive auto-construction of the city and analysis is one of our central propositions. We are interested in the perspective of auto-construction as a material metaphor for rendering visible how analysis itself is auto-constructed. We want to bring this book's foregoing reflections on the culture of prototyping—its methods in speculative solidarity and its experiments in collaborative concept work—to bear on some long-standing debates about the nature of the urban question.[7]

Despite some noteworthy and innovative proposals for making explicit "the strange language of urbanization," the fact remains that most recent urban theory has done little to explicate its own moments of articulation.[8] The nature of the empirical remains mostly unproblematized, and it is only the adequateness of this or that body of theory that has been highlighted for discussion. Thus, to this day, investigations into how the urban is rendered visible as method and field site remain conspicuously absent from the literature. The relation between the field as empirical site and the field as theoretical project remains largely hidden and unexplored. We have come to naturalize scholarly accounts as speaking *about* a place (geographical or epistemic), paying little or no attention to how such places must themselves be drawn together as empirical and pragmatic problems. The empirical problems of this or that place cover up the very operation of problematization as method.

Our proposal for using auto-construction as a heuristic centers on the concept's specific (recursive) twinning of method and theory. Auto-construction offers an image for understanding how empirical problems are auto-constructed into situated theories and theoretical navigations. More often than not, these theoretical designs are premised on a dynamic and collaborative accompaniment of inquiry that, as we have seen throughout the book, enlists local communities, researchers, multiple media, and mediators, working with and across a variety of genres and aesthetics of description.[9] Such pragmatic and inventive exercises in design and construction also render visible the nature of the city as a problem of method. That is, the city is a method—of designs, problematizations, and analyses—in constant auto-construction.[10]

The literature on urban auto-construction provides an especially poignant place for exploring these issues because it has traditionally been framed as a reservoir of cultural ingenuity and resilience. Auto-construction has provided scholars with an apparently natural metaphor for sociocultural creativity, thus justifying subsequent claims to analytical and theoretical invention. There is a wonderful passage in Marilyn Strathern's well-known reflection on "the ethnographic moment" that captures this slippage beautifully, noting how our capacity for ethnographic description is often preempted by our (Euro-American) expectations concerning what counts as an epistemic effect in the first place.[11] One "could refer to it as auto-dazzle," Strathern says, adding, "Knowledge involves creativity, effort, production; it loves to uncover creativity, effort, production!" Scholars are intent on staging the products of research in terms of "discovery and re-discovery," where our capacity to reveal something mirrors the "revelatory practices" that we encounter in the field itself.[12] We might say that the care with which we construct our ethnographic descriptions aims at dazzling (surprising, persuading, mystifying) our readers in terms symmetrical to how those moments of surprise took hold of us in the ethnographic encounter. And yet, as Roy Wagner long cautioned us, we should do well to avoid equating our understandings of surprise with our interlocutors' surprises with understanding.[13] Such symmetry is itself problematic and should not be taken at face value, for otherwise we risk falling in love, as Strathern puts it, with our own anticipations of consequence.

Auto-Construction

In his now-classic article on auto-construction, the anthropologist James Holston introduced the concept as a heuristic for thinking about the complex dynamics that subtend processes of peripheral urbanization in Brazil.[14] These processes, he noted, are at once capitalist- and state-driven, for through the process of building their homes, the inhabitants of peripheral and informal communities self-fashion a seemingly paradoxical type of political subjectivity for themselves as at once rights holders *and* consumer citizens: home building becomes for them an arena for the contestation and struggle over entitlements and rights to home ownership (and the matrix of public services and infrastructures wherein these are located, such as water sanitation, sewage, and so forth). It also becomes a template for drawing on and expressing a wide array of consumer desires and aesthetics, for example, in matters of interior decoration or material culture. The vitality of auto-construction—the desideratum that the house incarnates as a life project, the vibrancy and energetics of family and community commitments that underwrite it and the space of political urgency and fundamental needs that it indexes—protrudes into the political landscape of the modernist city, which otherwise crumbles and falls to pieces in the background. Self-built and auto-constructed, the city-yet-to-come advances, encroaching on, if not wholly in defiance of, the fatuous landscapes of modernity. The destruction and the auto-construction of the city as theory: few concepts can say so much with so little.

While originally deployed to describe a specific modality of housing projects in developing countries, auto-construction has today become very much a staple of urban theory.[15] From do-it-yourself urban designs to self-help housing, from community architectural projects to open-source urban infrastructures, from the right to the city to the right to infrastructure, auto-construction has become a sine qua non of the descriptive repertoire and analytical vocabulary of the informal city, if not its most promissory and fertile conceptual reservoir.[16] Under one guise or another, the literature on auto-construction has borne witness to the birth and rebirth of the city time and again: as a source of vitality and improvisation; of skill, craft, and tacit knowledge; of political acuity and community values; of autonomy and resistance; of resilience and resourcefulness; of perseverance, defiance, and irreductibility. Auto-construction and its proxies have been used to map and trace manifold topologies of epistemic overflow, where technical, environmental, and political relations fly below the radar of market and state practices or generate unsuspected, and yet productive, displacements and reconfigurations between them. They have provided a conceptual sensibility for framing the messy entanglements of material energies, affective relations, political capacities, and social creativity that make up city life.

There is a specific geopolitical history, however, to our contemporary state of fascination with the informal, the energetic, and the auto-constructed. In a recent and important piece on "slum as theory," the urbanist Vyjayanthi Rao has taken issue with some of the epistemological assumptions underlying the way in which we have come to grasp the urban condition.[17] "What," she asks, "counts as knowledge of the urban?"[18] She lays out her argument through a critical engagement with Mike Davis's well-known essay on the planetary urbanism of slums.[19] Davis's work has been criticized for presenting an apocalyptic and dystopian vision of urban development, where the reality of empire, global capital, and neoliberalism condemn a "surplus humanity," in Davis's disturbing formulation, to a future of misery, disease, crime, and desperation.[20] Apropos of auto-construction, Davis dedicates one chapter of his 2006 book *Planet of Slums* to criticizing what he calls the "illusions of self-help" that informed the World Bank's philosophical and programmatic approach to housing policies starting in the 1970s.[21] He traces the World Bank's vision to the ideas of the English anarchist architect John Turner who, after living in the squatter settlements of Lima from 1957 to 1965, developed an understanding of community self-organization and autonomy that led to various writings and proposals defending self-building as a policy alternative—so-called sites and services programs designed to provide land and basic infrastructural services that people would occupy to develop their own housing projects.[22] Yet while, for Davis, this "amalgam of anarchism and neoliberalism" [23] did little but legitimate the state's retreat as a provider of public services and infrastructure, Turner's work has otherwise been recuperated as a precursor to a type of activist architecture born out of the experience of Latin American informality that may hold global lessons for all: "If there is one area where Latin American experience contains a global lesson . . . it is its attitude to the informal city. What do we mean by 'informal'? The short answer is slums . . . [which] are far from chaotic. They may lack essential services, yet they operate under their own self-regulating systems."[24]

The Latin American slum thus stands as a metonym of entrepreneurial pragmatism—optimist, extrovert, hands-on—operating as an epistemic space: "active forms: systems, networks, connections, infrastructure—all of these are more important arguably than the dumb object-housing of the modernists."[25] Indeed, what draws Rao herself to the debate is the way in which Davis deploys the slum as a theoretical construct whose geographical and historical axes rest "upon the 'city of the South' as its proxy subject. A new understanding of the global emerges by situating the spaces of these cities at the epicenter of a certain catastrophic appetite of global capital flows and turning those spaces into a new territorial principle of order."[26] In its place, Rao offers an alternative theoretical figuration for the slum, where rather than a proxy for locating the pressure zones of empire and capital, the "slum becomes an epistemological shorthand for tracking the cracks . . . and for locating the mutations of the modern state."[27]

Slum as theory, slum as pragmatism: have we moved from the slum as an aftershock of capital to the slum as the auto-dazzle of theory?

Auto-Peripheries

As described in part 3, on May 15, 2011, following a public demonstration over the political management of the economic crisis, a group of protesters set up an encampment at Madrid's Puerta del Sol, the city's historic central square, which in a matter of days grew into a complex infrastructure and social movement, in due time transforming the nature of municipal politics in the city. The image of the encampment—rugged, provisional, auto-constructed—circulated around the globe and became an emblem of the Spanish 15M movement. The encampment organized itself into a "city in miniature," as people were fond of saying. It provided temporary food and shelter for the encampment; there was a kitchen and a refectory, a nursery, and a library, as well as an open-source infrastructure of solar panels and wireless networks. Protesters came together in a variety of assemblies and working groups to deal with matters such as long-term politics, feminism, a respect and care commission, and a task force dedicated to curating and preserving the movement's archives. Methodologies popped up everywhere—for assembling, for mediating conflicts, for cultivating the hospitality of strangers.

Having taken residence in the very geographical and political heart of the Spanish state, from day one the encampment faced up to its eventual dismantling and worked toward its future reappearance in more than a hundred popular assemblies across Madrid's neighborhoods. Therefore, when the encampment finally came down, a month into the inaugural occupation, it was the energy of this auto-peripheralization—a proliferation of assemblies, squatted social centers, urban community orchards, and commons networks across the city's hinterland—that took over and kept the momentum. As we described in chapters 6 and 7: the peripheries took center stage and resumed the work of—nurtured the capacity for—ambulation and self-peripheralization.

In her recent writings on subaltern urbanism, Ananya Roy has suggested that social theory may be at risk of fetishizing the slum as an epistemic and topological vector, noting how the metonym of the slum has become a conceptual reservoir from which to justify speaking of both "self-organizing economies of entrepreneurialism" and the "habitus of the dispossessed."[28] The slum, as Roy rightly observes, has become a dazzle for theory, which is why she calls for developing a more nuanced and subtle heuristics of subalternity, including an appeal to thinking with and across the zones of exception, gray spaces, and processes of urban informality inhabiting the interstices of the territorial, juridical, and legal/lethal regimes of capital and state sovereignty. One such other notion is the periphery, which, following AbdouMaliq Simone,[29] Roy defines as both "a space in the making and a form of making theory."[30]

We are taken by Roy's "intervention in the epistemologies and methodologies of urban studies."[31] Her outlining of the metonymic cul-de-sacs that slum urbanism has got us into is most pertinent and valuable. But let us pause for a moment to consider her focus on the periphery as heuristic. In the double sense that Roy attributes to the term—that is, as designating both a geographic and an epistemic space—we take it that the promise the periphery might hold for description lies in the fact that the two types of space (the geographic and the epistemic) do not, in fact, wholly coincide. The periphery, as we see it, is what holds both descriptive spaces together and, simultaneously, apart. The periphery works as a descriptive and epistemic figure insofar as it can keep the tension in place—such that one can imagine, for instance, what the work of auto-peripheralization might entail.[32] For this reason, we believe it is important to be able to specify under which conditions the periphery as a genre in description can describe the periphery as urban process: how does the operation of problematization for which the periphery stands as heuristic inhabit its field site?

These are questions, we would like to insist, that go to the heart of how social science research takes up residence in a field site—how it draws itself together as an inventive and pragmatic design, how it auto-constructs itself, and therefore how it relates to other methods of auto-construction and exploration. Let us be more specific.

In her deployment of the term as a double heuristic (now geographical territory, now concept), Roy recalls the work of James Holston and Teresa Caldeira, who make use of the ethnographic category *periferia* (periphery) to describe the "settlements of people beyond a city center's perimeter of urbanized and legalized services," which are characteristic of Brazilian urbanization.[33] The periphery does not signal a stable territorial demarcation but rather a shifting geo-epistemic operator: it is a dynamic vector that indexes the "relations of mutual dependence—a social production and circulation of space—in which centers and peripheries each define the other through an apparatus of domination . . . comprising political, legal, social, economic and infrastructural components whose interrelations constantly change. As a result, peripheries *as both place and concept* shift in location and meaning through time."[34]

Holston and Caldeira go on to show how urban experiences of peripheries sparked a variety of neighborhood-based social movements and grassroots mobilizations, whose claims and demands helped "mark a decisive moment in the constitution of a new conception of citizenship" in the history of Brazil.[35] Although the processes through which such experiences of what they call "insurgent citizenship" came to the fore were many and complex, the claims that residents have made to the city over time have often been specifically grounded in and through the experience of auto-construction: "Insurgent citizenship depends,"

Holston and Caldeira tell us, "on a sense of self-worth undeniably connected to property ownership and the auto-construction of houses."[36] Auto-construction thus provides a material and volitional locus for the self-expression of the city as an affective and political desideratum.

In his earlier work on auto-construction, however, Holston goes even further in specifying the "aesthetics of auto-construction" that animate and style such expressions of self-worth.[37] According to Holston, the question of aesthetics proves central to understanding the personal investments and challenges that people mobilize when projecting their houses as outward manifestations of their selves and markers of their relations to others. As he puts it, houses are "'good to think' because they channel personal experience into a public idiom, architecture. . . . This idiom is a visual calculus of appearances—a particular style of facade, certain decorations, the display of appliances, a specific finish or material, and so forth— widely intelligible as symbolic notations about self and society, present and future."[38] A crucial dimension of this visual calculus, he observes, relates to the repertoire of aesthetic designs and styles that people draw from to achieve "an intended effect."[39] The goal is to bring to fruition a sense of innovation, to showcase one's mastery of an idiom that will justify general approbation and the recognition that one's house has "personality."[40] One is almost tempted to say that such designs are aimed at dazzling one's neighbors.

Yet if dazzle is much sought after, no little amount of effort goes into controlling the effects of auto-dazzle as well. As Holston notes, it is of utmost importance to avoid imitation and, above everything else, to deflect any hint of suspicion that one may have been copying:

> People usually refuse, to the point of real irritation, to admit that they derive their house designs or decorations from any source other than pure inspiration. Yet, I have seen them exchanging house plans, perusing fashion and home-life magazines, taking field trips to shopping centers and elite neighborhoods, and making careful observations about the upper-class habits and décor presented in TV soap operas. Moreover, they have to use the same construction materials and household goods to make meaningful statements in the sign system of auto-construction. The problem is that they must, and do, avidly copy.[41]

This is why, as Holston underscores, "to question their sources is to tarnish their sense of personal distinction in which they have so heavily invested."[42] This is not, therefore, simply a question about what auto-construction accomplishes or what it stands for. It is not a question about auto-construction as object (housing) or auto-construction as process (self-help, self-organization). Rather, what we see here is how the city advances surreptitiously, as it simultaneously gropes and touts its way through waves of informality and trickery, of seduction and allure, glamor and imitation, production and predation. The city auto-constructs itself as a complex economy of urges and aspirations, a contradictory hide-and-seek of lure and abandonment, desire and affectation that impedes any definitive formalization of what the periphery does to the city or how it works. Here the city serves as "a kind of perceptual system, a way of seeing": an evanescent landscape whose outlines—the tricks and trades of mimesis and camouflage, of splendor or deception—one must constantly learn to see.[43] We may think of auto-construction, therefore, as a sort of auto-heuristics for the city, a device that can help us adumbrate, but also inhabit, the tensions and elisions that we all inevitably encounter between the city's moments of dazzle and our moments of auto-dazzle with the city. This is auto-construction as method.

Auto-Heuristics

Residents of the La Latina neighborhood remember the date of May 15, 2011 (the date of Puerta del Sol's occupation) for a different, if related reason. On that day, a group of neighbors, community activists, and artists took to the streets to occupy three thousand square meters of land that had been lying vacant ever since plans for a sports complex were brought to a halt in the aftermath of the economic crisis.

The reasons for the occupation were celebratory. The neighbors had been granted the management of the space after eight months of negotiations with the departments of Citizen Participation, Inland Revenue, and their local borough representatives from the municipal government. The residents had proven to be swift and perspicacious organizers. Back in September 2010, the government had authorized a makeshift occupation in the context of a weekend cultural festival—the White Night curated by Basurama. With the event over, and the site locked up and abandoned again, some neighbors "found" a copy of the key to the gates fencing in the space.

The festival had proven a success, and it took little imagination for the neighbors to realize the formidable community potential of the vacant lot. They organized an assembly that soon entered into negotiations and concerted action with a variety of neighborhood stakeholders, including the two local neighborhood associations, local schools and shopkeepers, nearby squatted social centers, and a variety of artistic and countercultural collectives. Impressed by the agility of the mobilization, and at any rate with no alternative plans for the site, the municipality agreed to an *acuerdo de cesión temporal* (temporary management permit) for the space.

This was an opportunity not to be missed. The neighbors moved swiftly, in a variety of registers and media. They set up an email distribution list, a Twitter account, and a Facebook page. They experimented with a variety of organizational formats—a Neighborhood Assembly, a Commission for Economic Affairs, and an Operations Commission—as well as a self-branded (if short-lived) hybrid governance structure that included representatives from the municipal government and delegates from the neighborhood assembly.

Within weeks the space acquired strange urban properties: this was a plaza, three thousand square meters in the heart of Madrid's old town no less, that had suddenly become an *espacio público de gestión ciudadana*, a public space managed by citizens. The space had been salvaged by the neighbors, and it proudly displayed the ruggedness and urgency of its salvage methodologies. We do not mean this derisively. On the contrary, El Campo boasted wooden planks and construction materials used by guerrilla architectural collectives in urbanism workshops. Passersby, architecture students, and local neighbors imagined, designed, and made unorthodox pieces of urban equipment later used in community gardening, in book fairs and organic food markets, in theatrical productions by local schools and political rallies by slumbering anarchist formations (see figure 15). El Campo stored paints, brushes, chairs, poly films (polyethylene sheeting), and urban waste with which children improvised playgrounds and battle scenes on its patio, with which scenographers traced the outlines of impossibly

FIGURE 15. Theatrical production at El Campo de Cebada. Photo by El Campo de Cebada is licensed under CC BY-SA 4.0: https://creativecommons.org /licenses/by-sa/4.0/.

allegorical cities, and amid whose forensic archaeologies teenage lovers sought refuge from the violent transparency of the society of control. Salvage methodologies had *liberado el espacio* (liberated the space), as neighbors proudly observed, and turned it into something at once more and less than public space.

On any Sunday morning, coinciding with a flea market next door, hundreds of thousands of people would walk past or into El Campo. The atmosphere was festive, joyous, and reminiscent of a bazaar, an exuberant public space. But it was also less than a public space, for the state was disappeared, an *auctoritas in absentia*. As a result, El Campo taxed the patience, resourcefulness, and intellectual powers of its citizen-managers. The group of barely twenty people who assiduously turned up at the weekly assembly meetings were overwhelmed and overworked. The daily chores of maintenance (opening the gates, sweeping and arranging the space, kicking people out when closing time approached), going through email correspondence, and keeping a lively digital community presence—for these chores, there never seemed to be enough people. On some occasions the space remained closed because no keyholders were around to open its gate. Events had to be postponed or canceled, people became angry, and discussions flared at the assembly, which in turn saw members leave and new ones arrive. Three thousand square meters of open-air space can take anyone's breath away.

That El Campo somewhat failed as a representational space, as a *political assembly*—as an organon for hearing matters of facts—did not otherwise prevent it from working as a lively *assemblage of the political*—an organon for reckoning with matters of sense. While it was, perhaps, incapable of centering itself as a conventional public space, of finding a language for itself as an agora of spectacle, El Campo otherwise succeeded in providing a platform for an intensive urbanization of outlook, a method for the city's self-peripheralization, for the improvisation and bricolage of autonomous apprenticeships.

As an example, El Campo hosted numerous debates and forums about the role of the academy and its relationship to the city, including the organization of a Popular University. One of the most interesting projects in this respect was the educational collective #edumeet. The initiative first met at El Campo in September 2011, following a Twitter exchange about matters of education and the city. The meeting brought together a group of some twenty people, including some of the original community of activists and architects who had occupied the site some months earlier, as well as newcomers to El Campo, including teachers, designers, and information technology consultants. The group convened thereafter every second Thursday evening, in meetings organized via Twitter, although without any expectation of attendance.

The conversations at #edumeet gravitated toward a concern with the nature of learning in the modern city, and in particular with the conditions—the built environment, the rhythms of capital, the social and technical forms of experience—that enabled or discouraged the awakening of the city's pedagogical capacities and affordances. People would often express concern about the fragility of a meeting that took place after hours, in the open air, not infrequently perambulating the nightly hospitality of bars or squatted social centers. It was a strange hospitality for which the meetings seemed to be groping. Yet it was also this transience and urban wildness that people most treasured, as they navigated and sounded out the landscapes, the penumbras, and the promises of shared learning (see figure 16). At the meetings, attendees voiced their dissatisfaction with formal education, not least with the role that the university played in the standardization and slumbering of urban experience. There was considerable discussion, for instance, about the kind of stance that research takes when it comes to the city: What does it mean to investigate the city? What types of relationships and bodies does the action of research elicit vis-à-vis the aesthetic inscriptions of artists, the nurturing accompaniments of teachers, or the literary curiosity of journalists? How does research take residence in the urban fabric, what sorts of traces does it leave, and what memories and awakenings does it excite? Some people would occasionally turn to us in our role as ethnographers with these and similar questions, curious to understand how ethnography shapes itself into a presence in the city—how it constructs a space of inquiry amid the vicissitudes and turmoil of a world in crisis. Where and how, they wanted to know, did ethnography fit into this budding, yet precarious infrastructure of feeling?

These were pressing questions for many participants, some of whom felt compelled to leave testimony, to *hacer visible* (make visible) that these discussions

FIGURE 16.   Meeting at El Campo de Cebada. Photo by El Campo de Cebada is licensed under CC BY-SA 4.0: https://creativecommons.org/licenses/by-sa/4.0/.

were being had, that they were taking place: indeed, that there were specific places in the city for them, or at least specific arrangements and possibilities. For instance, it became an established practice for attendees to report the discussions live on Twitter, embedding drawings and photographs of the group, excerpts from notes, images from the surrounding environment, and the like. Attendees would also write up the evening's discussions in blog posts or produce summaries for online architectural and urbanist forums; some would venture theoretical forays into the discursive realms of so-called peer-to-peer and do-it-yourself urbanism. These arrangements signaled specific distributions of presence and action, of bodies-in-place and bodies-across-space; directions to and swells of movement, excitement, expectation, and reward. They deployed summative systems and methods for intuiting and tracking, for knowing and acknowledging, for witnessing and learning. "The city," people would whisper to each other with sparkling eyes, "surges."

As time went by, #edumeet became a reference for discussions on free culture and the city. By 2012, *Arquitectura Viva*, Spain's most prestigious architectural journal, published a special issue on emerging architectural collectives that included an entry on #edumeet. The entry was self-curated by #edumeet's Twitter followers and read thus:

> #edumeet / learning ambiances, autonomous and temporal / people that talk about education at la Cebada every second Thursday / or in bars / ... affective space around learning / ... a #hashtag that belongs to no one / may well be happening right now without us knowing about it / ... unlearning by meeting new people who do not share your interests / every new tweet is a new render of #edumeet.[44]

There is another sense in which witnessing and learning became important operators in the organization of experience at El Campo. Ever since the space was liberated in February 2011, Basurama and Zuloark organized so-called Handmade Urbanism workshops at the site, where students of architecture, passersby, and neighbors were invited to design and construct pieces of urbanism for the city (see figure 17). As the architects liked to say, "today urbanism is brico-urbanism, a handmade job (*el urbanismo es brico-urbanismo, se hace con las manos*)." Following the architectural collective's own involvement in the open-source platform Inteligencias Colectivas (as described in chapter 5), a central pedagogical dimension of these workshops was that all designs were documented following an open-source philosophy. This required participants to make not just technical notes and instructional diagrams for every object or installation, but also explanations regarding the types of materials used, their affordances, how and where they were sourced, and the like. The documentation included photo-

FIGURE 17.   "Handmade Urbanism" workshop at El Campo de Cebada. Photo by Zuloark is licensed under CC BY-SA 4.0: https://creativecommons.org /licenses/by-sa/4.0/.

graphs, diagrams, videos, or 3D renderings, which were then uploaded and made available online in the hope that they would become methods or prototypes for the ongoing investigation of the city as an open-source environment. Some of these prototypes traveled to other parts of the city, such as when the prototype for an urban bench was disassembled and later used in the construction of community garden beds or used for furnishing a local school's playground in auto-construction workshops with students. The travels of these various objects and resources entangled the city in a thick texture of social and material relations, which people started to speak of as *metodologías para hacer ciudad*, methods for eliciting the city's capacities.

However, the documentation that participants produced at the workshops was erratic and inconsistent. Some relished the opportunity to document exhaustively their work and would even carry out interviews with local neighbors in an attempt to substantiate a design or aesthetic choice, while others would get away with little more than a couple of photographs or drawings. Such unevenness troubled the architectural collectives. We had long conversations with Manuel regarding the urban nature of these designs and objects, given that one could hardly speak of them as having standards of any kind. On one occasion, Manuel probed deeper than previously on the specific inflection that open-source designs brought to the relationship between knowledge and acknowledgment, between learning and witnessing in urban affairs: "The thing is," he said, "that when the municipality speaks of 'participatory design,' they are thinking how to embed representative voices into infrastructures and standards, say, for designing children's playgrounds or urban equipment for plazas and parks. We, on the other hand, are thinking of pedagogy and learning: how to design spaces and infrastructures so that communities can learn from one another." He continued: "So when we say that El Campo is *una infraestructura para la ciudad*, an infrastructure for the city, we don't just mean to say that it provides the space or materials for the community to carry out activities that were previously unimaginable. Rather, it is the learning processes that it enables and sets in circulation that we are interested in. It is the circulating economy of learning that *is* the infrastructure." Aurora, another member of Zuloark, joined in: "Everywhere you look, from urban community gardens to #edumeet or the 15M neighborhood assemblies, there is an explicit effervescence and consciousness regarding the apprenticeships that the city is deploying (*los aprendizajes que se despliegan por la ciudad*)." But, she added, "one also senses that much of it passes unnoticed, that we have no place from where to make all those learning processes learnable: what does it mean to make an urban apprenticeship legible? What kind of learning is the city?"[45]

The Arts of Bricolage

Auto-construction has a long tradition in urban studies and anthropology. By 1984, the urbanist Alberto Arecchi had pointed out the significance of auto-construction as an empirical system of problem solving in African cities, although he likewise alerted readers to the risks of invoking auto-construction as a romanticized, neocolonial trope for indigenous self-empowerment: "Where auto-construction is a traditional symptom of poverty, where new governments are anxious to modernize, to make slums and huts a thing of the past, one sometimes risks sounding neo-colonialist when propounding the advantages of auto-construction."[46] The allure and the perils of auto-construction have remained with urban theory ever since. The metonym of the slum, in Ananya Roy's description, remains a powerful placeholder for both dystopian and inventive accounts of the urban: for the retrograde, the resilient, and the resourceful.

Inspired by recent scholarship that seeks in the periphery, the informal, and the subaltern new perceptual systems for thinking (with) the city, we have offered here an argument for the use of auto-construction as a double heuristic of method and theory for the urban condition. "Rather than the city being somehow read through particular schemes of power," the anthropologist Morten Nielsen wrote in his study of auto-construction in Maputo, Mozambique, the lens of *inverse governmentality* (as he cleverly describes such self-help housing projects) offers a perspective in which "the city consequently reads itself."[47] Similarly, we have tried to show how auto-construction may work as an auto-heuristic, not just for urban theory but also for social analysis more broadly. As we have seen, the work of auto-constructing El Campo de Cebada, of furnishing both a material and social ecology for it, also became a method for describing the political and epistemic liberation of the space. The inhabitants of El Campo experimented with various technologies and genres for registering the obligations and requirements, as well as the aspirations and expectations, that they deposited on the site as a space of autonomy, learning, and mutual witnessing. Their auto-construction functioned as a method of description and a design for theory, of the city they have at hand and of the city they would like to build: a city-specific and a city-in-abstraction. Let us bring this chapter to a close with some reflections on the panoply of methods inhabiting, intermediating, and upending how the city-specific and the city-in-abstraction relate to one another.

Few distinctions have drawn as engaged and exhaustive scrutiny and criticism as that between the specific and abstract qualities of conceptual reasoning. No lesser text than *The Savage Mind* famously opens with a disquisition on the spurious differentiation between specific and abstract thought when applied, respectively, to primitive and scientific reasoning.[48] Claude Lévi-Strauss suggested that the savage mind is fueled by bricolage, an operation of inventiveness that draws on a heterogeneous yet limited set of tools and materials for laying out novel arrangements with which to navigate the world. The operation of bricolage exemplified, for Lévi-Strauss, "a science of the concrete," where the abstract or specific qualities of conceptual maneuvering are superseded by a method of empirical pragmatics and potentiality.[49]

The image of the bricoleur recalls the method of brico-urbanism that guerrilla architectural collectives single out as characteristic of their practice in Madrid. However, if for Lévi-Strauss bricolage makes for an operation that lies "half-way between percepts and concepts," it has been our purpose to show how, in the context of guerrilla urbanism, the method of bricolage is itself auto-constructed in an operation that recursively problematizes the very status of the city as method.[50] Thus, when people summoned the ghosts of the economic crisis at the Puerta del Sol's city in miniature or when they speculated on the oligarchic alliance between real estate interests and corrupt politicians that haunted the future of El Campo, they were invoking an image of the city that made itself felt as both a specific and a generic presence in their lives. The generic and the specific appear entangled and muddled, and the experience of navigating and moving between them is rendered as an experience of method, of sharing-with, moving-toward, mobilizing-for, immersing-in, and systematizing-out-from—for example, through the use of specific languages and interfaces of description, archival and documentary technologies, or systems and infrastructures for learning together. We may say that the city appears as "a figure seen twice"—an object at once specific and abstract—yet it does so only while in motion as a method in auto-construction.[51] For some scholars, this rehearses and invites reformulations of the problem of the epistemology of the urban—the categories and concepts with which to apprehend the city. Instead of lingering with this problem, though, we suggest considering and exploring the methods, designs, and "trajectories of apprenticeships" through which the city and its stories auto-construct one another.[52] In other words, this is the art of urban theory as an art of bricolage.

Conclusion

NOTES ON INTRANSITIVE URBANISM

In 1978, the Italian urbanist Giuseppe Campos Venuti published *Urbanistica e austerità* (Urbanism and austerity).[1] A longtime member of the Italian Communist Party and, throughout the 1960s, the person behind the recuperation of Bologna's historic city center from the compulsions of real estate and capitalist accumulation, Campos Venuti was an iconic figure in left-wing urban circles across Europe at the time. In the 1960–1970s, he had been an early analyst of the consequences brought about by the legacy of Italian fascism's predilection for real estate capital speculation. In *Urbanistica e austerità* he favored in its place a view of urban planning "that is no longer a plan for the expansion of the city but, on the contrary, a plan for its renovation, for the so-called 'active safeguarding' of those factors that are crucial for urban life: the public, the social, the productive, the environment, and the programmatic."[2]

These five safeguards articulated a model for "austerity urbanism" that is very different from how the concept was reintroduced into urban theory in the wake of the financial crisis in 2008.[3] For Campos Venuti, austerity urbanism offered a pathway for resisting capitalist speculation by nurturing instead the already existing social, communal, and public resources working latently in cities. It was this vision for public urbanism that appealed left-wing Spanish planners when, following the death of dictator Francisco Franco in 1975, the country ushered in a timorous and uncertain path towards democratization. Thus, when in 1979 a coalition formed by the Spanish Socialist and Workers Party (Partido Socialista Obrero Español [PSOE]) and the Spanish Communist Party (Partido Comunista de España [PCE]) won the first democratic municipal elections in Madrid, the new government rushed to set up a working group to draft a new urban plan for the city that drew heavily on Campos Venuti's ideas (to the extent that he joined the project as a consultant).[4]

Austerity urbanism offered a venue for integrating a deeply public approach to municipal governance with the barrio-centered approach developed by the many-headed hydra of the neighborhood movement in the early 1970s. By the time the Communist and Socialist Parties took office in 1979, the neighborhood movement had become a formidable presence to reckon-with in urban politics. The movement first saw the light in the late 1960s amidst struggles against slum urbanization, a side-effect of the massive rural-urban migration triggered by the large-scale capitalist industrialization programs of Francoist development (*desarrollismo franquista*). By 1968, aided by underground communist and revolutionary parties and grassroots apostolic collectives, slum dwellers had organized into *asociaciones de vecinos* (neighborhood associations) whose original demands called for decent housing, public schools, and basic urban infrastructure.[5] However, in a very short time the movement also developed technical skills for negotiating land expropriations, property evaluations, or the establishment of housing cooperatives with government, real estate developers, and landlords.[6] Moreover, by 1972 activists were already describing the movement's own praxis as a mobilization for the "right to the city."[7] Thus, some neighborhood associations went on to develop claims for making room "for fantasy and hope . . . and children's right to play" in our cities, while others successfully campaigned to have the history of the neighborhood's struggle included in the syllabi of local schools.[8] In 1968, to give a final example, the residents of the slum settlement of Palomeras Bajas joined a group of architects and lawyers to draft an urban plan to counter the Ministry of Housing's own program to expropriate the settlement. As the neighborhood association's text put it: "We want houses *for everyone*. . . . We want houses *soon*. . . . We want houses *here*. Our neighborhood is the expression of our efforts. We have come a long way to make a life of our own in the city, to build a new human community of people that know and help each other. We treasure our social and human richness, which we have built with great sacrifice of time, patience, and trust. . . . We are working toward the *auto-transformation* of the whole community."[9]

When the Socialist and Communist Parties took office in 1979, the conditions therefore seemed ripe for setting in motion a profound process of municipalist democratization, as Murray Bookchin might have once imagined it.[10] But this was not to be. The oil crisis had hit Spain particularly hard. By 1977, with over two thirds of energy consumption hinging on oil imports, the annual inflation rate neared 42 percent while unemployment entered a structural downward turn that would peak in 1985 at almost 3 million people (21.5 percent).[11] In this crisis scenario, all political parties, both left and right, subscribed in October 1977 the Pactos de la Moncloa (Moncloa Pacts), which tied the political transition to democracy to the economy's structural stabilization in the world system. As we noted in the introduction, in this fashion the transition to democracy—*la Transición*, in its capitalized, self-important historical designation—was spun and co-opted by a regime of technocratic governance that under the mantle of a pact of amnesty and consensus buried all hints and promises of radical and revolutionary democracy.

It was hardly a smooth transition. There were industrial strikes and mass demonstrations, in a few cases leading to fatal encounters with the police. While some people tried to "break the consensus," the terms of the transition seemed, however, finally set in stone.[12] Within this wider definition of how democracy was to be operationalized as a *transitional form* to a liberal economy, there were, however, some actors who partially succeeded in demonstrating, or at least retaining for themselves, a sense of relevance and capacity as *intransitive subjects*. The term "intransitive culture" was advanced by the cultural historian Germán Labrador in 2017 to draw attention to a neglected generation of artists and poets whose fatal destinies marked agonistically and dramatically the violent biopolitics of the "culture of the *Transición*."[13] Labrador's careful and attentive reading of the interstitial and precarious survival of such an intransitive generation is admirable; yet there are grounds for suggesting that the neighborhood movement managed to carve out an analogous form of *intransitive urbanism* too. This much was insinuated by the sociologist Tomás Villasante in 1989 in what remains one of the most substantive reviews of the movement's history. We quote at length:

> The neighborhood movement's struggle for housing remains a largely atypical factor in the history of a political transition characterized as a bartering agreement between two historical agencies. Neither those who supported the dictatorship, nor those who opposed it, had enough endorsements to overpower the other side. Therefore, they were forced to reach an agreement. There would be democracy, yes, there would be elections, political parties, and free trade unions, but in exchange the structural foundations of the system would remain intact. That is to say: Spain would remain aligned with the Western bloc, the Monarchy would remain foundational to all political legitimacy, the unity of the State sacrosanct, and the economy indissolubly tied to market forces. This is what has come to be known as the Constitutional Pact, which required of an underlying social pact. It has become a popular expression to remark that anyone who moved a little bit too much [i.e., whose

demands exceeded what the liberal consensus had allocated for them], wouldn't show up in the final picture. And indeed, no one moved, *but for the neighbors.*[14]

We have argued in this book that the history of free culture activism in the first two decades of the twenty first century partook of this larger impetus for intransitive urbanism. Ours is not a historical argument. We have no interest in sustaining a direct genealogy between the neighborhood movement of the 1970s and the free culture movement of the 2000s.[15] Our attention has been drawn instead to the drives for autonomy and liberation that resonate throughout, including the skepticism that free culture activists and the neighborhood movement shared toward the "transitional" as a narrative and framework of political hope and progress. As Germán Labrador has pointed out, one finds echoes in both periods of "people making a historical recollection of how to come together *as a commons to the defense of the public.*"[16] The intransitive is marked by this double movement: an intensive orientation that is at once a form of defense of the public and a form of liberation for the commons.

In the case of the neighborhood associations, their intransigence referred, on the one hand, to a specific historical formation—a constitutional framework of liberal consensus fabricated in 1979—regarding the conditions and limits to urban justice and democracy. On the other hand, and by the same token, the imposition of this framework is exactly what prompted the redescription of the movement's practices of reclamation as practices of *auto-transformation*, that is, as intransitive practices.

The experiences of free culture activists, we have seen throughout the book, also took such a double form, in each case marking a type of negative and positive freedom: *liberation from* the long shadows of post-Francoist culture, including most prominently its regimes of authorial and technocratic governance and expertise; as well as *liberation for* experimenting with new forms of autonomous designs, assembly democracy, and infrastructural sovereignty. Inasmuch as in their different ways these various actors were pushing against the transitional legacies of Spain's post-dictatorial culture, it is therefore not unreasonable to describe their efforts as building up into a form of intransitive urbanism, too.

In an Intransitive Mood

As we noted in the introduction, intransitive urbanism speaks to tactical designs and practices of inhabitation that are nervously posed between the near-Norths of modernization and the near-Souths of peripheralization—an urbanism that is *in transit* between antithetical and otherwise unreal poles.[17] It is neither of them, but to some extent it is also both. This is a story, then, that sits somewhat uncomfortably next to existing accounts of makeshift and informal urbanisms in the Global South and insurrectionary and indignant urbanisms in the Global North. All along, our story has drawn attention to the commons-public assemblages subscribing cultura libre: where the public sometimes rushed to the defense or enablement of the commons (for example, the Spanish fork of Wikipedia, La Casa Encendida, and Medialab), or where the commons sometimes aided in the protection or enhancement of the public (the 15M assembly movement, Campo de Cebada), or, more often than not, where the public, the commons, and cultura libre were blurred and exchanged in ways that were indistinguishable, entangled, and intransitive. Therefore, as we bring our book to a close, let us sketch some final arguments for the intransitive as a sensibility for urban and social theory more broadly.[18]

Transitivity is a mode of relation between actions and things. This is its definition in grammar, where transitive verbs are said to transfer the action to external objects while intransitive verbs carry the action themselves. As such, intransitive verbs do not require a direct object to complete their meaning. In the sentence, "The bird flies," the verb "flies" is intransitive, whereas in the sentence, "He makes pies," the verb "make" is transitive. Although there are plenty of nuances and complexities to the nature of transitivity in grammar, here we wish to build on the resonances of the term to articulate a theoretical sensibility for the intransitive as a specific orientation to movement, becoming, and inhabitation. Whereas transitive verbs, we might say, mark a split between an action and its worlding, it is in the nature of the intransitive to sense and cause to drift a mode of worlding all along.

We appeal thus to a notion of the intransitive to more broadly describe modes of comportment and anticipation that are partly skeptical about transitional orientations, that is, orientations that move through or aim for the arcs of promissory and felicitous arrivals, and partly skeptical, also, about transitive arguments—that is, arguments that are conformed through, or arranged by the predictable concatenation of consequential objects and reasons. Purposely designed and justified transitions, history has long taught us, tend to end calamitously.

The intransitive has, in this sense, a touch of intransigence also, of rebellious dignity and joyous tenacity. Since there is no direct object to an intransitive verb, only ex post facto can one clear a space for asking where, when, how, or how long. Take the case of the city. In an intransitive mode, one's relation to the city is rushed, felt, modulated or inchoated through expressions that only vaguely, almost imperceptibly, take a recognizable urban form, sometimes through second-guessing or retrospective recomposition—these are forms that are not in any obvious way about (say) housing, public space, or informality. These are categories that aim too neatly, it seems to us, for transitional objects.

We are not disingenuous about the nature of the intransitive. We are well aware that activists' claims are nothing if not specific and concrete. This book is replete with examples: demands for decent housing, to end precarious employment, for a free internet, and so on. Yet it is not just what activists struggle for that we wish to highlight here but also how they comport and bear themselves in doing so. The intransitive aims for a mode of description that helps us thicken and give texture to such tactical worldings.

The conceptual triad we have proposed in this book—climates of methods, matters of sense, bricolages of apprenticeships—comprises one such attempt at analyzing how intransitive movements ground their capacities and aspirations for auto-transformation. They are categories suggested to us by our ethnography as we looked into the interstices of description for different enunciations and orchestrations of the informal, the material, and the affective—the making and remaking of a free/libre urbanism.

Cities have a tendency to impose their own categories of adjudication and classification on us: space and scale, network and infrastructure, use value and exchange value, public and private, institutional and collective action. We have presented many of these categories in the preceding pages. In an intransitive mood, however, we have opted for a different register of description. In opening up a space for speaking about climates of methods, matters of sense, and bricolages of apprenticeships, we have found inspiring companionship in the work of Alexander Vasudevan and his exploration of how the logics of autonomy in the squatters' movement, as well as its logistics of infrastructural maintenance and improvisation, amount to a sort of makeshift urbanism. Likewise we have been inspired by the work of Stavros Stavrides, for whom the operations of commoning are always driven at some level by an exciting crossing of thresholds and the juxtaposition of liminal, sometimes secrete passageways within the cartographies of capital; the work of Ananya Roy, who insists that we look for the gray spaces and zones of exception produced by the double work of peripheralization—as a geographical and epistemic frontier—in between capital and state sovereignty; and the work of AbdouMaliq Simone, who insists that cityness always and everywhere drifts and creeps up through dashes of improvisation and provisional lattices of alliance. All these works strike us as manifestations of intransitive urbanisms, too, blurring, trespassing, and endlessly redescribing the transitive grammars (subject-object, culture-nature, human-nonhuman, and so on) of neoliberal urban governance.

The intransitive, therefore, signposts not just a sensorium, a movement-assemblage of bodies and inclinations, but also a material culture. Indeed, a running interest of ours throughout the book has been to describe in detail the material designs of activists' hopes—what free culture activists in Madrid referred to as the *culture of prototyping*. Prototypes, we have seen, are intransitive designs, aiming less for description than redescription. They serve as technologies of hospitality, inasmuch as they enable difficult conversations between public culture, free culture, and the commons. In this sense, we feel it does not do justice to describe the culture of prototyping as partaking of contemporary calls for "transitional designs." Of course, they have much in common. Both prototypes and transitional designs are passionately committed to the reconception of lifestyles, by means both speculative and material, in the pursuance of a future worth living. The anthropologist Arturo Escobar, who produced an authoritative account of how transitional discourses have been variously theorized across disciplines, noted that, "While the age to come is described in the North as being postgrowth, postmaterialist, posteconomic, postcapitalist, and posthuman, for the South it is expressed in terms of being postdevelopment, nonliberal, postcapitalist/noncapitalist, biocentric, and postextractivist."[19] Escobar is particularly interested in how transitional designs, notwithstanding their variance, offer templates for ideas "about emergence, self-organization, and autopoiesis" to drive militant theories of social change.[20] One would be foolish not to subscribe to that view.

However, perhaps because our ethnography of free culture activism is nervously posed between near-Norths and near-Souths, between fatuous horizons of Europeanization and the lurking shame of a retrograde dictatorial past, and in this context strained and stretched between the defense of the public, the liberation of the commons, and the presentiments of cultura libre—perhaps for all these reasons, activists expressed a desire to recast the hopes of the transitional through the warmth and accompaniments of the intransitive. There is a history, it seems, of how climates of methods, matters of sense, and bricolages of apprenticeships can still enchant what we learn from all transitions, whether future or past.

Notes

INTRODUCTION

1. Unless otherwise stated, all translations from Spanish sources, including academic texts, interviews, archival materials, and ethnographic exchanges, are our own.

2. Vicente Rubio-Pueyo, "Municipalism in Spain: From Barcelona to Madrid, and Beyond," City Series, Rosa Luxemburg Stiftung (New York), 2017.

3. *Indignados* (outraged) became the media label for the movement, echoing the title of Stephan Hessel's manifesto published earlier that year. Hessel was a French diplomat, who participated in the drafting of the Universal Human Rights Declaration of 1948. He wrote *Time for Outrage* at the age of ninety-three. The book quickly became a bestseller in France and has since been translated into other languages; see Stephane Hessel, *Time for Outrage!* (London: Quartet Books, 2011). In Spain, however, participants preferred to refer to themselves as the 15M movement, a designation that marked a moment of initiation, joy, and possibility, rather than outrage or despair. We follow this convention here too.

4. See, for example, Guillem Martínez, ed., *CT o la cultura de la Transición: Crítica a 35 años de cultura española* (Madrid: Penguin Random House, 2012).

5. Guillermo Zapata, "La CT como marco: Un caso de éxito no CT: el 15M. O de cómo puede suceder un éxito no previsto en una cultura, como la CT, que controla los accesos al éxito y al fracaso," in *CT o la cultura de la Transición: Crítica a 35 años de cultura española*, ed. Guillem Martínez (Madrid: Penguin Random House, 2012), 145.

6. See the opening epigraph. See also Michel Foucault, "What Is Enlightenment?," in *The Foucault Reader*, ed. Paul Rabinow (New York: Pantheon Books, 1984), 32–50.

7. We are inspired here by AbdouMaliq Simone's theoretical formulation of the "near-South" as a geography of inchoations of global urban trends that is, however, always tensed by movements-toward rather than complete realizations; see AbdouMaliq Simone, *Jakarta, Drawing the City Near* (Minneapolis: University of Minnesota Press, 2014).

8. For the question, see, for example, Erik Swyngedouw, *Promises of the Political: Insurgent Cities in a Post-Political Environment* (Cambridge, MA: MIT Press, 2018).

9. Red de Espacios Ciudadanos, "Marco Común I.4: Esbozo de un marco común para la cesión de espacios destinados a la autogestión ciudadana con el objetivo de fomentar el desarrollo de los bienes comunes en los barrios de Madrid," 2016, http://www.espaciosciudadanos.org/wp-content/uploads/2016/01/Marco-Comun-v1-4.pdf. A much paler version of the statute was approved and signed into an ordinance on public-social cooperation by the Ahora Madrid government on May 30, 2018. The final text of the ordinance was poorly received by activists.

10. As Debbie Bookchin and Blair Taylor have explained, Murray Bookchin was a pioneer of the ecology movement, his 1964 pamphlet, "Ecology and Revolutionary Thought" being "the first to equate the grow-or-die logic of capitalism with the ecological destruction of the planet"; see Debbie Bookchin and Blair Taylor, "Introduction," in *The Next Revolution: Popular Assemblies and the Promise of Direct Democracy*, by Murray Bookchin, ed. Debbie Bookchin and Blair Taylor (London: Verso, 2015), xv. In his later writings, Bookchin developed a revolutionary theory of democracy founded on the promises of confederate face-to-face assemblies and autonomous grassroots projects.

Although Bookchin only sparsely employed the term "free city" in his writings, for all intents and purposes the concept of libertarian municipalism, which played a central part in his thought, functions as a synonym of the free city, the *liber municipium*. For his part, in *The City and the Grassroots*, Manuel Castells surveyed a variety of case studies in social protest to propose a model of collective organization and action founded on a particular attribution of historical praxis to urban social movements, namely, their capacity to articulate three basic goals: (i) to fight for the use value rather than the exchange value of the city; (ii) a sense of cultural autonomy and community; and (iii) a search for increased political self-management; see Castells, *The City and the Grassroots: A Cross-Cultural Theory of Urban Social Movements* (Berkeley: University of California Press, 1984), 319–21. The shape of the free city, Castells suggested, always and everywhere takes a particular form, a form that is lent to it by the undeterred aspirations of social movements: "We call the struggle for a free city, a citizen movement" (320, emphasis removed).

11. Patrick Joyce, *The Rule of Freedom: Liberalism and the Modern City* (London: Verso, 2003).

12. Henri Lefebvre, "Right to the City," in *Writings on Cities*, ed. Eleonore Kofman and Elizabeth Lebas (Oxford: Blackwell, 1996), 79.

13. Lefebvre, "Right to the City," 65–66.

14. Lefebvre, "Right to the City," 77.

15. Lefebvre, "Right to the City," 158, emphasis in the original.

16. David Harvey, *Rebel Cities: From the Right to the City to the Urban Revolution* (London: Verso Books, 2012), xv.

17. See Kafui A. Attoh, "What Kind of Right Is the Right to the City?," *Progress in Human Geography* 35, no. 5 (October 1, 2011): 669–85, https://doi.org/10.1177/0309132510394706.

18. James Holston, "Metropolitan Rebellions and the Politics of Commoning the City," *Anthropological Theory* 19, no. 1 (March 1, 2019): 127, https://doi.org/10.1177/1463499618812324.

19. Holston, "Metropolitan Rebellions," 127.

20. Holston, "Metropolitan Rebellions," 129.

21. Holston, "Metropolitan Rebellions," 123, 125, and throughout.

22. See for example Efrat Eizenberg, "Actually Existing Commons: Three Moments of Space of Community Gardens in New York City," *Antipode* 44, no. 3 (2012): 764–82, https://doi.org/10.1111/j.1467-8330.2011.00892.x; Stavros Stavrides, *Common Space: The City as Commons* (London: Zed Books, 2016).

23. Eizenberg, "Actually Existing Commons," 778.

24. Stavrides, *Common Space*, 5, 56, and throughout.

25. On assemblage urbanism, see, for example, Neil Brenner, David J. Madden, and David Wachsmuth, "Assemblage Urbanism and the Challenges of Critical Urban Theory," *City* 15, no. 2 (April 1, 2011): 225–40, https://doi.org/10.1080/13604813.2011.568717; Ignacio Farías, "The Politics of Urban Assemblages," *City* 15, nos. 3–4 (Agosto 2011): 365–74, https://doi.org/10.1080/13604813.2011.595110; Colin McFarlane, "Assemblage and Critical Urbanism," *City* 15, no. 2 (April 1, 2011): 204–24, https://doi.org/10.1080/13604813.2011.568715.

26. Ignacio Farías and Anders Blok, "Introducing Urban Cosmopolitics: Multiplicity and the Search for a Common World," in *Urban Cosmopolitics: Agencements, Assemblies, Atmospheres*, ed. Anders Blok and Ignacio Farías (London: Routledge, 2016), 1.

27. See, for example, Luis I. Prádanos, *Postgrowth Imaginaries: New Ecologies and Counterhegemonic Culture in Post-2008 Spain* (Liverpool: Liverpool University Press, 2018).

28. Bruno Latour, "From Realpolitik to Dingpolitik or How to Make Things Public," in *Making Things Public: Atmospheres of Democracy*, ed. Bruno Latour and Peter Weibel (Cambridge, MA: MIT Press, 2005), 16.

29. Bruno Latour, "Why Has Critique Run Out of Steam? From Matters of Fact to Matters of Concern," *Critical Inquiry* 30, no. 2 (January 1, 2004): 225–48, https://doi .org/10.1086/421123.

30. María Puig de la Bellacasa, *Matters of Care: Speculative Ethics in More Than Human Worlds* (Minneapolis: University of Minnesota Press, 2017).

31. On the distribution of the sensible, see Jacques Rancière, *The Politics of Aesthetics* (London: Bloomsbury, 2004).

32. Ivan Illich, *Tools for Conviviality* (New York: Harper & Row, 1973).

33. Eduardo Viveiros de Castro, "On Models and Examples: Engineers and Bricoleurs in the Anthropocene," *Current Anthropology* 60, no. S20 (April 1, 2019): S296–308, https://doi.org/10.1086/702787.

34. Viveiros de Castro, "On Models and Examples," S300.

35. Amador Fernández-Savater, "¿Cómo se organiza un clima?," *Fuera de lugar* (blog), January 9, 2012, https://blogs.publico.es/fueradelugar/1438/%c2%bfcomo-se-organiza-un -clima. See also Fernández-Savater, *Habitar y gobernar: Inspiraciones para una nueva concepción política* (Barcelona: NED Ediciones, 2020), 136, 246.

36. Murray Bookchin, *The Ecology of Freedom: The Emergence and Dissolution of Hierarchy* (Palo Alto: Cheshire Books, 1982), 46.

37. Bookchin's theory of libertarian municipalism remains somewhat problematic on account of his rationalistic and evolutionary concept of social life. For Bookchin, hidden in the nature of the city lies dormant a historical potency for human emancipation. Cities, he argues, are units of political association where freedom can emerge naturally out from a dialectics of reason and creative communality. There seems to be little scope in Bookchin's theory for conceptions of urban life that are not rooted in Enlightened social theory, where individuals and communities do not of necessity seek to shape and transcend one another in a dialectic of rational emancipation.

38. Isabelle Stengers, *Cosmopolitics I* (Minneapolis: University of Minnesota Press, 2010), 56–57.

39. Collettivo A/traverso, *Alicia es el diablo: Radio libre*, trans. Paco Quintana (Barcelona: Ed. Ricou [Hacer], 1981), 50.

40. Dipesh Chakrabarty, "The Climate of History: Four Theses," *Critical Inquiry* 35, no. 2 (January 1, 2009): 197–222, https://doi.org/10.1086/596640.

41. AbdouMaliq Simone and Edgar Pieterse, *New Urban Worlds: Inhabiting Dissonant Times* (Cambridge, MA: Polity Press, 2017), 15.

42. Stevphen Shukaitis and David Graeber, "Introduction," in *Constituent Imagination: Militant Investigations, Collective Theorization*, ed. Stevphen Shukaitis, David Graeber, and Erika Biddle (Oakland: AK Press, 2007), 31.

43. John Perry Barlow, "A Declaration of the Independence of Cyberspace," Electronic Frontier Foundation, 1996, https://www.eff.org/es/cyberspace-independence.

44. Christopher M. Kelty, *Two Bits: The Cultural Significance of Free Software* (Durham, NC: Duke University Press, 2008), 5.

45. Richard Stallman, *Free Software, Free Society: Selected Essays of Richard M. Stallman* (Boston: GNU Press, 2006), 35.

46. Hector Postigo, *The Digital Rights Movement: The Role of Technology in Subverting Digital Copyright* (Cambridge, MA: MIT Press, 2012).

47. Postigo, *Digital Rights Movement*, 5.

48. Lawrence Lessig, *Code and Other Laws of Cyberspace* (New York: Basic Books, 1999); Lawrence Lessig, *Free Culture: The Nature and Future of Creativity* (New York: Penguin, 2004).

49. E. Gabriella Coleman, *Coding Freedom: The Ethics and Aesthetics of Hacking* (Princeton, NJ: Princeton University Press, 2012), 19.

50. E. Gabriella Coleman, *Coding Freedom*, 95.

51. Jeffrey S. Juris, *Networking Futures: The Movements against Corporate Globalization* (Durham, NC: Duke University Press, 2008), 11 and throughout.

52. Kelty, *Two Bits*, 264.

53. John Postill, *The Rise of Nerd Politics: Digital Activism and Political Change* (London: Pluto Press, 2018).

54. Postill, *Rise of Nerd Politics*, 13.

55. Postill, *Rise of Nerd Politics*, 12.

56. Postigo, *Digital Rights Movement*, 179.

57. Between 2006 and 2010, income inequality increased in Spain more than in any other developed economy; see International Labor Organization (ILO), "Global Wage Report 2014/2015: Wages and Income Inequality," Geneva, 23, http://ilo.org/global /research/global-reports/global-wage-report/2014/lang--en/index.htm. As the right-wing Partido Popular government set the benchmark for austerity policies, by 2011 the population at risk of poverty had already increased by 23.3 percent in absolute terms, compared with 6.6 percent in Western Europe; see Emmanuele Pavolini, Margarita León, Ana M. Guillén, and Ugo Ascoli, "From Austerity to Permanent Strain? The EU and Welfare State Reform in Italy and Spain," *Comparative European Politics* 13, no. 1 (January 1, 2015): 60, https://doi.org/10.1057/cep.2014.41. Moreover, "young people [replaced] the elderly as the group most at risk of poverty"; see Organization for Economic Cooperation and Development (OECD), "In It Together: Why Less Inequality Benefits All," Paris, 2015, 25, https://doi.org/10.1787/9789264235120-en.

58. "Every 15 minutes," Eduardo Romanos estimated in 2014, "a family is evicted from their home in Spain because they are unable to meet their mortgage payments"; see Romanos, "Evictions, Petitions and Escraches: Contentious Housing in Austerity Spain," *Social Movement Studies* 13, no. 2 (April 3, 2014): 296, https://doi.org/10.1080 /14742837.2013.830567. The grassroots housing organization Plataforma de Afectados por la Hipoteca (Platform for Mortgage Victims) calculated that between 2007 and 2011 banks in Spain initiated 349,438 foreclosure proceedings, while between 2008 and 2011 courts ordered repossession and eviction in 166,716 proceedings. See Ada Colau and Adrià Alemany, *Vidas hipotecadas* (Barcelona: Angle Editorial, 2012), 228, 231.

59. Jamie Peck, "Austerity Urbanism," *City* 16, no. 6 (December 1, 2012): 651, https:// doi.org/10.1080/13604813.2012.734071.

60. Fran Tonkiss, "Austerity Urbanism and the Makeshift City," *City* 17, no. 3 (June 1, 2013): 313, https://doi.org/10.1080/13604813.2013.795332.

61. Martínez, "El concepto CT"; Pablo Sánchez León, "Desclasamiento y desencanto: La representación de las clases medias como eje de una relectura generacional de la Transición española," *Kamchatka: Revista de análisis cultural*, no. 4 (December 4, 2014): 63–99, https://doi.org/10.7203/KAM.4.4145.

62. Germán Labrador, "¿Lo llamaban democracia? La crítica estética de la política en la Transición española y el imaginario de la historia en el 15-M.," *Kamchatka: Revista de análisis cultural*, no. 4 (December 4, 2014): 21, https://doi.org/10.7203/KAM.4.4296.

63. Luis Moreno-Caballud, *Cultures of Anyone: Studies on Cultural Democratization in the Spanish Neoliberal Crisis* (Liverpool: Liverpool University Press, 2015), 93.

64. Germán Labrador Méndez, *Culpables por la literatura: Imaginación política y contracultura en la Transición española (1968–1986)* (Madrid: Ediciones Akal, 2017), 342.

65. Gonzalo Wilhelmi, *Romper el consenso: La izquierda radical en la Transición española (1975–1982)* (Madrid: Siglo XXI de España Editores, 2016).

66. Andrea A. Davis, "Enforcing the Transition: The Demobilization of Collective Memory in Spain, 1979–1982," *Bulletin of Hispanic Studies (Liverpool, 2002)* 92, no. 6 (2015): 685.

67. Germán Labrador Méndez, "La cultura en transición y la cultura de la Transición (CT)," *La Circular*, 2015, 46.

68. Labrador Méndez, *Culpables por la literatura*, 86 and throughout.

69. Moreno-Caballud, *Cultures of Anyone*, 6 and throughout.

70. Kostis Kornetis, "'Is There a Future in This Past?' Analyzing 15M's Intricate Relation to the Transición," *Journal of Spanish Cultural Studies* 15, nos. 1–2 (April 3, 2014): 95, https://doi.org/10.1080/14636204.2014.938432.

PART I. THE CULTURES OF THE FREE CITY

1. Margarita Padilla, Interview with Margarita Padilla, March 29, 2017.

2. Subcomandante Marcos, "El EZLN acude al encuentro intercontinental por la humanidad y contra el neoliberalismo a presentar la imagen del otro México, El México indígena, El México rebelde y digno," *Enlace Zapatista* (blog), July 18, 1997, http://enlacezapatista .ezln.org.mx/1997/07/17/el-ezln-acude-al-encuentro-intercontinental-por-la-humanidad-y -contra-el-neoliberalismo-a-presentar-la-imagen-del-otro-mexico-el-mexico-indigena-el -mexico-rebelde-y-digno/.

3. Margarita Padilla, "¿Y si partimos en dos la red?," *Contrapoder* (2005): 85, 92.

4. Padilla, Interview.

1. FREE NEIGHBORHOODS

1. Francois Dosse, *Gilles Deleuze and Félix Guattari: Intersecting Lives* (New York: Columbia University Press, 2010), 288.

2. Collettivo A/traverso, *Alice è il diavolo* (Milano: Edizioni L'Erba Voglio, 1977).

3. Collettivo A/traverso, *Alicia es el diablo: Radio libre*, trans. Paco Quintana (Barcelona: Ed. Ricou [Hacer], 1981), 68, 101–2.

4. Félix Guattari, *Molecular Revolution: Psychiatry and Politics*, trans. Rosemary Sheed (Harmondsworth: Penguin Books, 1984), 236.

5. Franco Bifo Berardi, *Félix Guattari: Thought, Friendship, and Visionary Cartography* (New York: Palgrave Macmillan, 2008), 31.

6. Guattari, *Molecular Revolution*, 238.

7. Lester Golden, "The Libertarian Movement in Contemporary Spanish Politics," *Antipode* 10–11, no. 3-1 (December 1, 1978): 115, https://doi.org/10.1111/j.1467-8330.1978 .tb00120.x.

8. Jordi Mir García, "Salir de los márgenes sin cambiar de ideas: Pensamiento radical, contracultural y libertario en la Transición española," *Ayer*, no. 81 (2011): 90–91.

9. Manuel Castells, *The City and the Grassroots: A Cross-Cultural Theory of Urban Social Movements* (Berkeley: University of California Press, 1983).

10. Castells, *The City and the Grassroots*, 287.

11. Marcello Caprarella and Fanny Hernández Brotons, "La lucha por la ciudad: Vecinos-trabajadores en las periferias de Madrid, 1968–1982," in *Memoria ciudadana y movimiento vecinal: Madrid, 1968–2008*, ed. Vicente Pérez Quintana and Pablo Sánchez León (Madrid: Los Libros de la Catarata, 2008), 52.

12. Manuel Castells, "Productores de ciudad: El movimiento ciudadano de Madrid," in *Memoria ciudadana y movimiento vecinal: Madrid, 1968–2008*, ed. Vicente Pérez Quintana and Pablo Sánchez León (Madrid: Los Libros de la Catarata, 2008), 22.

13. Miguel Ángel Martínez López and Ángela García Bernardos, eds., *Okupa Madrid (1985–2011): Memoria, reflexión, debate y autogestión colectiva del conocimiento* (Madrid: Seminario de Historia Política y Social de las Okupaciones en Madrid-Metrópolis, 2014), 24; Miguel Ángel Martínez López, "Socio-Spatial Structures and Protest Cycles of

Squatted Social Centres in Madrid," in *The Urban Politics of Squatters' Movements*, ed. Miguel Ángel Martínez López (New York: Palgrave Macmillan, 2018), 28.

14. Castells, *The City and the Grassroots*, 278.

15. Andrea A. Davis, "Enforcing the Transition: The Demobilization of Collective Memory in Spain, 1979–1982," *Bulletin of Hispanic Studies (Liverpool, 2002)* 92, no. 6 (2015): 686.

16. Vicente Pérez Quintana and Pablo Sánchez León, eds., *Memoria ciudadana y movimiento vecinal: Madrid, 1968–2008* (Madrid: Los Libros de la Catarata, 2008).

17. Gonzalo Wilhelmi Casanova, *Armarse sobre las ruinas: Historia del movimiento autónomo en Madrid (1985–1999)* (Madrid: Potencial Hardcore, 2000), 28.

18. Wilhelmi Casanova, *Armarse sobre las ruinas*, 31.

19. Wilhelmi Casanova, *Armarse sobre las ruinas*, 31.

20. Wilhelmi Casanova, *Armarse sobre las ruinas*, 31.

21. Martínez López and García Bernardos, *Okupa Madrid*, 153.

22. Martínez López and García Bernardos, *Okupa Madrid*, 147.

23. Cristina Flesher Eguiarte, "The Logic of Autonomy: Principles, Praxis, and Challenges of Autonomous Anti-Capitalist Movement: Three Case Studies from Madrid" (University of California, Berkeley, 2005); see also, for example, George N. Katsiaficas, *The Subversion of Politics: European Autonomous Social Movements and the Decolonization of Everyday Life* (Oakland, CA: AK Press, 2006); Geronimo, *Fire and Flames: A History of the German Autonomist Movement* (Oakland, CA: PM Press, 2012).

24. Wilhelmi Casanova, cited in Martínez López and García Bernardos, *Okupa Madrid*, 136.

25. Wilhelmi Casanova, *Armarse sobre las ruinas*, 62.

26. Wilhelmi Casanova, *Armarse sobre las ruinas*, 59.

27. Jesús Ibáñez, *Por una sociología de la vida cotidiana* (Madrid: Siglo XXI de España Editores, 1994).

28. Ibáñez, *Por una sociología*, 13–15.

29. Ibáñez, *Por una sociología*, 17.

30. Ibáñez, *Por una sociología*, 16.

31. José Luis Moreno Pestaña, *Filosofía y sociología en Jesús Ibáñez: Genealogía de un pensador crítico* (Madrid: Siglo XXI de España Editores, 2008).

32. Jesús Ibáñez, *Más allá de la sociología. el grupo de discusión técnica y crítica* (Madrid: Siglo XXI, 1979).

33. Gabriel Albiac, "Jesús Ibáñez, testigo de cargo," *El mundo (la esfera de los libros)*, June 14, 1997.

34. "Autobiografía (Los años de aprendizaje de Jesús Ibáñez)," *Anthropos: Revista de documentación científica de la cultura* 113 (1990): 16.

35. Martínez López and García Bernardos, *Okupa Madrid*, 151.

36. Wilhelmi Casanova, *Armarse sobre las ruinas*, 52.

37. Gonzalo Wilhelmi Casanova, *Lucha autónoma: Una visión de la coordinadora de colectivos, 1990–1997* (Madrid: Aurora Ediciones, 1998).

38. Jacobo Rivero, cited in Martínez López and García Bernardos, *Okupa Madrid*, 173.

39. The place of students in the shaping of an autonomous consciousness and politics has traditionally been a source of academic and conceptual discomfort. Students played a crucial part in the formation of autonomous groups in Italy and Germany in the late 1960s, yet notwithstanding their organizational and affective input, they rarely brought a direct experience of factory-floor alienation or confrontation to these groups' struggles. For example, as Geronimo put it in his personal memoir of autonomous activism in Germany in the second half of the twentieth century, by 1969 most "student activists shied away from the 'tedious' daily work in the factories. Eventually, this caused deep

alienation between the university and the factory committees"; see Geronimo, *Fire and Flames*, 37. The Italian scene was different. The *autonomia operaia* movement was a direct response by unskilled assembly line workers to their conditions of production, soon joined by left-wing intellectuals and students. In the late 1970s, a second wave of autonomous activism—the so-called "diffused" or "creative" autonomy—expanded the field of action beyond the factory-floor to incorporate students and the unemployed, as well as gay, feminist, and other countercultural groups. The experience of Radio Alice has sometimes been singled out as a watershed moment in the "diffusion" of autonomy from the factory to the street; see Patrick Cuninghame, "Autonomia in the 1970s: The Refusal of Work, the Party and Power," *Cultural Studies Review* 11, no. 2 (October 25, 2013): 77–94, https://doi.org/10.5130/csr.v11i2.3660.

40. In the words of one of the founding members of the Laboratory: "We set out on a political search, in part through our encounter with new actors, such as the non-violent antimilitarist movement, the ecological and feminist movements, but also deeply moved by a sense of uncertainty, whilst simultaneously spurred by debates, readings, and a close observation of the political thought and praxis taking place around us, in new contexts such as the Italian autonomist movement"; see Carlos Vidania Domínguez, "Fragmentación, red, autonomía," in *Tomar y hacer en vez de pedir y esperar: Autonomía y movimientos sociales: Madrid, 1985–2011*, ed. Francisco Salamanca and Gonzalo Wilhelmi Casanova (Madrid: Solidaridad Obrera, 2012), 51.

41. Martínez López and García Bernardos, *Okupa Madrid*, 151.

42. Jacobo Rivero, cited in Martínez López and García Bernardos, *Okupa Madrid*, 206.

43. Jacobo Rivero, cited in Martínez López and García Bernardos, *Okupa Madrid*, 209.

44. Visits were still being organized in the early 2000s. Pablo Iglesias, the leader of the left-wing populist party Podemos who raised to become Spain's Second Deputy Prime Minister in 2020–2021, has written about his own visit to Italian squatted social centers as a young "disobedient" and autonomist activist in the summer of 2003; see Pablo Iglesias Turrión, *Desobedientes: De Chiapas a Madrid* (Madrid: Editorial Popular, 2011), 134. The circulation and exchange of activists between Italy and Spain, he observed, took place over at least a ten-year period, facilitated, he noted with a dose of amusement, "by the Erasmus exchange program" (23).

45. "In the second half of the 1980s," write Andrea Membretti and Pierpaolo Mudu of the transversal orientation of Italian autonomism, "a second generation of *Centri Sociali* materialized. . . . In big Italian cities, autonomists, punks, and underground cultures were intermixed, originating a new wave of *Centri Sociali*. This 'contamination' had been built through a conscious spatial strategy where *Centri Sociali* constituted spaces of 'amalgamation' for self-management practices"; see Andrea Membretti and Pierpaolo Mudu, "Where Global Meets Local: Italian Social Centres and the Alterglobalization Movement," in *Understanding European Movements: New Social Movements, Global Justice Struggles, Anti-Austerity Protest*, ed. Cristina Flesher Fominaya and Laurence Cox (Oxford: Routledge, 2013), 79.

46. Jacobo Rivero, cited in Martínez López and García Bernardos, *Okupa Madrid*, 174.

47. Guattari, *Molecular Revolution*, 11–23. In the words of the Radio Alice collective: "The collective transformation of existence runs transversally across behaviors found in different social strata, fueled by a process that is neither mechanic nor additive (that is, an extension of the organization) but *transversal* (where new desires are expressed and new groups formed), leading to the diffusion and unfolding of subversive and liberatory behaviors across different planes"; see Collettivo A/traverso, *Alicia es el diablo*, 69, emphasis added.

48. For an excellent account of Radio Alice and the influence of Mao-Dadaist insurgent aesthetics in the shaping of Italian autonomous media activism at the turn of the

century, see Alessandra Renzi, *Hacked Transmissions: Technology and Connective Activism in Italy* (Minneapolis: University of Minnesota Press, 2020), 50–53.

49. William Chislett, *The Internationalization of the Spanish Economy* (Madrid: Real Instituto Elcano de Estudios Internacionales y Estratégicos, 2002), 150.

50. Greig Charnock, Thomas Purcell, and Ramón Ribera-Fumaz, *The Limits to Capital in Spain: Crisis and Revolt in the European South* (New York: Palgrave Macmillan, 2014), 66–67.

51. Maribel Casas-Cortés, "A Genealogy of Precarity: A Toolbox for Rearticulating Fragmented Social Realities in and out of the Workplace," *Rethinking Marxism* 26, no. 2 (April 3, 2014): 208, https://doi.org/10.1080/08935696.2014.888849.

52. Instituto Nacional de Estadística, "Anuario estadístico de España: Año 1995" (Madrid, 1995), http://www.ine.es/inebaseweb/treeNavigation.do?tn=151078.

53. The pioneering work of Spanish squatted social centers in articulating "early alter-globalization protest campaigns" has been described by Miguel Ángel Martínez; see Miguel Ángel Martínez López, "The Squatters' Movement: Urban Counter-Culture and Alter-Globalization Dynamics," *South European Society and Politics* 12, no. 3 (September 1, 2007): 390–91, https://doi.org/10.1080/13608740701495285.

54. Casas-Cortés, "A Genealogy of Precarity."

55. José Luis Carretero, "La apuesta autónoma (LA reloaded)," in *Tomar y hacer en vez de pedir y esperar: Autonomía y movimientos sociales: Madrid, 1985–2011*, ed. Francisco Salamanca and Gonzalo Wilhelmi Casanova (Madrid: Solidaridad Obrera, 2012), 50.

56. Alberto Melucci, *Nomads of the Present: Social Movements and Individual Needs in Contemporary Society* (London: Hutchinson Radius, 1989), 60, 208.

57. Michael Hardt, "Introduction: Laboratory Italy," in *Radical Thought in Italy: A Potential Politics*, ed. Paolo Virno and Michael Hardt (Minneapolis: University of Minnesota Press, 1996), 4.

58. Pablo Ximénez de Sandoval, "Salen de prisión los últimos cuatro insumisos de la mili," *El país*, May 26, 2002, sec. Espana, https://elpais.com/diario/2002/05/26/espana/1022364010_850215.html.

59. Gonzalo Wilhelmi Casanova, "Todo parecía posible," in *Tomar y hacer en vez de pedir y esperar: Autonomía y movimientos sociales: Madrid, 1985–2011*, ed. Francisco Salamanca and Gonzalo Wilhelmi Casanova (Madrid: Solidaridad Obrera, 2012), 84.

60. Vidania Domínguez, "Fragmentación, Red, autonomía," 61, n. 5.

61. Wilhelmi Casanova, "Todo parecía posible," 91.

62. Phoolan Delvi, "Mujeres sin hombres y peces sin bicicletas: Mirando Hacia Atrás: Experiencias de autonomía y feminismo," in *Tomar y hacer en vez de pedir y esperar: Autonomía y movimientos sociales: Madrid, 1985–2011*, ed. Francisco Salamanca and Gonzalo Wilhelmi Casanova (Madrid: Solidaridad Obrera, 2012), 25. Elizabeth Lorenzi has written a moving and remarkable first-person account of what it felt like being a young woman in the climate of agonistic masculinity that characterized the early years of the autonomous movement in Madrid in the 1990s; see Elisabeth Lorenzi Fernández, "Un cóctel contra la indiferencia, el Molotov," in *Tomar y hacer en vez de pedir y esperar: Autonomía y movimientos sociales: Madrid, 1985–2011*, ed. Francisco Salamanca and Gonzalo Wilhelmi Casanova (Madrid: Solidaridad Obrera, 2012), 117–38.

63. Paolo Virno, "Virtuosity and Revolution: The Political Theory of Exodus," in *Radical Thought in Italy: A Potential Politics*, ed. Paolo Virno and Michael Hardt (Minneapolis: University of Minnesota Press, 1996), 199.

64. David Graeber, *Fragments of an Anarchist Anthropology* (Chicago: Prickly Paradigm Press, 2004), 60.

65. Graeber, *Fragments*, 62.

66. Hakim Bey, *Taz: The Temporary Autonomous Zone, Ontological Anarchy, Poetic Terrorism* (New York: Autonomedia, 2003).

67. Bey, *Taz*, 100. "The TAZ agrees with the hackers because it wants to come into being—in part—through the Net" (109).

68. Bey, *Taz*, 99, emphasis in the original.

69. To follow Sara Evans and Harry Boyte's now-classic definition, free spaces "are the environments in which people are able to learn a new self-respect, a deeper and more assertive group identity, public skills, and values of cooperation and civic virtue. Put simply, free spaces are settings between private lives and large-scale institutions where ordinary citizens can act with dignity, independence, and vision. These are, in the main, voluntary forms of association with a relatively open and participatory character—many religious organizations, clubs, self-help and mutual aid societies, reform groups, neighborhood, civic, and ethnic groups, and a host of other associations grounded in the fabric of community life"; see Sara M. Evans and Harry C. Boyte, *Free Spaces: The Sources of Democratic Change in America* (New York: Harper & Row, 1986), 17–18.

70. Francesca Polletta, "'Free Spaces' in Collective Action," *Theory and Society* 28, no. 1 (1999): 7.

71. Polletta, "Free Spaces," 9–12.

72. Bey, *Taz*, 99.

73. Beatriz Plaza, "The Guggenheim-Bilbao Museum Effect: A Reply to María V. Gomez' 'Reflective Images: The Case of Urban Regeneration in Glasgow and Bilbao,'" *International Journal of Urban and Regional Research* 23, no. 3 (1999): 589–92, https://doi.org/10.1111/1468-2427.00215.

74. Eugenio L. Burriel de Orueta, "La 'década prodigiosa' del urbanismo español (1997–2006)," *Scripta nova: Revista electrónica de geografía y ciencias sociales* 12, no. 270 (August 28, 2008), https://doi.org/10.1344/sn2008.12.1489.

75. Emmanuel Rodríguez López, "La ciudad global o la nueva centralidad de Madrid," in *Madrid: ¿La suma de todos? Globalización, territorio, desigualdad*, ed. Observatorio Metropolitano (Madrid: Traficantes de sueños, 2007), 65.

76. Jorge Martínez Pagés and Luis Ángel Maza, "Análisis del precio de la vivienda en España" (Madrid: Banco de España, 2003), 11, https://www.bde.es/f/webbde/SES/Secciones/Publicaciones/PublicacionesSeriadas/DocumentosTrabajo/03/Fic/dt0307.pdf.

77. Martínez López, "Socio-Spatial Structures," 37.

78. Ayuntamiento de Madrid, "Memoria del plan general de ordenación Urbana 1997" (1997), 89.

79. Observatorio Metropolitano, ed., *Madrid: ¿La suma de todos? Globalización, territorio, desigualdad* (Madrid: Traficantes de sueños, 2007), 233.

80. Julio Vinuesa Angulo and José María De la Riva Ámez, "Los 'grandes desarrollos' del PG97, un grave error de planteamiento y una amenaza para el futuro urbanístico de Madrid," in *Reflexiones a propósito de la Revisión del Plan General de Madrid*, ed. Julio Vinuesa Angulo, David Porras Alfaro, José María De la Riva Ámez, and Felipe Fernández García (Madrid: Grupo TRyS, 2013), 497, 498.

81. Vinuesa Angulo and De la Riva Ámez, "Los 'grandes desarrollos,'" 498–99.

82. Vicente Pérez Quintana, "Lavapiés: Intervención y rehabilitación (1998–2008)" (Madrid: Empresa Municipal de la Vivienda y Suelo, 2008), 225, https://aavvmadrid.org/intercambio/FEC/EstudioARI%20Lavapies_1998-%202008.pdf.

83. At a meeting commemorating the twentieth anniversary of the occupation of the Laboratory, Carlos Vidania Domínguez, a longtime activist and original resident of the squat, noted: "The Laboratory was planned. The idea of meddling and confounding the metropolitan and the territorial dimensions of the city—that was planned. The idea of focusing

on affects and desire as vectors of social change (say, by opening up spaces to new electronic music and rave parties)—that was planned. The idea of opening up the squat, to liberate it as a 'free house'—that was planned"; fieldwork diary, Alberto Corsín Jiménez, May 11, 2017. The audio recordings of the meeting are available at https://archive.org/details/AudioLaboIngobernable11Mayo.

84. Carlos Vidania Domínguez and Margarita Padilla, "Okupar el vacío desde el vacío," in *Autonomía y metropolis: Del movimiento okupa a los centros sociales de segunda generación.*, ed. Javier Toret, Nicolás Sguiglia, Santiago Fernández Patón, and Mónica Lama, (Málaga: CEDMA, 2008), 54.

85. Vidania Domínguez, "Fragmentación, red, autonomía," 70. Cuninghame, "Autonomia in the 1970s."

86. Vidania Domínguez and Padilla, "Okupar el vacío desde el vacío," 54–55.

87. Silvia López Gil, "Reordenación de territorios," 2003, https://sindominio.net/karakola/antigua_casa/textos/brumaria.htm, order of the passages altered.

88. Cited in Alexander Vasudevan, *The Autonomous City: A History of Urban Squatting* (London: Verso, 2017), 35. See also Roberto González García and Alejandra Araiza Díaz, "Feminismo y okupación en España: El caso de la Eskalera Karakola," *Sociológica* 31, no. 87 (2016), http://www.scielo.org.mx/scielo.php?pid=S0187-01732016000100007&script=sci_arttext.

89. Precarias a la deriva, *A la deriva por los circuitos de la precariedad femenina* (Madrid: Traficantes de Sueños, 2004), 249 and throughout.

90. Montserrat Cañedo Rodríguez, "Multitudes urbanas: De las figuras y lógicas prácticas de la identificación política," *Revista de dialectología y tradiciones populares* 67, no. 2 (December 30, 2012): 367, https://doi.org/10.3989/rdtp.2012.13.

91. Pérez Quintana, "Lavapiés: Intervención y rehabilitación (1998–2008)," 165–68. For a history of the network, see Jesús Carrillo, *Space Invaders: Intervenciones artístico-políticas en un territorio en disputa: Lavapiés (1997–2004)* (Madrid: Brumaria, 2018), 55–86.

92. Carlos Vidania Domínguez, "¿Han oído hablar de Lavapiés? Historia de una ruina provocada," in *El cielo está enladrillado: Entre el mobbing y la violencia inmobiliaria y urbanística* (Barcelona: Edicions Bellaterra, 2006), 137.

93. Carrillo, *Space Invaders*, 89–142.

94. Santiago Barber Cortés, Curro Aix Gracia, and Marcelo Expósito, "Entrevista a Santiago Barber y Curro Aix: La fiambrera barroca," *Desacuerdos: Sobre arte, política y esfera pública en el estado español* 1 (2004): 167–73.

95. On the politics of ruin declaration, see Vidania Domínguez, "¿Han oído hablar de Lavapiés?"

96. See http://www.sindominio.net/fiambrera/convocatoria.html.

97. The video recording of the festival is available at https://archive.org/details/jornadasrehabilitarlavapiesnov1998.

98. Vasudevan, *The Autonomous City.*

99. Cited in Vasudevan, *The Autonomous City*, 145, 146.

100. Vasudevan, *The Autonomous City*, 175.

101. Gianni Piazza and Miguel Ángel Martínez López, "More than Four Decades of Squatting: Cycles, Waves and Stages of Autonomous Urban Politics in European Cities," in *The Urban Politics of Squatters' Movements*, ed. Miguel Ángel Martínez López (New York: Palgrave Macmillan, 2018), 229–45.

102. See Harvey, *Rebel Cities.*

103. Martínez López, "Socio-Spatial Structures."

104. Vidania Domínguez and Padilla, "Okupar el vacío desde el vacío," 55.

2. THE COPYLEFT AND THE (COPY) RIGHT TO THE CITY

1. Margarita Padilla, "Por qué nodo50 ha dejado de interesarme," 1999, http://biblioweb
.sindominio.net/telematica/nonodo50.html; Mercé Molist Ferrer, "Hackstory.Es: La historia nunca contada del underground hacker en la península Ibérica," 2008, https://
hackstory.net/Nodo50.

2. See, for example, the website of the Fourth Annual State Gathering of Counterinformation (Encuentro Estatal de Contrainformación): https://www.nodo50.org/contrainfos
/home.htm.

3. Nanni Balestrini, *The Unseen* (London: Verso Books, 1989), 133. The first hackmeeting in Spain was organized in the squatted social center Les Naus, Barcelona, in October 20–22, 2000. The meeting was organized by hackers and activists who had attended the first Italian hackmeeting organized by the counterinformation network StranoNetwork and the Centro Popolare Autogestito di Firenze Sud in Florence in June 1998; see Molist Ferrer, "Hackstory.Es." The manifesto for the Barcelona meeting consisted of a long passage from *The Unseen*, a novel by the Italian poet and writer Nanni Balestrini that recounts the vagaries of a young autonomist activist in the late 1970s as he attempts to set up a free radio station and is eventually imprisoned. The original passage cited by the manifesto reads: "to generalize the offensive means to radicalize disaffection with whichever hierarchy you choose to exercise our destructive creativity against the society of the spectacle to sabotage the machines and goods that sabotage our lives to promote indefinite wildcat general strikes always to have mass meetings in all the separate factories to elect delegates who can be recalled by the base *to keep continuous links between all the places of struggle to overlook no useful technical means of free communication* to give a direct use value to everything that has an exchange value to occupy permanently the factories and the public buildings to organize self-defence of the conquered territories and on with the music"; see Balestrini, *The Unseen*, 133; emphasis in the manifesto, not the original.

4. Padilla, "Por qué nodo50 ha dejado de interesarme," order of passages inverted.

5. The archive of the área telemática is available at http://www.sindominio.net
/laboratorio/atl/home.htm, which includes information on its manifesto, workshops, interviews, news, and so on.

6. Miquel Vidal, "Liberar el ciberespacio: Reflexiones sobre un lustro de comunidades políticas virtuales: Entrevista con Miquel Vidal," *Contrapoder*, 2005, 73.

7. Renzi, *Hacked Transmissions*, 97.

8. sinDominio.net, "Preguntas frecuentes sobre el proyecto SinDominio.Net,"
2004, http://sindominio.net/article.php3?id_article=31.

9. The complicities between hacker communities and squatted social centers is well known in the European social movement scene, especially in Italy and the Netherlands; see Stefania Milan, *Social Movements and Their Technologies: Wiring Social Change* (Houndmills: Palgrave Macmillan, 2013), 47, 66. As Caroline Nevejan and Alexander Badenoch have explained in the case of Amsterdam: "The social actors who would go on to shape Amsterdam's Internet infrastructure node in Europe and make it publicly available came from the city's countercultural and squatter movement. Creating new media spaces was part and parcel of the movement—and the struggles—to create new forms of urban space"; see Caroline Nevejan and Alexander Badenoch, "How Amsterdam Invented the Internet: European Networks of Significance, 1980–1995," in *Hacking Europe: From Computer Cultures to Demoscenes*, ed. Gerard Alberts and Ruth Oldenziel (London: Springer, 2014), 193. Indeed, along the many English words imported to describe the practices of hacking, "came a Dutch translation: *computerkraken*, best translated as 'computer squatting,'" Nevejan and Badenoch, 199. In the Spanish context, the strong connection between the worlds of hacking and the world of squatted social centers has

been described by Igor Sábada and Gustavo Roig Rodríguez in "El movimiento de okupación ante las nuevas tecnologías: Okupas en las redes," in *¿Dónde están las llaves? El
movimiento Okupa: Prácticas y contextos sociales*, ed. Ramón Adell Argilés and Miguel
Ángel Martínez López (Madrid: Los Libros de la Catarata, 2004), 267–91.

10. Zapatistas, *Zapatista encuentro: Documents from the First Intercontinental Encounter for Humanity and against Neoliberalism* (New York: Seven Stories Press, 1998), 53.

11. Todd Wolfson, *Digital Rebellion: The Birth of the Cyber Left* (Champaign: University of Illinois Press, 2014).

12. Wolfson, *Digital Rebellion*, 45–46.

13. Gabriella Coleman, "From Internet Farming to Weapons of the Geek," *Current
Anthropology* 58, no. S15 (November 22, 2016): S94, https://doi.org/10.1086/688697.

Gabriella Coleman, "Hacker," in *Digital Keywords: A Vocabulary of Information Society
and Culture*, ed. Benjamin Peters (Princeton, NJ: Princeton University Press, 2016), 167.

14. Vidal, "Liberar el ciberespacio: Reflexiones sobre un lustro de comunidades
políticas virtuales. Entrevista con Miquel Vidal," 74.

15. Yonderboy [Miguel Vidal], "La ACP vuelve por fin a la luz como nuevo nodo de indymedia," *Barrapunto*, April 24, 2002, http://barrapunto.com/articles/02/04/24/0038227.shtml.

16. Our reconstruction of the story of the ACP's closure is based on interviews that
Margarita Padilla ("¿Y si partimos en dos la red?") and Miguel Vidal ("Liberar el ciberespacio") conducted with the grassroots philosopher and editor Amador Fernández Savater in
2005.

17. Vidal, "Liberar el ciberespacio," 77–78.

18. In the original, the word "enablement" is not one that Margarita uses. She modulates the word "power" into various significations, not easily translated into English. The
original reads: "La asamblea tiene que 'poder.' 'Poder' no es tomar decisiones, 'poder' es
decidir qué tipo de decisiones, en qué lenguaje las tomas, poder deconstruir las propias
decisiones . . . poder de poder.' Padilla, "¿Y si partimos en dos la red?," 84.

19. Padilla, "¿Y si partimos en dos la red?," 85–86.

20. The software they used was based on slashcode, the program underpinning the social news website Slashdot. Miguel Vidal joined the Spanish version of Slashdot, Barrapunto,
in 2001 and worked as its system administrator until 2008. For a history of Barrapunto, see
Javier Lacort, "En el principio fue barrapunto: 'Llenamos un vacío que nadie ha recuperado,'" Xataka, October 10, 2017, https://www.xataka.com/empresas-y-economia/en-el
-principio-fue-barrapunto-llenamos-un-vacio-que-nadie-ha-recuperado.

21. Vidal, "Liberar el ciberespacio," 78–79.

22. Vidal, "Liberar el ciberespacio," 78. We have opted here for a somewhat liberal
translation of a number of colloquial turns. The original reads: "se piensa que cualquier
filtrado es censura, pero la censura en Internet es un contrasentido porque es un espacio
donde si no publicas en un sitio puedes en otro. . . . Este tipo de prejuicios, en los sitios
más vinculados a comunidades técnicas (comunidades de hackers y software libre),
quienes iniciaron este tipo de herramientas colaborativas, no se da. Lo que yo he visto
en los foros más técnicos en que se puede determinar de forma más ecuánime quién lleva
razón y quién no, eso suele ser más productivo; pero, en cambio, en esos mismos foros
cuando se deriva hacia la discusión política es igual de desastroso que Indymedia (el
mismo desmadre, el 'opinódromo' . . .)"; see Vidal, 78.

23. Nathaniel Tkacz, "The Spanish Fork: Wikipedia's Ad-Fuelled Mutiny," Wired
UK, January 20, 2011, http://www.wired.co.uk/article/wikipedia-spanish-fork.

24. Robert W. Gehl, *Reverse Engineering Social Media: Software, Culture, and Political
Economy in New Media Capitalism* (Philadelphia: Temple University Press, 2014), 119.

25. Tiziana Terranova, "Free Labor: Producing Culture for the Digital Economy,"
Social Text 18, no. 2 (June 1, 2000): 33–58.

26. Terranova, "Free Labor," 33.

27. Terranova, "Free Labor," 39, 54.

28. Terranova, "Free Labor," 35.

29. Terranova, "Free Labor," 41 and throughout.

30. Franco Bifo Berardi, "What Is the Meaning of Autonomy Today?," in *Precarious Rhapsody: Semiocapitalism and the Pathologies of the Post-Alpha Generation* (London: Minor Compositions, 2009), 81.

31. Berardi, "What Is the Meaning," 82.

32. Michael Hardt and Antonio Negri, *Multitude: War and Democracy in the Age of Empire* (New York: Penguin, 2005).

33. Gehl, *Reverse Engineering Social Media*, 122.

34. Javier de la Cueva, Interview with Javier de la Cueva, February 16, 2017.

35. Gehl, *Reverse Engineering Social Media*, 131, 134; Tkacz, "The Spanish Fork."

36. de la Cueva, Interview with Javier de la Cueva.

37. Postigo, *The Digital Rights Movement*.

38. "Un juez ratifica que los cd grabables deben pagar derechos de autor," *La vanguardia*, January 14, 2002, https://www.lavanguardia.com/internet/20020114/51262748891/un-juez-ratifica-que-los-cd-grabables-deben-pagar-derechos-de-autor.html.

39. Christopher M. Kelty, *Two Bits: The Cultural Significance of Free Software* (Durham: Duke University Press, 2008), 243–68.

40. The 2002 ruling over the "digital canon" sparked a war over digital rights that lasted for well over a decade, and twisted, morphed, and extended to include battles for free speech and against the oligarchic and plutocratic alliance between politicians and media moguls. In 2009, the government drafted a bill that included a provision to create an intellectual property commission invested with the power to take down websites or service providers that infringed on copyright. Named after the minister of culture who championed it, the Sinde Law was widely criticized for violating basic human rights because it invested a ministerial authority with a power that should be confined to the judiciary. By 2011, when the Sinde Law was finally passed in parliament, the momentum of the protests had grown and mutated into a movement for Democracia Real Ya (Real Democracy Now) that converged with other movements against corruption and for the right to housing and eventually culminated in the May 15 demonstrations. "In some respects, the FCM [Free Culture Movement]," the political scientist Mayo Fuster Morell wrote, "is considered a predecessor of the 15M mobilization in Spain. More concretely, the formats of the Sinde Law campaign . . . were a reference point for designing the 15M demonstration"; see Mayo Fuster Morell, "From Digital Commons to Society Commons: Influence of the Free Culture Movement in the 15M Mobilization," in *Crisis and Social Mobilization in Contemporary Spain: The 15M Movement*, ed. Benjamín Tejerina and Ignacia Perugorría (Oxford: Routledge, 2018), 68. For a detailed history of how networked opposition to the Sinde Law converged with other social movements and culminated in the 15M protests, see Adriana Razquin Mangado, *Didáctica ciudadana: La vida política en las plazas. etnografía del movimiento 15M* (Granada: Editorial Universidad de Granada, 2017) chap. 1.

41. David García Aristegui, "Haciendo ruido con las rejas de la jaula: Semana de lucha social 'rompamos el silencio' 2005–2011," in *Tomar y hacer en vez de pedir y esperar: Autonomía y movimientos sociales: Madrid, 1985–2011*, ed. Francisco Salamanca and Gonzalo Wilhelmi Casanova (Madrid: Solidaridad Obrera, 2012), 240, 246.

42. Laia Reventós, "Una demanda contra el canon de los cd y dvd circula por Internet," *El País*, July 29, 2004, https://elpais.com/diario/2004/07/29/ciberpais/1091065228_850215.html.

43. de la Cueva, Interview.

44. de la Cueva, Interview.

45. Manuela Villa, Interview with Manuela Villa, March 9, 2017.

46. Villa, Interview.

47. Villa, Interview.

48. Villa, Interview.

49. Villa, Interview.

50. Villa, Interview.

51. Villa, Interview.

52. Adolfo Estalella, "Dorkbot inicia en Madrid sesiones alternativas de artistas y 'hackers,'" *El País*, November 4, 2004, https://elpais.com/diario/2004/11/04/ciberpais /1099537343_850215.html.

53. On the history of Barrapunto, see Lacort, "En el principio fue Barrapunto."

54. Francesco Manetto, "Reportaje | ¿El motor del barrio? En un bajo, junto al chino," *El País*, March 3, 2007, https://elpais.com/diario/2007/03/03/madrid/1172924663_850215 .html.

55. Villa, Interview

56. Villa, Interview.

57. de la Cueva, Interview.

58. de la Cueva, Interview.

59. de la Cueva, Interview.

60. See, for example, Mercé Molist, "Por primera vez una sentencia judicial española cita el 'Copyleft,'" *El País*, February 16, 2006, https://elpais.com/diario/2006/02/16 /ciberpais/1140058946_850215.html.

61. de la Cueva, Interview.

62. Manetto, "Reportaje | ¿El motor del barrio?"

63. Luis Sánchez-Moliní, "'Hay que pensar en cómo redistribuir la riqueza que se genera en las redes,'" *Diario de Sevilla*, January 13, 2019, https://www.diariodesevilla .es/rastrodelafama/Arquitectura-bioclimatizacion-redes-ETSA_0_1318068491.html.

64. José Pérez de Lama, Interview with José Pérez de Lama, January 24, 2017.

65. José Pérez de Lama, "Entre Blade Runner y Mickey Mouse: Nuevas condiciones urbanas: Una perspectiva desde Los Angeles, California (1999–2002)" (Universidad de Sevilla, 2006), https://idus.us.es/xmlui/handle/11441/24254.

66. Burriel de Orueta, "La 'década prodigiosa' del urbanismo español (1997–2006)."

67. Santiago Barber, Victoria Frensel, and María José Romero, eds., *Cómo nació, creció y se resiste a ser comido EL GRAN POLLO DE LA ALAMEDA: Una docena de años de lucha en el barrio de la Alameda, Sevilla* (Sevilla: Consejo de Redacción del Gran Pollo de la Alameda, 2006).

68. Santiago Barber, Victoria Frensel, and María José Romero, "Urban: Hasta aquí llegó el nivel de escombro: Introducción.," in *Cómo nació, creció y se resiste a ser comido EL GRAN POLLO DE LA ALAMEDA. Una docena de años de lucha en el barrio de la Alameda, Sevilla* (Sevilla: Consejo de Redacción del Gran Pollo de la Alameda, 2006), 60.

69. Ibán Díaz, "Bienvenido Mr. Hurgan: El urban, de la palabra a los hechos," in *Cómo nació, creció y se resiste a ser comido EL GRAN POLLO DE LA ALAMEDA: Una docena de años de lucha en el barrio de la Alameda, Sevilla* (Sevilla: Consejo de Redacción del Gran Pollo de la Alameda, 2006), 66.

70. José Pérez de Lama and Sergio Moreno Páez, "Request for Comments," in *Wikiplaza: Request for Comments* (Barcelona: dpr-barcelona, 2011), 12–13.

71. Jason Logan [Sack], "Take the Skinheads Bowling," *InfoNation*, 1995.

72. Logan [Sack], "Take the Skinheads Bowling," 13.

73. Critical Art Ensemble, *Electronic Civil Disobedience and Other Unpopular Ideas* (Brooklyn, NY: Autonomedia, 1996), 11 and 19.

74. Tim Jordan, *Activism!: Direct Action, Hacktivism and the Future of Society* (London: Reaktion Books, 2002), 119.

75. John D. H. Downing, Tamara Villarreal Ford, Genève Gil, and Laura Stein, *Radical Media: Rebellious Communication and Social Movements* (Thousand Oaks, CA: SAGE Publications, 2001).

76. Milan, *Social Movements and Their Technologies*, 48.

77. Milan, *Social Movements and Their Technologies*, 47.

78. Around the time when Pérez de Lama encouraged his students to stage theatrical urban climates, the Critical Art Ensemble (CAE) was expanding its repertoire of electronic resistance methods to incorporate broader tactical media interventions, including biotechnology or the "foundational environment . . . of street theater." Streets, the CAE intuited, offered scenographic resources for digital rebellion too. See Critical Art Ensemble, *Digital Resistance: Explorations in Tactical Media* (Brooklyn, NY: Autonomedia, 2001), 96.

3. THE CITY IN FLAMES

1. Cristina Flesher Fominaya, "The Madrid Bombings and Popular Protest: Misinformation, Counter-Information, Mobilisation and Elections after '11-M,'" *Contemporary Social Science* 6, no. 3 (November 1, 2011): 290, https://doi.org/10.1080/21582041.2011.603910.

2. Jeffrey S. Juris, *Networking Futures: The Movements against Corporate Globalization* (Durham, NC: Duke University Press, 2008).

3. Guillem Martínez, ed., *CT o la cultura de la Transición: Crítica a 35 años de cultura española* (Madrid: Penguin Random House, 2012).

4. Jorge Luis Marzo, "Política cultural del gobierno español en el exterior (2000–2004)," *Desacuerdos. Sobre arte, política y esfera pública en el estado español* 2 (2005): 58–121.

5. Ángel Badillo, "Las políticas públicas de acción cultural exterior de España," Estrategia Exterior Española (Real Instituto Elcano, 2014).

6. Carlos Alberdi, Interview with Carlos Alberdi, November 10, 2017.

7. Rafael Doctor Roncero, ed., *Nuevas cartografías de Madrid* (Madrid: La Casa Encendida y Casa de América, 2003).

8. Gloria G. Durán and Alan W. Moore, "La tabacalera of Lavapiés: A Social Experiment or a Work of Art?," *FIELD: A Journal of Socially-Engaged Art Criticism* 2 (Fall 2015): 72 n. 13.

9. Carlos Alberdi, Interview.

10. Andrés Padilla, "Dos focos culturales, pared con pared," *El País*, January 3, 2003, https://elpais.com/diario/2003/01/03/madrid/1041596669_850215.html.

11. The classic text on relational aesthetics is Nicolas Bourriaud, *Relational Aesthetics* (Dijon: Les Presses du réel, 2002). On participatory and community art, see Grant H. Kester, *The One and the Many: Contemporary Collaborative Art in a Global Context* (Durham, NC: Duke University Press, 2011); Kate Crehan, *Community Art: An Anthropological Perspective* (Oxford: Berg, 2013). For a well-known critique of these approaches, see Claire Bishop, *Artificial Hells: Participatory Art and the Politics of Spectatorship* (New York: Verso Books, 2012).

12. Jorge Ribalta, "Experimentos para una nueva institucionalidad," in *Objetos relacionales: Colección MACBA 2002–2007*, ed. Manuel Borja-Villel, Kaira M. Cabañas, and Jorge Ribalta (Barcelona: MACBA, 2010), 225–65.

13. Ribalta, "Experimentos," 234–35.

14. Juris, *Networking Futures*, 275.

15. Lucie Kolb and Gabriel Flückiger, "New Institutionalism Revisited," *On Curating | Special Issue on (New) Institution (Alism)*, December 2013, 9; Jesús Carrillo, *Space Invaders:*

Intervenciones artístico-políticas en un territorio en disputa: Lavapiés (1997–2004) (Madrid: Brumaria, 2018), 161.

16. Juris, *Networking Futures*, 197.

17. Casilda Cabrerizo Sanz, Azucena Klett, and Pablo García Bachiller, "De alianzas anómalas a nuevos paisajes políticos: Madrid, Lavapiés y otras geografías de lo común," *URBS: Revista de estudios urbanos y ciencias sociales* 5, no. 2 (November 4, 2015): 163–78.

18. Marcos Serrano, "Fw: [Wh2001] Reu de las jornadas de propiedad intelectual," *Copyleft*, December 16, 2002, https://listas.sindominio.net/mailman/private/copyleft /2002-December/000002.html.

19. Universidad Nómada, "Universidad Nómada," 2002, https://sindominio.net /unomada/.

20. See https://sindominio.net/unomada/patentes.html; https://sindominio.net/unom ada/migraciones/planjornadas.pdf.

21. Pablo Iglesias Turrión, *Desobedientes: De Chiapas a Madrid* (Madrid: Editorial Popular, 2011), 23.

22. Juris, *Networking Futures*; Iglesias Turrión, *Desobedientes*.

23. Jesús Ibáñez, "Autobiografía (Los años de aprendizaje de Jesús Ibáñez)," *Anthropos: Revista de documentación científica de la cultura* 113 (1990): 21.

24. Cristina Flesher Eguiarte, "The Logic of Autonomy: Principles, Praxis, and Challenges of Autonomous Anti-Capitalist Movement: Three Case Studies from Madrid" (University of California, Berkeley, 2005), 250.

25. Fieldwork diary, Alberto Corsín Jiménez, May 11, 2017. The audio recordings of the meeting are available at https://archive.org/details/AudioLaboIngobernable11Mayo.

26. Serrano, "Fw: [Wh2001] Reu de las jornadas de propiedad intelectual."

27. Miguel Vidal, "[Copyleft] Creative Commons y licencias Copyleft," *Copyleft*, December 17, 2002, https://listas.sindominio.net/mailman/private/copyleft/2002-December /000003.html.

28. Amador Fernández-Savater, "[Copyleft] Perfil jornadas," *Copyleft*, December 18, 2002, https://listas.sindominio.net/mailman/private/copyleft/2002-December/000006 .html.

29. See https://sindominio.net/copyleft-old/index-2.html.

30. Desacuerdos Colectivo Editorial, "Desacuerdos: Sobre arte, políticas y esfera pública en el estado Español," *Desacuerdos: Sobre arte, política y esfera pública en el estado español* 1 (2004): 12.

31. Javier de la Cueva, "[OT] Competencias de las entidades de gestión," *Copyleft*, June 11, 2004, https://listas.sindominio.net/mailman/private/copyleft/2004-June/001470 .html.

32. Javier de la Cueva, "[OT] Competencias de las entidades de gestión," June 11, 2004, https://listas.sindominio.net/mailman/private/copyleft/2004-June/001477.html.

33. Miguel Vidal, "Re: Competencias de las entidades de gestión," *Copyleft*, June 11, 2004, https://listas.sindominio.net/mailman/private/copyleft/2004-June/001471.html.

34. Javier de la Cueva, "Re: Competencias de las entidades de gestión," *Copyleft*, June 11, 2004, https://listas.sindominio.net/mailman/private/copyleft/2004-June/001472 .html.

35. See https://lists.ibiblio.org/pipermail/cc-es/.

36. Miguel Vidal, "Charla movilizaciones canon bibliotecas," *Copyleft*, March 9, 2005, https://listas.sindominio.net/mailman/private/copyleft/2005-March/002105.html.

Defunkid, "La Elena Francis del Copyleft," *Copyleft*, August 23, 2004, https://listas .sindominio.net/mailman/private/copyleft/2004-August/001802.html.

37. copyleft@sueltate.es, "[Copyleft] Discutiendo sobre las FAQ," *Copyleft*, July 5, 2004, https://listas.sindominio.net/mailman/private/copyleft/2004-July/001671.html.

38. Javier Candeira, "Yendo al grano," *Copyleft*, July 2, 2004, https://listas.sindominio
.net/mailman/private/copyleft/2004-July/001642.html.

39. Miguel Vidal, "[Copyleft] Discutiendo sobre las FAQ," *Copyleft*, July 2, 2004, https://
listas.sindominio.net/mailman/private/copyleft/2004-July/001630.html.

40. Miguel Vidal, "Comentarios a las FAQ y estructura," *Copyleft*, July 10, 2004, https://
listas.sindominio.net/mailman/private/copyleft/2004-July/001713.html.

41. Elinor Ostrom, *Governing the Commons: The Evolution of Institutions for Collective Action* (New York: Cambridge University Press, 1990).

42. Yochai Benkler, "Overcoming Agoraphobia: Building the Commons of the Digitally Networked Environment," *Harvard Journal of Law & Technology* 11, no. 2 (1998): 287–400.

43. Lawrence Lessig, *Code and Other Laws of Cyberspace* (New York: Basic Books, 1999); Lawrence Lessig, "Keynote Address: Commons and Code," *Fordham Intellectual Property, Media and Entertainment Law Journal* 9, no. 2 (December 1, 1999): 405. See also Lawrence Lessig, *The Future of Ideas: The Fate of the Commons in a Connected World* (New York: Knopf Doubleday Publishing Group, 2002). Yochai Benkler's influential early articulation of a digitally networked commons can be found in Benkler, "Overcoming Agoraphobia."

44. Naomi Klein, "Reclaiming the Commons," *New Left Review* 2, no. 9 (2001): 81–89.

45. Rafael Fernández Calvo, ed., *Conocimiento abierto*, vol. 163 (Novática, Revista de la Asociación de Técnicos Informáticos, 2003).

46. Javier Candeira, "[Copyleft] Resumen de Copyleft, Vol 57, Envío 6," *Copyleft*, March 31, 2008, https://listas.sindominio.net/mailman/private/copyleft/2008-March
/002488.html.

47. Miguel Vidal, "[Copyleft] Resumen de Copyleft, Vol 57, Envío 6," *Copyleft*, March 31, 2008, https://listas.sindominio.net/mailman/private/copyleft/2008-March
/002498.html.

48. Javier Candeira, "[Copyleft] Resumen de Copyleft, Vol 57, Envío 6," *Copyleft*, April 1, 2008, https://listas.sindominio.net/mailman/private/copyleft/2008-April/002499
.html.

49. María José Canel and Karen Sanders, "Crisis Communication and Terrorist Attacks: Framing a Response to the 2004 Madrid Bombings and 2005 London Bombings," in *The Handbook of Crisis Communication*, ed. W. Timothy Coombs and Sherry J. Holladay (Malden: Wiley-Blackwell, 2010), 455, https://doi.org/10.1002/9781444314885.ch22.

50. Colectivo Editorial Indymedia Madrid, "Atentado contra la sociedad civil de Madrid," in *¡Pásalo! Relatos y análisis sobre El 11-M y los días que le siguieron* (Madrid: Traficantes de Sueños, 2004), 28.

51. Collettivo A/traverso, *Alicia es el diablo: Radio libre*, 50, emphasis removed.

52. Gustavo Roig Domínguez and Sara López Martín, "Del desconcierto emocional a la movilización política: Redes sociales y medios alternativos Del 11-M al 13-M," in *13-M. Multitudes Online*, ed. Víctor Sampedro Blanco (Madrid: Los Libros de la Catarata, 2005), 212.

53. Fominaya, "The Madrid Bombings and Popular Protest," 297.

54. Fominaya, "The Madrid Bombings and Popular Protest," 290.

55. Pablo Francescutti, Alejandro Baer, José María García de Madariaga, and Paula López, "La 'noche de los móviles': Medios, redes de confianza y movilización juvenil," in *13-M. Multitudes Online*, ed. Víctor Sampedro Blanco (Madrid: Los Libros de la Catarata, 2005), 63.

56. Roig Domínguez and López Martín, "Del desconcierto emocional a la movilización política: Redes sociales y medios alternativos del 11-M al 13-M," 216.

57. Jacobo Rivero, cited in Martínez López and García Bernardos, eds., *Okupa Madrid (1985–2011): Memoria, reflexión, debate y autogestión colectiva del conocimiento* (Madrid:

Seminario de Historia Política y Social de las Okupaciones en Madrid-Metrópolis, 2014), 206.

58. Various Authors, ¡Pásalo! *Relatos y análisis sobre el 11-M y los días que le siguieron* (Madrid: Traficantes de Sueños, 2004), 13–14.

PART 2. CLIMATES OF METHODS

1. For a recent account of the history of Spanish historiographical exceptionalism, see, for example, Juan Pimentel and José Pardo-Tomás, "And Yet, We Were Modern: The Paradoxes of Iberian Science after the Grand Narratives," *History of Science* 55, no. 2 (June 1, 2017): 133–47, https://doi.org/10.1177/0073275316684353.

2. Antonio Lafuente, Interview with Antonio Lafuente, July 4, 2007.

3. Antonio Lafuente and Antonio Jesús Delgado, *La geometrización de la tierra (1735–1744)*, vol. 3 of *Cuadernos Galileo de historia de la ciencia* (Madrid: Consejo Superior de Investigaciones Científicas, 1984).

4. Antonio Lafuente, *Las dos orillas de la ciencia: La traza pública e imperial de la ilustración española* (Madrid: Marcial Pons, 2012).

5. Antonio Lafuente and Javier Moscoso, *Georges-Louis Leclerc conde de Buffon (1707–1788)* (Madrid: Consejo Superior de Investigaciones Científicas, 1999).

6. Antonio Lafuente and Nuria Valverde, "Las políticas del Sentido Común: Feijoo contra los dislates del rigor," in *Feijoo, hoy*, ed. Inmaculada Urzainqui (Oviedo: Fundación Gregorio Marañón-Instituto Feijoo de Estudios del siglo XVIII, 2003), 131–57.

7. In later conversations Lafuente would often draw on the work of Hans-Jörg Rheinberger to describe the commons as an "experimental system": a collective design to, as Rheinberger puts it, "move around by means and by virtue of checking out, of groping, of *tâtonnement.*" See Hans-Jörg Rheinberger, *Toward a History of Epistemic Things: Synthesizing Proteins in the Test Tube* (Stanford. CA: Stanford University Press, 1997), 74. On free software as an experimental system, see, in particular, Christopher M. Kelty, *Two Bits: The Cultural Significance of Free Software* (Durham, NC: Duke University Press, 2008).

8. Antonio Lafuente, "El museo como casa de los comunes," *Claves de razón práctica*, no. 157 (2005): 24.

9. Lafuente, "El museo," 29.

10. Lafuente, "El museo," 31.

11. Antonio Lafuente, "Foros híbridos" (Madrid, La Casa Encendida, 2004), 4.

12. Red de Lavapiés, "La Tabacalera a debate," 2004, http://latabacalera.net/web2004/info/index.html.

13. Aitor, "Fwd: Marzo," *Copyleft*, February 24, 2004, https://listas.sindominio.net/mailman/private/copyleft/2004-February/000953.html.

14. Antonio Lafuente, "Jornada sobre el procomún, Mesa 1 | Medialab Prad Madrid," May 17, 2007, https://www.medialab-prado.es/videos/jornada-sobre-el-procomun-mesa-1.

15. Antonio Lafuente, Interview with Antonio Lafuente, June 4, 2018; on the commons as a laboratory, see also Adolfo Estalella Fernández, Jara Rocha, and Antonio Lafuente, "Laboratorios de Procomún: Experimentación, recursividad y activismo," *Teknokultura: Revista de cultura digital y movimientos sociales* 10, no. 1 (March 31, 2013): 21–48.

4. MORE THAN MANY AND LESS THAN ONE

1. The relocation to the Sawmill finally took place in April 2013. However, at the time of making the final edits to the book, in spring 2021, MLP was once again relocated, against the will of its employees and users, to another location on the outskirts of the city.

2. Participants in the debates included the historian of science Antonio Lafuente, the art professor and former member of La Fiambrera Obrera Jordi Claramonte, and the

guerrilla philosopher and former member of Universidad Nómada Amador Fernández-Savater—to cite but a few of the names mentioned in part 1.

3. Marcos was appointed Medialab Prado's director in 2014.

4. Marcos García, Interview with Marcos García, July 12, 2018.

5. Marcos García, Interview.

6. Originally the center opened under the name MediaLab Madrid and operated as an artistic partnership between cultural producers Karin Ohlenschläger and Luis Rico and Madrid's municipality. In 2006, the municipality took full control of the project under the directorship of Juan Carrete.

7. The workshop was presented by David Cuartielles, one of the cofounders of the Arduino project and a long-time associate of MLP.

8. Fieldwork diary, Alberto Corsín Jiménez, November 30, 2010.

9. Jara Rocha, Interview with Jara Rocha, April 16, 2010.

10. Jara Rocha, Interview.

11. From 2004 to 2010, Antonio Lafuente kept a blog, *Tecnocidanos* (Citizen-scientists), which was one of the most visited science blogs in Spain. He first wrote "Neighborhood Science" for the blog on March 22, 2006. The text is also available in Antonio Lafuente, *El carnaval de la tecnociencia: Diario de una navegación entre las nuevas tecnologías y los nuevos patrimonios* (Madrid: Gadir, 2007), 77–79.

12. In 2010, for instance, the mentors were Douglas Repetto, an American artist well-known for founding the art/community group Dorkbot, and Olivier Schulbaum, founder of the commons design firm Platoniq and the crowdfunding platform Goteo. Langdon Winner, professor of social studies of science at Rensselaer Polytechnic Institute, was the invited speaker.

13. Matt Ratto, "Critical Making: Conceptual and Material Studies in Technology and Social Life," *Information Society* 27, no. 4 (2011): 252–60, https://doi.org/10.1080/01972243.2011.583819.

14. Anthony Dunne, *Hertzian Tales: Electronic Products, Aesthetic Experience, and Critical Design* (Cambridge, MA: MIT Press, 2008); Karin Knorr-Cetina, *Epistemic Cultures: How the Sciences Make Knowledge* (Cambridge, MA: Harvard University Press, 1999); Ratto, "Critical Making," 254, 253.

15. Fieldwork diary, Adolfo Estalella, June 7, 2010.

16. Fieldwork diary, Adolfo Estalella, June 14, 2010.

17. See http://meipi.org/.

18. Mary Douglas, *Purity and Danger: An Analysis of Concepts of Pollution and Taboo* (London: Routledge & Kegan Paul, 1966), 35.

19. La Tabacalera, "Guía copyfight para CSA | dirección general de autogestión cultural," 2010, http://blogs.latabacalera.net/dgac/tabacalera-copyfight/.

20. Marcos García, Interview.

21. Lilly Irani, "Hackathons and the Making of Entrepreneurial Citizenship," *Science, Technology & Human Values*, April 8, 2015, 800, https://doi.org/10.1177/0162243915578486, emphasis in the original.

22. Irani, "Hackathons," 811–12, 14.

23. Renzi, *Hacked Transmissions*, 133, 150, 171, and throughout.

24. Suchman joined Xerox's Palo Alto Research Center (PARC) in 1979 as one of a team of social scientists dedicated to producing ethnographically rich accounts of the transformation of administrative work. While anthropologists were initially tasked with producing culturally sensitive accounts of the design of the "office of the future," over the years their ethnographic practice was enlisted as one of a suite of prototyping procedures for the participatory design of industrial technologies; see, for example, Lucy Suchman, "Consuming Anthropology," in *Interdisciplinarity: Reconfigurations of the Social and*

Natural Sciences, ed. Andrew Barry and Georgina Born (Oxford: Routledge, 2013), 141–60. As Suchman would hear repeatedly over the years, "the future arrived sooner" at PARC; see Lucy Suchman, "Anthropological Relocations and the Limits of Design," *Annual Review of Anthropology* 40, no. 1 (2011): 2, https://doi.org/10.1146/annurev.anthro .041608.105640. Yet this was a future, as Suchman has insisted throughout her work, that for many years demanded an "artful integration . . . of laborious reconfigurations— always partial, provisional, and precarious—[of] familiar arrangements and modes of ac- tion" (15). It was a future that was always located at the crossroads of specific intensive arrangements of labor, sensitivity, and care and that required on-going attention and in- terrogation of its changing circumstances. As a region of aspiration, then, the future at PARC was for many years one that demanded ongoing performance for its sustainability rather than a temporal horizon to which one could fast-forward.

25. Maxigas, "Hacklabs and Hackerspaces—Tracing Two Genealogies," *Journal of Peer Production* 2 (2012), http://peerproduction.net/issues/issue-2/peer-reviewed-papers/hack labs-and-hackerspaces/.

26. As we mentioned in part 1 and will describe further in the next chapter, the work of transforming and blurring the boundaries between public culture and free culture took place across numerous Spanish cultural institutions, including Arteleku, MACBA, La Casa Encendida, and Intermediae-Matadero. The work of MLP is exemplary but not exceptional in this context.

27. Medialab-Prado, *Pensando y haciendo Medialab-Prado: Conclusiones. | Medialab- Prado Madrid*, 2011, https://www.medialab-prado.es/videos/pensando-y-haciendo-medialab -prado-conclusiones-0.

28. Padilla and Fernández-Savater spent over a month working hand-in-hand with MLP's staff reviewing the video recordings of the previous sessions, studying various written pieces contributed by MLP associates, meeting weekly with staff and regular participants in MLP activities, and developing a SWOT (strengths, weaknesses, oppor- tunities, and threats) analysis and visual ontology of MLP's cultural system.

29. Amador Fernández-Savater and Franco Ingrassia, "Pensar (en) la dispersión Ent- revista con Franco Ingrassia," *Espai en blanc*, October 1, 2012, http://espaienblanc.net/?page _id=605.

30. Fieldwork diary, Alberto Corsín Jiménez, March 4, 2011. The video recording of the workshop is available at https://www.medialab-matadero.es/videos/pensando-y -haciendo-medialab-prado-conclusiones.

31. Fieldwork diary, Alberto Corsín Jiménez, March 4, 2011.

32. Fieldwork diary, Alberto Corsín Jiménez, March 4, 2011.

33. Lauren Berlant, "The Commons: Infrastructures for Troubling Times," *Envi- ronment and Planning D: Society and Space* 34, no. 3 (June 1, 2016): 397, https://doi.org /10.1177/0263775816645989.

34. Berlant, "The Commons," 399.

35. Anna Lowenhaupt Tsing, *The Mushroom at the End of the World: On the Possibil- ity of Life in Capitalist Ruins* (Princeton: Princeton University Press, 2015), 278.

36. Donna Haraway, "A Manifesto for Cyborgs: Science, Technology, and Socialist Feminism in the 1980s," *Socialist Review* 80 (1985): 92.

37. Haraway, "Manifesto for Cyborgs," 96.

38. Marilyn Strathern, *Partial Connections* (Walnut Creek, CA: AltaMira Press, 2004), 36; see also Annemarie Mol and John Law, "Complexities: An Introduction," in *Complexi- ties: Social Studies of Knowledge Practices*, ed. John Law and Annemarie Mol (Durham, NC: Duke University Press, 2002), 11 and throughout. To paraphrase Marilyn Strathern: "I pre- ferred complex trajectories to blurred genres. They give us marginally more purchase for

dealing with the unpredictable"; see Marilyn Strathern, *Property, Substance, and Effect: Anthropological Essays on Persons and Things* (London: Athlone Press, 1999), 25.

39. Christopher M. Kelty, *Two Bits: The Cultural Significance of Free Software* (Durham, NC: Duke University Press, 2008).

5. FREEDOM IN 3D

1. See Alberto Corsín Jiménez and Zuloark, *Caja de herramientas de Ciudad Escuela. Guía de aprendizaje* (Madrid: Ciudad Escuela, 2017), https://digital.csic.es/bitstream/10261/173847/1/170613-CajaHerramientas.pdf.

2. See http://www.inteligenciascolectivas.org/ic-sol-15m-cubrir-la-plaza/.

3. See https://inteligenciascolectivas.org/es/inicio/.

4. Iván López Munuera, "Notas sobre el 'bum': Los colectivos españoles, un ecosistema plural," *Arquitectura viva*, no. 145 (2012): 16.

5. Sindicato de Arquitectos, "III Estudio laboral sobre el sector de la arquitectura," 2013, https://sindicatoarquitectos.wordpress.com/2013/10/07/iii-estudio-laboral-sobre-el-sector-de-la-arquitectura/.

6. Domenico di Siena, "Creatividad horizontal: Redes, conectores y plataformas," *Arquitectura viva*, no. 145 (2012).

7. James Secord, "Monsters at the Crystal Palace," in *Models: The Third Dimension of Science*, ed. Soraya de Chadarevian and Nick Hopwood (Stanford: Stanford University Press, 2004), 139.

8. Nick Hopwood and Soraya de Chadarevian, "Dimensions of Modelling," in *Models: The Third Dimension of Science*, ed. Soraya de Chadarevian and Nick Hopwood, 1st ed. (Stanford: Stanford University Press, 2004), 1–15.

9. Hopwood and de Chadarevian, "Dimensions of Modelling," 10.

10. Zoohaus Collective, Interview with Zoohaus Collective, July 17, 2012.

11. See https://inteligenciascolectivas.org/es/inicio/.

12. We follow the project's convention and hereafter refer to each such design or device as an *intelligence*.

13. We described the influence of the Spanish Development Agency in the shaping of the New Institutionalist cultural agenda in chapter 3.

14. Zoohaus Collective, Interview.

15. Mario Biagioli, "Patent Specification and Political Representation," in *Making and Unmaking Intellectual Property: Creative Production in Legal and Cultural Perspective*, ed. Mario Biagioli, Peter Jaszi, and Martha Woodmansee (Chicago: University of Chicago Press, 2011), 25–39.

16. Zoohaus Collective, Interview.

17. Zoohaus Collective, Interview.

18. Bruno Latour, "From Multiculturalism to Multinaturalism: What Rules of Method for the New Socio-Scientific Experiments?," *Nature and Culture* 6, no. 1 (2011): 1–17, https://doi.org/10.3167/nc.2011.060101.

19. Biagioli, "Patent Specification and Political Representation," 26–27.

20. Biagioli, "Patent Specification and Political Representation," 27.

21. Mario Biagioli, "Patent Republic: Representing Inventions, Constructing Rights and Authors," *Social Research: An International Quarterly* 73 (December 2006): 1129–72.

22. Alain Pottage, "Law Machines: Scale Models, Forensic Materiality and the Making of Modern Patent Law," *Social Studies of Science* 41, no. 5 (October 1, 2011): 622, https://doi.org/10.1177/0306312711408484.

23. Pottage, "Law Machines," 627.

24. Biagioli, "Patent Specification and Political Representation," 27.

25. Zoohaus Collective, Interview.

26. Zoohaus, "Inteligencia colectiva [officina OTICAM]: Proyecto desarrollado por Zoohaus para el ranchito, Matadero Madrid, comisariado por Iván López Munuera," 2010, 3.

27. Zoohaus, "Inteligencia colectiva," 3.

28. Zoohaus, "Inteligencia colectiva," 6.

29. Zoohaus, "Inteligencia colectiva," 8.

30. Zoohaus Collective, Interview.

31. Zoohaus Collective, Interview.

32. Zoohaus Collective, Interview.

33. James Holston, *Insurgent Citizenship: Disjunctions of Democracy and Modernity in Brazil* (Princeton: Princeton University Press, 2007), 260–63.

34. Zoohaus Collective, Interview.

35. Zoohaus Collective, Interview.

36. See, for example, James Holston, "Autoconstruction in Working-Class Brazil," *Cultural Anthropology* 6, no. 4 (November 1, 1991): 447–65, https://doi.org/10.1525/can.1991.6.4.02a00020.

37. Zoohaus Collective, Interview.

38. Zoohaus Collective, Interview.

39. Zoohaus Collective, Interview.

40. McKenzie Wark, *50 Years of Recuperation of the Situationist International* (New York: Princeton Architectural Press, 2008), 7.

41. We follow here Gernot Böhme's important writings apropos the way in which "atmospheres" are bodied forth and "created by things, persons or their constellations." Böhme's essay, which is a contribution to a new aesthetics (understood as a general theory of perception), makes an original argument for thinking of atmospheres as a crucial piece in any ontology's furniture. For Böhme, the atmospheric is irradiated as the "ecstasies of the thing[s]" that make up a spatial and infrastructural environment. "The primary 'object' of perception," he writes, "is atmospheres." The atmospheric, then, is a quality of the arrangement and choreography of objects and things in an interior design; see Gernot Böhme, "Atmosphere as the Fundamental Concept of a New Aesthetics," *Thesis Eleven* 36, no. 1 (August 1, 1993): 122, 121, 125, https://doi.org/10.1177/072551369303600107.

42. Zoohaus Collective, Interview.

43. Zoohaus Collective, Interview.

44. Secord, "Monsters at the Crystal Palace," 148.

45. Secord, "Monsters at the Crystal Palace," 143, 141.

46. Wark, *50 Years of Recuperation*, 21.

47. Wark, *50 Years of Recuperation*, 24.

48. Fieldwork diary, Alberto Corsín Jiménez, May 10, 2017.

49. Marc Dessauce, ed., *The Inflatable Moment: Pnuematics and Protest in '68* (New York: Princeton Architectural Press and Architectural League of New York, 1999).

50. Fred Turner, *The Democratic Surround: Multimedia and American Liberalism from World War II to the Psychedelic Sixties* (Chicago: University of Chicago Press, 2013).

51. Javier Lezaun, "Democracy in America 3D," *Journal of Cultural Economy* 8, no. 2 (2015): 243, https://doi.org/10.1080/17530350.2014.948482.

52. Craig Buckley, "Introduction: The Echo of Utopia," in *Utopie: Texts and Projects, 1967–1978* (Cambridge, MA: MIT Press, 2011), 17.

PART 3. MATTERS OF SENSE

1. Ander Contel, Interview with Ander Contel, May 10, 2018.

2. Contel, Interview.

3. Contel, Interview.
4. Contel, Interview.

6. ASSEMBLING NEIGHBORS

1. We have anonymized all names in this chapter and chapter 7.

2. We can hardly provide here a sociological overview of the hundreds of assemblies that popped up in Madrid. Generally speaking, assemblies reproduced the demographic and socioeconomic backgrounds of the neighborhoods wherein they took residence. In response to the specific needs of each neighborhood, some assemblies developed stronger working groups than others. For example, in Prosperidad, a neighborhood at the epicenter of a large and socially diverse district (Chamartín), where there are known to be large differences in the quality of education provided by local state schools, the assembly became known across the city for its Education Working Group. The Lavapiés Assembly, on the other hand, became well-known for its Immigration and Housing Working Groups. On the whole, assemblies reproduced the rich heterogeneity of urban life.

3. Adam Reed, "'Blog This': Surfing the Metropolis and the Method of London," *Journal of the Royal Anthropological Institute* 14, no. 2 (June 1, 2008): 392, https://doi.org/10.1111/j.1467-9655.2008.00508.x.

4. Manuel Castells, *The City and the Grassroots: A Cross-Cultural Theory of Urban Social Movements* (Berkeley: University of California Press, 1983).

5. Castells, *The City and the Grassroots*, 51.

6. Alfonso Pérez-Agote, Benjamín Tejerina, and Margarita Barañano, eds., *Barrios multiculturales: Relaciones interétnicas en los barrios de San Francisco (Bilbao) y Embajadores/Lavapiés (Madrid)* (Madrid: Trotta, 2010).

7. See https://lavapies.tomalosbarrios.net/.

8. Asamblea Popular de Madrid, "Metodología asamblearia," 2011, https://madrid.tomalosbarrios.net/metodologia-asamblearia/.

9. Asamblea Popular de Madrid, "¿Qué es la comisión de barrios?," June 12, 2011, https://madrid.tomalosbarrios.net/%c2%bfque-es-la-comision-de-barrios/.

10. AcampadaSol, "Guía rápida para la dinamización de asambleas populares," May 31, 2011, https://madrid.tomalaplaza.net/2011/05/31/guia-rapida-para-la-dinamizacion-de-asambleas-populares/.

11. Ana Rosa Lorenzo Vila and Miguel Ángel Martínez López, *Asambleas y reuniones: Metodologías de autoorganización* (Madrid: Traficantes de Sueños, 2005).

12. AcampadaSol, "Guía rápida."

13. AcampadaSol, "Guía rápida."

14. AcampadaSol, "Guía rápida."

15. Toma los barrios, "Asamblea Popular de Lavapiés," lavapies.tomalosbarrios.net/category/actas (accessed December 1, 2011).

16. AcampadaSol, "Guía rápida."

17. AcampadaSol, "Guía rápida."

18. AcampadaSol, "Guía rápida."

19. For an account of the relationship between the squatter movement and the 15M movement in Madrid see Miguel Ángel Martínez López and Ángela García Bernardos, "Converging Movements: Occupations of Squares and Buildings," in *Crisis and Social Mobilization in Contemporary Spain: The 15M Movement*, ed. Benjamín Tejerina and Ignacia Perugorría (Oxford: Routledge, 2018), 95–118.

20. Fieldwork diary, Alberto Corsín Jiménez, May 28, 2011.

21. Fieldwork diary, Adolfo Estalella, June 16, 2011.

22. Fieldwork diary, Alberto Corsín Jiménez, June 11, 2011.

23. For an object-oriented politics, see Noortje Marres and Javier Lezaun, "Materials and Devices of the Public: An Introduction," *Economy and Society*, October 17, 2011, 1–21, https://doi.org/10.1080/03085147.2011.602293.

24. Vivienda y desahucios de Lavapiés, "Bando alquiler. 17/9," n-1.cc/pg/file/read/761 216/bado-alquiler-1709 (accessed December 1, 2011).

25. Tony Crook, *Anthropological Knowledge, Secrecy and Bolivip, Papua New Guinea: Exchanging Skin* (Oxford: British Academy/Oxford University Press, 2007), 218.

26. Crook, *Anthropological Knowledge*, 218.

27. Fieldwork diary, Adolfo Estalella, August 7, 2011.

28. Fieldwork diary, Adolfo Estalella, August 7, 2011.

29. Vyjayanthi Rao, "Embracing Urbanism: The City as Archive," *New Literary History* 40, no. 2 (2009): 371–83, https://doi.org/10.1353/nlh.0.0085.

30. Rao, "Embracing Urbanism," 381–82.

31. Toma los barrios, Asamblea Popular de Lavapiés, Acta de la chiqui-asamblea 01/10/2011," lavapies.tomalosbarrios.net/2011/10/05/acta-de-la-chiqui-asamblea-01102011/ (accessed October 10, 2011).

32. Fieldwork diary, Adolfo Estalella, October 1, 2011.

33. Henri Lefebvre, "Right to the City," in *Writings on Cities*, edited by Eleonore Kofman and Elizabeth Lebas (Oxford: Blackwell, 1996), 61–181.

34. David Harvey, "The Right to the City," *New Left Review* 53 (2008): 37.

35. Don Mitchell, *The Right to the City: Social Justice and the Fight for Public Space* (New York: Guilford Press, 2003).

36. Kafui A. Attoh, "What Kind of Right Is the Right to the City?," *Progress in Human Geography* 35, no. 5 (October 1, 2011): 678, https://doi.org/10.1177/0309132510394706.

37. Henri Lefebvre, "Theoretical Problems of Autogestion," in *State, Space, World: Selected Essays*, ed. Neil Brenner and Stuart Elden (Minneapolis: University of Minnesota Press, 2009), 138–52; see also Mark Purcell, "The Right to the City: The Struggle for Democracy in the Urban Public Realm," *Policy & Politics* 41, no. 3 (July 1, 2013): 317, https://doi.org/10.1332/030557312X655639.

7. AMBULATIONS

1. Judith Butler, *Notes toward a Performative Theory of Assembly* (Cambridge, MA: Harvard University Press, 2015), 11, 18, and throughout.

2. Butler, *Notes*, 85.

3. Michael Hardt and Antonio Negri, *Assembly* (Oxford: Oxford University Press, 2017), 295.

4. Juan Méndez, "Solidaridad y ayuda mutua: El grupo de Migración y convivencia de la Asamblea Popular de Lavapiés," *Teknokultura: Revista de cultura digital y movimientos sociales* 9, no. 2 (December 23, 2012): 51–52.

5. Méndez, "Solidaridad y ayuda mutua," 50.

6. Méndez, "Solidaridad y ayuda mutua," 56.

7. Ernesto García López, "'Unidos por el sentido común': Identidad(es) cultural(es) y participación política en el 15M: preguntas para una reflexión etnográfica," *Revista de antropología experimental*, special issue 13 (2013): 41–71.

8. Richard Sennett, *The Fall of Public Man* (Cambridge: Cambridge University Press, 1977).

Erving Goffman, *Relations in Public: Microstudies of the Public Order* (New York: Basic Books, 1971).

9. Aristotle, *Aristotle's "Politics,"* 2nd ed., trans. Carnes Lord (Chicago: University of Chicago Press, 2013), 41.

10. Jürgen Habermas, *The Structural Transformation of the Public Sphere: An Inquiry into a Category of Bourgeois Society*, ed. Frederick Lawrence (Cambridge: Polity Press, 1989).

11. Benjamin Barber, *Strong Democracy: Participatory Politics for a New Age* (Berkeley: University of California Press, 2003), 175.

12. Ludwig Schwarte, "Parliamentary Public," in *Making Things Public: Atmospheres of Democracy*, ed. Bruno Latour and Peter Weibel (Cambridge, MA: MIT Press, 2005), 786–94.

13. Paulo Tavares, "General Essay on Air: Probes into the Atmospheric Conditions of Liberal Democracy" (Centre for Research Architecture, University of London, 2008), http://www.paulotavares.net/air/.

14. Peter Sloterdijk, "Atmospheric Politics," in *Making Things Public: Atmospheres of Democracy*, ed. Bruno Latour and Peter Weibel (Cambridge, MA: MIT Press, 2005), 944–51.

15. John Parkinson, *Democracy and Public Space: The Physical Sites of Democratic Performance* (Oxford: Oxford University Press, 2012).

16. John Holloway, *Crack Capitalism* (London: Pluto Press, 2010), 45.

17. Marianne Maeckelbergh, "Doing Is Believing: Prefiguration as Strategic Practice in the Alterglobalization Movement," *Social Movement Studies* 10, no. 1 (January 1, 2011): 4, 15, https://doi.org/10.1080/14742837.2011.545223.

18. David Graeber, *Direct Action: An Ethnography* (Oakland, CA: AK Press, 2009), 210.

19. Stine Krøijer, *Figurations of the Future: Forms and Temporalities of Left Radical Politics in Northern Europe* (New York: Berghahn Books, 2015), 105.

20. Krøijer, *Figurations of the Future*, 120.

21. Krøijer, *Figurations of the Future*, 122–23.

22. Krøijer, *Figurations of the Future*, 135.

23. Krøijer, *Figurations of the Future*, 209.

24. Krøijer, *Figurations of the Future*, 83 and throughout.

25. Henri Lefebvre, *Rhythmanalysis: Space, Time, and Everyday Life* (Continuum International Publishing Group, 2004), 93.

26. Gilles Deleuze and Félix Guattari, *A Thousand Plateaus: Capitalism and Schizophrenia* (Minneapolis: University of Minnesota Press, 1987), 373.

27. Deleuze and Guattari, *A Thousand Plateaus*, 372.

28. On the different ways in which issues of concern become material publics, see Noortje Marres, *Material Participation: Technology, the Environment and Everyday Publics* (London: Palgrave Macmillan, 2012).

29. After Jacques Rancière's notion of the *partage du sensible* (the distribution of the sensible), with which he names the politico-aesthetic regimes that partition the legibility and experience of the world for us: what can be said, heard and seen, and what cannot. Politics emerges when the partition is disrupted; see Jacques Rancière, *The Politics of Aesthetics* (London: Bloomsbury, 2004).

30. Bruno Latour, "Why Has Critique Run Out of Steam?" From Matters of Fact to Matters of Concern." *Critical Inquiry* 30, no. 2 (January 1, 2004): 225–48, https://doi.org/10.1086/421123.

31. Mary Puig de la Bellacasa, *Matters of Care: Speculative Ethics in More Than Human Worlds* (Minneapolis: University of Minnesota Press, 2017).

PART 4. BRICOLAGES OF APPRENTICESHIPS

1. Ciudad Escuela, http://ciudad-escuela.org/.

2. Aurora Adalid, Interview with Aurora Adalid, April 15, 2019.

3. Adalid, Interview.
4. Adalid, Interview.
5. Adalid, Interview.
6. Adalid, Interview.
7. Adalid, Interview.
8. Adalid, Interview.
9. See https://urbanrights.org/.
10. Aurora Adalid, Interview.

8. AUTO-CONSTRUCTION REDUX

1. The unemployment rate in San Cristóbal is 17.85 percent, Madrid's highest. Less than half of the neighborhood's population has any formal education, with only 4.8 percent having completed a higher education qualification. Average income in 2015 reached €15,594.

2. Justin McGuirk, *Radical Cities: Across Latin America in Search of a New Architecture* (London: Verso, 2014), 15.

3. Here, we are inspired by Raymond Williams's (1961) well-known description of the cultural vectors—the structures of feeling—shaping class dynamics, but also Abdou-Maliq Simone's recent reappropriation of the term to describe the "urban majorities" that come together and take shape as a "densification of techniques . . . calculations, impulses, screens, surfaces . . . tears," such that "things get their 'bearings' by having 'bearing' on each other"; see Simone, *Jakarta, Drawing the City Near* (Minneapolis: University of Minnesota Press, 2014), 84. William's concept of "structures of feeling" is found in Raymond Williams, *The Long Revolution* (London: Chatto & Windus, 1961).

4. We hyphenate this term, although scholars like James Holston do not, to highlight its recursive logic: a language of the city that does double duty as a language for the city.

5. An ethnographic account of El Campo's soundscape can be found in Jorge Martín Sainz de los Terreros, "Welcoming Sound: The Case of a Noise Complaint in the Weekly Assembly of El Campo de Cebada," *Social Movement Studies* 17, no. 3 (May 4, 2018): 269–81, https://doi.org/10.1080/14742837.2018.1456328.

6. AbdouMaliq Simone, "Pirate Towns: Reworking Social and Symbolic Infrastructures in Johannesburg and Douala," *Urban Studies* 43, no. 2 (February 1, 2006): 359, https://doi.org/10.1080/00420980500146974.

7. See also George Marcus, "Prototyping and Contemporary Anthropological Experiments with Ethnographic Method," *Journal of Cultural Economy* 7, no. 4 (October 2, 2014): 399–410, https://doi.org/10.1080/17530350.2013.858061; Celia Lury and Nina Wakeford, eds., *Inventive Methods: The Happening of the Social* (London: Routledge, 2012).

8. Nathalie Boucher, Mariana Cavalcanti, Stefan Kipfer, Edgar Pieterse, Vyjayanthi Rao, and Nasra Smith, "Writing the Lines of Connection: Unveiling the Strange Language of Urbanization," *International Journal of Urban and Regional Research* 32, no. 4 (December 1, 2008): 989–1027, https://doi.org/10.1111/j.1468-2427.2008.00827.x.

9. Paul Rabinow, *The Accompaniment: Assembling the Contemporary* (Chicago: University of Chicago Press, 2011).

10. In this guise, auto-construction helps us move away from questions of representation in urban theory, not just by drawing attention to the vectors of affect, desire, or vitality that traverse city life nor by focusing on the complex, heterogeneous, and fuzzy assemblages that constantly compose and recompose the urban condition, but rather by paying attention to the ecologies of practice through which the city is auto-constructed as method of inquiry and exploration. On nonrepresentational theory in urban studies, see Nigel Thrift, *Non-Representational Theory: Space, Politics, Affect* (London: Routledge,

2008). On the urbanization of affect and vitality, see Daniella Gandolfo, *The City at Its Limits: Taboo, Transgression, and Urban Renewal in Lima* (Chicago: University of Chicago Press, 2009); AbdouMaliq Simone, *City Life from Jakarta to Dakar: Movements at the Crossroads* (New York: Routledge, 2009). On urban assemblages, see Ignacio Farias and Thomas Bender, eds., *Urban Assemblages: How Actor-Network Theory Changes Urban Studies* (London: Routledge, 2009); Colin McFarlane, *Learning the City: Knowledge and Translocal Assemblage* (New York: John Wiley & Sons, 2011).

11. Marilyn Strathern, *Property, Substance, and Effect: Anthropological Essays on Persons and Things* (London: Athlone Press, 1999), 6.

12. Strathern, *Property, Substance, and Effect*, 20.

13. "Their misunderstanding of me was not the same as my misunderstanding of them," Wagner famously noted in his magisterial *The Invention of Culture*; see Roy Wagner, *The Invention of Culture* (Chicago: University of Chicago Press, 1981), 24.

14. James Holston, "Autoconstruction in Working-Class Brazil," *Cultural Anthropology* 6, no. 4 (November 1, 1991): 447–65. https://doi.org/10.1525/can.1991.6.4.02a00020.

15. See, for example, Alberto Arecchi, "Auto-Construction in Africa," *Cities* 1, no. 6 (November 1, 1984): 575–79, https://doi.org/10.1016/0264-2751(84)90065-9; Geert A. Banck, "Poverty, Politics and the Shaping of Urban Space: A Brazilian Example," *International Journal of Urban and Regional Research* 10, no. 4 (December 1, 1986): 522–40, https://doi.org/10.1111/j.1468-2427.1986.tb00027.x.

16. See, for example, Alberto Corsín Jiménez, "The Right to Infrastructure: A Prototype for Open-Source Urbanism," *Environment and Planning D: Society and Space* 32, no. 2 (2014); Gordon C. C. Douglas, *The Help-Yourself City: Legitimacy and Inequality in DIY Urbanism* (New York: Oxford University Press, 2018); Eizenberg, "Actually Existing Commons"; Kurt Iveson, "Cities within the City: Do-It-Yourself Urbanism and the Right to the City," *International Journal of Urban and Regional Research* 37, no. 3 (May 1, 2013): 941–56, https://doi.org/10.1111/1468-2427.12053; McGuirk, *Radical Cities: Across Latin America in Search of a New Architecture*.

17. Vyjayanthi Rao, "Slum as Theory: The South/Asian City and Globalization," *International Journal of Urban and Regional Research* 30, no. 1 (March 1, 2006): 225–32, https://doi.org/10.1111/j.1468-2427.2006.00658.x.

18. Rao, "Slum as Theory," 225.

19. Mike Davis, "Planet of Slums: Urban Involution and the Informal Proletariat," *New Left Review* 26 (March–April 2004): 5–34; See also Mike Davis, *Planet of Slums* (New York: Verso, 2006).

20. Davis, *Planet of Slums*, 174–98.

21. Davis, *Planet of Slums*, 70–94.

22. John F. C. Turner and Robert Fichter, eds., *Freedom to Build: Dweller Control of the Housing Process* (New York: Macmillan, 1972); John F. C. Turner, *Housing by People: Towards Autonomy in Building Environments* (New York: Pantheon Books, 1976).

23. Davis, *Planet of Slums*, 72.

24. McGuirk, *Radical Cities*, 25.

25. McGuirk, *Radical Cities*, 33.

26. Rao, "Slum as Theory," 227.

27. Rao, "Slum as Theory," 232.

28. Ananya Roy, "Slumdog Cities: Rethinking Subaltern Urbanism," *International Journal of Urban and Regional Research* 35, no. 2 (March 1, 2011): 227, 231, https://doi.org/10.1111/j.1468-2427.2011.01051.x.

29. Simone, *City Life from Jakarta to Dakar*.

30. Roy, "Slumdog Cities," 232.

31. Roy, "Slumdog Cities," 224.

32. Note how the periphery is made to work in this context as *a figure seen twice*: now territory, now concept. Annelise Riles uses this phrase to describe the complex heuristics of the network age, where social and analytical forms often substitute for each other; see Annelise Riles, *The Network Inside Out* (Ann Arbor: University of Michigan Press, 2001).

33. James Holston and Teresa Caldeira, "Urban Peripheries and the Invention of Citizenship," *Harvard Design Magazine* 28 (2008): 21.

34. Holston and Caldeira, "Urban Peripheries," 21, emphasis added.

35. Holston and Caldeira, "Urban Peripheries," 21.

36. Holston and Caldeira, "Urban Peripheries," 2.

37. Holston, "Autoconstruction in Working-Class Brazil," 456.

38. Holston, "Autoconstruction in Working-Class Brazil," 456.

39. Holston, "Autoconstruction in Working-Class Brazil," 460.

40. Holston, "Autoconstruction in Working-Class Brazil," 460.

41. Holston, "Autoconstruction in Working-Class Brazil," 461.

42. Holston, "Autoconstruction in Working-Class Brazil," 461.

43. Simone, "Pirate Towns," 359.

44. edumeet, "Edumeet," *Arquitectura Viva* 145 (2012): 26.

45. Fieldwork diary, Alberto Corsín Jiménez, December 22, 2013. Aurora's final question, in the original Spanish, was *"¿qué significa aprender ciudad?" Aprender ciudad* and *hacer ciudad*, learning and making cityness, have become two of the most popular idioms in use among grassroots community projects.

46. Arecchi, "Auto-Construction in Africa," 575–76.

47. Morten Nielsen, "Inverse Governmentality: The Paradoxical Production of Peri-Urban Planning in Maputo, Mozambique," *Critique of Anthropology* 31, no. 4 (December 1, 2011): 352, https://doi.org/10.1177/0308275X11420118.

48. Claude Lévi-Strauss, *The Savage Mind* (Oxford: Oxford University Press, 1996), 1–9.

49. Lévi-Strauss, *Savage Mind*, 16.

50. Lévi-Strauss, *Savage Mind*, 18.

51. Riles, *The Network Inside Out*, 91.

52. Phillipe Pignarre and Isabella Stengers, *Capitalist Sorcery: Breaking the Spell* (London: Palgrave Macmillan, 2011), 44 and throughout.

CONCLUSION

1. Giuseppe Campos Venuti, *Urbanistica e austerità* (Milan: Feltrinelli, 1978).

2. Federico Camerin, "Giuseppe Campos Venuti en el urbanismo Italiano del siglo XX y los desafíos 'de austeridad' para el futuro," *Investigaciones geográficas*, no. 95 (2018): 7, https://doi.org/10.14350/rig.59534.

3. See, for example, Jamie Peck, "Austerity Urbanism," *City* 16, no. 6 (December 1, 2012): 626–55, https://doi.org/10.1080/13604813.2012.734071.

4. Carlos Sambricio, "El urbanismo de la Transición: Madrid, 1979–1983: El Plan General de Ordenación Urbana," in *El urbanismo de la Transición: El Plan General de Ordenación Urbana de Madrid de 1985. Volumen I*, ed. Carlos Sambricio and Paloma Ramos (Madrid: Ayuntamiento de Madrid, 2019), 44–50.

5. Javier Angulo Uribarri, *Cuando los vecinos se unen* (Madrid: Propaganda Popular Católica, 1972), 53.

6. Nina Schierstaedt, "Los barrios madrileños como áreas de confrontación social durante el tardofranquismo y la Transición: Los casos de la Meseta de Orcasitas, Palomeras, San Blas y El Pilar," *Historia, trabajo y sociedad*, no. 7 (2016): 63–66.

7. These activists were deliberately echoing Henri Lefebvre's text, whose Spanish translation appeared only a year after its original publication in 1968; see Angulo Uribarri, *Cuando*, 34.

8. Cited in Angulo Uribarri, *Cuando,* 82, 66.

9. Cited in Angulo Uribarri, *Cuando,* 46, emphasis added.

10. To be clear, the neighborhood movement was hardly exempt from internal tensions and contradictions. Some of its members were active in various political parties and contended for positions of power and influence within the movement. In the wake of the first wave of democratic elections, nationally in 1977 and municipally in 1979, these various factions and positions were made dramatically explicit and tore many associations apart; see, for example, Vincente Pérez Quintana and Pablo Sánchez León, *Memoria ciudadana y movimiento vecinal: Madrid, 1968–2008* (Madrid: Los Libros de la Catarata, 2008).

11. See Carles Sudrià, "El ajuste económico de la Transición," *El País*, February 13, 2012, Economia sect., https://elpais.com/economia/2012/02/10/actualidad/1328871012 _734915.html; José María Serrano Sanz, "Crisis económica y transición política," *Ayer*, no. 15 (1994): 147, 158.

12. Gonzalo Wilhelmi, *Romper el consenso: La izquierda radical en la Transición española (1975–1982)* (Madrid: Siglo XXI de España Editores, 2016).

13. Germán Labrador Méndez, *Culpables por la literature: Imaginación política y contracultura en la Transición española (1968–1986)* (Madrid: Ediciones Akal, 2017), 86 and throughout.

14. Tomás Rodríguez-Villasante, Tomás, Julio Alguacil, Concha Denche, Agustín Hernández Aja, Concha León, and Isabel Velázquez, *Retrato de Chabolista Con Piso: Análisis de redes sociales en la remodelación de barrios de Madrid* (Madrid: Revista Alfoz-CIDUR, 1989), 20, emphasis added.

15. In fact, as we made clear in chapter 1, by the 1990s the memory of the neighborhood movement had largely faded among young activists, who were drawn instead to the Italian and German autonomous movements for inspiration. The teachings of Jesús Ibáñez and Tomás Villasante, who were involved in the neighborhood movement in the 1970s, were somewhat of an exception, offering their sociology students at Universidad Complutense an inkling of the resonances and continuities between urban struggles in post-Francoist Spain.

16. Labrador Méndez, "La cultura en transición y la cultura de la Transición (CT)," *La Circular* (2015): 46, emphasis in the original.

17. Alternatively, we may think of it as a story from "middle Earth" (Medi-terraneum), although we prefer to take such geopolitical fetishizations with a grain of salt; compare Lila Leontidou, *The Mediterranean City in Transition: Social Change and Urban Development* (Cambridge: Cambridge University Press, 1990).

18. On the use of transitivity and intransitivity as a sociological heuristic, see also Stef Jansen, "For a Relational, Historical Ethnography of Hope: Indeterminacy and Determination in the Bosnian and Herzegovinian Meantime," *History and Anthropology* 27, no. 4 (August 7, 2016): 448–49, https://doi.org/10.1080/02757206.2016.1201481.

19. Arturo Escobar, *Designs for the Pluriverse: Radical Interdependence, Autonomy, and the Making of Worlds* (Durham, NC: Duke University Press, 2018), 140.

20. Escobar, *Designs for the Pluriverse*, 152.

Bibliography

AcampadaSol. "Guía rápida para la dinamización de asambleas populares," May 31, 2011. https://madrid.tomalaplaza.net/2011/05/31/guia-rapida-para-la-dinamizacion-de-asambleas-populares/.

Adalid, Aurora. Interview with Aurora Adalid, April 15, 2019.

Aitor. "Fwd: Marzo." *Copyleft*, February 24, 2004. https://listas.sindominio.net/mailman/private/copyleft/2004-February/000953.html.

Alberdi, Carlos. Interview with Carlos Alberdi, November 10, 2017.

Albiac, Gabriel. "Jesús Ibáñez, testigo de cargo." *El mundo (la esfera de los libros)*, June 14, 1997.

Angulo Uribarri, Javier. *Cuando los vecinos se Unen*. Madrid: Propaganda Popular Católica, 1972.

Arecchi, Alberto. "Auto-Construction in Africa." *Cities* 1, no. 6 (November 1, 1984): 575–79. https://doi.org/10.1016/0264-2751(84)90065-9.

Aristotle. *Aristotle's "Politics,"* 2nd ed. Translated by Carnes Lord. Chicago: University of Chicago Press, 2013.

Asamblea Popular de Madrid. "Metodología asamblearia," 2011. https://madrid.tomalosbarrios.net/metodologia-asamblearia/.

——. "¿Qué es la Comisión de Barrios?," June 12, 2011. https://madrid.tomalosbarrios.net/%c2%bfque-es-la-comision-de-barrios/.

Attoh, Kafui A. "What Kind of Right Is the Right to the City?" *Progress in Human Geography* 35, no. 5 (October 1, 2011): 669–85. https://doi.org/10.1177/0309132510394706.

Ayuntamiento de Madrid. Memoria del Plan General de Ordenación Urbana 1997 (1997).

Badillo, Ángel. "Las políticas públicas de acción cultural exterior de España." Estrategia Exterior Española. Real Instituto Elcano, 2014.

Balestrini, Nanni. *The Unseen*. London: Verso Books, 1989.

Banck, Geert A. "Poverty, Politics and the Shaping of Urban Space: A Brazilian Example." *International Journal of Urban and Regional Research* 10, no. 4 (December 1, 1986): 522–40. https://doi.org/10.1111/j.1468-2427.1986.tb00027.x.

Barber, Benjamin. *Strong Democracy: Participatory Politics for a New Age*. Berkeley: University of California Press, 2003.

Barber, Santiago, Victoria Frensel, and María José Romero, eds. *Cómo nació, creció y se resiste a ser comido EL GRAN POLLO DE LA ALAMEDA: Una docena de años de lucha en el barrio de la Alameda, Sevilla*. Sevilla: Consejo de Redacción del Gran Pollo de la Alameda, 2006.

Barber, Santiago, Victoria Frensel, and María José Romero. "Urban: Hasta aquí llegó el nivel de escombro: Introducción." In *Cómo nació, creció y se resiste a ser comido EL GRAN POLLO DE LA ALAMEDA: Una docena de años de lucha en el barrio de la Alameda, Sevilla*, 60–61. Sevilla: Consejo de Redacción del Gran Pollo de la Alameda, 2006.

Barber Cortés, Santiago, Curro Aix Gracia, and Marcelo Expósito. "Entrevista a Santiago Barber y Curro Aix: La fiambrera barroca." *Desacuerdos: Sobre arte, política y esfera pública en el estado español* 1 (2004): 167–73.

Barlow, John Perry. "A Declaration of the Independence of Cyberspace." Electronic Frontier Foundation, 1996. https://www.eff.org/es/cyberspace-independence.

Benkler, Yochai. "Overcoming Agoraphobia: Building the Commons of the Digitally Networked Environment." *Harvard Journal of Law & Technology* 11, no. 2 (1998): 287–400.

Berardi, Franco Bifo. *Félix Guattari: Thought, Friendship, and Visionary Cartography.* Basingstoke, UK: Palgrave Macmillan, 2008.

——. "What Is the Meaning of Autonomy Today?" In *Precarious Rhapsody: Semiocapitalism and the Pathologies of the Post-Alpha Generation*, 74–83. London: Minor Compositions, 2009.

Berlant, Lauren. "The Commons: Infrastructures for Troubling Times." *Environment and Planning D: Society and Space* 34, no. 3 (June 1, 2016): 393–419. https://doi.org/10.1177/0263775816645989.

Bey, Hakim. *Taz: The Temporary Autonomous Zone, Ontological Anarchy, Poetic Terrorism.* New York: Autonomedia, 2003.

Biagioli, Mario. "Patent Republic: Representing Inventions, Constructing Rights and Authors." *Social Research: An International Quarterly* 73 (December 2006): 1129–72.

——. "Patent Specification and Political Representation." In *Making and Unmaking Intellectual Property: Creative Production in Legal and Cultural Perspective*, edited by Mario Biagioli, Peter Jaszi, and Martha Woodmansee, 25–39. Chicago: University of Chicago Press, 2011.

Bishop, Claire. *Artificial Hells: Participatory Art and the Politics of Spectatorship.* New York: Verso Books, 2012.

Böhme, Gernot. "Atmosphere as the Fundamental Concept of a New Aesthetics." *Thesis Eleven* 36, no. 1 (August 1, 1993): 113–26. https://doi.org/10.1177/072551369303600107.

Bookchin, Debbie, and Blair Taylor. "Introduction." In *The Next Revolution: Popular Assemblies and the Promise of Direct Democracy*, by Murray Bookchin. Edited by Debbie Bookchin and Blair Taylor. New York: Verso, 2015, xv.

Bookchin, Murray. *The Ecology of Freedom: The Emergence and Dissolution of Hierarchy.* Palo Alto, CA: Cheshire Books, 1982.

Boucher, Nathalie, Mariana Cavalcanti, Stefan Kipfer, Edgar Pieterse, Vyjayanthi Rao, and Nasra Smith. "Writing the Lines of Connection: Unveiling the Strange Language of Urbanization." *International Journal of Urban and Regional Research* 32, no. 4 (December 1, 2008): 989–1027. https://doi.org/10.1111/j.1468-2427.2008.00827.x.

Bourriaud, Nicolas. *Relational Aesthetics.* Dijon: Les Presses du réel, 2002.

Brenner, Neil, David J. Madden, and David Wachsmuth. "Assemblage Urbanism and the Challenges of Critical Urban Theory." *City* 15, no. 2 (April 1, 2011): 225–40. https://doi.org/10.1080/13604813.2011.568717.

Buckley, Craig. "Introduction: The Echo of Utopia." In *Utopie: Texts and Projects, 1967–1978*, 9–21. Cambridge, MA: MIT Press, 2011.

Burriel de Orueta, Eugenio L. "La 'década prodigiosa' del urbanismo español (1997–2006)." *Scripta nova: Revista electrónica de geografía y ciencias sociales* 12, no. 270 (August 28, 2008). https://doi.org/10.1344/sn2008.12.1489.

Butler, Judith. *Notes toward a Performative Theory of Assembly.* Cambridge, MA: Harvard University Press, 2015.

Camerin, Federico. "Giuseppe Campos Venuti en el urbanismo italiano del siglo XX y los desafíos 'de austeridad' para el futuro." *Investigaciones geográficas*, no. 95 (April 2018). https://doi.org/10.14350/rig.59534.

Campos Venuti, Giuseppe. *Urbanistica e austerità.* Milan: Feltrinelli, 1978.

Candeira, Javier. "[Copyleft] Resumen de Copyleft, Vol 57, Envío 6." *Copyleft*, April 1, 2008. https://listas.sindominio.net/mailman/private/copyleft/2008-April/002499.html.

——. "[Copyleft] Resumen de Copyleft, Vol 57, Envío 6." *Copyleft*, March 31, 2008. https:// listas.sindominio.net/mailman/private/copyleft/2008-March/002488.html.

——. "Yendo al grano." *Copyleft*, July 2, 2004. https://listas.sindominio.net/mailman /private/copyleft/2004-July/001642.html.

Canel, María José, and Karen Sanders. "Crisis Communication and Terrorist Attacks: Framing a Response to the 2004 Madrid Bombings and 2005 London Bombings." In *The Handbook of Crisis Communication*, edited by W. Timothy Coombs and Sherry J. Holladay, 449–66. Malden, UK: Wiley-Blackwell, 2010. https://doi.org /10.1002/9781444314885.ch22.

Caprarella, Marcello, and Fanny Hernández Brotons. "La lucha por la ciudad: Vecinos-Trabajadores en las periferias de Madrid. 1968–1982." In *Memoria ciudadana y movimiento vecinal: Madrid, 1968–2008*, edited by Vicente Pérez Quintana and Pablo Sánchez León, 33–53. Madrid: Los Libros de la Catarata, 2008.

Carretero, José Luis. "La apuesta autónoma (LA Reloaded)." In *Tomar y hacer en vez de pedir y esperar: Autonomía y movimientos sociales. Madrid, 1985–2011*, edited by Francisco Salamanca and Gonzalo Wilhelmi Casanova, 35–50. Madrid: Solidaridad Obrera, 2012.

Carrillo, Jesús. *Space Invaders: Intervenciones artístico-políticas en un territorio en disputa: Lavapiés (1997–2004)*. Madrid: Brumaria, 2018.

Casas-Cortés, Maribel. "A Genealogy of Precarity: A Toolbox for Rearticulating Fragmented Social Realities in and out of the Workplace." *Rethinking Marxism* 26, no. 2 (April 3, 2014): 206–26. https://doi.org/10.1080/08935696.2014.888849.

Castells, Manuel. *The City and the Grassroots: A Cross-Cultural Theory of Urban Social Movements*. Berkeley: University of California Press, 1983.

——. "Productores de ciudad: El movimiento ciudadano de Madrid." In *Memoria ciudadana y movimiento vecinal: Madrid, 1968–2008*, edited by Vicente Pérez Quintana and Pablo Sánchez León, 21–32. Madrid: Los Libros de la Catarata, 2008.

Chakrabarty, Dipesh. "The Climate of History: Four Theses." *Critical Inquiry* 35, no. 2 (January 1, 2009): 197–222. https://doi.org/10.1086/596640.

Charnock, Greig, Thomas Purcell, and Ramón Ribera-Fumaz. *The Limits to Capital in Spain: Crisis and Revolt in the European South*. London: Palgrave Macmillan, 2014.

Chislett, William. *The Internationalization of the Spanish Economy*. Madrid: Real Instituto Elcano de Estudios Internacionales y Estratégicos, 2002.

Colau, Ada, and Adrià Alemany. *Vidas hipotecadas*. Barcelona: Angle Editorial, 2012.

Colectivo Editorial Indymedia Madrid. "Atentado contra la sociedad civil de Madrid." In *¡Pásalo! Relatos y análisis sobre el 11-m y los días que le siguieron*, 28–30. Madrid: Traficantes de Sueños, 2004.

Coleman, E. Gabriella. *Coding Freedom: The Ethics and Aesthetics of Hacking*. Princeton: Princeton University Press, 2012.

Coleman, Gabriella. "From Internet Farming to Weapons of the Geek." *Current Anthropology* 58, no. S15 (November 22, 2016): S91–102. https://doi.org/10.1086 /688697.

——. "Hacker." In *Digital Keywords: A Vocabulary of Information Society and Culture*, edited by Benjamin Peters, 158–72. Princeton: Princeton University Press, 2016.

Collettivo A/traverso. *Alice è il diavolo*. Milano: Edizioni L'Erba Voglio, 1977.

——. *Alicia es el diablo: Radio libre*. Translated by Paco Quintana. Barcelona: Ed. Ricou (Hacer), 1981.

Contel, Ander. Interview with Ander Contel, May 10, 2018.

copyleft@sueltate.es. "[Copyleft] Discutiendo sobre las FAQ." *Copyleft*, July 5, 2004. https://listas.sindominio.net/mailman/private/copyleft/2004-July/001671.html.

Corsín Jiménez, Alberto. "The Right to Infrastructure: A Prototype for Open-Source Urbanism." *Environment and Planning D: Society and Space* 32, no. 2 (2014).

Corsín Jiménez, Alberto, and Zuloark. *Caja de herramientas de Ciudad Escuela. Guía de aprendizaje.* Madrid: Ciudad Escuela, 2017. https://digital.csic.es/bitstream /10261/173847/1/170613-CajaHerramientas.pdf

Crehan, Kate. *Community Art: An Anthropological Perspective.* Oxford: Berg, 2013.

Critical Art Ensemble. *Digital Resistance: Explorations in Tactical Media.* Brooklyn, NY: Autonomedia, 2001.

——. *Electronic Civil Disobedience and Other Unpopular Ideas.* Brooklyn, NY: Autonomedia, 1996.

Crook, Tony. *Anthropological Knowledge, Secrecy and Bolivip, Papua New Guinea: Exchanging Skin.* Oxford: British Academy and Oxford University Press, 2007.

Cuninghame, Patrick. "Autonomia in the 1970s: The Refusal of Work, the Party and Power." *Cultural Studies Review* 11, no. 2 (October 25, 2013): 77–94. https://doi.org /10.5130/csr.v11i2.3660.

Davis, Andrea A. "Enforcing the Transition: The Demobilization of Collective Memory in Spain, 1979–1982." *Bulletin of Hispanic Studies (Liverpool, 2002)* 92, no. 6 (2015): 667–90.

Davis, Mike. *Planet of Slums.* New York: Verso, 2006.

——. "Planet of Slums: Urban Involution and the Informal Proletariat." *New Left Review* 26 (March–April 2004): 5–34.

Defunkid. "La Elena Francis del Copyleft." *Copyleft,* August 23, 2004. https://listas .sindominio.net/mailman/private/copyleft/2004-August/001802.html.

de la Cueva, Javier. Interview with Javier de la Cueva, February 16, 2017.

——. "[OT] Competencias de las entidades degestión," *Copyleft,* June 11, 2004. https:// listas.sindominio.net/mailman/private/copyleft/2004-June/001477.html.

——. "[OT] Competencias de las entidades degestión." *Copyleft,* June 11, 2004. https:// listas.sindominio.net/mailman/private/copyleft/2004-June/001470.html.

——. "Re: Competencias de las entidades de gestión." *Copyleft,* June 11, 2004. https://listas .sindominio.net/mailman/private/copyleft/2004-June/001472.html.

Deleuze, Gilles, and Félix Guattari. *A Thousand Plateaus: Capitalism and Schizophrenia.* Minneapolis: University of Minnesota Press, 1987.

Delvi, Phoolan. "Mujeres Sin hombres y peces sin bicicletas: Mirando Hacia Atrás: Experiencias de autonomía y feminismo." In *Tomar y hacer en vez de pedir y esperar: Autonomía y movimientos sociales: Madrid, 1985–2011,* edited by Francisco Salamanca and Gonzalo Wilhelmi Casanova, 9–34. Madrid: Solidaridad Obrera, 2012.

Desacuerdos Colectivo Editorial. "Desacuerdos: Sobre arte, políticas y esfera pública en el estado español." *Desacuerdos: Sobre arte, política y esfera pública en el estado español* 1 (2004): 11–13.

Dessauce, Marc, ed. *The Inflatable Moment: Pnuematics and Protest in '68.* New York: Princeton Architectural Press and Architectural League of New York, 1999.

Díaz, Ibán. "Bienvenido Mr. Hurgan: El urban, de la palabra a los hechos." In *Cómo nació, creció y se resiste a ser comido EL GRAN POLLO DE LA ALAMEDA: Una docena de años de lucha en el barrio de La Alameda, Sevilla,* 62–66. Sevilla: Consejo de Redacción del Gran Pollo de la Alameda, 2006.

Doctor Roncero, Rafael, ed. *Nuevas cartografías de Madrid.* Madrid: La Casa Encendida y Casa de América, 2003.

Dosse, Francois. *Gilles Deleuze and Félix Guattari: Intersecting Lives.* New York: Columbia University Press, 2010.

Douglas, Gordon C. C. *The Help-Yourself City: Legitimacy and Inequality in DIY Urbanism.* New York: Oxford University Press, 2018.

Douglas, Mary. *Purity and Danger: An Analysis of Concepts of Pollution and Taboo*. London: Routledge & Kegan Paul, 1966.

Downing, John D. H., Tamara Villarreal Ford, Genève Gil, and Laura Stein. *Radical Media: Rebellious Communication and Social Movements*. Thousand Oaks, CA: SAGE Publications, 2001.

Dunne, Anthony. *Hertzian Tales: Electronic Products, Aesthetic Experience, and Critical Design*. Cambridge, MA: MIT Press, 2008.

Durán, Gloria G., and Alan W. Moore. "La Tabacalera of Lavapiés: A Social Experiment or a Work of Art?" *FIELD. A Journal of Socially-Engaged Art Criticism* 2 (Fall 2015): 49–75.

edumeet. "Edumeet." *Arquitectura viva* 145 (2012): 26.

Eizenberg, Efrat. "Actually Existing Commons: Three Moments of Space of Community Gardens in New York City." *Antipode* 44, no. 3 (2012): 764–82. https://doi.org/10.1111/j.1467-8330.2011.00892.x.

Escobar, Arturo. *Designs for the Pluriverse: Radical Interdependence, Autonomy, and the Making of Worlds*. Durham, NC: Duke University Press, 2018.

Estalella, Adolfo. "Dorkbot inicia en Madrid Sesiones Alternativas de Artistas y 'Hackers.'" *El País*, November 4, 2004. https://elpais.com/diario/2004/11/04/ciberpais/1099537343_850215.html.

Estalella Fernández, Adolfo, Jara Rocha, and Antonio Lafuente. "Laboratorios de procomún: Experimentación, recursividad y activismo." *Teknokultura: Revista de cultura digital y movimientos sociales* 10, no. 1 (March 31, 2013): 21–48.

Evans, Sara M., and Harry C. Boyte. *Free Spaces: The Sources of Democratic Change in America*. New York: Harper & Row, 1986.

Farías, Ignacio. "The Politics of Urban Assemblages." *City* 15, no. 3–4 (August 2011): 365–74. https://doi.org/10.1080/13604813.2011.595110.

Farías, Ignacio, and Thomas Bender, eds. *Urban Assemblages: How Actor-Network Theory Changes Urban Studies*. London: Routledge, 2009.

Farías, Ignacio, and Anders Blok. "Introducing Urban Cosmopolitics: Multiplicity and the Search for a Common World." In *Urban Cosmopolitics: Agencements, Assemblies, Atmospheres*, 1–22. London and New York: Routledge, 2016.

Fernández Calvo, Rafael, ed. *Conocimiento abierto*. Vol. 163. Novática: Revista de la Asociación de Técnicos Informáticos, 2003.

Fernández-Savater, Amador. "¿Cómo se organiza un clima?" *Fuera de lugar* (blog), January 9, 2012. https://blogs.publico.es/fueradelugar/1438/%c2%bfcomo-se-organiza-un-clima.

———. "[Copyleft] Perfil jornadas." *Copyleft*, December 18, 2002. https://listas.sindominio.net/mailman/private/copyleft/2002-December/000006.html.

———. *Habitar y gobernar: Inspiraciones para una nueva concepción política*. Barcelona: NED Ediciones, 2020.

Fernández-Savater, Amador. "Pensar (en) la dispersión entrevista con Franco Ingrassia." *Espai en blanc*, nos. 9, 10, 11 (2011). http://espaienblanc.net/?page_id=605.

Flesher Eguiarte, Cristina. "The Logic of Autonomy: Principles, Praxis, and Challenges of Autonomous Anti-Capitalist Movement. Three Case Studies from Madrid." University of California, Berkeley, 2005.

Fominaya, Cristina Flesher. "The Madrid Bombings and Popular Protest: Misinformation, Counter-Information, Mobilisation and Elections after '11-M.'" *Contemporary Social Science* 6, no. 3 (November 1, 2011): 289–307. https://doi.org/10.1080/21582041.2011.603910.

Foucault, Michel. "What Is Enlightenment?" In *The Foucault Reader*, edited by Paul Rabinow, 32–50. New York: Pantheon Books, 1984.

Francescutti, Pablo, Alejandro Baer, José María García de Madariaga, and Paula López. "La 'Noche de Los Móviles': Medios, Redes de Confianza y Movilización Juvenil." In *13-M: Multitudes Online*, edited by Víctor Sampedro Blanco, 63–83. Madrid: Los Libros de la Catarata, 2005.

Fuster Morell, Mayo. "From Digital Commons to Society Commons: Influence of the Free Culture Movement in the 15M Mobilization." In *Crisis and Social Mobilization in Contemporary Spain: The 15M Movement*, edited by Benjamín Tejerina and Ignacia Perugorría, 54–72. Oxford: Routledge, 2018.

Gandolfo, Daniella. *The City at Its Limits: Taboo, Transgression, and Urban Renewal in Lima*. Chicago: University of Chicago Press, 2009.

García, Jordi Mir. "Salir de los márgenes sin cambiar de ideas: Pensamiento radical, contracultural y libertario en la Transición española." *Ayer*, no. 81 (2011): 83–108.

García, Marcos. Interview with Marcos García, July 12, 2018.

García Aristegui, David. "Haciendo ruido con las rejas de la jaula: Semana de lucha social 'rompamos el silencio' 2005–2011." In *Tomar y hacer en vez de pedir y esperar: Autonomía y movimientos sociales: Madrid, 1985–2011*, edited by Francisco Salamanca and Gonzalo Wilhelmi Casanova, 239–52. Madrid: Solidaridad Obrera, 2012.

García López, Ernesto. "'Unidos por el sentido común': Identidad(es) cultural(es) y participación política en el 15M: Preguntas para una reflexión etnográfica." *Revista de antropología experimental*, special issue 13 (2013): 41–71.

Gehl, Robert W. *Reverse Engineering Social Media: Software, Culture, and Political Economy in New Media Capitalism*. Philadelphia: Temple University Press, 2014.

Geronimo. *Fire and Flames: A History of the German Autonomist Movement*. Oakland, CA: PM Press, 2012.

Goffman, Erving. *Relations in Public: Microstudies of the Public Order*. New York: Basic Books, 1971.

Golden, Lester. "The Libertarian Movement in Contemporary Spanish Politics." *Antipode* 10–11, no. 3-1 (December 1, 1978): 114–18. https://doi.org/10.1111/j.1467-8330 .1978.tb00120.x.

González García, Roberto, and Alejandra Araiza Díaz. "Feminismo y Okupación En España: El Caso de La Eskalera Karakola." *Sociológica* 31, no. 87 (2016). http://www .scielo.org.mx/scielo.php?pid=S0187-01732016000100007&script=sci_arttext.

Graeber, David. *Direct Action: An Ethnography*. Oakland, CA: AK Press, 2009.

——. *Fragments of an Anarchist Anthropology*. Chicago: Prickly Paradigm Press, 2004.

Guattari, Félix. *Molecular Revolution: Psychiatry and Politics*. Translated by Rosemary Sheed. Hardmondsworth, UK: Penguin Books, 1984.

Habermas, Jürgen. *The Structural Transformation of the Public Sphere: An Inquiry into a Category of Bourgeois Society*. Edited by Frederick Lawrence. Cambridge: Polity Press, 1989.

Haraway, Donna. "A Manifesto for Cyborgs: Science, Technology, and Socialist Feminism in the 1980s." *Socialist Review* 80 (1985): 65–107.

Hardt, Michael. "Introduction: Laboratory Italy." In *Radical Thought in Italy: A Potential Politics*, edited by Paolo Virno and Michael Hardt, 1–10. Minneapolis and London: University of Minnesota Press, 1996.

Hardt, Michael, and Antonio Negri. *Assembly*. Oxford: Oxford University Press, 2017.

——. *Multitude: War and Democracy in the Age of Empire*. New York: Penguin, 2005.

Harvey, David. *Rebel Cities: From the Right to the City to the Urban Revolution*. London: Verso Books, 2012.

——. "The Right to the City." *New Left Review* 53 (2008): 23–40.

Hessel, Stephane. *Time for Outrage!* New York: Quartet Books, 2011.

Holloway, John. *Crack Capitalism*. London: Pluto Press, 2010.

Holston, James. "Autoconstruction in Working-Class Brazil." *Cultural Anthropology* 6, no. 4 (November 1, 1991): 447–65. https://doi.org/10.1525/can.1991.6.4.02a00020.

———. *Insurgent Citizenship: Disjunctions of Democracy and Modernity in Brazil.* Princeton: Princeton University Press, 2007.

———. "Metropolitan Rebellions and the Politics of Commoning the City." *Anthropological Theory* 19, no. 1 (March 1, 2019): 120–42. https://doi.org/10.1177/1463499618812324.

Holston, James, and Teresa Caldeira. "Urban Peripheries and the Invention of Citizenship." *Harvard Design Magazine* 28 (2008): 18–23.

Hopwood, Nick, and Soraya de Chadarevian. "Dimensions of Modelling." In *Models: The Third Dimension of Science*, edited by Soraya de Chadarevian and Nick Hopwood, 1–15. Stanford, CA: Stanford University Press, 2004.

Ibáñez, Jesús. "Autobiografía (los años de aprendizaje de Jesús Ibáñez)." *Anthropos: Revista de documentación científica de la cultura* 113 (1990): 9–25.

———. *Más allá de la sociología: El grupo de discusión técnica y crítica.* Madrid: Siglo XXI, 1979.

———. *Por una sociología de la vida cotidiana.* Madrid: Siglo XXI de España Editores, 1994.

Iglesias Turrión, Pablo. *Desobedientes: De Chiapas a Madrid.* Madrid: Editorial Popular, 2011.

Illich, Ivan. *Tools for Conviviality.* New York: Harper & Row, 1973.

Instituto Nacional de Estadística. "Anuario Estadístico de España. Año 1995." Madrid, 1995. http://www.ine.es/inebaseweb/treeNavigation.do?tn=151078.

International Labor Organization (ILO). "Global Wage Report 2014/2015: Wages and Income Inequality." Geneva. http://ilo.org/global/research/global-reports/global-wage-report/2014/lang--en/index.htm. Accessed January 21, 2019.

Irani, Lilly. "Hackathons and the Making of Entrepreneurial Citizenship." *Science, Technology & Human Values*, April 8, 2015, 0162243915578486. https://doi.org/10.1177/0162243915578486.

Iveson, Kurt. "Cities within the City: Do-It-Yourself Urbanism and the Right to the City." *International Journal of Urban and Regional Research* 37, no. 3 (May 1, 2013): 941–56. https://doi.org/10.1111/1468-2427.12053.

Jansen, Stef. "For a Relational, Historical Ethnography of Hope: Indeterminacy and Determination in the Bosnian and Herzegovinian Meantime." *History and Anthropology* 27, no. 4 (August 7, 2016): 447–64. https://doi.org/10.1080/02757206.2016.1201481.

Jordan, Tim. *Activism!: Direct Action, Hacktivism and the Future of Society.* London: Reaktion Books, 2002.

Joyce, Patrick. *The Rule of Freedom: Liberalism and the Modern City.* London: Verso, 2003.

"Un juez ratifica que los cd grabables deben pagar derechos de autor." *La vanguardia*, January 14, 2002. https://www.lavanguardia.com/internet/20020114/51262748891/un-juez-ratifica-que-los-cd-grabables-deben-pagar-derechos-de-autor.html.

Juris, Jeffrey S. *Networking Futures: The Movements against Corporate Globalization.* Durham, NC: Duke University Press, 2008.

Katsiaficas, George N. *The Subversion of Politics: European Autonomous Social Movements and the Decolonization of Everyday Life.* Oakland, CA: AK Press, 2006.

Kelty, Christopher M. *Two Bits: The Cultural Significance of Free Software.* Durham, NC: Duke University Press, 2008.

Kester, Grant H. *The One and the Many: Contemporary Collaborative Art in a Global Context.* Durham, NC: Duke University Press, 2011.

Klein, Naomi. "Reclaiming the Commons." *New Left Review* 2, no. 9 (2001): 81–89.

Knorr-Cetina, Karin. *Epistemic Cultures: How the Sciences Make Knowledge.* Cambridge, MA: Harvard University Press, 1999.

Kolb, Lucie, and Gabriel Flückiger. "New Institutionalism Revisited." *On Curating | Special Issue on (New) Institution (Alism)*, December 2013.

Kornetis, Kostis. "'Is There a Future in This Past?' Analyzing 15M's Intricate Relation to the Transición." *Journal of Spanish Cultural Studies* 15, nos. 1–2 (April 3, 2014): 83–98. https://doi.org/10.1080/14636204.2014.938432.

Krøijer, Stine. *Figurations of the Future: Forms and Temporalities of Left Radical Politics in Northern Europe.* New York: Berghahn Books, 2015.

Labrador, Germán. "¿Lo llamaban democracia? La crítica estética de la política en la Transición española y el imaginario de la historia en el 15-M." *Kamchatka: Revista de análisis cultural*, no. 4 (December 4, 2014): 11–61. https://doi.org/10.7203/KAM.4.4296.

Labrador Méndez, Germán. *Culpables por la literatura: Imaginación política y contracultura en la Transición española (1968–1986).* Madrid: Ediciones Akal, 2017.

——. "La cultura en transición y la cultura de la Transición (CT)." *La circular*, 2015.

Lacort, Javier. "En el principio fue barrapunto: 'Llenamos un vacío que nadie ha recuperado.'" *Xataka*, October 10, 2017. https://www.xataka.com/empresas-y-economia/en-el-principio-fue-barrapunto-llenamos-un-vacio-que-nadie-ha-recuperado.

Lafuente, Antonio. *El carnaval de la tecnociencia: Diario de una navegación entre las nuevas tecnologías y los nuevos patrimonios.* Madrid: Gadir, 2007.

——. "El museo como casa de los comunes." *Claves de razón práctica*, no. 157 (2005): 24–31.

——. "Foros híbridos." La Casa Encendida (Madrid), 2004.

——. Interview with Antonio Lafuente, July 4, 2007.

——. Interview with Antonio Lafuente, June 4, 2018.

——. "Jornada sobre el procomún, mesa 1 | Medialab-Prado Madrid," May 17, 2007. https://www.medialab-prado.es/videos/jornada-sobre-el-procomun-mesa-1.

——. *Las dos orillas de la ciencia: La traza pública e imperial de la ilustración española.* Madrid: Marcial Pons, 2012.

Lafuente, Antonio, and Antonio Jesús Delgado. *La geometrización de la tierra (1735–1744).* Vol. 3 of *Cuadernos Galileo de historia de la ciencia.* Madrid: Consejo Superior de Investigaciones Científicas, 1984.

Lafuente, Antonio, and Javier Moscoso. *Georges-Louis Leclerc Conde de Buffon (1707–1788).* Madrid: Consejo Superior de Investigaciones Científicas, 1999.

Lafuente, Antonio, and Nuria Valverde. "Las políticas del sentido común: Feijoo contra los dislates del rigor." In *Feijoo, Hoy*, edited by Inmaculada Urzainqui, 131–57. Oviedo: Fundación Gregorio Marañón-Instituto Feijoo de Estudios del Siglo XVIII, 2003.

La Tabacalera. "Guía Copyfight para CSA | Dirección General de Autogestión Cultural," 2010. http://blogs.latabacalera.net/dgac/tabacalera-copyfight/.

Latour, Bruno. "From Multiculturalism to Multinaturalism: What Rules of Method for the New Socio-Scientific Experiments?" *Nature and Culture* 6, no. 1 (2011): 1–17. https://doi.org/10.3167/nc.2011.060101.

——. "From Realpolitik to Dingpolitik or How to Make Things Public." In *Making Things Public: Atmospheres of Democracy*, edited by Bruno Latour and Peter Weibel, 14–43. Cambridge, MA: MIT Press, 2005.

——. "Why Has Critique Run Out of Steam? From Matters of Fact to Matters of Concern." *Critical Inquiry* 30, no. 2 (January 1, 2004): 225–48. https://doi.org/10.1086/421123.

Lefebvre, Henri. *Rhythmanalysis: Space, Time, and Everyday Life.* Continuum International Publishing Group, 2004.

——. "Right to the City." In *Writings on Cities*, edited by Eleonore Kofman and Elizabeth Lebas, 61–181. Oxford: Blackwell, 1996.

——. "Theoretical Problems of Autogestion." In *State, Space, World: Selected Essays*, edited by Neil Brenner and Stuart Elden, 138–52. Minneapolis: University of Minnesota Press, 2009.

Leontidou, Lila. *The Mediterranean City in Transition: Social Change and Urban Development*. Cambridge: Cambridge University Press, 1990.

Lessig, Lawrence. *Code and Other Laws of Cyberspace*. New York: Basic Books, 1999.

——. *Free Culture: The Nature and Future of Creativity*. New York: Penguin, 2004.

——. *The Future of Ideas: The Fate of the Commons in a Connected World*. New York: Knopf Doubleday Publishing Group, 2002.

——. "Keynote Address: Commons and Code." *Fordham Intellectual Property, Media and Entertainment Law Journal* 9, no. 2 (December 1, 1999): 405.

Lévi-Strauss, Claude. *The Savage Mind*. Oxford: Oxford University Press, 1996.

Lezaun, Javier. "Democracy in America 3D." *Journal of Cultural Economy* 8, no. 2 (2015): 235–44. https://doi.org/10.1080/17530350.2014.948482.

Logan [Sack], Jason. "Take the Skinheads Bowling." *InfoNation*, 1995.

López Gil, Silvia. "Reordenación de Territorios," 2003. https://sindominio.net/karakola /antigua_casa/textos/brumaria.htm.

López Munuera, Iván. "Notas sobre el 'bum': Los colectivos españoles, un ecosistema plural." *Arquitectura viva*, no. 145 (2012).

Lorenzi Fernández, Elisabeth. "Un cóctel contra la indiferencia, el Molotov." In *Tomar y hacer en vez de pedir y esperar: Autonomía y movimientos sociales: Madrid, 1985–2011*, edited by Francisco Salamanca and Gonzalo Wilhelmi Casanova, 117–38. Madrid: Solidaridad Obrera, 2012.

Lorenzo Vila, Ana Rosa, and Miguel Ángel Martínez López. *Asambleas y reuniones: Metodologías de autoorganización*. Madrid: Traficantes de Sueños, 2005.

Lury, Celia, and Nina Wakeford, eds. *Inventive Methods: The Happening of the Social*. London: Routledge, 2012.

Maeckelbergh, Marianne. "Doing Is Believing: Prefiguration as Strategic Practice in the Alterglobalization Movement." *Social Movement Studies* 10, no. 1 (January 1, 2011): 1–20. https://doi.org/10.1080/14742837.2011.545223.

Manetto, Francesco. "Reportaje | ¿El motor del barrio? En un bajo, junto al chino." *El País*, March 3, 2007. https://elpais.com/diario/2007/03/03/madrid/1172924663 _850215.html.

Marcos, Subcomandante. "El EZLN Acude al Encuentro Intercontinental Por La Humanidad y Contra El Neoliberalismo a Presentar La Imagen Del Otro México, El México Indígena, El México Rebelde y Digno." *Enlace Zapatista* (blog), July 18, 1997. http://enlacezapatista.ezln.org.mx/1997/07/17/el-ezln-acude-al-encuentro -intercontinental-por-la-humanidad-y-contra-el-neoliberalismo-a-presentar-la -imagen-del-otro-mexico-el-mexico-indigena-el-mexico-rebelde-y-digno/.

Marcus, George. "Prototyping and Contemporary Anthropological Experiments with Ethnographic Method." *Journal of Cultural Economy* 7, no. 4 (October 2, 2014): 399–410. https://doi.org/10.1080/17530350.2013.858061.

Marres, Noortje. *Material Participation: Technology, the Environment and Everyday Publics*. London: Palgrave Macmillan, 2012.

Marres, Noortje, and Javier Lezaun. "Materials and Devices of the Public: An Introduction." *Economy and Society*, October 17, 2011, 1–21. https://doi.org/10.1080 /03085147.2011.602293.

Martínez, Guillem, ed. *CT o la cultura de la Transición: Crítica a 35 años de cultura española*. Madrid: Penguin Random House, 2012.

——. "El concepto CT." In *CT o la cultura de la Transición: Crítica a 35 años de cultura española*, 13–23. Madrid: Penguin Random House, 2012.

Martínez López, Miguel Ángel. "Socio-Spatial Structures and Protest Cycles of Squatted Social Centres in Madrid." In *The Urban Politics of Squatters' Movements*, edited by Miguel Ángel Martínez López, 25–49. New York: Palgrave Macmillan, 2018. // www.palgrave.com/gp/book/9781349953134.

———. "The Squatters' Movement: Urban Counter-Culture and Alter-Globalization Dynamics." *South European Society and Politics* 12, no. 3 (September 1, 2007): 379–98. https://doi.org/10.1080/13608740701495285.

Martínez López, Miguel Ángel, and Ángela García Bernardos. "Converging Movements: Occupations of Squares and Buildings." In *Crisis and Social Mobilization in Contemporary Spain: The 15M Movement*, edited by Benjamín Tejerina and Ignacia Perugorría, 95–118. Oxford and New York: Routledge, 2018.

———, eds. *Okupa Madrid (1985–2011): Memoria, reflexión, debate y autogestión colectiva del conocimiento*. Madrid: Seminario de Historia Política y Social de las Okupaciones en Madrid-Metrópolis, 2014.

Martínez Pagés, Jorge, and Luis Ángel Maza. "Análisis del precio de la vivienda en españa." Banco de España (Madrid), 2003. https://www.bde.es/f/webbde/SES/Secciones/Publicaciones/PublicacionesSeriadas/DocumentosTrabajo/03/Fic/dt0307.pdf.

Martín Sainz de los Terreros, Jorge. "Welcoming Sound: The Case of a Noise Complaint in the Weekly Assembly of El Campo de Cebada." *Social Movement Studies* 17, no. 3 (May 4, 2018): 269–81. https://doi.org/10.1080/14742837.2018.1456328.

Marzo, Jorge Luis. "Política cultural del gobierno español en el exterior (2000–2004)." *Desacuerdos: Sobre arte, política y esfera pública en el estado español* 2 (2005): 58–121.

Maxigas. "Hacklabs and Hackerspaces—Tracing Two Genealogies." *Journal of Peer Production* 2 (2012). http://peerproduction.net/issues/issue-2/peer-reviewed-papers/hacklabs-and-hackerspaces/.

McFarlane, Colin. "Assemblage and Critical Urbanism." *City* 15, no. 2 (April 1, 2011): 204–24. https://doi.org/10.1080/13604813.2011.568715.

———. *Learning the City: Knowledge and Translocal Assemblage*. New York: John Wiley & Sons, 2011.

McGuirk, Justin. *Radical Cities: Across Latin America in Search of a New Architecture*. London: Verso, 2014.

Medialab-Prado. *Pensando y haciendo Medialab-Prado: Conclusiones. | Medialab-Prado Madrid*, 2011. https://www.medialab-prado.es/videos/pensando-y-haciendo-medialab-prado-conclusiones-0.

Melucci, Alberto. *Nomads of the Present: Social Movements and Individual Needs in Contemporary Society*. London: Hutchinson Radius, 1989.

Membretti, Andrea, and Pierpaolo Mudu. "Where Global Meets Local: Italian Social Centres and the Alterglobalization Movement." In *Understanding European Movements: New Social Movements, Global Justice Struggles, Anti-Austerity Protest*, edited by Cristina Flesher Fominaya and Laurence Cox, 76–93. Oxford and New York: Routledge, 2013.

Méndez, Juan. "Solidaridad y ayuda mutua. El grupo de Migración y convivencia de la Asamblea Popular de Lavapiés." *Teknokultura. Revista de Cultura Digital y Movimientos Sociales* 9, no. 2 (December 23, 2012): 267–86.

Milan, Stefania. *Social Movements and Their Technologies: Wiring Social Change*. Houndmills, UK: Palgrave Macmillan, 2013.

Mitchell, Don. *The Right to the City: Social Justice and the Fight for Public Space*. New York: Guilford Press, 2003.

Mol, Annemarie, and John Law. "Complexities: An Introduction." In *Complexities: Social Studies of Knowledge Practices*, edited by John Law and Annemarie Mol, 1–22. Durham, NC: Duke University Press, 2002.

Molist, Mercé. "Por primera vez una sentencia judicial española cita el 'Copyleft.'" *El país*, February 16, 2006. https://elpais.com/diario/2006/02/16/ciberpais/1140058946 _850215.html.

Molist Ferrer, Mercé. "Hackstory.es: La historia nunca contada del underground hacker en la península ibérica," 2008. https://hackstory.net/Nodo50.

Moreno-Caballud, Luis. *Cultures of Anyone: Studies on Cultural Democratization in the Spanish Neoliberal Crisis*. Liverpool: Liverpool University Press, 2015.

Moreno Pestaña, José Luis. *Filosofía y Sociología En Jesús Ibáñez: Genealogía de Un Pensador Crítico*. Madrid: Siglo XXI de España Editores, 2008.

Nevejan, Caroline, and Alexander Badenoch. "How Amsterdam Invented the Internet: European Networks of Significance, 1980–1995." In *Hacking Europe: From Computer Cultures to Demoscenes*, edited by Gerard Alberts and Ruth Oldenziel, 189–217. London: Springer, 2014.

Nielsen, Morten. "Inverse Governmentality: The Paradoxical Production of Peri-Urban Planning in Maputo, Mozambique." *Critique of Anthropology* 31, no. 4 (December 1, 2011): 329–58. https://doi.org/10.1177/0308275X11420118.

Observatorio Metropolitano, ed. *Madrid: ¿La suma de todos? Globalización, territorio, desigualdad*. Madrid: Traficantes de sueños, 2007.

Organization for Economic Cooperation and Development (OECD). "In It Together: Why Less Inequality Benefits All." Paris: OECD Publishing, 2015. https://doi.org /10.1787/9789264235120-en.

Ostrom, Elinor. *Governing the Commons: The Evolution of Institutions for Collective Action*. New York: Cambridge University Press, 1990.

Padilla, Andrés. "Dos focos culturales, pared con pared." *El país*, January 3, 2003. https:// elpais.com/diario/2003/01/03/madrid/1041596669_850215.html.

Padilla, Margarita. Interview with Margarita Padilla, March 29, 2017.

——. "Por qué nodo50 ha dejado de interesarme," 1999. http://biblioweb.sindominio.net /telematica/nonodo50.html.

——. "¿Y si partimos en dos la Red?" *Contrapoder*, 2005.

Parkinson, John. *Democracy and Public Space: The Physical Sites of Democratic Performance*. Oxford: Oxford University Press, 2012.

Pavolini, Emmanuele, Margarita León, Ana M Guillén, and Ugo Ascoli. "From Austerity to Permanent Strain? The EU and Welfare State Reform in Italy and Spain." *Comparative European Politics* 13, no. 1 (January 1, 2015): 56–76. https://doi.org/10 .1057/cep.2014.41.

Peck, Jamie. "Austerity Urbanism." *City* 16, no. 6 (December 1, 2012): 626–55. https:// doi.org/10.1080/13604813.2012.734071.

Pérez-Agote, Alfonso, Benjamín Tejerina, and Margarita Barañano, eds. *Barrios multiculturales: Relaciones interétnicas en los barrios de San Francisco (Bilbao) y Embajadores/Lavapiés (Madrid)*. Madrid: Trotta, 2010.

Pérez de Lama, José. "Entre Blade Runner y Mickey Mouse: Nuevas condiciones urbanas: Una perspectiva desde Los Angeles, California (1999–2002)." Universidad de Sevilla, 2006. https://idus.us.es/xmlui/handle/11441/24254.

——. Interview with José Pérez de Lama, January 24, 2017.

Pérez de Lama, José, and Sergio Moreno Páez. "Request for Comments." In *Wikiplaza: Request for Comments*. Barcelona: dpr-barcelona, 2011.

Pérez Quintana, Vicente. "Lavapiés: Intervención y rehabilitación (1998–2008)." Madrid: Empresa Municipal de la Vivienda y Suelo, 2008. https://aavvmadrid.org/intercam bio/FEC/EstudioARI%20Lavapies_1998-%202008.pdf.

Pérez Quintana, Vicente, and Pablo Sánchez León, eds. *Memoria Ciudadana y Movimiento Vecinal. Madrid, 1968–2008*. Madrid: Los Libros de la Catarata, 2008.

Piazza, Gianni, and Miguel Ángel Martínez López. "More than Four Decades of Squatting: Cycles, Waves and Stages of Autonomous Urban Politics in European Cities." In *The Urban Politics of Squatters' Movements*, edited by Miguel Ángel Martínez López, 229–45. New York: Palgrave Macmillan, 2018. //www.palgrave .com/gp/book/9781349953134.

Pignarre, Phillipe, and Isabella Stengers. *Capitalist Sorcery: Breaking the Spell*. London: Palgrave Macmillan, 2011.

Pimentel, Juan, and José Pardo-Tomás. "And Yet, We Were Modern: The Paradoxes of Iberian Science after the Grand Narratives." *History of Science* 55, no. 2 (June 1, 2017): 133–47. https://doi.org/10.1177/0073275316684353.

Plaza, Beatriz. "The Guggenheim-Bilbao Museum Effect: A Reply to María V. Gomez' 'Reflective Images: The Case of Urban Regeneration in Glasgow and Bilbao.'" *International Journal of Urban and Regional Research* 23, no. 3 (1999): 589–92. https:// doi.org/10.1111/1468-2427.00215.

Polletta, Francesca. "'Free Spaces' in Collective Action." *Theory and Society* 28, no. 1 (1999): 1–38.

Postigo, Hector. *The Digital Rights Movement: The Role of Technology in Subverting Digital Copyright*. Cambridge, MA: MIT Press, 2012.

Postill, John. *The Rise of Nerd Politics: Digital Activism and Political Change*. London: Pluto Press, 2018.

Pottage, Alain. "Law Machines: Scale Models, Forensic Materiality and the Making of Modern Patent Law." *Social Studies of Science* 41, no. 5 (October 1, 2011): 621–43. https://doi.org/10.1177/0306312711408484.

Prádanos, Luis I. *Postgrowth Imaginaries: New Ecologies and Counterhegemonic Culture in Post-2008 Spain*. Liverpool: Liverpool University Press, 2018.

Precarias a la deriva. *A la deriva por los circuitos de la precariedad femenina*. Madrid: Traficantes de Sueños, 2004.

Puig de la Bellacasa, María. *Matters of Care: Speculative Ethics in More Than Human Worlds*. Minneapolis: University of Minnesota Press, 2017.

Purcell, Mark. "The Right to the City: The Struggle for Democracy in the Urban Public Realm." *Policy & Politics* 41, no. 3 (July 1, 2013): 311–27. https://doi.org/10.1332 /030557312X655639.

Rabinow, Paul. *The Accompaniment: Assembling the Contemporary*. University of Chicago Press, 2011.

Rancière, Jacques. *The Politics of Aesthetics*. London: Bloomsbury, 2004.

Rao, Vyjayanthi. "Embracing Urbanism: The City as Archive." *New Literary History* 40, no. 2 (2009): 371–83. https://doi.org/10.1353/nlh.0.0085.

——. "Slum as Theory: The South/Asian City and Globalization." *International Journal of Urban and Regional Research* 30, no. 1 (March 1, 2006): 225–32. https://doi.org /10.1111/j.1468-2427.2006.00658.x.

Ratto, Matt. "Critical Making: Conceptual and Material Studies in Technology and Social Life." *The Information Society* 27, no. 4 (2011): 252–60. https://doi.org/10.1080 /01972243.2011.583819.

Razquin Mangado, Adriana. *Didáctica ciudadana: La vida política en las plazas. etnografía del movimiento 15M*. Granada: Editorial Universidad de Granada, 2017.

Red de Espacios Ciudadanos. "Marco común i.4. esbozo de un marco común para la cesión de espacios destinados a la autogestión ciudadana con el objetivo de fomentar el desarrollo de los bienes comunes en los barrios de Madrid," 2016. http://www .espaciosciudadanos.org/wp-content/uploads/2016/01/Marco-Comun-v1-4.pdf.

Red de Lavapiés. "La tabacalera a debate," 2004. http://latabacalera.net/web2004/info /index.html.

Reed, Adam. "'Blog This': Surfing the Metropolis and the Method of London." *Journal of the Royal Anthropological Institute* 14, no. 2 (June 1, 2008): 391–406. https://doi .org/10.1111/j.1467-9655.2008.00508.x.

Renzi, Alessandra. *Hacked Transmissions: Technology and Connective Activism in Italy.* Minneapolis: University of Minnesota Press, 2020.

Reventós, Laia. "Una demanda contra el canon de los cd y dvd circula por internet." *El pais,* July 29, 2004. https://elpais.com/diario/2004/07/29/ciberpais/1091065228 _850215.html.

Rheinberger, Hans-Jörg. *Toward a History of Epistemic Things: Synthesizing Proteins in the Test Tube.* Stanford, CA: Stanford University Press, 1997.

Ribalta, Jorge. "Experimentos para una nueva institucionalidad." In *Objetos relacionales. colección MACBA 2002–2007,* edited by Manuel Borja-Villel, Kaira M. Cabañas, and Jorge Ribalta, 225–65. Barcelona: MACBA, 2010.

Riles, Annelise. *The Network Inside Out.* Ann Arbor: University of Michigan Press, 2001.

Rocha, Jara. Interview with Jara Rocha, April 16, 2010.

Rodríguez, Montserrat Cañedo. "Multitudes urbanas: De las figuras y lógicas prácticas de la identificación política." *Revista de dialectología y tradiciones populares* 67, no. 2 (December 30, 2012): 359–84. https://doi.org/10.3989/rdtp.2012.13.

Rodríguez López, Emmanuel. "La ciudad global o la nueva centralidad de Madrid." In *Madrid: ¿La suma de todos? Globalización, territorio, desigualdad,* edited by Observatorio Metropolitano, 41–93. Madrid: Traficantes de sueños, 2007.

Rodríguez-Villasante, Tomás, Julio Alguacil, Concha Denche, Agustín Hernández Aja, Concha León, and Isabel Velázquez. *Retrato de chabolista con piso: Análisis de redes sociales en la remodelación de barrios de Madrid.* Madrid: Revista Alfoz-CIDUR, 1989.

Roig Domínguez, Gustavo, and Sara López Martín. "Del desconcierto emocional a la movilización política: Redes sociales y medios alternativos del 11-M al 13-M." In *13-M: Multitudes Online,* edited by Víctor Sampedro Blanco, 183–228. Madrid: Los Libros de la Catarata, 2005.

Romanos, Eduardo. "Evictions, Petitions and Escraches: Contentious Housing in Austerity Spain." *Social Movement Studies* 13, no. 2 (April 3, 2014): 296–302. https:// doi.org/10.1080/14742837.2013.830567.

Roy, Ananya. "Slumdog Cities: Rethinking Subaltern Urbanism." *International Journal of Urban and Regional Research* 35, no. 2 (March 1, 2011): 223–38. https://doi.org /10.1111/j.1468-2427.2011.01051.x.

Rubio-Pueyo, Vicente. "Municipalism in Spain. From Barcelona to Madrid, and Beyond." City Series. Rosa Luxemburg Stiftung (New York), 2017.

Sádaba Rodríguez, Igor, and Gustavo Roig Domínguez. "El movimiento de okupación ante las nuevas tecnologías: Okupas en las redes." In *¿Dónde están las llaves? El movimiento Okupa: Prácticas y contextos sociales,* edited by Ramón Adell Argilés and Miguel Ángel Martínez López, 267–91. Madrid: Los Libros de la Catarata, 2004.

Sambricio, Carlos. "El urbanismo de la Transición: Madrid, 1979–1983. El Plan General de Ordenación Urbana." In *El urbanismo de la Transición: El Plan General de Ordenación Urbana de Madrid de 1985. Volumen 1,* edited by Carlos Sambricio and Paloma Ramos, 14–71. Madrid: Ayuntamiento de Madrid, 2019.

Sánchez León, Pablo. "Desclasamiento y desencanto: La representación de las clases medias como eje de una relectura generacional de la Transición española." *Kamchatka" Revista de análisis cultural,* no. 4 (December 4, 2014): 63–99. https://doi.org/10.7203 /KAM.4.4145.

Sánchez-Moliní, Luis. "'Hay que pensar en cómo redistribuir la riqueza que se genera en las redes.'" Diario de Sevilla, January 13, 2019. https://www.diariodesevilla.es

/rastrodelafama/Arquitectura-bioclimatizacion-redes-ETSA_0_1318068491
.html.

Sanz, Casilda Cabrerizo, Azucena Klett, and Pablo García Bachiller. "De alianzas anómalas a nuevos paisajes políticos. Madrid, Lavapiés y otras geografías de lo común." *URBS. Revista de estudios urbanos y ciencias sociales* 5, no. 2 (November 4, 2015): 163–78.

Sanz, José María Serrano. "Crisis económica y transición política." *Ayer*, no. 15 (1994): 135–64.

Schierstaedt, Nina. "Los barrios madrileños como áreas de confrontación social durante el tardofranquismo y la Transición: Los casos de la Meseta de Orcasitas, Palomeras, San Blas y El Pilar." *Historia, trabajo y sociedad*, no. 7 (2016): 55–75.

Schwarte, Ludwig. "Parliamentary Public." In *Making Things Public: Atmospheres of Democracy*, edited by Bruno Latour and Peter Weibel, 786–94. Cambridge, MA: MIT Press, 2005.

Secord, Nick. "Monsters at the Crystal Palace." In *Models: The Third Dimension of Science*, edited by Soraya de Chadarevian and Nick Hopwood, 138–69. Stanford, CA: Stanford University Press, 2004.

Sennett, Richard. *The Fall of Public Man*. Cambridge: Cambridge University Press, 1977.

Serrano, Marcos. "Fw: [Wh2001] Reu de Las Jornadas de Propiedad Intelectual." *Copyleft*, December 16, 2002. https://listas.sindominio.net/mailman/private/copyleft/2002 -December/000002.html.

Shukaitis, Stevphen, and David Graeber. "Introduction." In *Constituent Imagination: Militant Investigations, Collective Theorization*, edited by Stevphen Shukaitis, David Graeber, and Erika Biddle. Oakland: AK Press, 2007.

Siena, Domenico di. "Creatividad horizontal: Redes, conectores y plataformas." *Arquitectura viva*, 2012.

Simone, AbdouMaliq. *City Life from Jakarta to Dakar: Movements at the Crossroads*. New York: Routledge, 2009.

——. *Jakarta, Drawing the City Near*. Minneapolis: University of Minnesota Press, 2014.

——. "Pirate Towns: Reworking Social and Symbolic Infrastructures in Johannesburg and Douala." *Urban Studies* 43, no. 2 (February 1, 2006): 357–70. https://doi.org /10.1080/00420980500146974.

Simone, AbdouMaliq, and Edgar Pieterse. *New Urban Worlds: Inhabiting Dissonant Times*. Cambridge: Polity Press, 2017.

Sindicato de Arquitectos. "III Estudio laboral sobre el sector de la arquitectura," 2013. https://sindicatoarquitectos.wordpress.com/2013/10/07/iii-estudio-laboral-sobre -el-sector-de-la-arquitectura/.

sinDominio.net. "Preguntas frecuentes sobre el proyecto sindominio.net," 2004. http:// sindominio.net/article.php3?id_article=31.

Sloterdijk, Peter. "Atmospheric Politics." In *Making Things Public: Atmospheres of Democracy*, edited by Bruno Latour and Peter Weibel, 944–51. Cambridge, MA: MIT Press, 2005.

Stallman, Richard. *Free Software, Free Society: Selected Essays of Richard M. Stallman*. Boston: GNU Press, 2006.

Stavrides, Stavros. *Common Space: The City as Commons*. London: Zed Books, 2016.

Stengers, Isabelle. *Cosmopolitics I*. Minneapolis: University of Minnesota Press, 2010.

Strathern, Marilyn. *Partial Connections*. Walnut Creek, CA: AltaMira Press, 2004.

——. *Property, Substance, and Effect: Anthropological Essays on Persons and Things*. London: Athlone Press, 1999.

Suchman, Lucy. "Anthropological Relocations and the Limits of Design." *Annual Review of Anthropology* 40, no. 1 (2011): 1–18. https://doi.org/10.1146/annurev.anthro.0416 08.105640.

——. "Consuming Anthropology." In *Interdisciplinarity: Reconfigurations of the Social and Natural Sciences*, edited by Andrew Barry and Georgina Born, 141–60. Oxford: Routledge, 2013.

Sudrià, Carles. "El ajuste económico de la Transición." *El país*. February 13, 2012, sec. Economia. https://elpais.com/economia/2012/02/10/actualidad/1328871012_734915.html.

Swyngedouw, Erik. *Promises of the Political: Insurgent Cities in a Post-Political Environment*. Cambridge, MA: MIT Press, 2018.

Tavares, Paulo. "General Essay on Air: Probes into the Atmospheric Conditions of Liberal Democracy." University of London, Centre for Research Architecture, 2008. http://www.paulotavares.net/air/.

Terranova, Tiziana. "Free Labor: Producing Culture for the Digital Economy." *Social Text* 18, no. 2 (June 1, 2000): 33–58.

Thrift, Nigel. *Non-Representational Theory: Space, Politics, Affect*. London: Routledge, 2008.

Tkacz, Nathaniel. "The Spanish Fork: Wikipedia's Ad-Fuelled Mutiny." *Wired UK*, January 20, 2011. http://www.wired.co.uk/article/wikipedia-spanish-fork.

Tonkiss, Fran. "Austerity Urbanism and the Makeshift City." *City* 17, no. 3 (June 1, 2013): 312–24. https://doi.org/10.1080/13604813.2013.795332.

Tsing, Anna Lowenhaupt. *The Mushroom at the End of the World: On the Possibility of Life in Capitalist Ruins*. Princeton: Princeton University Press, 2015.

Turner, Fred. *The Democratic Surround: Multimedia and American Liberalism from World War II to the Psychedelic Sixties*. Chicago: University of Chicago Press, 2013.

Turner, John F. C. *Housing by People: Towards Autonomy in Building Environments*. New York: Pantheon Books, 1976.

Turner, John F. C., and Robert Fichter, eds. *Freedom to Build: Dweller Control of the Housing Process*. New York: Macmillan, 1972.

Universidad Nómada. "Universidad Nómada," 2002. https://sindominio.net/unomada/.

Various authors. *¡Pásalo! Relatos y Análisis Sobre El 11-M y Los Días Que Le Siguieron*. Madrid: Traficantes de Sueños, 2004.

Vasudevan, Alexander. *The Autonomous City: A History of Urban Squatting*. London: Verso, 2017.

Vidal, Miguel. "Charla movilizaciones canon bibliotecas." *Copyleft*, March 9, 2005. https://listas.sindominio.net/mailman/private/copyleft/2005-March/002105.html.

——. "Comentarios a las FAQ y estructura." *Copyleft*, July 10, 2004. https://listas.sindominio.net/mailman/private/copyleft/2004-July/001713.html.

——. "[Copyleft] Creative Commons y licencias Copyleft." *Copyleft*, December 17, 2002. https://listas.sindominio.net/mailman/private/copyleft/2002-December/000003.html.

——. "[Copyleft] Discutiendo sobre las FAQ." *Copyleft*, July 2, 2004. https://listas.sindominio.net/mailman/private/copyleft/2004-July/001630.html.

——. "[Copyleft] Resumen de Copyleft, Vol 57, Envío 6." *Copyleft*, March 31, 2008. https://listas.sindominio.net/mailman/private/copyleft/2008-March/002498.html.

——. "Liberar el ciberespacio: Reflexiones sobre un lustro de comunidades políticas virtuales: Entrevista con Miquel Vidal." *Contrapoder*, 2005.

——. "Re: Competencias de las entidades degestión." *Copyleft*, June 11, 2004. https://listas.sindominio.net/mailman/private/copyleft/2004-June/001471.html.

Vidania Domínguez, Carlos. "Fragmentación, red, autonomía." In *Tomar y hacer en vez de pedir y esperar: Autonomía y movimientos sociales: Madrid, 1985–2011*, edited by Francisco Salamanca and Gonzalo Wilhelmi Casanova, 51–71. Madrid: Solidaridad Obrera, 2012.

———. "¿Han oído hablar de Lavapiés? Historia de una ruina provocada." In *El cielo está enladrillado: Entre el mobbing y la violencia inmobiliaria y urbanística*, 135–45. Barcelona: Edicions Bellaterra, 2006.

Vidania Domínguez, Carlos, and Margarita Padilla. "Okupar el vacío desde el vacío." In *Autonomía y metrópolis: Del movimiento okupa a los centros sociales de segunda generación*, edited by Javier Toret, Nicolás Sguiglia, Santiago Fernández Patón, and Mónica Lama, 53–56. Málaga: CEDMA, 2008.

Villa, Manuela. Interview with Manuela Villa, March 9, 2017.

Vinuesa Angulo, Julio, and José María De la Riva Ámez. "Los 'grandes desarrollos' del PG97, un grave error de planteamiento y una amenaza para el futuro urbanístico de Madrid." In *Reflexiones a propósito de la Revisión del Plan General de Madrid*, edited by Julio Vinuesa Angulo, David Porras Alfaro, José María De la Riva Ámez, and Felipe Fernández García, 493–511. Madrid: Grupo TRyS, 2013.

Virno, Paolo. "Virtuosity and Revolution: The Political Theory of Exodus." In *Radical Thought in Italy: A Potential Politics*, edited by Paolo Virno and Michael Hardt, 189–210. Minneapolis and London: University of Minnesota Press, 1996.

Viveiros de Castro, Eduardo. "On Models and Examples: Engineers and Bricoleurs in the Anthropocene." *Current Anthropology* 60, no. S20 (April 1, 2019): S296–308. https://doi.org/10.1086/702787.

Wagner, Roy. *The Invention of Culture*. Chicago: University of Chicago Press, 1981.

Wark, McKenzie. *50 Years of Recuperation of the Situationist International*. New York: Princeton Architectural Press, 2008.

Wilhelmi, Gonzalo. *Romper el consenso: La izquierda radical en la Transición española (1975–1982)*. Madrid: Siglo XXI de España Editores, 2016.

Wilhelmi Casanova, Gonzalo. *Armarse sobre las ruinas: Historia del movimiento autónomo en Madrid (1985–1999)*. Madrid: Potencial Hardcore, 2000.

———. *Lucha autónoma: Una visión de la coordinadora de colectivos, 1990–1997*. Madrid: Aurora Ediciones, 1998.

———. "Todo parecía posible." In *Tomar y hacer en vez de pedir y esperar: Autonomía y movimientos sociale: Madrid, 1985–2011*, edited by Francisco Salamanca and Gonzalo Wilhelmi Casanova, 73–102. Madrid: Solidaridad Obrera, 2012.

Williams, Raymond. *The Long Revolution*. London: Chatto & Windus, 1961.

Wolfson, Todd. *Digital Rebellion: The Birth of the Cyber Left*. Champaign: University of Illinois Press, 2014.

Ximénez de Sandoval, Pablo. "Salen de prisión los últimos cuatro insumisos de la mili." *El País*. May 26, 2002, sec. Espana. https://elpais.com/diario/2002/05/26/espana /1022364010_850215.html.

Yonderboy [Miguel Vidal]. "La ACP vuelve por fin a la luz como nuevo nodo de indy-media." *Barrapunto*, April 24, 2002. http://barrapunto.com/articles/02/04/24 /0038227.shtml.

Zapata, Guillermo. "La CT como marco: Un caso de éxito no CT: el 15M. O de cómo puede suceder un éxito no previsto en una cultura, como la CT, que controla los accesos al éxito y al fracaso." In *CT o la cultura de la Transición: Crítica a 35 años de cultura española*, ed. Guillem Martínez 141–50. Madrid: Penguin Random House, 2012.

Zapatistas. *Zapatista Encuentro: Documents from the First Intercontinental Encounter for Humanity and against Neoliberalism*. New York: Seven Stories Press, 1998.

Zoohaus. "Inteligencia colectiva [Officina OTICAM]: Proyecto desarrollado por Zoohaus para el ranchito: Matadero Madrid: Comisariado Por Iván López Munuera," 2010.

Zoohaus Collective. Interview with Zoohaus Collective, July 17, 2012.

Index

Page numbers in italics indicate figures

CPSIA information can be obtained
at www.ICGtesting.com
Printed in the USA
LVHW041055010223
738319LV00003B/185